NETSCAPE NAVIGATOR™ 2.0

Surfing the Web and Exploring the Internet

Windows® Version

NETSCAPE NAVIGATOR™ 2.0

Surfing the Web and Exploring the Internet

Windows® Version

Bryan Pfaffenberger

University of Virginia
Charlottesville, Virginia

AP PROFESSIONAL

Boston San Diego New York
London Sydney Tokyo Toronto

This book is printed on acid-free paper. 

AP PROFESSIONAL
1300 Boylston Street, Chestnut Hill, MA 02167
World Wide Web page at http://www.apnet.com

An imprint of ACADEMIC PRESS, INC.
A Division of HARCOURT BRACE & COMPANY

United Kingdom Edition published by
ACADEMIC PRESS LIMITED
24–28 Oval Road, London NW1 7DX

Library of Congress Cataloging-in-Publication Data
Pfaffenberger, Bryan, 1949–
Netscape navigator 2.0 : surfing the web and exploring the Internet / Bryan Pfaffenberger.
p. cm.
Includes index.
ISBN 0-12-553145-1 (alk. paper). -- ISBN 0-12-553146-X (CD-ROM)
1. Netscape. 2. World Wide Web (Information retrieval system)
3. Internet (Computer network)
TK5105.882.P42 1996
025.04--dc20 96-6177
CIP

International Edition: ISBN 0-12-784847-9 (alk. paper) ISBN 0-12-784848-7 (CD-ROM)

Printed in the United States of America
96 97 98 99 IP 9 8 7 6 5 4 3 2 1

For Suzanne, always

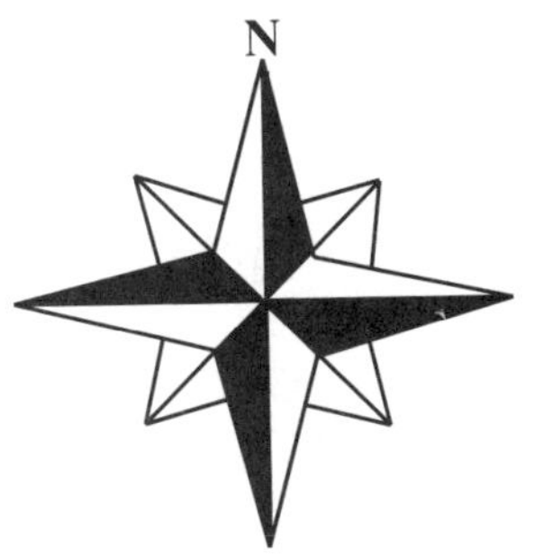

Contents

Introduction

It's the fastest growing communication system in human history. It's loaded with useful information. And, it's fun. It's the World Wide Web. Academics, in their professorial way, call it a global hypermedia system. For you and me, it's an incredibly fun way that you can jump from one Internet computer to the next, just by clicking an underlined word or phrase called a *hyperlink*. After clicking the hyperlink, the Web goes to work, accessing the information you requested—which might be a document, a sound, an animation, or a movie clip. And who knows where you'll wind up? You might wind up browsing multimedia resources on a computer across the street—or halfway around the world.

The Web is entertaining, useful, fun, and—increasingly—just about indispensable. Many people, myself included, think that the World Wide Web is the opening salvo in the development of a global "information superhighway,"

knowledge of which will be required of any educated person. The time to start is now. And the perfect tool is Netscape Navigator.

What Is Netscape Navigator?

To access the World Wide Web, you need an Internet connection and a program called a *browser.* A browser decodes the hidden symbols in Web documents, turning them into richly formatted documents replete with fonts and graphics. In addition, browsers also originate messages that locate and retrieve documents, every time you click a hyperlink. Many people believe that Netscape Navigator is the best Web browser available—and I concur.

New for 2

This book shows you how to master Netscape Navigator Version 2, the exciting new version of Netscape. You'll learn about all the new features of this major release, including the program's ability to run Java applets (miniature programs) right on your screen. You'll also learn about all the exciting new plug-ins (accessory programs) that extend Netscape's capabilities. They enable you to view animations, 3-D virtual reality scenes, and live-action movies right on the Web pages you're accessing!

Why Do You Need This Book?

You've probably heard that Netscape is easy to use. It is, up to a point. But Netscape is a tool for accessing the World Wide Web (and indeed, the whole Internet). When you learn Netscape, you learn the Web *and* you learn the Internet. That's a lot to learn, and you'll need some help. You've come to the right place.

This isn't just a book about learning Netscape Version 2, although we somewhat immodestly feel that it does a pretty good job in that department. It's about mastering Netscape *and* surfing the Web *and* exploring the Internet. It's three books in one—and you need all three. Web surfing is more complicated than it appears on the surface, and the going gets rough when you're trying to use the Web to retrieve needed information. Moreover, Netscape provides the tools you need to access all of the Internet's riches, including Gopher menus, FTP file archives (free software!), Usenet newsgroups, and Telnet resources, including bulletin board systems (BBSs) and freenets.

So this book teaches three essential skills:

- Becoming an absolute, flat-out master of Netscape, using the tricks and techniques known only to those who grow pale from all-night Netscape sessions.
- Surfing the Web with an unerring aim, locating the cool, the informative, the useful, the wacky, and the irreverent.
- Using Netscape to harvest the incredible information and entertainment resources of the entire Internet, including Gopher, FTP, Usenet, and Telnet.

No matter whether you're a beginner with Netscape or a seasoned vet of all-night surf sessions, you'll find that this book is packed with knowledge, strategies, techniques, and cunning tricks. It presents a comprehensive strategy for total mastery of the Internet!

What's on the CD-ROM Disc?

While we're on the sales pitch here—you *are* reading this in the bookstore, aren't you?—let me mention this book's CD-ROM disc. Even if this book were full of patent nonsense (which it isn't, I hasten to add), it would still be worth buying just for this disc alone. You may not realize this just yet, but Netscape needs help if you want to access all the Web's riches. It needs helper applications and plug-in programs. In fact, you need to choose, obtain, install, and configure at least a half dozen helper applications to bring Netscape to its full potential. To obtain all of these programs from the Internet, you'd need to spend hours—even days—researching the best helper program options, finding them on the Internet, and downloading them in a tedious, byte-by-byte process.

But not with this book! We've packed the CD-ROM disc with the best helper and plug-in applications available for use with Netscape. You'll find programs for listening to sounds of every conceivable kind, software for viewing movies and animations (including MPEG and QuickTime movies), a fully functional version of Adobe's Acrobat Reader for viewing richly formatted documents, the incredible new version of WinZip (which can unpack any of the different types of compressed files you'll encounter on the Internet), Telnet helpers, plug-ins and much, much more.

To access all the goodies on the disc, just slip it into your CD-ROM drive. Use Netscape's File Open command to locate the file named WELCOME.HTM—after that, it's self-explanatory.

Don't have Internet connectivity yet? This book includes everything you need to access the Internet from anywhere in the United States with EarthLink Network TotalAccess. If you subscribe to EarthLink's high-speed Net access service, you can use the special version of Netscape Navigator Version 2 that's included with this book. (If you already have an Internet service provider, ask your service provider to help you obtain Netscape from Netscape Communication's FTP server; see Appendix A.)

Netscape's the ideal tool for surfing the Web and exploring the Internet. This book makes this tool come to life, putting you in touch with the fun, the knowledge, the resources, and—yes—the wonderful zaniness of the World Wide Web.

How This Book Is Organized

This book is designed for a fast start with Netscape. As the need arises, you can use the additional chapters to round out your knowledge of this fantastic program, the Web, and the Internet. Before getting started, though,

- Do you need an Internet connection and a copy of Netscape? If you haven't got your Internet connection yet, be sure to read Appendix A.
- Do you already have an Internet connection and Netscape Version 2? Flip to Appendix E, which tells you how to install all the cool plug-ins and helper applications on this book's CD-ROM disc.

Part I: Netscape Quick Start

Part I serves as an introduction to this entire book—and if you're strapped for time, you can learn about 80% of what you'll need to know just by reading these three chapters.

In Chapter 1, "Getting Started with Netscape Navigator," you'll learn the parts of Netscape's screen, including what all those buttons do. It's worth a skim, even if you've already played with the program a bit. If you've used earlier versions of Netscape before, this chapter introduces the new features of the Version 2 interface.

Chapter 2, "The Gentle Art of Web Surfing," provides an introduction for much of the rest of the book. You'll learn all the fundamentals of Web navigation the Netscape way. In addition, this chapter shows you some of the advanced functions of Netscape, which is a very powerful tool for accessing all kinds of Internet resources.

Chapter 3, "When the Surf Gets Rough," shows you how to deal with common error messages and other problems you'll encounter while you're surfing the Net.

Part II: Mastering Netscape

To get the most out of any fine computer program, you need guidance and tons of tips. You'll find what you're looking for in Part II, "Mastering Netscape." Even experienced Netscape mavens concede that they learn quite a bit from these chapters! When you finish reading them, you'll be an expert at using this outstanding program.

Chapter 4, "Change That Start Page," gets you started the right way, namely, with a default home page that's much more useful than the one Netscape accesses automatically. You'll find this home page on this book's CD-ROM disc, and it's jammed with useful tools for navigating the Web.

Chapter 5, "Improving Netscape's Performance," shows you how to extract the maximum Web-surfing speed out of Netscape. You'll learn all of the tricks that experienced Netscape users discover the hard way, through experience. Even if you're using Netscape over a relatively slow modem (14.4 Kbps), you'll be able to browse the Web at a very good clip after reading this chapter.

New for 2 Chapter 6, "Creating and Using Bookmarks," fully explores Netscape's improved Bookmarks menu, which enables you to save location information about Web sites you've visited. You'll learn how to organize your Bookmarks menu so that it becomes a treasure trove of Web information that you find useful.

New for 2 Chapter 7, "Using SmartMarks," introduces the SmartMarks plug-in program, which adds advanced features to Netscape's already impressive bookmarks capability.

Chapter 8, "Managing Documents," shows you how to save and print those fantastic documents you're downloading from the Net.

Chapter 9, "Customizing and Configuring Netscape," walks you through all those Preferences dialog boxes, highlighting the customization options that can really make a difference for you.

Part III: Grooving on Multimedia

New for 2 With Version 2 of Netscape, you can add plug-in programs that greatly extend the program's multimedia capabilities. In addition, you can also use helper applications—programs that deal with the sounds, movies, and animations that plug-ins can't handle. Part III shows you how to explore the rich multimedia resources of the Web.

If you haven't yet done so, flip to Appendix B to learn how to configure Netscape for the use of helper applications. Appendix E provides step-by-step instructions for installing the plug-ins and helper apps that you'll find on this book's CD-ROM disc.

New for 2 Chapter 10, "Understanding Helper Apps and Plug-Ins," thoroughly surveys the helper applications and plug-in programs that you'll find on this book's CD-ROM disc. You'll learn what they do and why they're so cool to use!

New for 2 Chapter 11, "Playing Sounds and Watching Movies," shows you how to harness the multimedia potential of the Web. You'll know how to deal with just about any sound or movie format that the Web can sling at you, including the new streaming sounds and live-action movies.

New for 2 Chapter 12, "Viewing Adobe Acrobat Documents," shows you how to open and read richly formatted Adobe Acrobat documents. You'll also learn how to use the Amber reader, which enables you to display Acrobat documents within Netscape's window.

New for 2 Chapter 13, "Taking a Sip of Java," introduces the amazing new Web experiences made possible by Java, the new cross-platform programming language created by Sun Microsystems. Because Netscape Version 2 can read and execute Java programs, you can access Web pages that contain Java code—and see amazing things happen on the Web pages you're viewing. Take the tour!

New for 2 Chapter 14, "How Shocking! (Viewing Animations with Shockwave)," thoroughly explores the new Macromedia plug-in for Netscape, Shockwave. With Shockwave installed, you can view professionally produced animations on the Web pages you're viewing. The era of flat, static Web presentations is drawing to a close, you'll surely agree.

New for 2 Chapter 15, "Exploring Virtual Worlds with Live3D," shows you how to navigate three-dimensional spaces with Live3D, a virtual reality plug-in for Netscape. The three dimensional worlds will appear within the Web pages you're viewing with Netscape. With Live3D installed, you can "walk" or "fly" through these spaces. Suddenly, the Web has three dimensions instead of two.

Part IV: It's Out There *Somewhere!*

Netscape isn't just a browser. Increasingly, it's an interface to everything the Internet has to offer. Part IV and Part V show you how to put all of the Internet's resources at your fingertips!

Chapter 16, "Explore the Web," shows you how to start exploring the World Wide Web. You'll get expert help from some of the Web's most ingenious and experienced travel guides!

Chapter 17, "Find It on the Web! (Search Engines and Subject Trees)," shows you how to find the information for which you're looking. The skills this chapter teaches are absolutely indispensable.

Part V: Exploring the Internet with Netscape

New for 2

Chapter 18, "Sending and Receiving E-mail," shows you how to use Netscape's great built-in electronic mail capabilities, which rival the best e-mail programs now available.

New for 2

Chapter 19, "Chat It Up," covers Netscape Chat, an add-on program that lets you get involved in real-time conferencing via Internet Relay Chat.

Chapter 20, "Digging Around in Gopher," shows you how to use Netscape to find and access the rich resources of Gopher, a menu-based Internet information system. You'll learn how to search with Veronica and how to find Gopher Jewels.

Chapter 21, "Ransacking FTP File Archives," shows you how to navigate the file systems of distant computers, finding and retrieving useful files and software. Special emphasis is placed on the Virtual Software Library, your key to more than 90,000 shareware programs.

New for 2

Chapter 22, "Ranting and Raving in Usenet Newsgroups," fully covers the completely redesigned Netscape Version 2 approach to Usenet. You'll learn how to post your own messages as well as read those placed by others.

Chapter 23, "Surviving Telnet and 3270 Sessions," shows you how to use Netscape to access the information stored in text-based computers, such as mainframe computers and bulletin board systems. With Telnet, another door opens to a huge variety of information, which you can access with Netscape.

Part VI: The Netscape Marketplace

Netscape isn't just a great Web browser and a tool for accessing Internet information. It's also the pathway to an amazing new world of Internet

commerce, all based on secure, encrypted transmissions made possible by Netscape's Secure Sockets Layer (SSL) technology. In Chapter 24, you'll find a nontechnical, easy-to-understand introduction to this technology and why it's needed. In Chapter 25, you'll find an introduction to some of the first commercial sites on the Web—sites that enable you to use your credit card to order on-line. Let's go shopping!

Part VII: The Appendices

This book includes five useful appendices, which will help you round out your knowledge and enjoyment of Netscape:

- **Get connected** Appendix A helps you get connected to the Internet with the CD-ROM software packaged with this book.
- **Configure Netscape** Appendix B shows you how to configure Netscape to work with helper applications and plug-ins.
- **What does that command do?** Appendix C presents a quick reference guide to Netscape's menu commands
- **Can't I use the keyboard?** Appendix D summarizes Netscape's keyboard commands in a handy table.
- **How do I install the CD-ROM software?** Appendix E fully covers the installation of all those great helper programs on this book's CD-ROM disc.

How to Read This Book

With Netscape Navigator close by, naturally. Also, I recommend Mountain Dew for those all-night sessions (yawn). Check out the From Here section at the end of every chapter of this book for pathways to follow.

In addition, keep your eye out for icons. They provide cues and clues that help you find your way through this book. Here's a quick overview of this book's icons:

Here you'll find tips, shortcuts, suggestions, insights, and other helpful information about Netscape.

We've tried to anticipate the problems you'll run into—and this icon shows where to look for solutions.

The Treasure Trove icon marks a cool Internet resource of some kind. Check it out!

This icon marks one of the fantastic new features of Netscape Navigator Version 2!

Look here for inside information on the way the Web works and for fairly advanced information that might be of interest to you if you'd like to master Netscape.

Acknowledgments

Writing a book such as this one isn't a solitary job for which an author should take sole credit—we get lots of help. I'd particularly like to thank Jenifer Niles (Sponsoring Editor), Jacqui Young (Editorial Assistant), and Cindy Kogut (Production Editor). Many other people at AP Professional contributed as well; thanks to all. I would also like to thank my agent, Carole McClendon of Waterside Productions, for linking me up with AP Professional, and the great people at Netscape for making such a fantastic program!

Let Me Hear From You!

If you have suggestions for the next edition of *Netscape Navigator: Surfing the Web and Exploring the Internet,* please let me hear from you. My e-mail address is bp@virginia.edu. Please bear in mind, though, that it's just me, my family, and the cat, and we don't have the resources to provide technical support for Netscape or the programs on the CD-ROM disc!

Part I

NETSCAPE QUICK START

Chapter 1

Getting Started with Netscape Navigator

On-screen, Netscape Navigator looks like most other Windows applications—with a few strange twists. What's the big "N," and why do comets shoot past it sometimes? And what's that funny broken key thing?

Whether or not you've already started surfing with Netscape (I'll bet you have), sooner or later you will want answers to such questions. You'll find them here, arranged for quick look-up. And if you're really busy, just scan "For the Time-Challenged," at the beginning of each chapter. This section hits the high points succinctly.

Are you a seasoned Windows user? You'll find lots of important stuff in this chapter about the features that differentiate Netscape from other Windows applications, such as the

Toolbar's navigation buttons, the directory buttons, the broken key, and the hyperlinks. You can skim this chapter to get the information you need.

Are you a beginning Windows user? I'm going to assume that you know the fundamentals of using Windows 3.1 or Windows 95, such as how to start a program. But you'll find plenty of help for getting started with Netscape.

This chapter has the following sections:

- **What's on the Screen?** A visual guide to the features you see in Netscape's window. Get a quick overview!
- **Basic Window Calisthenics** Minimize, maximize, stretch, shrink—until you get it just right.
- **Quitting Netscape Navigator** Mommy, Daddy stayed up all night again!

Which Version of Windows Are You Using?

This book covers both Windows versions of Netscape, the 16-bit version for Windows 3.1, and the 32-bit version for Windows 95. The two versions of the program are almost identical, so all the instructions work for both versions of Netscape Navigator. If you're using Windows 3.1, don't be put off by the screen illustrations in this book—your version of Netscape will look almost exactly the same, except that you'll see the old, familiar Windows 3.1 interface.

Starting Netscape Navigator

Assuming you've already installed Netscape Navigator and are connected to the Internet (see Appendix A), you're ready to surf the Web.

For the Time-Challenged

- Netscape is preset to display the Netscape welcome page as its default home page. (You can change this if you want, as explained in Chapter 4.)
- Don't spend too much time trying to learn all the options on the menu bar. You won't use them frequently. With the exception of Bookmarks, the options you'll frequently use are available on the Toolbar.
- The Netsite box displays the URL (Uniform Resource Locator, the Web address) of the document you are currently viewing. (This box is called Location if you're accessing a server other than those made by Netscape Communications.)
- The doorkey icon tells you whether you're accessing a secure server (if it's broken, you're not).
- Hyperlinks, shown in color and underlining on color monitors, enable you to access another Web document. Just move the pointer to the hyperlink, and click the left mouse button once.
- The big "N" (the status indicator) displays an animation while Netscape is downloading a document you've requested. At the bottom of the screen, the status bar tells you what you're downloading, and the progress bar tells you how much of the job is finished.
- Netscape doesn't save your window-sizing and positioning options until you choose Save Options from the Options menu.

To start Netscape Navigator:

1. Click the icon that connects you to your Internet service provider or the Microsoft Network.
2. Double-click the Netscape Navigator icon. If you're using Windows 95, you can choose Netscape from the Program menu, which you can access through the Start menu.

You'll see Netscape on-screen (Figure 1.1). To find out what you're looking at, read on.

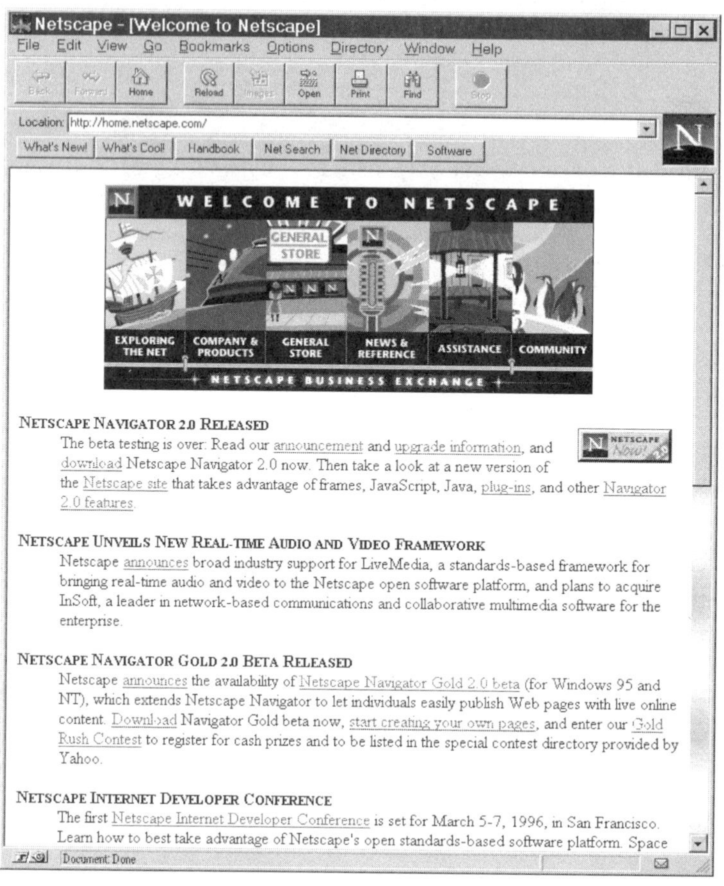

Figure 1.1 Netscape Navigator

WHAT'S ON THE SCREEN?

When Netscape Navigator starts, you'll see the program's window on-screen. The program icon (the big "N") displays an animation, informing you that Netscape is downloading information. In about a minute (or less, if you have a fast connection), you'll see the default *start page,* the page that appears when you start Netscape (or click the Home button).

Appearing within Netscape's application workspace, the default start page (see Figure 1.1) comes to you from Netscape Communications Corporation's headquarters in sunny California. In Netscape, as in any graphical Web browser, the default home page is the Web document that the program is preset to display when started.

My screen doesn't have some of the things shown in Figure 1.1! Somebody has messed with your Options menu, baby. On the menu bar, click Options. Below the first separator bar, look for options that don't have a check mark. These have been turned off. To turn them on, just click the option. Continue doing this until all the options have been turned on. Then open the Options menu one more time and choose Save Options.

The following sections detail the rest of the Netscape window, shown in Figure 1.2.

Title Bar

At the top of Netscape's window is the title bar, a standard Windows feature. Here, Netscape displays its own name. In addition, you see the title of the document you are currently viewing.

Menu Bar

Below the title bar is the menu bar, which is just down the street from the neighborhood bar—but it's not five yet, is it? On the menu bar, you'll find the titles of Netscape's menus, from which you can choose additional

Where does the title come from? Web documents are written in the HyperText Markup Language (HTML), which enables Web authors to identify specific parts of the document, such as the title, headings, body text, and lists. The title bar displays the text that's marked with the <TITLE>...</TITLE> tags. If the document you're displaying contains the title "Sailing Page," you'll see "Netscape – [Sailing Page]" on the title bar.

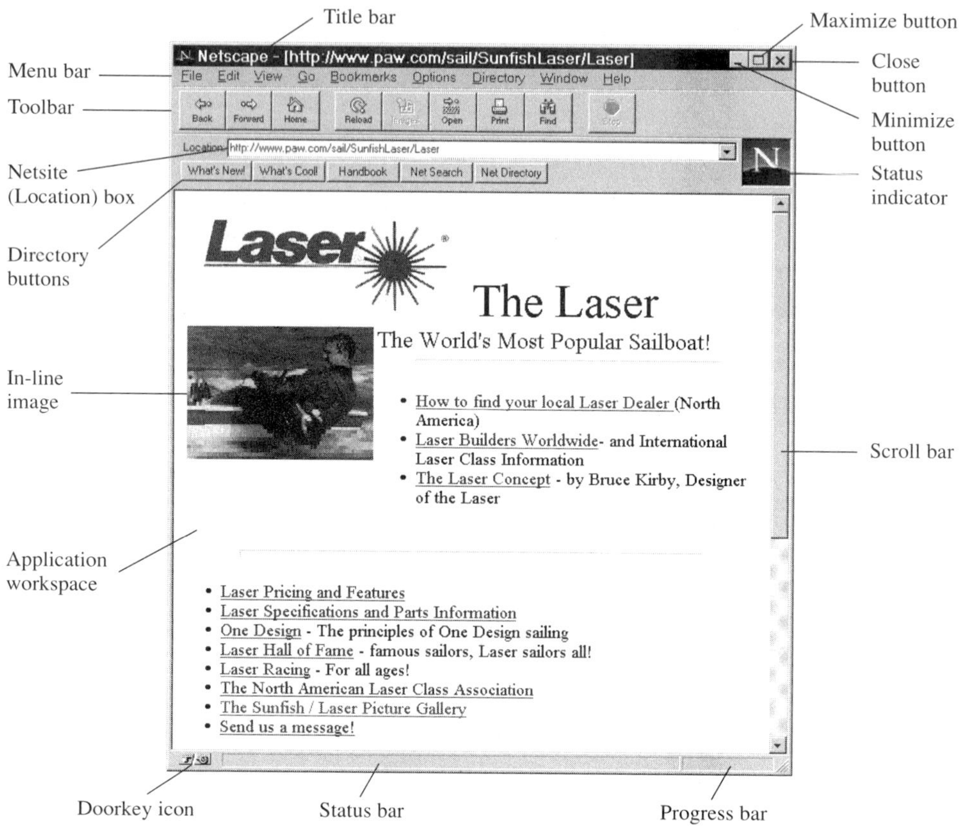

Title bar
Maximize button
Menu bar
Close button
Toolbar
Minimize button
Netsite (Location) box
Status indicator
Directory buttons
In-line image
Scroll bar
Application workspace
Doorkey icon
Status bar
Progress bar

Figure 1.2 The parts of Netscape's program window

options. Frankly, you won't use the menu bar very often—most of Netscape's most useful tools are available on the Toolbar (see the next section).

Here's a very quick overview of what's on these menus:

New for 2

- **File** This menu enables access to a grab bag of display, storage, and printing options. You'll use it most frequently to open local files. A new feature with Version 2: You can use this menu to open new Web or Mail windows.

- **Edit** This menu contains the standard Windows editing options, including Undo, Cut, Copy, Paste, and Find. The keyboard shortcuts are faster and easier. To use them, you hold down the Ctrl key and press the indicated key (for example, if you press Ctrl + F, you see the Find dialog box).
- **View** From this menu, you can choose options controlling the way Netscape obtains documents, but most of them can be chosen more quickly by using the Toolbar (discussed in the next section).
- **Go** Like the View menu, this menu contains several commands that are more easily accessed by clicking buttons on the Toolbar. But there's one gem: At the bottom of the menu, you see a list of the documents you've accessed recently. To go back to any of them, you just choose the document's name from the menu.

- **Bookmarks** This is probably the most useful menu of all. From it, you can choose options that enable you to create bookmarks. A bookmark is a saved document address that enables you to return to this document quickly, just by choosing it from the Bookmarks menu. You'll learn more about bookmarks in Chapter 6. *Note:* If you've installed Netscape's new SmartMarks add-on, this menu has different commands. These commands give you direct access to SmartMark's enormously cool features. You'll learn more about SmartMarks in Chapter 7.
- **Options** This menu enables you to choose the way Netscape appears on-screen. Netscape is preset to display all of its optional screen features, such as the Toolbar, and that's the way I recommend that you use the program. In addition, you'll find lots of options for customizing Netscape, which are fully covered in Chapter 9.
- **Directory** This menu enables you to go directly to valuable Web resources, including search services. It duplicates the Directory buttons and gives a few additional options.
- **Window** This menu enables you to open new Mail and News windows, and also provides access to the Address Book, the bookmarks you've chosen, and the history list. You'll learn more about these features later in this book.
- **Help** This menu offers access to Netscape Navigator's on-line help directory—but hey, you've got this book. Much of the rest of this menu is a rather thinly disguised marketing tool.

I've got tennis elbow from using this darned mouse! I like to keep the use of my mouse to the minimum—and to do so, I make full use of keyboard commands. Look for the underlined letter in menu and option names. You can use these letters with the Alt key to select commands and options—without touching the mouse! To choose the View menu, hold down the Alt key and press V (uppercase or lowercase). To choose the Reload option in this menu, just press R.

Toolbar

The Toolbar contains buttons, or tools, that enable easy access to frequently used Netscape commands. Here's a very quick once-over-lightly (you'll learn how to use these buttons in this chapter and the next):

Back	Go back to the document you just viewed.
Forward	Return to the document you went back from. This button isn't available unless you've displayed a document and then clicked the Back tool.
Home	Redisplay the default home page.
Reload	Retrieve the currently displayed document again.
Images	Turn off the automatic downloading of in-line images.
Open	Type a URL (Web address) directly.
Print	Print the document that Netscape is currently displaying.
Find	Find text in the current document.
Stop	Stop downloading the current document.

Netsite (Location) Box

The Netsite box indicates the Web address (the URL) of the document you are currently viewing. When you access a non-Netscape Communications server, this box is called Location instead of Netsite.

Directory Buttons

The Directory buttons enable you to access Web resources quickly. All of these options are also available on the Directory menu.

Button	Name	Description
What's New!	What's New	Displays a list of new and interesting Web sites.
What's Cool!	What's Cool	Here are some Web sites that Mozilla likes. See you in a couple of hours.
Handbook	Handbook	Click here to see Netscape's on-line documentation.
Net Search	Net Search	Displays a great list of Web search engines (programs that search databases of Web documents). You'll learn more about searching the Web in Chapter 17.
Net Directory	Net Directory	Displays a page that provides access to the Yahoo subject tree (which is like a library subject catalog). Through Yahoo, you can access other equally useful Web subject trees. You'll learn more about subject trees in Chapter 17.
Software	Software	Click here to find out about Netscape's software upgrades.

Status Indicator

The big "N" lets you know when Netscape is downloading a document from the Web—it plays an animation (currently, comets shooting over the earth). When the document is finished downloading, you see "Document Done" on the status bar (at the bottom of the screen).

What's in a URL? A URL has three parts. The first part (http://) indicates the type of resource you're viewing. If you're viewing an FTP file archive, the first part of the URL reads "ftp://," while a Gopher menu's URL reads "gopher://."

The second part of the URL indicates the name of the computer you're accessing (such as home.netscape.com).

The third part of the directory indicates the path that Netscape must take to locate the document, and it also includes the document name (/home/welcome.html). Sometimes the third part of a URL is missing, which tells Netscape to look for and obtain the default document.

Do you really need to know all this? Not really, but sometimes you'll need to type URLs and it's important to do so correctly. For more information, check out Chapter 2.

To return to Netscape's home page, just click the status indicator.

Application Workspace

Here, Netscape displays the document you're currently viewing. You'll see text and hyperlinks, and you may also see in-line images (graphics that appear along with the text). If the document is bigger than the available window space, the scroll bars activate. You can click the scroll arrows, or drag the scroll bars, to bring hidden portions of the document into view.

Doorkey Icon

This icon indicates whether you're accessing a secure server. If you're not, the key is broken. Don't give your credit card number to any on-line vendor unless the connection is secure! If you're accessing a secure site, the key is unbroken.

Status Bar and Progress Bar

Next to the doorkey icon, there's a panel called the *status bar*. Netscape uses the status bar to display messages about what the program is doing. Most of the time, you can ignore these messages, unless you're curious to know what the program is doing.

Next to the status bar, you see a blank panel called the *progress bar*. When Netscape retrieves a document from the Internet, you'll see a graphical display indicating how much of the document has been obtained.

Mail Icon

New for 2 If you've set up Netscape to read your Internet mail, you'll know when there's mail waiting for you: you'll see a little yellow letter on the status bar. To open a mail window, just double-click the mail icon.

Hyperlinks: The Basics

Note that some of the words and phrases you see are highlighted with colors and underlining (if you're using a monochrome monitor, you'll see only underlining). These are *hyperlinks* (also called *anchors* or just *links*).

When you click on a hyperlink, Netscape locates the Web document that is linked to this hyperlink and initiates the transfer.

Try clicking one of the hyperlinks now:

1. Move the tip of the mouse pointer so that it's positioned over the hyperlink, and take a look at the status bar at the bottom of the screen. This displays the URL of the document to which this anchor is linked.
2. With the left mouse button, click the link. Forget all that double-clicking stuff; you just click once.

Several things happen now:

- The big "N" displays an animation (shooting comets). This tells you that Netscape is obtaining the document you requested, through a

process called *downloading*. Incidentally, the official name for the big "N" is *status indicator.* (I like "Big 'N'" better.)

- The status bar indicates that Netscape is downloading a document.
- You see the new document within Netscape's application workspace.

What does "downloading" mean? When downloading occurs, Netscape transfers an entire document to your computer's memory, along with any associated graphics. This is called "downloading" because the information is coming from a distant computer to your computer. (As you might guess, the term *uploading* means sending information from your computer to a distant computer.) Once the document is in your computer's memory, you can scroll through it quickly. In addition, Netscape stores recently accessed documents in memory so that you can redisplay them quickly, should you wish to return to them.

Now try going back to the document you displayed previously. To do so, just click the Back button on the Toolbar. Take a look at the hyperlink you just clicked.

If you're viewing Netscape on a color monitor, note that the hyperlink you just clicked has changed color. This is a *visited* hyperlink, a hyperlink to a document that you've already seen. You can still click the hyperlink to redisplay the visited document, but Netscape wants you to know that you've been down that road before.

Basic Window Calisthenics

Like the window of any fine Windows application, Netscape's window can be adjusted until it suits your fancy. You can also minimize the program to an icon or maximize it to full size. The following instructions quickly detail these procedures; Figure 1.3 shows the on-screen window controls. P.S.—The Do-Nothing button really *doesn't* do anything. Access it at

http://www.wam.umd.edu/~twoflowr/button.htm

by typing this address exactly in the Location box and pressing Enter.

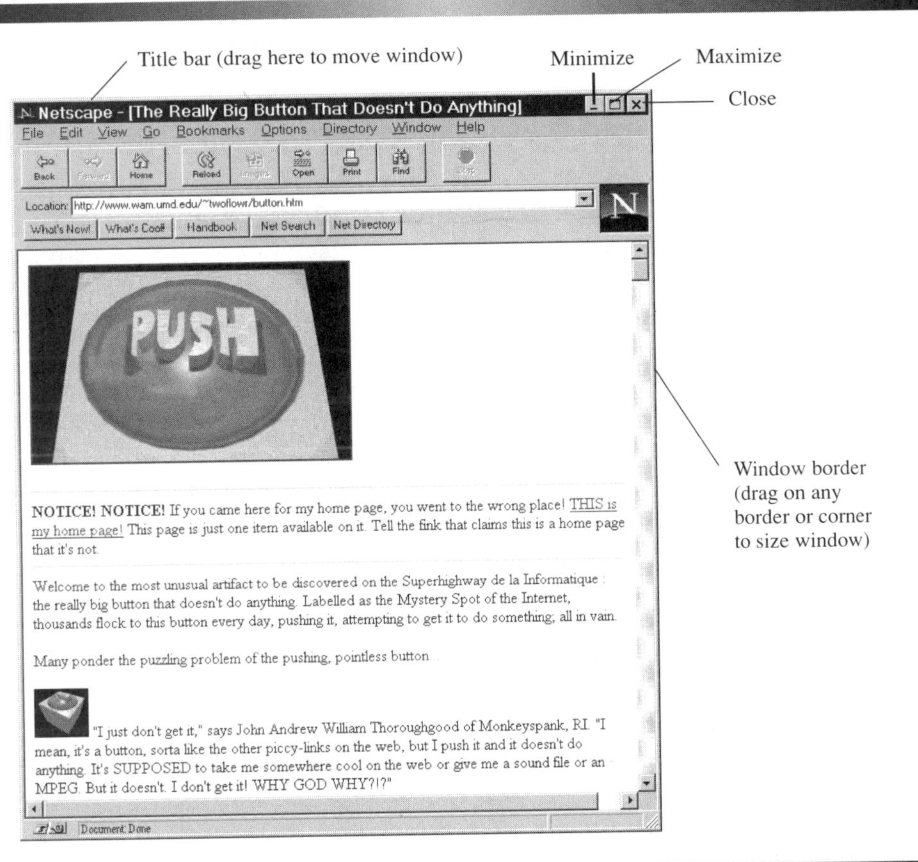

Figure 1.3 On-screen window controls

Moving the Window

To move Netscape's window on the screen:

1. Move the mouse pointer to the title bar, hold down the left mouse button, and drag. You'll move the whole window.
2. When you've moved the window to where you want it to appear, release the mouse button.

Sizing the Window

To size Netscape's window:

1. Move the mouse pointer to one of the window's borders until the pointer changes shape, and drag the border.
2. When you've sized the window the way you want, release the mouse button.

Here's a neat trick: To size two borders at once, click on one of the corners and drag.

Minimizing the Window

To minimize Netscape's window:

1. Click the Minimize button. This shrinks Netscape down to an icon on the desktop (Windows 3.1) or a button on the taskbar (Windows 95).
2. To redisplay Netscape, double-click the minimized program icon (Windows 3.1) or the taskbar button (Windows 95).

Maximizing the Window

To maximize Netscape's window:

1. Click the Maximize button.
2. After you've maximized the window, you can restore the window to its previous size by clicking the same button.

Save those window positions! Now that you've gone to all the trouble to position the window the way you want, why not save your choices? From the Options menu, choose Save Options. (If you don't use this command, you'll see the default window position the next time you open Netscape Navigator.)

Quitting Netscape Navigator

So, you're done. It's about 5 AM, isn't it? Hope you had fun.

To quit Netscape Navigator:

- From the File menu, choose Exit
  or
- Press Alt + F4

From Here

- Surf's up! Explore the Web, and access Internet resources, in Chapter 2.
- Running into problems—like that horrible "403—Access Forbidden" message? Check out Chapter 3, "When the Surf Gets Rough."
- Like to master Netscape, using the tricks known only to late-night confirmed hyperlink addicts? Check out Part II.

Chapter 2

The Gentle Art of Web Surfing

Wouldn't it be cool to learn how to surf the Web with the best of 'em, and in just an hour or two? If you agree, read this chapter. Sure, there's more to learn than this chapter covers, but you'll learn 90% of what you need to have some serious fun with Netscape. Plus, this chapter serves as a guide to much of the rest of this book. Later chapters explore its topics in more detail. By reading this chapter, you can learn which subjects you'd like to explore more deeply.

Just what does surfing the Web mean? It means exploring, discovering, navigating—and above all, being swept away by a series of awesome hyperlinks that you can ride all over cyberspace.

Netscape's your surfboard. You start by finding a cool Web document, one that's loaded with hyperlinks, and then begin exploring. As you navigate link after link, you'll connect with computers all over North America, Europe, Australia, and even more remote places. You can look forward to countless hours of discovery, fun, and even enchantment, with a bit of boredom thrown in (admittedly, not every Web site is worth accessing).

The surfing metaphor is darned appropriate: Sometimes you'll put your "board" on an amazing series of hyperlinks, and they'll carry you off to who-knows-where. And sometimes, admittedly, the hyperlinks you'll ride aren't very interesting, although (happily) some of them are so stupid that they are truly hilarious (see the following Treasure Trove). But there's gold in those links, as you'll surely agree. Have fun, and be sure to cancel tomorrow's appointments.

If you're curious to know what a really dumb Web site looks like, you'll find lots of links to dum-dum pages at the wonderful Useless Pages site,

http://www.primus.com/staff/paulp/useless.html

Webmaster Paul Phillips created this site after discovering that somebody named Kenny Z had typed his entire CD collection in an HTML document and made it available on the Web. Paul reflects that this was the first Web document that, as he puts it, "overtly crossed the line from tolerably frivolous to truly inane." Paul has since collected dozens of useless pages—you just have to check this out. For some reason, one of Paul's finds, the National Texture Administration's home page,

http://ftp.std.com/homepages/stevec/NTA/intro.html

just kills me. Maybe it's the link to "Man, the texturing animal." Read a treatise on fish and whale regurgitation, talk to Michael's cat, visit Edward's Scratch-n-Sniff Theater, read Dan's Dream Journal, and identify Ferret-Free Zones. To learn how to access a Web page by typing a URL directly, see the section titled "Typing a Web Address Directly," later in this chapter.

This chapter will benefit every reader of this book, and that's true even if you've already done some Web surfing with

Netscape. In this chapter, you'll find a Web-savvy approach to Netscape, the approach that experienced Netscape mavens use every day. Working through this chapter, even the stuff that seems obvious, will reveal the Netscape secrets and strategies that make this program the Web browser of choice.

For the Time-Challenged

- Remember to click just once when you click a hyperlink.
- A graphic with a blue border contains a hyperlink.
- Some graphics contain hyperlinks but don't have blue borders. To tell whether a graphic contains a hyperlink, move the mouse pointer over the graphic. If it changes to a hand shape, the graphic contains a hyperlink.
- To return to a document you've previously displayed, click Back or choose the document's name from the Go menu. To redisplay the document you were just viewing, click Forward.
- If you've accessed a multi-part Web page that has internal navigation buttons, learn how to use them. For finding your way around this web site, these buttons are much better than Netscape's Back and Forward buttons.

- When you access a document that contains frames, Netscape's window splits into two or more independently scrollable panels. To work with one of the panels, click within it.
- To access a Web page by typing its Web address directly, type it in the Location box and press Enter.
- If you get lost, click the Home button.
- To view movies, you need to install a helper application (see Chapter 11). Netscape is preset to play certain sounds.
- To locate documents on the Web, learn how to use search engines and subject trees.

A Word about Web Terminology

The Web's grown so fast that there hasn't been time to develop a consistent nomenclature—which doesn't help people who are trying to learn how to use it. Here are a few definitions to help you get started.

Page A Web document. Of course, many of these documents are longer than one page.

Home Page A Web document that's a "home" or a headquarters for a certain type of information. People like to set up home pages containing information about themselves, for example. Netscape has its own home page, the one you see every time you start the program.

Start Page The Web document that you see every time you start Netscape (or click the Home button). By default, this is Netscape's home page. You can change this, as explained in Chapter 4.

Web Browser A program that enables you to surf the Internet in search of Web pages.

Web Server A program that makes Web pages available to people who are browsing the Web.

Web Site A computer that's running a Web server. A Web site may contain lots of pages—maybe thousands of them. Unfortunately, many people use the term "site" as if it were synonymous with "page" ("That's a cool *site*" usually means "That's a cool *page*.")

URL The Web address of a Web page. I'll use the terms "Web address" and "URL" interchangeably.

There are more Web terms to learn, but these are more than sufficient to get you going.

Starting Netscape

Assuming you've already installed Netscape and configured your Internet connection (see Appendix A), you're ready to go.

Starting Netscape with Windows 3.1

In Program Manager, locate the Netscape program group, and double-click the Netscape Navigator program icon.

Starting Netscape with Windows 95

In the Start menu of Windows 95, click Programs, and then click Netscape to open the Netscape program group. Double-click the Netscape Navigator icon to start Netscape. You'll see Netscape on-screen, and the program displays the default start page (see Figure 2.1).

Using Windows 95? Eliminate all this Start-menu fussing by creating a shortcut for Netscape. The shortcut will appear on the desktop, where you can position it next to the Microsoft Network and Internet icons so thoughtfully provided by Microsoft (icons, I hasten to add, that you can't get rid of without knowing some system-level programming tricks.) To create a Netscape shortcut, click on the Netscape Navigator program icon and drag it to the desktop.

Netscape likes visitors—it helps them sell advertising space on their home page—but you should eventually change the default start page to something more tailored to your needs. It's really easy to do. For the low-down, see Chapter 4.

The Fundamental Maneuvers of Web Surfing

What makes the Web so much *fun* is its unpredictability—you start out clicking links from Netscape's home page (suggestion: click the What's Cool button to see a list of neat sites), and who knows where you'll wind up?

Experienced surfers know, though, that there are two kinds of surfing:

- **Grooving** This is good. Seriously good. When you're in a groove, you just can't seem to do anything wrong—you keep finding these *tremendous* sites, and the links from these sites take you to even more tremendous sites.

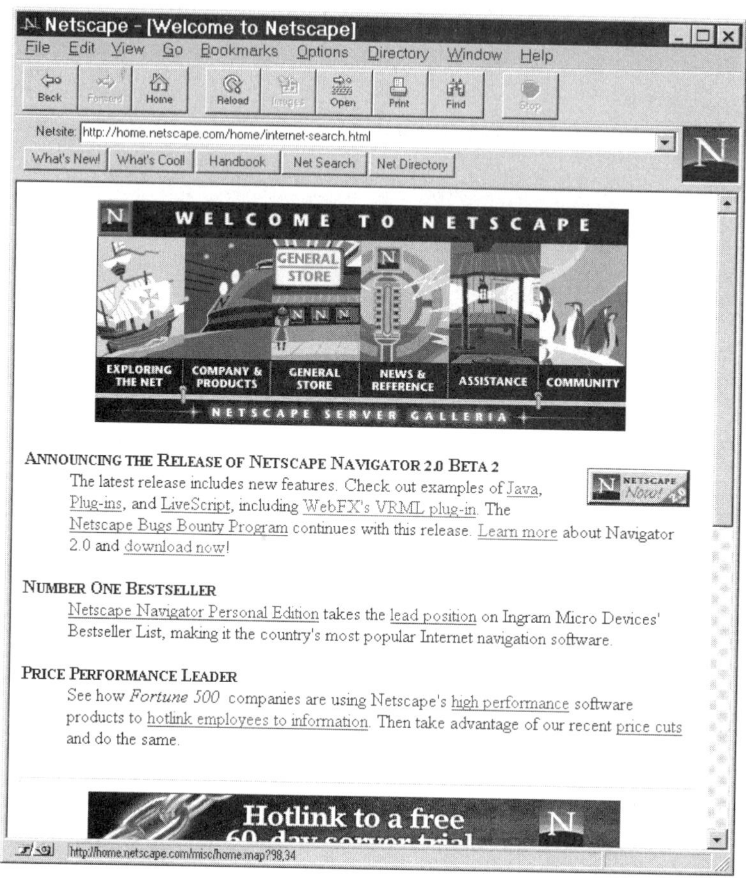

Figure 2.1 Default start page (Netscape Communications Corporation)

- **Thrashing** Everything you see is junk. On top of that, you're lost. You click and click, but there's nothing worth seeing.

Caught in a thrash? Get out of it by clicking the What's Cool button. You'll see Netscape's What's Cool page again. Try surfing from there—you can't go wrong. Check out a page, and click the Back button to go back to the What's Cool page again.

The Subtle Mysteries and Finer Points of Hyperlinks

You already know that hyperlinks appear in distinctive formatting (color and underlining, if you're using a color monitor). In addition, visited hyperlinks (ones you've clicked before) appear in a different, distinctive color. Here are a couple of additional points you need to know about hyperlinks:

- **Click *once*** To activate a hyperlink, you just move the pointer to it, and click. Yes, that's right—click once. Because many Macintosh and Windows functions are initiated by double-clicking something, you may have to unlearn the tendency to double-click. That second click may activate an unwanted hyperlink on the page that's about to be displayed, taking you to who-knows-where.
- **Some graphics contain hyperlinks** You can click these pictures to display a Web document. Here's how to tell whether an in-line graphic is a hyperlink: Look for a border around the graphic. With most browsers, the border appears in blue. Note, though, that Web authors are increasingly hiding the blue border (there's a way you can do this), since they believe that it's unaesthetic. When this is done, though, there's usually some indication on the graphic itself that it's really a hyperlink. In Figure 2.1, for example, the Netscape Now graphic is a button—just the sort of thing you'd want to click.
- **Learn to use image maps** Some Web pages include graphics that have clickable regions, each associated with its own hyperlink. Such graphics are called *image maps*, although they don't necessarily look like a map. An example is the beautiful graphic at the top of Netscape's home page, which has a number of distinct areas. If you click one of these areas, Netscape displays the linked document. A great example of an image map is the White House Home Page (Figure 2.2). The whole screen is a clickable image map.

I can't tell whether this graphic contains a hyperlink or not! No blue border? It might still contain one or more hyperlinks. To find out, move the mouse pointer over the graphic. If it changes shape to a hand with one finger extended, then you know that the graphic contains a hyperlink.

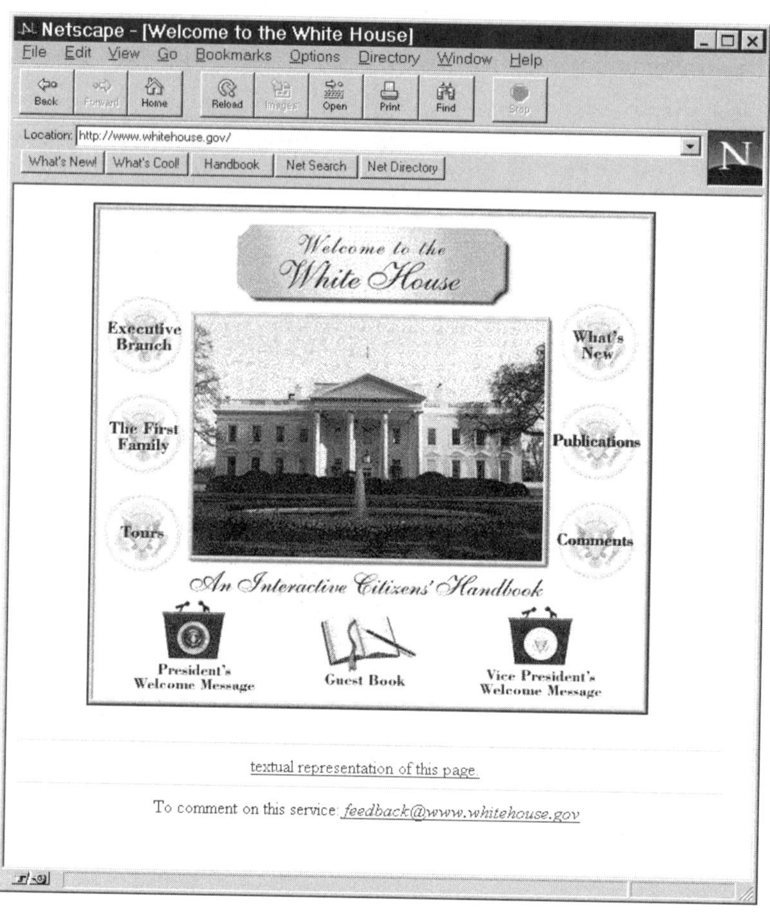

Figure 2.2 White House Home Page (http://www.whitehouse.gov/)

I'M LOST! (NAVIGATION FUNDAMENTALS)

Two exclamations are heard from beginning Web surfers: "Cool!" followed shortly by "Where am I!!?" Here's a very quick mini-course in Web navigation.

Going Back

At any time, you can go back to see a document you previously viewed. To go back, you click the Back button. If you just love toying with Windows' menus, you could choose Back from the Go menu, but mouse-haters are cheerfully invited to use the Alt + < keyboard shortcut. (< is the less-than symbol, which you'll find to the right of the letter M on your keyboard.)

Mouse lovers, here's a neat trick. To go back, just click the *right* mouse button anywhere within the document. From the pop-up menu, click Back.

You can keep clicking Back to return to previously viewed documents, but if you're going back more than two or three documents, there's a better way. See "There's a History to This," in Chapter 5.

Notice that going back is a lot faster than downloading the document in the first place? That's because Netscape stores a copy of recently accessed documents in a special memory area called a *cache*. The program can retrieve documents from the cache much faster than it can retrieve them from the network.

If you're trying to redisplay a document that you viewed several clicks ago, don't waste time by clicking the Back button repeatedly. Instead, open the Go menu and look for the document's name at the bottom of this menu. Note that sometimes Netscape doesn't save the names of all the documents you've visited. To find out why, see "There's a History to This," in Chapter 5.

Going Forward

Once you've gone back by clicking the Back button, the Forward button becomes available. Try it now (or press Alt + >).

If you like using the mouse, try this: Right-click anywhere within the document, and choose Forward.

So what does the Forward button do? It lets you return to the document you just went Back from. Oh, heck, it's easier to do than talk about.

The Forward button is dimmed! You're viewing the most recent document you downloaded, which means that you can't go forward. You can go back, or you can access a new Web document by clicking a hyperlink or typing a Web address.

Look for Internal Navigation Buttons!

Many Web sites offer more than just a page; they offer a *web*, and within this web each page has navigation buttons to help you find your way. A web (as opposed to *the* Web, the World Wide Web) is a collection of related Web documents, all stored on a single site; each document explores one facet of the topic at hand. Internal navigation aids help you find your way around in a web. Ideally, navigation buttons appear on every page of the web and look just the same, so you quickly learn how to navigate within the web.

If the web you're browsing has internal navigation buttons, by all means use them! Internal navigation buttons always give you the best way of navigating within a multidocument web. That's because the web's author knows just how the web is structured. The navigation buttons have been designed to help you navigate the web logically. You can use Netscape's Back and Forward buttons to redisplay pages you just accessed, if you wish, but the internal navigation buttons are your best bet.

You'll quickly learn to recognize navigation buttons, which are of two kinds:

- **Graphical Buttons** These are popular because they look neat, but they take forever to download on slow SLIP/PPP lines using modems. See Figure 2.3 for an example.
- **Text Buttons** These navigation aids download much more quickly because they're made from ordinary characters. See Figure 2.4 for an example.

I don't know what this darned navigation button does! Too many Web authors use button graphics that don't really suggest what's going to happen when you click on the navigation buttons—so don't feel bad, it's not you. Thoughtful Web authors include explanatory text along with the buttons, unless the buttons' meanings are so clear that it's obvious what they do.

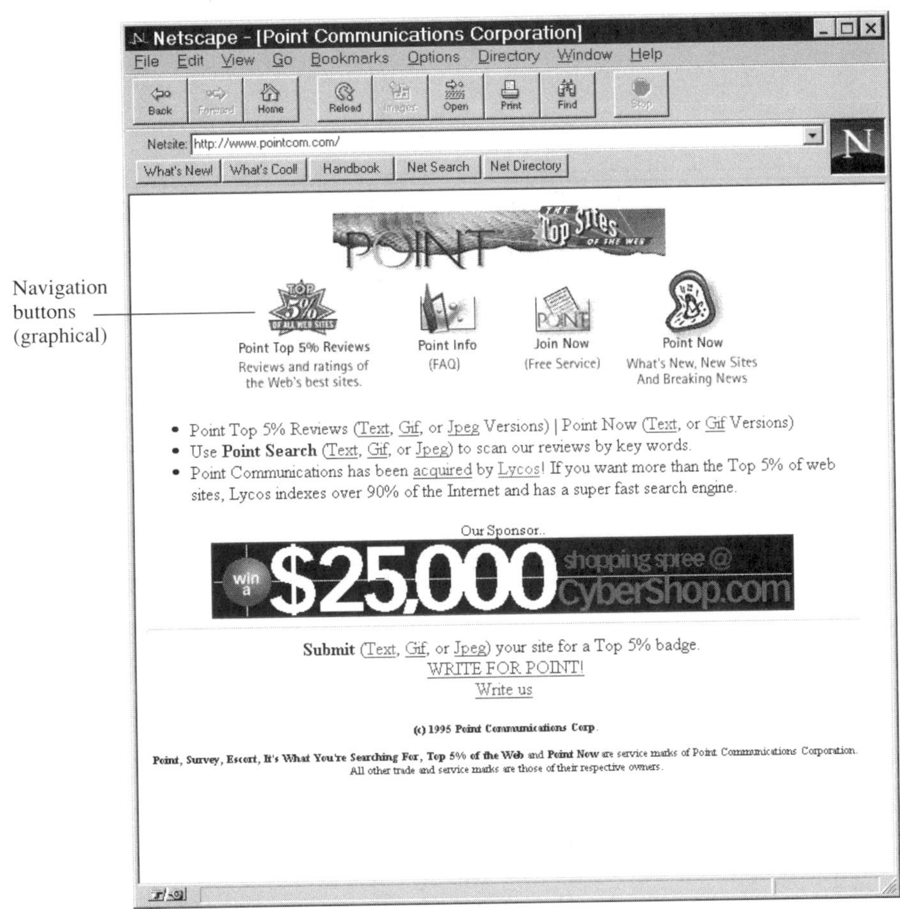

Figure 2.3 Graphical navigation buttons

IT'S A FRAME-UP (USING FRAMES)

New for 2

A very nice new feature of Netscape 2.0 is support of *frames*, a set of HTML tags that enable Web authors to divide a page into several independently scrollable panels. When you access a document that contains frames,

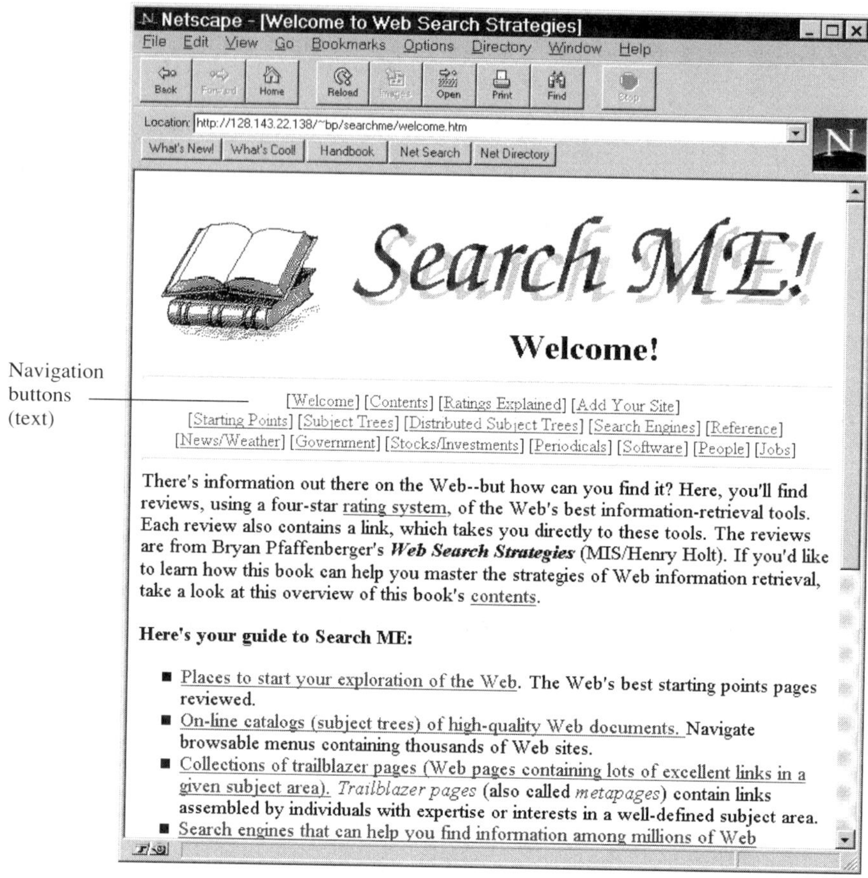

Figure 2.4 Text-based navigation buttons

Netscape divides the application workspace into two or more panels. If there's more text in one of the panels than Netscape can display, the program automatically includes a scroll bar. You can use the scroll bar to bring the hidden parts of the panel into view.

Some Web authors may give you the option of repositioning the frame borders. If you'd like to do so, move the pointer to the border. If the pointer changes shape to a bidirectional arrow, you can adjust the border's position.

An obvious and appropriate use for frames is to keep navigation buttons on-screen at all times. With a one-page display, the buttons scroll out of sight as the user reads the document. With frames, a Web author can position the frame in a panel that stays put, even if the user scrolls the other panel (see Figure 2.5). Another obvious application of frames lies in computer-aided instruction. In Figure 2.6, you see an interesting explanation of the human eye; when you click on one of the features of the eye, you see an explanation in the right-hand panel.

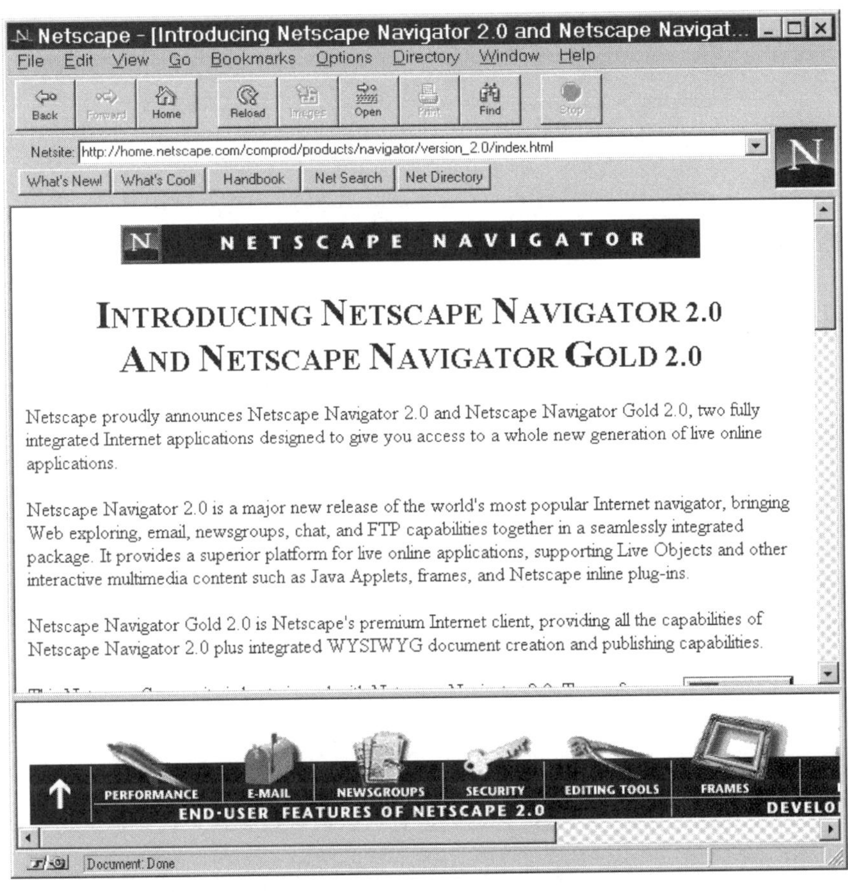

Figure 2.5 Navigation buttons positioned in bottom panel

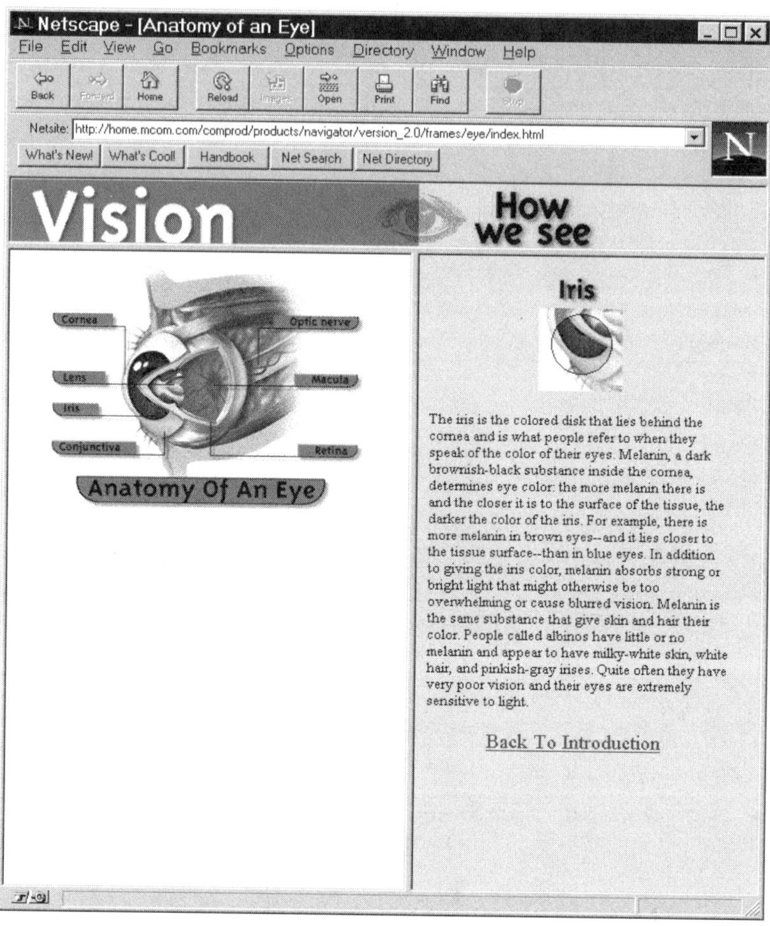

Figure 2.6 Frames used for computer-aided instruction

JAVA!

New for 2

Here's the latest and probably the neatest thing on the Web. Java is a new programming language that is being developed by Sun Microsystems. Based on the popular C++ language, widely used by professional programmers, Java enables professional programmers to prepare mini-programs called

Java applets. New HTML tags enable Web developers to embed Java applets into Web pages—when you access such a page, things happen!

On pages containing Java applets, you'll see action where there was once nothing but static text and graphics—for example, words will whirl, blink, and fade. One of the coolest demonstration sites shows a simulated stock ticker tape, which scrolls past the screen at an impressive clip.While it does, three charts track your favorite stocks' price movements throughout the day. Most exciting, though, are a whole range of planned Web applications that will enable you to interact with a Web page and see the results immediately.

Netscape Version 2 can run Java applets, and does so automatically. You don't need to do anything special, or learn any new commands. You'll just notice that the pages you download have added functionality.

This Java applet is taking forever to load! Some Java applets require downloading graphics and sounds in addition to the Java code, and this might require a minute or two. Be patient—chances are that the wait will be worth it!

Typing a Web Address Directly

You've picked up your copy of *Netguide*, and you've read about this seriously cool Web site. The only problem is, there's no hyperlink to this site on Netscape's default home page. How do you get there? You can type the Web address directly and go straight to the site.

Don't waste time trying to find a site by clicking hyperlink after hyperlink. Chances are you'll never make it: At this writing, there are over 8 million Web documents in existence! If you know the site's URL (Uniform Resource Locator), you can type the URL in Netscape and access the site directly.

Understanding Web Addresses

A Web address (URL) has three parts:

- **Protocol Name** This is the first part of the URL. It specifies the type of Internet communication standard (protocol) that's used to obtain this document. Web documents use the HTTP (World Wide

Web) protocol, so you'll see *http://* at the beginning of Web addresses. You may also encounter *gopher://, ftp://,* and other protocol names.

- **Internet Address** In the second part of the URL, you see the Internet *domain name* of the computer that stores the resource you're accessing. The parts of the domain name are separated by dots, as in *www.yahoo.com.*
- **File Location** The third part of a URL specifies the location of the resource within the file system of the computer you're accessing. You may see one or more subdirectory (folder) names in this section. The final component of the URL is the file name of the resource you're accessing. If it's a Web document, the file will end in *.htm or *.html.

A URL looks like this:

http://dmf.culture.fr/files/imaginary_exhibition.html

Using the Open Location Dialog Box

To access a Web address by typing it directly, follow these steps:

1. From the File menu, choose Open Location, or use the Ctrl + L keyboard shortcut, or click the Open button.
2. In the Open Location dialog box, carefully type the URL. Be sure to copy the URL exactly, including the exact pattern of capitalization. Don't include any spaces.
3. Click Open.

I typed the URL, but it didn't work! Whoops. Well, there are several possible reasons. Here's a rundown:

- **You may have typed the URL wrong.** Even a little tiny mistake, like putting a period at the end of the URL or adding a space, can mess things up. Remember, too, that URLs are case-sensitive (uppercase and lowercase letters are different). If you find a mistake, just edit and correct it within the Netsite box, and press Enter to try again.

- **The author or site administrator may have pulled the plug on this site.** That wasn't very nice, was it? But it happens. Incidentally, some of the URLs in this book may have gone bye-bye in the interval between my writing and your reading—if you run into any of these, let me know (bp@virginia.edu).
- **Too many people are trying to access the site.** Netscape is trying, trying, trying to access the site; the comets keep shooting, but nothing appears . . . minutes go by, fruitlessly. Give up, and click Stop. Try again later—like 2 AM. So many people are surfing the Web that it's sometimes hard to get through to popular sites during prime daytime hours (10 AM to 4 PM).

Typing the URL in the Location Box

Here's a faster way to type the URL:

1. Click within the Location box. Netscape selects the current Web address.
2. Just start typing the new URL. The name of the Location box changes to Go to.
3. Press Enter when you're done typing the URL.

You can sometimes tell a lot about a Web resource by looking at its URL. For example, the URL on page 34 tells me that the document is located in a computer in France (the "fr" part of the domain name is a code name for France). I'll bet that the document is stored on a UNIX machine, too, since UNIX computers can handle long file names ("imaginary_exhibition.html"). A short file name with the *.htm extension is a dead giveaway that the computer is a Windows 3.1 system. Some more tips: In domain names, "edu" indicates a college or university, while "com" indicates a private company, "org" indicates a nonprofit organization, and "gov" indicates a government office of some kind.

Don't retype a URL if you want to revisit a site you previously accessed by typing the URL directly—Netscape remembers the last ten URLs that you directly typed in the Location box. To choose one of them, click the down arrow at the right edge of the Location box.

How I Got Here, I Haven't a Clue (Go Home)

If you're really lost, you'll know it: hyperdisorientation sets in. (Hyperdisorientation is a well-documented malady of cyberspace, a recently discovered syndrome with distressing symptoms: Patients do not know how they got to where they are, haven't the foggiest idea how to retrace their steps, and babble incessantly about lost URLs.) Netscape provides a quick cure: Click the Home button. You'll see the Netscape welcome page again.

Help Me, Helper Applications!

Netscape can't do everything by itself, although it does a great job of displaying GIF and JPEG graphics. Sounds, movies, and animations are dinosaurs of a different color, though—the program needs helper applications, programs that start when they're needed in order to play a movie or sound.

Netscape comes with a cool sound player (Netscape Audio Player); it's already set up and ready to go, so let's give it a whirl. How about a selection from Neil Young's *Sleeps with Angels*? To access the *Sleeps with Angels* page, type the following URL directly:

http://www.iuma.com/Warner/html/Young,_Neil.html

By the way, note the comma after "Young"—you need to type this URL exactly.

This is legit, incidentally; it's a 30-second excerpt from "Change Your Mind," one of the cuts from the album, and it's offered by Warner Brothers—for promotional purposes, obviously.

To hear the mono version of "Change Your Mind," click the Sun-AU (271K) option. (The other option, an 800K-plus stereo MPEG file, requires a custom sound player.) Netscape downloads the sound (this takes a while), and then displays the Netscape Audio Player application. You'll see a row of VCR-like controls; just click the Play control to start the sound.

It won't play through my PC's little speaker! To hear the sound, your system must be equipped with a sound card and speakers.

When you're finished listening to the sound, you can "rewind" it and play it again, or just quit (double-click the application's Control menu icon, or click the Close button).

I Want to See You Again, or, Setting Bookmarks

You've found a cool Web site, haven't you? And you want to know how to get back without having to click for six months, or type the URL, don't you? That's why Netscape lets you set bookmarks.

A bookmark is a URL that you've saved to a special list of ultra-cool Web sites, a list you have constructed yourself. Whenever you run across a Web site you like, just set a bookmark, as explained here.

To set a bookmark:

1. Display the Web page that you want to mark.
2. From the Bookmarks menu, choose Add Bookmark, or use the Ctrl + D keyboard shortcut.

Netscape adds the name of the document you're displaying to the Bookmarks menu. To visit this document again, just open the Bookmarks menu and choose the document's name.

I've added too many documents to my Bookmarks menu! This happens pretty fast, you'll find. Once you've added one or two dozen documents to your Bookmarks menu, it isn't very much fun to use anymore. Time to get organized! Netscape provides a cool way to create submenus, so that you can pack dozens and dozens of bookmarks in this

menu without creating something overwhelming to the eye. Flip to Chapter 6 for the lowdown on organizing your Bookmarks menu.

The Bookmarks menu is loaded with SmartMarks options—but no Bookmarks options! Great—you've installed SmartMarks. You'll be glad you did. To find out how to save bookmark items with SmartMarks, see Chapter 7.

Excuse Me, Where's the Subject Catalog? (Subject Trees and Search Engines)

Let's start with the bad news. It's really difficult to find information on the Web. Here's why. You've probably heard that the Internet is an experiment in controlled anarchy—there's no central headquarters of Internet, Inc. You don't have to get anyone's permission to hook up your computer or network to the Internet. So the Internet just grows and grows, hooking up an estimated 35 million people so far.

Because the Web uses the Internet for its communication base, the Web's just as gloriously disorganized—you don't have to ask anyone's permission to put documents on the Web. There's no single, central repository of records concerning Web documents.

With some 8 million Web documents now in existence (make that 12 million by the time you read this), we're talking about an information-retrieval nightmare. There's stuff on the Web concerning the chardonnays of Western Australia, the role of community networks in improving health care delivery, or the history of punk rock in the funkier districts of London—but good luck finding it, unless you're lucky enough to stumble on a trailblazer document that summarizes all the relevant links. (A trailblazer document, discussed in Chapter 16, stems from some charitable individual's attempts to sum up a number of interesting links, often on a single subject area such as gardening.)

Although there's no official, central database of Web documents, lots of clever computer people have been trying to solve the information-retrieval problem. They've taken two approachs, called *subject trees* and *search engines*.

- **Subject Trees** A subject tree is a subject-oriented catalog of URLs, organized by topic (such as "Astrology," "Astronomy," "Astrophysics," etc.). The "tree" part of the name comes from the catalog's hierarchical organization; under "music," for instance, you find branches of the tree, such as classical music, folk music, and techno-rave music. No subject tree is complete; it is a really big pain to keep one of these things updated. Most of the work is done by civic-minded volunteers, who have only so much time for such things. Out of some 2 million Web documents, for example, Yahoo—one of the best subject trees—indexes only about 32,000. On the bright side, though, Yahoo contains 32,000 *good* URLs. There's a lot of junk out there, but it doesn't pass the subject tree's screening mechanisms.

- **Search Engine** A search engine provides keyword searching of a database that has been compiled by a spider or worm (a program that automatically "crawls" the Web, finding Web documents and recording information about them). A search engine enables you to type in one or more search words (such as "Neil" and "Young"). The search engine then tries to match these search terms against a database of URL names and topics. Search engines and spiders are helpful tools, but bear in mind that they retrieve the chaff as well as the wheat: A search for CDs, for instance, will retrieve Kenny Z's useless list of his CD collection along with some on-line compact disc vendors and an unbelievable assortment of other stuff.

Let's take a look at subject trees in more detail; Chapter 17 delves into the mysteries of search engines.

Introducing Yahoo

No subject tree can hope to keep up with the thousands of new Web pages that appear every week. Every subject tree is therefore a selection from what's out there, and some are hipper than others. The hippest? Yahoo.

The name "Yahoo" stands for Yet Another Hierarchically Officious Oracle. On Yahoo's help page, you'll find a pull-down box that lets you choose words other than "Officious" if you like, including "Obstreperous" and "Odiferous." Self-effacing Yahoo may be, but you'll probably supply another "O" word: Outstanding. Actually, Yahoo means "a member of a race of brutes in Swift's *Gulliver's Travels* who have the form and all the vices of man"—but none of the virtues. Yahoo was created by David Filo and Jerry Yang, formerly computer science graduate students at Stanford University (until Yahoo swallowed them whole).

Accessing Yahoo

To access Yahoo, use this URL:

http://www.yahoo.com/

You'll see Yahoo's main subject tree (Figure 2.7).

Note the navigation buttons at the top of the page; you'll find them at the top of every Yahoo page. If you get lost, you can click "Yahoo!" to redisplay this page.

Exploring Yahoo

Now you'll see why Yahoo is called a subject tree. Click Government, and you'll see some of the main Government "branches" (subheadings), as shown in Figure 2.8. And if you click one of these subheadings, you'll see a page like the one shown in Figure 2.9; here you see document names.

Here's the cool part. These document names are living, breathing hyperlinks, which you can click just like any other hyperlink.

Have fun. There are over 50,000 hyperlinks in Yahoo!

Using Yahoo

Like all excellent webs, Yahoo offers a set of internal navigation buttons. Here's what the buttons do:

Yahoo	Displays the top-level Yahoo subject headings.
Up	If you've gone down into the subheadings, this button takes you back up one level.
Help	Get help with Yahoo's features.
Search	Type one or more keywords to see if there's a match somewhere in Yahoo. You'll learn more about searching Yahoo in Chapter 17.

Yahoo explorers, look for a pair of eyglasses next to a document's name. This indicates an especially good document of its type.

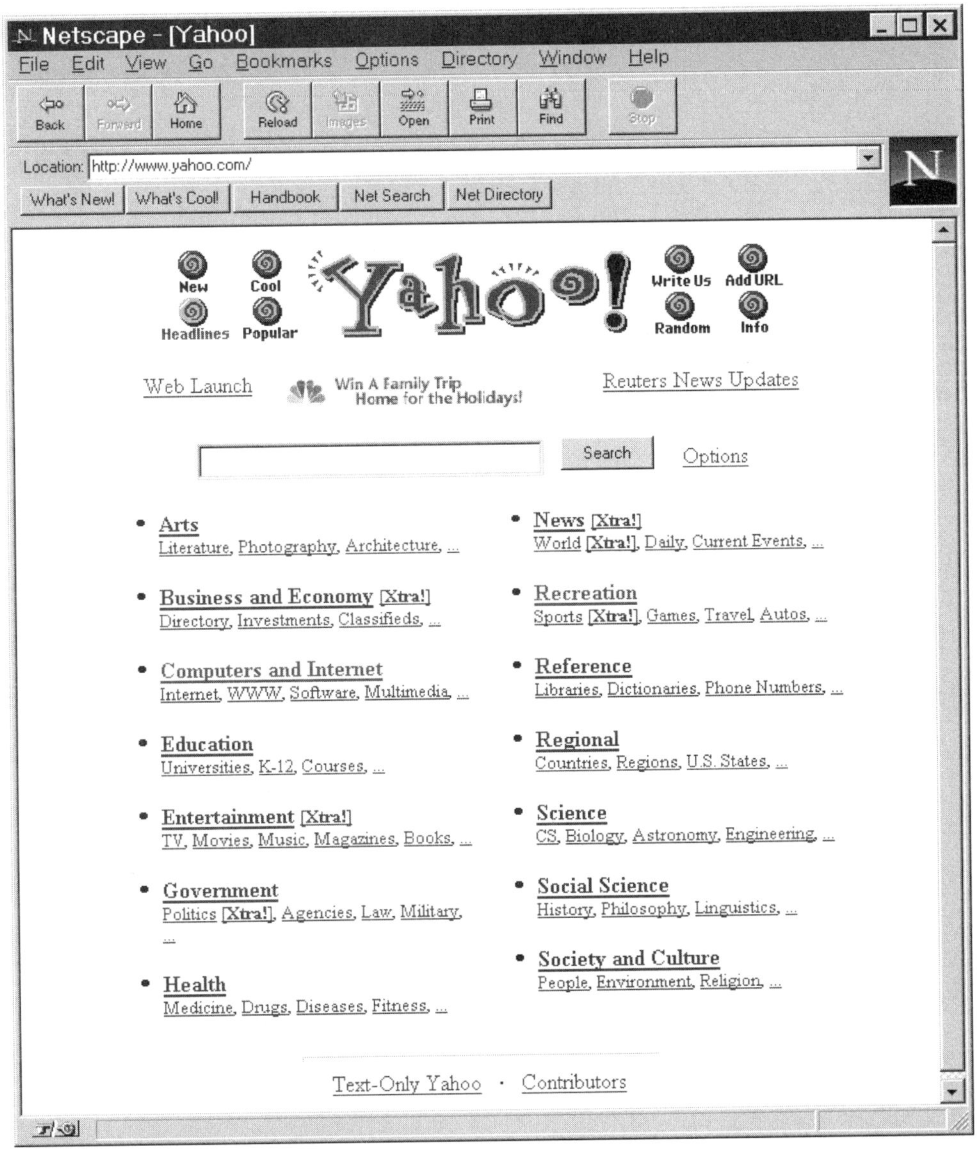

Figure 2.7 Yahoo subject tree

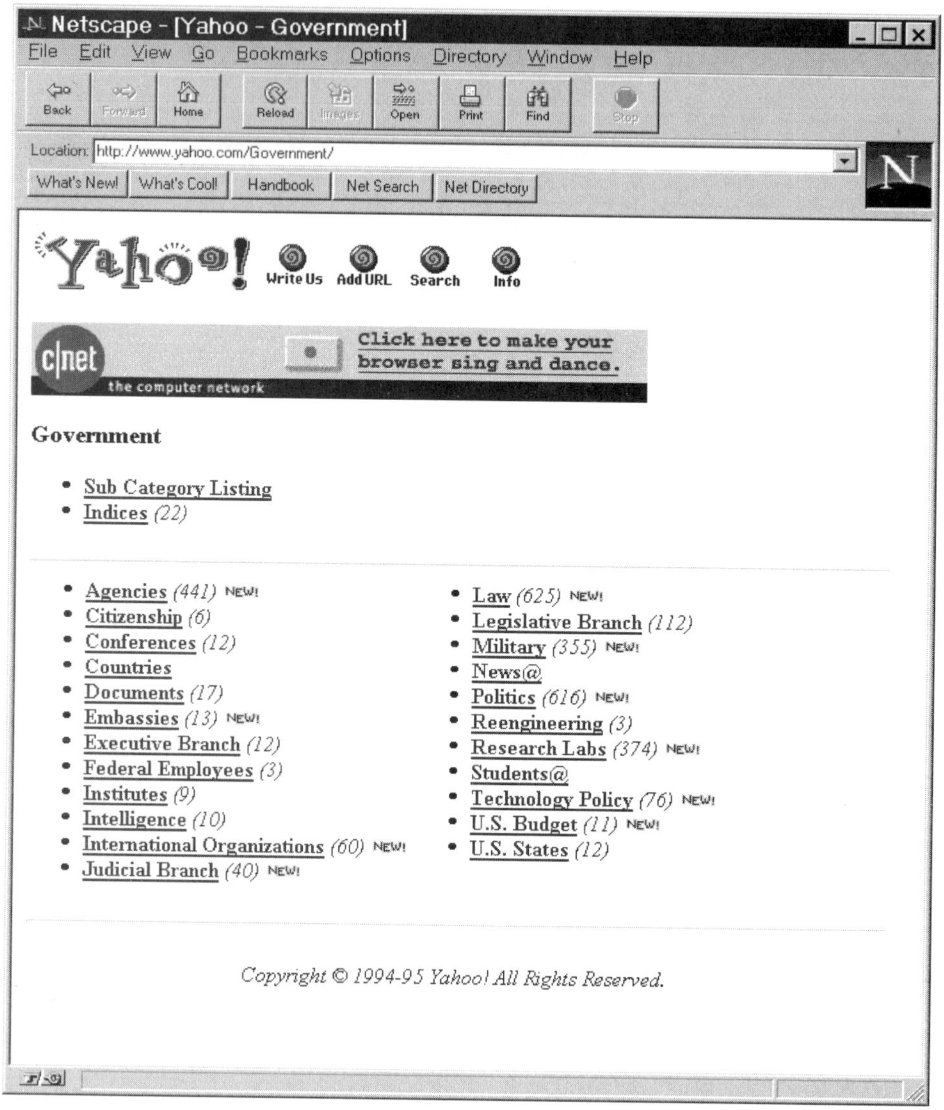

Netscape - [Yahoo - Government]

File Edit View Go Bookmarks Options Directory Window Help

Back Forward Home Reload Images Open Print Find Stop

Location: http://www.yahoo.com/Government/

What's New! What's Cool! Handbook Net Search Net Directory

Yahoo! Write Us Add URL Search Info

c|net the computer network — Click here to make your browser sing and dance.

Government

- Sub Category Listing
- Indices *(22)*

- Agencies *(441)* NEW!
- Citizenship *(6)*
- Conferences *(12)*
- Countries
- Documents *(17)*
- Embassies *(13)* NEW!
- Executive Branch *(12)*
- Federal Employees *(3)*
- Institutes *(9)*
- Intelligence *(10)*
- International Organizations *(60)* NEW!
- Judicial Branch *(40)* NEW!
- Law *(625)* NEW!
- Legislative Branch *(112)*
- Military *(355)* NEW!
- News@
- Politics *(616)* NEW!
- Reengineering *(3)*
- Research Labs *(374)* NEW!
- Students@
- Technology Policy *(76)* NEW!
- U.S. Budget *(11)* NEW!
- U.S. States *(12)*

Copyright © 1994-95 Yahoo! All Rights Reserved.

Figure 2.8 Goverment "branch" of Yahoo subject tree

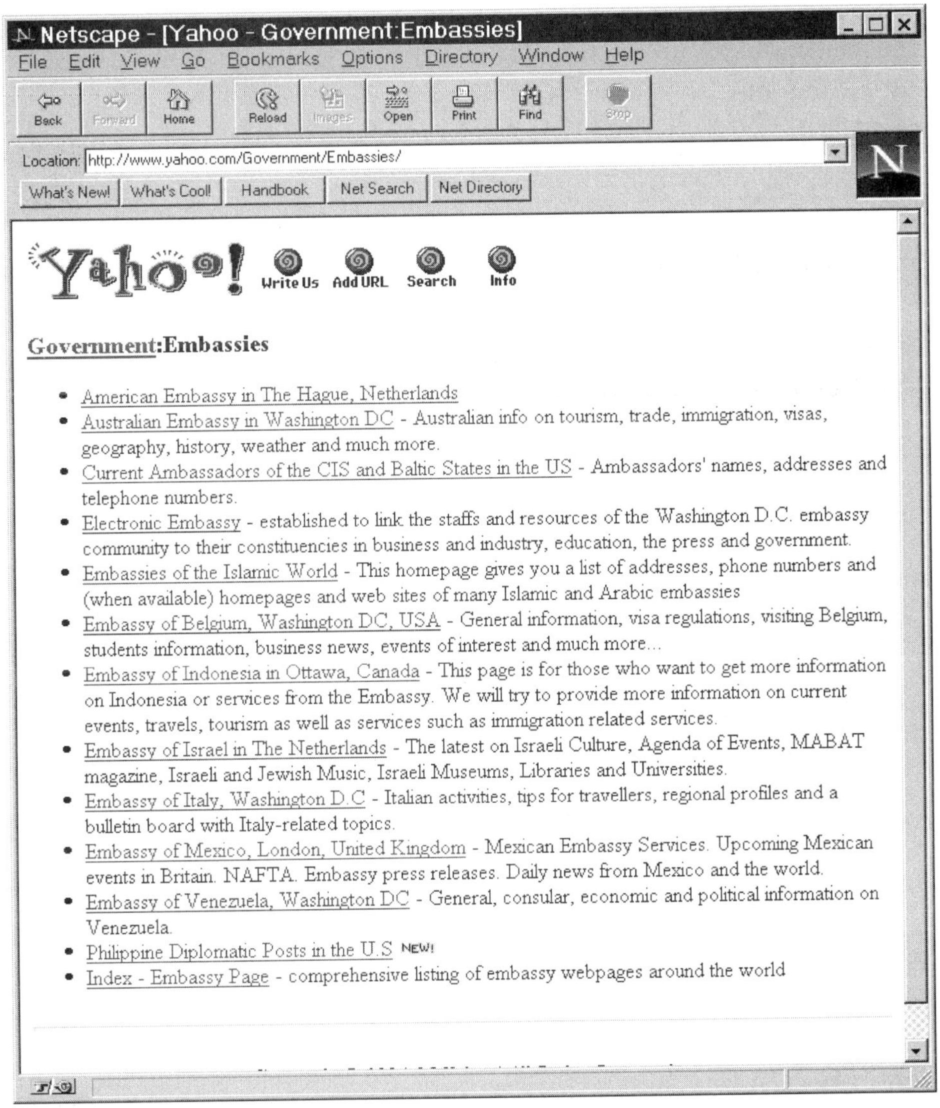

Netscape - [Yahoo - Government:Embassies]

File Edit View Go Bookmarks Options Directory Window Help

Back Forward Home Reload Images Open Print Find Stop

Location: http://www.yahoo.com/Government/Embassies/

What's New! What's Cool! Handbook Net Search Net Directory

Yahoo! Write Us Add URL Search Info

Government:Embassies

- American Embassy in The Hague, Netherlands
- Australian Embassy in Washington DC - Australian info on tourism, trade, immigration, visas, geography, history, weather and much more.
- Current Ambassadors of the CIS and Baltic States in the US - Ambassadors' names, addresses and telephone numbers.
- Electronic Embassy - established to link the staffs and resources of the Washington D.C. embassy community to their constituencies in business and industry, education, the press and government.
- Embassies of the Islamic World - This homepage gives you a list of addresses, phone numbers and (when available) homepages and web sites of many Islamic and Arabic embassies
- Embassy of Belgium, Washington DC, USA - General information, visa regulations, visiting Belgium, students information, business news, events of interest and much more...
- Embassy of Indonesia in Ottawa, Canada - This page is for those who want to get more information on Indonesia or services from the Embassy. We will try to provide more information on current events, travels, tourism as well as services such as immigration related services.
- Embassy of Israel in The Netherlands - The latest on Israeli Culture, Agenda of Events, MABAT magazine, Israeli and Jewish Music, Israeli Museums, Libraries and Universities.
- Embassy of Italy, Washington D.C - Italian activities, tips for travellers, regional profiles and a bulletin board with Italy-related topics.
- Embassy of Mexico, London, United Kingdom - Mexican Embassy Services. Upcoming Mexican events in Britain. NAFTA. Embassy press releases. Daily news from Mexico and the world.
- Embassy of Venezuela, Washington DC - General, consular, economic and political information on Venezuela.
- Philippine Diplomatic Posts in the U.S NEW!
- Index - Embassy Page - comprehensive listing of embassy webpages around the world

Figure 2.9 Documents listed in Yahoo

FROM HERE

- Change the default start page. To do so, flip to Chapter 4.
- Run into some trouble navigating the Web? Check out Chapter 3.
- Deal with an unwieldy Bookmarks menu in Chapter 6—or better yet, install SmartMarks and learn how to use this much-improved bookmark organizer (Chapter 7).
- Learn how to save and print the documents you display on the Web (Chapter 8).
- Learn more about starting points, subject trees, and search engines in Part IV.

Chapter 3

When the Surf Gets Rough

Netscape is loads of fun to use, but the Web isn't perfect. You will encounter many network-related problems while you're surfing. These aren't Netscape's fault, but part of Netscape mastery involves knowing what to do about them. This chapter discusses the things that can go wrong while you're surfing the Web—the black holes, the forbidden zones, the unplugged sockets, and more.

Even if you haven't run into the problems discussed in this chapter, it's still a good idea to skim it.

For the Time-Challenged

- If a site doesn't respond after a minute or two, give up.
- If you type a URL directly, make sure you type it correctly. A typing error could produce a DNS error message (the domain name is incorrect) or a 404 Not Found message (the document name is incorrect). Correct your typing and try again.
- Still getting a DNS or 404 error message? The site's down or the document's gone. Sorry.
- Accessing an erotica site could very well get you a 403 Forbidden message. Try again later, or just buy a copy of *Playboy.*
- Socket error messages generally indicate a temporary problem: Try clicking the hyperlink again.
- The other stuff discussed in this chapter falls into the minor nuisance category.

I Clicked the Hyperlink – and Nothing Happened!

The site you're trying to access is busy, busy, busy—so busy in fact, that it can't even transmit a message that it's too busy! Pathetic. Try again later—like at 2:30 AM.

If you're determined to get through to a site, open a new window in Netscape and let the original window keep on tryin'. Maybe the document you want will appear after a few minutes. Maybe not.

A site that just never responds is known to Web surfers as a Black Hole. If you've never had this experience, but would like to give it a try, there is a Black Hole simulation at the following URL:

http://www.ravenna.com/blackhole.html

Please do not click the Black Hole link (Figure 3.1). You will be caught in the Hole and unable to get out. Somehow, resist the temptation! (Actually, you can just click Stop and then Back to get out of the Hole.)

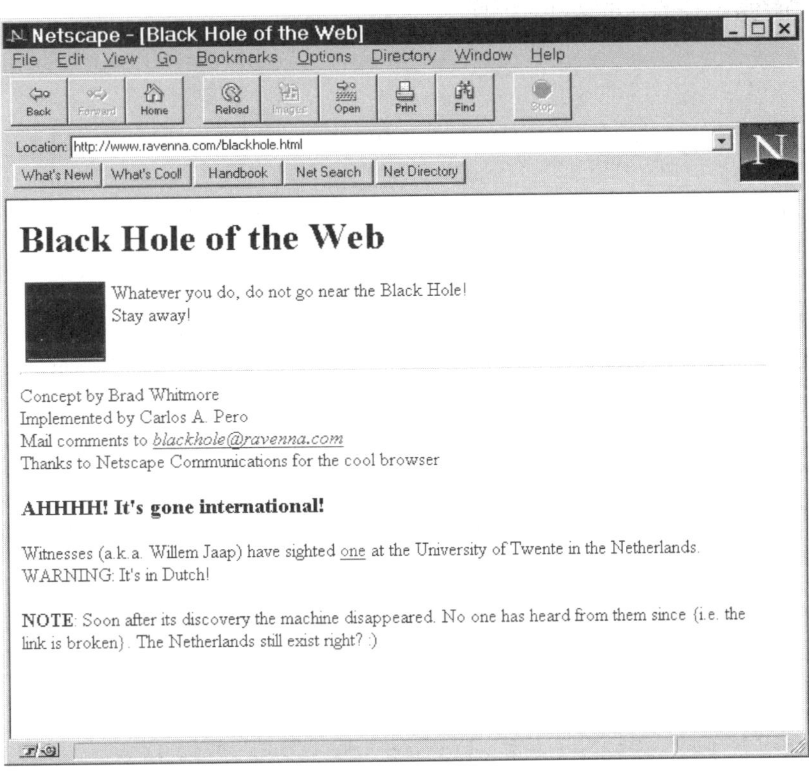

Figure 3.1 The Black Hole

It Says the DNS Lookup Failed!

Netscape tried to access a Web site, but nothing happened, and then you see a dialog box with the message that the DNS lookup went awry (Figure 3.2). There are several possibilities here:

- Are you using a SLIP or PPP connection? Check to make sure that you're still connected. Many dial-in systems are set up to hang up on you if there is no activity for a specified period of time, such as 10 minutes. (After all, other people are trying to access the system, and

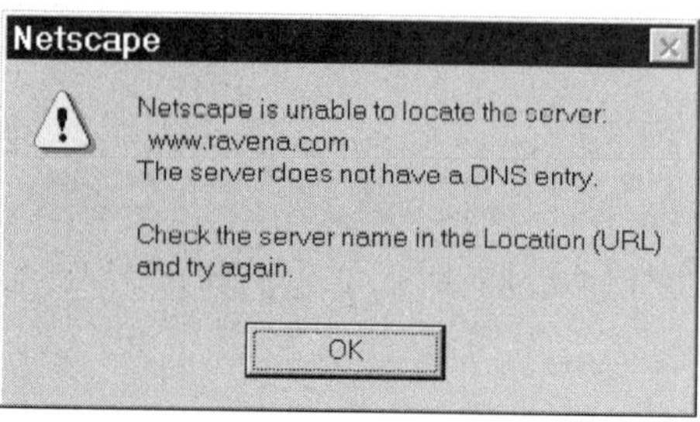

Figure 3.2 A DNS lookup gone astray

as far as anyone knows, you've probably gone fishing or something.) Use your SLIP/PPP dialer to re-establish the connection, and click the hyperlink again.

- Did you type the URL? You may have mistyped the domain name part of the URL (the part that contains the name of the computer you're trying to access).
- The computer you're trying to answer may have gone "Whoomp!" (That's the noise a computer makes when it's taken out of service and permanently disconnected from the Internet, in case you were wondering.)
- The DNS server might be overloaded. Try again later.

It Says "Not Found (Error 404)"!

The domain name's all right—Netscape was able to contact the computer you're looking for—but, sorry to say, there's no document by that name located on the machine you've accessed (Figure 3.3). Did you type the URL yourself? If so, carefully check your typing, and make any corrections, if necessary, right in the Location box. Press Enter to try again.

If you get the 404 Not Found message again, the document has probably been withdrawn from the server.

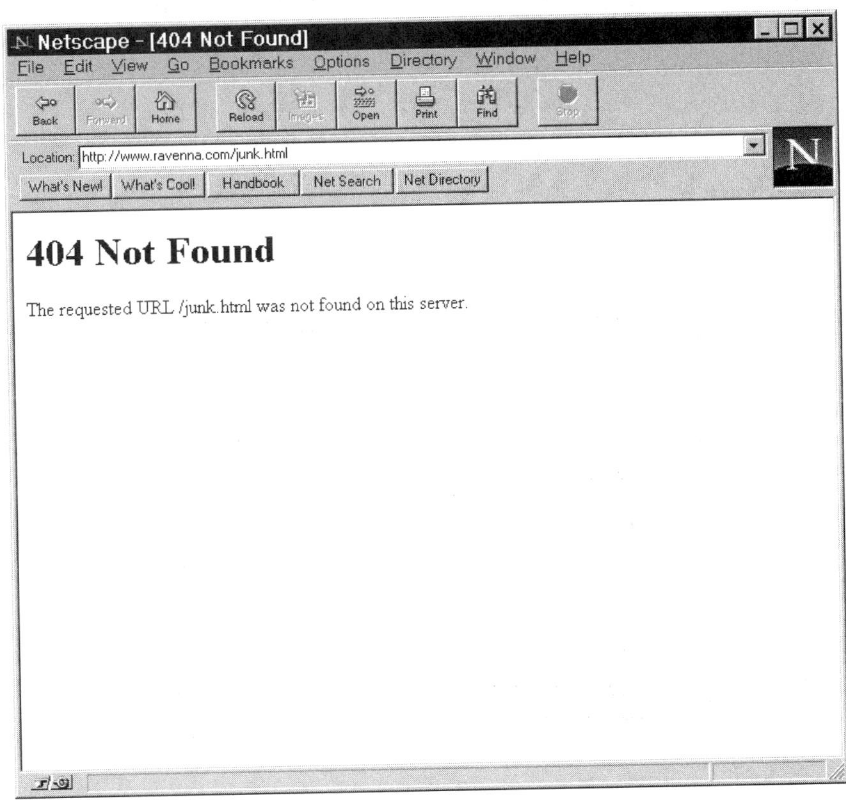

Figure 3.3 404 Not Found

Wow! "Forbidden"! (Error 403)

Naughty, naughty! You weren't trying to access a sex site, were you? Sites with naughty pictures tend to get shut down by system administrators, thanks to the fact that there are, apparently, about 20 million Web users with nothing better to do than hunt down erotic Web sites. With so many people trying to access the document, its host system can't function. Irate, the system administrator removes the offending document and places a restriction on its access, producing this sternly worded message (Figure 3.4).

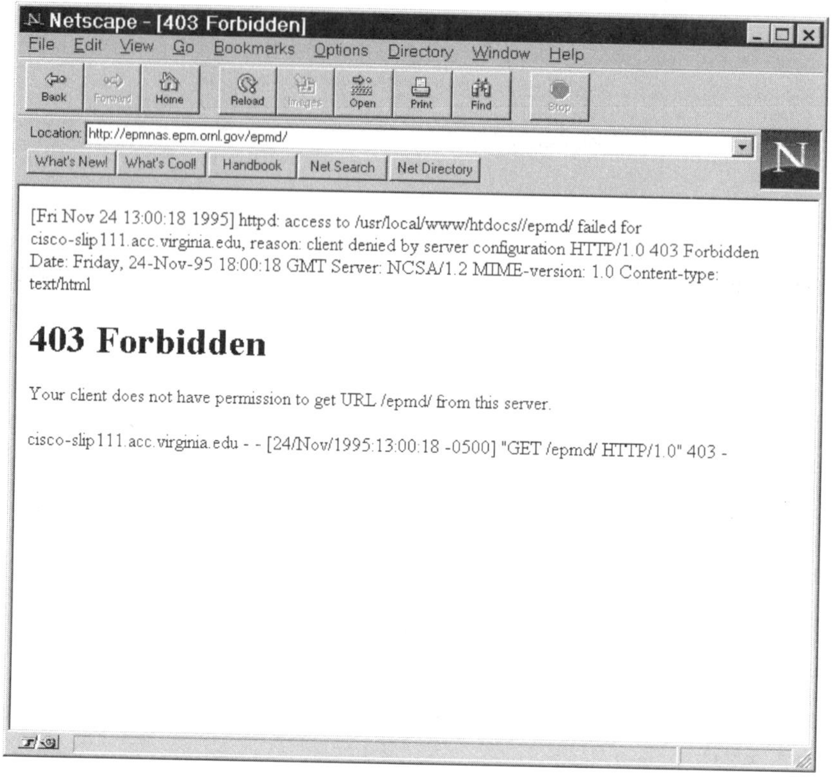

Figure 3.4 403 Forbidden

Sometimes you'll get this message when you're trying to access a non-naughty site. It probably means that the document you're looking for no longer exists.

Horrors! A Network Error

Something went wrong with the network connection (Figure 3.5). Chances are good it's a temporary problem. Just click the hyperlink again.

If that doesn't work, check to see whether you're still on-line. High-speed modems are sensitive creatures—if there's a big-time error transmitting

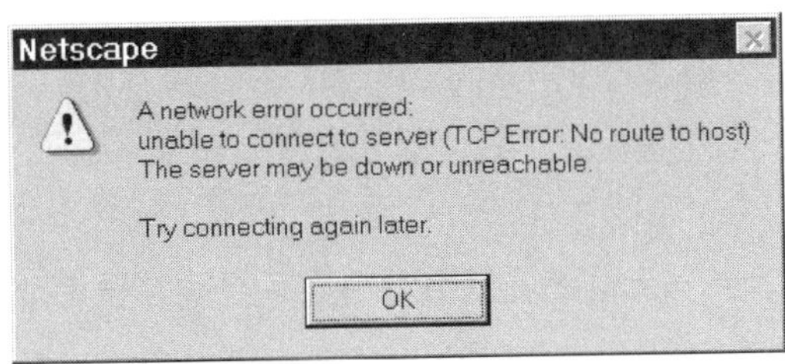

Figure 3.5 Socket disconnected

data, usually caused by a noisy line, they may down the connection without giving you any warning (thanks). Try reconnecting and accessing the site again.

It Says "This Site Has Moved"!

Well, make a note of the new hyperlink. Usually, pages such as this one include something you can click to get to the right place (see Figure 3.6).

They're Demanding a Password!

They can do that, if they like. And you can't access the page unless you type the correct login name and password (Figure 3.7). Probably, there's information on how to register—if you want to gain access to the site, do it.

It Says "The Information You Have Submitted Is Not Secure"!

And it isn't (Figure 3.8). Any message you send on the Web can be quite easily intercepted and read. That's why you should never, never, never send your

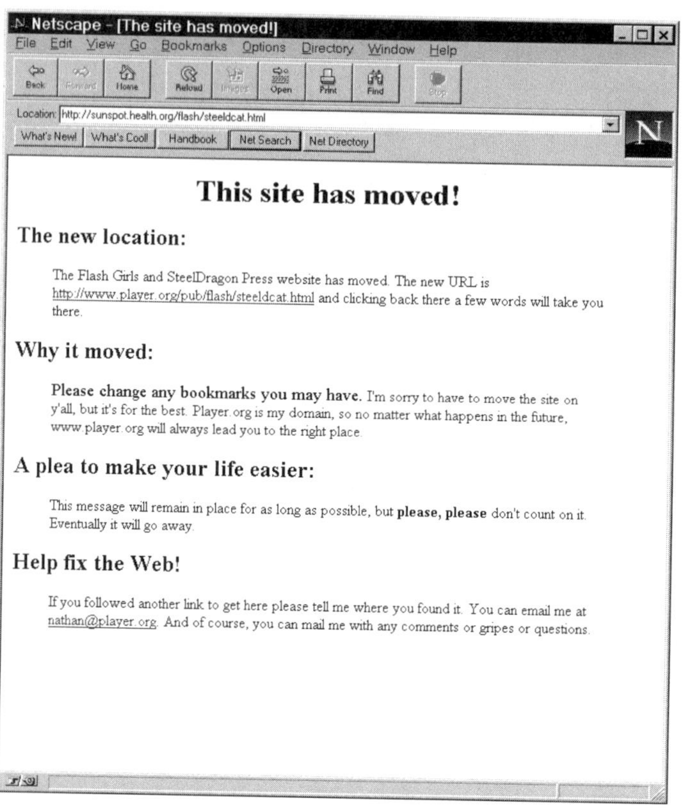

Figure 3.6 Forwarding address

credit card information, or any other personal information, via forms that you fill out in Web documents—unless, that is, you're accessing a secure document (see Chapter 24). This message is telling you that you're uploading (sending) information to a server that isn't secure. (Netscape knows.)

This message gets a bit boring after a while. If you're tired of seeing it, and know better than to upload sensitive information to servers that aren't secure, you can stop Netscape from displaying it. From the Options menu, choose Security

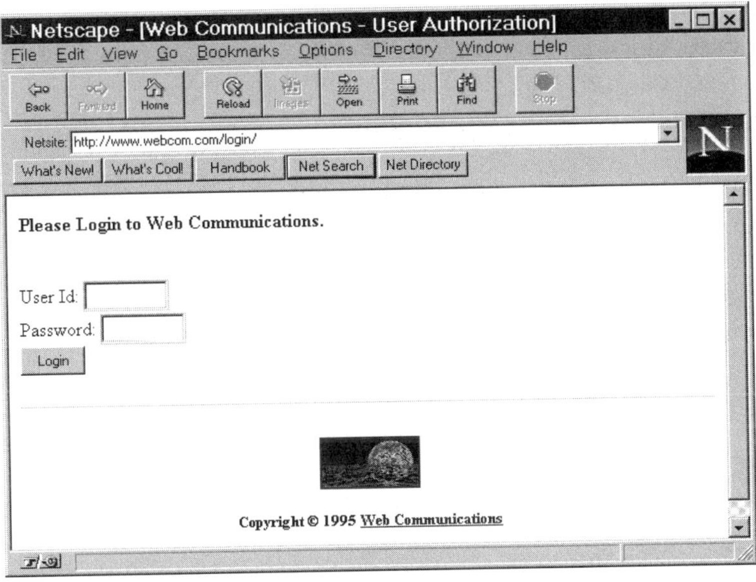

Figure 3.7 Login name and password required for access

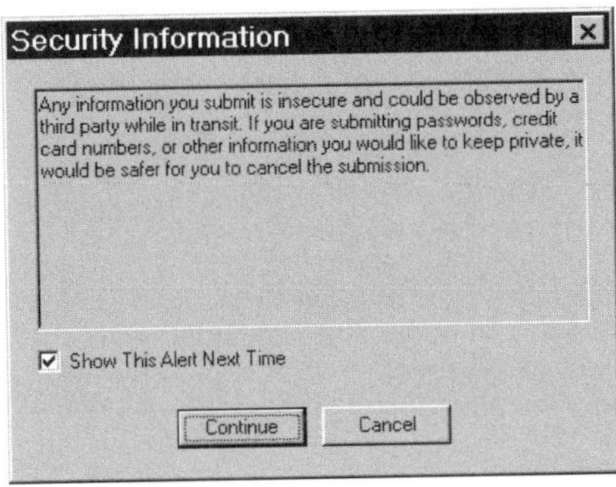

Figure 3.8 Warning about uploading information

Preferences. In the General area, deselect Submitting a Form Insecurely. Click OK to confirm the change, and choose Save Options from the Options menu just to make sure your choice gets saved (normally, your option choices are saved when you quit Netscape, but they won't get saved if Netscape crashes for some reason—so do it now, and you won't have to repeat these steps).

From Here

- Make the Web more accessible by changing your start page. Find out how in Chapter 4.
- Is Netscape running too sluggishly for your taste? Soup it up in Chapter 5, "Improving Netscape's Performance."
- Can't find your way back to a favorite site? Check out Chapter 6, "Creating and Using Bookmarks."

Part II

Mastering Netscape

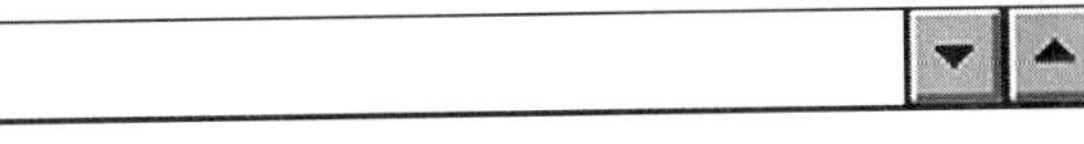

Chapter 4

Change That Start Page!

You start Netscape, and every time you do, you see Netscape's default start page, at Netscape's headquarters in Menlo Park, California. Wouldn't you like to see something more useful, something more tailored to your Web-browsing needs? If so, you've come to the right place: This chapter shows you how to change the default start page, the page you'll see every time Netscape starts. (You also see this page when you click the Home button.)

What's the point of changing the start page? The improvement is more than cosmetic. A good start page gives you instant access to a huge variety of resources: starting points, subject trees, search engines, news, weather, sports, time-wasting diversions, humor, entertainment, and more.

You can choose any home page you like—this chapter shows you how to hunt down cool home pages and make them your own—or you can use the

For the Time-Challenged

- A start page is what you see when you start Netscape or click the Home button. You should change the default start page (Netscape's welcome page), substituting something of more personal value to you.
- This book comes with a home page called HOME.HTM, and it's a good choice. It's packed with useful hyperlinks that enable you to search for information, obtain news and weather reports, check out movie and video reviews, and much more.
- To install HOME.HTM as your home page, flip to the section "Changing Your Home Page," and follow the instructions carefully.
- You can use someone else's home page as your own. A great place to hunt for home pages is Who's Who on the Internet, http://web.city.ac.uk/citylive/pages.html. This is a good option for hobbyists and enthusiasts of all kinds.
- Another good home page option is to use one of the many subject-oriented trailblazer pages of the Virtual Library, http://info.cern.ch/hypertext/DataSources/bySubject/Overview.html. This is a good option for students, teachers, and professionals.
- You can save your bookmark list and make it your home page. For more information, see Chapter 6.

home page included on this book's disc, HOME.HTM. Either way, your enjoyment of Netscape and the Web will increase by leaps and bounds.

Every reader of this book should check out this chapter and change Netscape's default home page. It's easy, and you don't need to know any HTML. The home page that's included with this book will really increase your enjoyment of the Web.

Have We Got a Home Page for You!

On this book's CD-ROM disc is one heck of a nice home page called (you guessed it) HOME (actually, HOME.HTM). Part of it is shown in Figure 4.1.

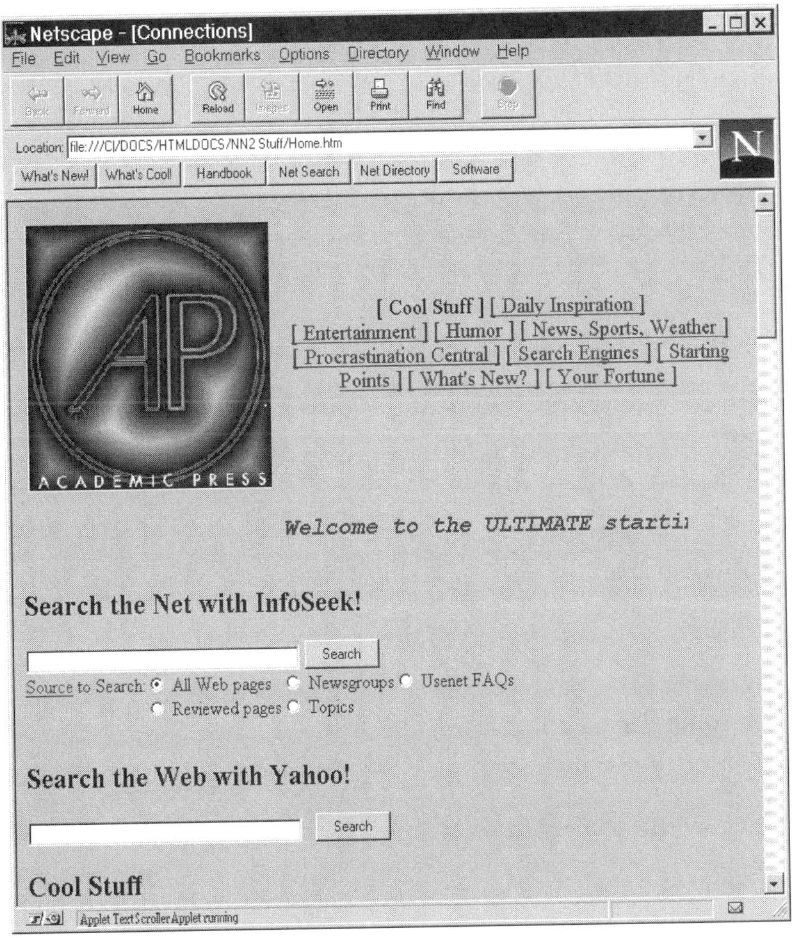

Figure 4.1 The home page that comes with this book (HOME.HTM)

At the top of this home page are two search engines: Infoseek and Yahoo. Below the search engines, you'll find links to the main subheadings. In Figure 4.1, you can see the Cool Stuff heading. Here's an overview of the rest of HOME.HTM:

Cool Stuff — Some of the most impressive and popular Web pages. If you're curious about what the Web

	should be like, take a look at these sites. You'll find a good selection of some of the Web's hottest sites, in a variety of subject areas.
Daily Inspiration	Check out the Deep Thought of the day, the quotations of the day, and more—including the Shakespearean insult of the day. Lots of fun stuff, and it changes every day.
Entertainment	The latest reviews of movies, videos, and music of all kinds.
Humor	Search for lightbulb jokes, play MadLib, and find out what happened to the guy who tried to use a $2 bill at Taco Bell.
News, Sports, Weather	Find out what's going on, from sources such as CBS News, the *San Francisco Chronicle*, and the *San Jose Mercury-News*.
Procrastination Central	You didn't *really* want to get any work done, did you? Mr. Potato Head and Tic Tac Toe will make sure that you don't.
Search Engines	The best search engines, a click away.
Starting Points	Some great starting points pages.
What's New	All kinds of new Web sites to explore.
Your Fortune	The Magic 8 Ball knows all, and if it doesn't, there's always the Fortune Cookie Server, an online Tarot reading, and the I Ching.

HOME.HTM doesn't contain thousands or even hundreds of hyperlinks; it contains just a few dozen. Apart from the hyperlinks in Cool Stuff, most of them share one element in common: They aren't boring, static pages that just show you the same text and graphics every time you access them. In Daily Inspiration, for example, you'll find lots of links that display something completely different at each access. Many other links connect you with fast-breaking news pages, which are updated frequently, and still others access databases that permit you to search for information.

HOME.HTM isn't perfect, since there's no way I could have anticipated all of your interests and hobbies. But it points the way. Learn a little HTML, and create your own start page!

Changing the Default Start Page

To change your default home page to HOME.HTM, follow these instructions:

1. From the Options menu, choose General Preferences. You'll see the Preferences dialog box, which has seven tabbed pages.
2. Choose the Appearance page (Figure 4.2) by clicking the Appearance tab, if necessary (this page may already be on top of the "stack" of tabbed pages).
3. In the text box below Start With, select the existing URL. If you prefer to not use the mouse, just press Tab until the URL is highlighted.
4. Assuming that your CD-ROM drive is drive D, carefully type the following:

   file:///D|/home/home.htm

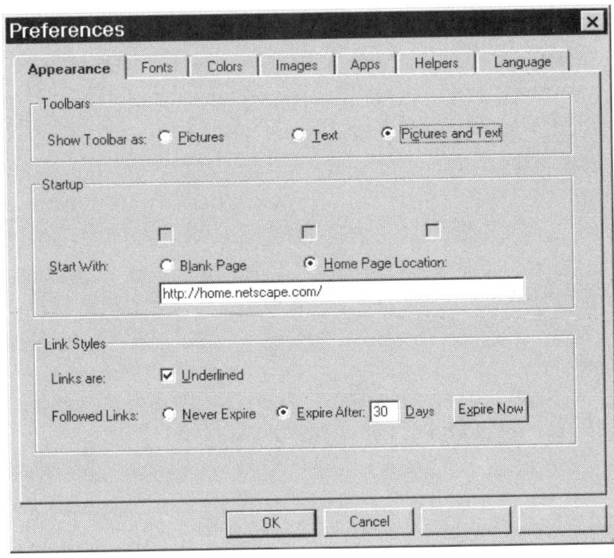

Figure 4.2 Appearance page (Preferences dialog box)

If your CD-ROM drive is accessed by means of a different drive letter, substitute that letter for the D.

Note that *three* slash marks come after "file:" and that there's a vertical bar character after "D."

Use this setup to try out HOME.HTM—but if you like it, consider copying the HOME directory to your hard disk. After doing so, you will not need to keep this book's CD-ROM disc in the disk drive. Repeat these instructions, but specify HOME.HTM's new location.

5. Click the Home Page Location option button, if necessary. (The other option is Blank Page, which isn't very much fun.)
6. Click OK or just press Enter to confirm your choice and return to Netscape.
7. Click the Home button to test your new start page.

It doesn't work! If you see a message stating that Netscape cannot find the file, check to see whether the CD-ROM disc is in the drive and that your drive is accessible. Open the Preferences dialog box again, display the Appearance page again, and carefully check your typing. Did you place three slashes after "file:"? Did you forget the colon after "file"? Did you spell the name of the document correctly? Did you use a vertical line character after the "D"? Did you add any spaces? (No spaces are allowed.) If you find a mistake, correct it, click OK, and click the Home button again. Still having problems? Make sure the file is in Netscape's directory.

More Great Start Pages

You'll find lots of great start pages on the Web. Here's a list of some of my favorites:

- **Nerd World Media** (http://www.nerdworld.com/) Here's a fun starting point that divides more than 8,000 sites into two major cat-

egories, Leisure and Knowledge; these categories are further broken down into a variety of subject headings. Hip and fun.

- **PC Computing's Web Map** (http://www.ziff.com/~pccomp/webmap/) Organized as a clickable image map, this starting points page provides a graphical entry point for popular sites in areas of interest to personal computer users, consumers, computer hobbyists, and parents.
- **Point** (http://www.pointcom.com/) Point is famous for its "top 5% of the Web" awards, which purport to identify the cream of the Web crop. A subject-oriented starting points page containing high-quality Web sites, Point indexes sites in the following subject areas: education, business/finance, entertainment, news/info, leisure activities, government and politics, science/technology, computers/Internet, shopping, arts/humanities, health/medicine, global village, kids, and "the road less traveled."
- **Search ME!** (http://watt.seas.virginia.edu/~bp/searchme/welcome.html) Here's the place to start your search of the Web. You'll find pages that list, review, and provide links to dozens of information-seeking services, including search engines, subject trees, reference, news, periodicals, and more.
- **The Starting Point** (http://www.stpt.com/welcome.html) A very nice starting points page is called, appropriately enough, Starting Point, and it's made available by Superhighway Consulting, Inc. You'll find links to news, weather, sports, entertainment, business, investing, professional, reference, shopping, travel, magazine, and education sites.
- **The Whole Internet Catalog** (http://gnn.digital.com/gnn/wic/index.html) A part of the Global Network Navigator (GNN) service, the Whole Internet Catalog (WIC) lists 1200 of the best sites on the Web. Organized like a subject tree, but with far fewer entries, WIC groups sites according to the following subject categories: arts/entertainment, business/finance, daily news, education, government/politics, health/medicine, humanities/social sciences, Internet, life/culture, recreation/sports/hobbies, science/technology, and travel.

To make any of these great pages your default start page, just type its URL in the Home Page Location box in the Appearance page in the Preferences dialog box, as described in the previous section.

Using Personal Home Pages

Somewhere out there, somebody shares a lot of your interests. And just possibly, this someone has created a publicly accessible home page—one of those "aren't-I-cool personal home pages for the masses," discussed earlier. You can make it your home page (that is, your default home page) easily enough; you just type the page's URL in the Preferences dialog box, as explained earlier in this chapter. The trick lies in finding a useful page. Here are some good bets:

- **John S. Makulowich's Awesome Lists,** http://www.clark.net/pub/journalism/awesome.html An alphabetized list of useful Web sites, created by an Internet trainer.
- **Meng Weng Wong's Home Page,** http:///www.seas.upenn.edu/~mengwong/meng.html A very useful page, created by a brilliant University of Pennsylvania graduate student.
- **Lorrie Cranor's Home Page,** http://dworkin.wustl.edu/pub/lorracks/home.html Lorrie's picks of the Web; a great page.

How can you learn about additional personal home pages? Thanks to a very remarkable on-line resource, the task of finding home pages has just gotten a lot easier. Here it is, folks: Who's Who on the Internet (formerly the Complete Home Page Directory) at http://web.city.ac.uk/citylive/pages.html (Figure 4.3). This web contains a list of hyperlinks to several thousand individuals' home pages, which you can access alphabetically, if you wish, by clicking the alphabet buttons.

The best way to search WWOTI is to use its search capabilities, which you can access from the site's welcome page. Unfortunately, WWOTI does not permit searches unless your site is registered (and it probably isn't). Paging through the alphabetical listings manually is time-consuming, but it's quite an interesting diversion, a classic Internet time-waster in itself. Here are a few jewels, including the description that the page authors themselves posted:

- **Anders Pages** Big sections about Transhumanism and the role-playing game Mage: The Ascension. Also information about General Weirdness, Magick, and Weird Science.
- **Arachnaut's Lair** The Arachnaut's Lair is the home page of Jim Hurley. The focus of the page is on electronic music and aquariums. You'll also find an assortment of links cataloged there.

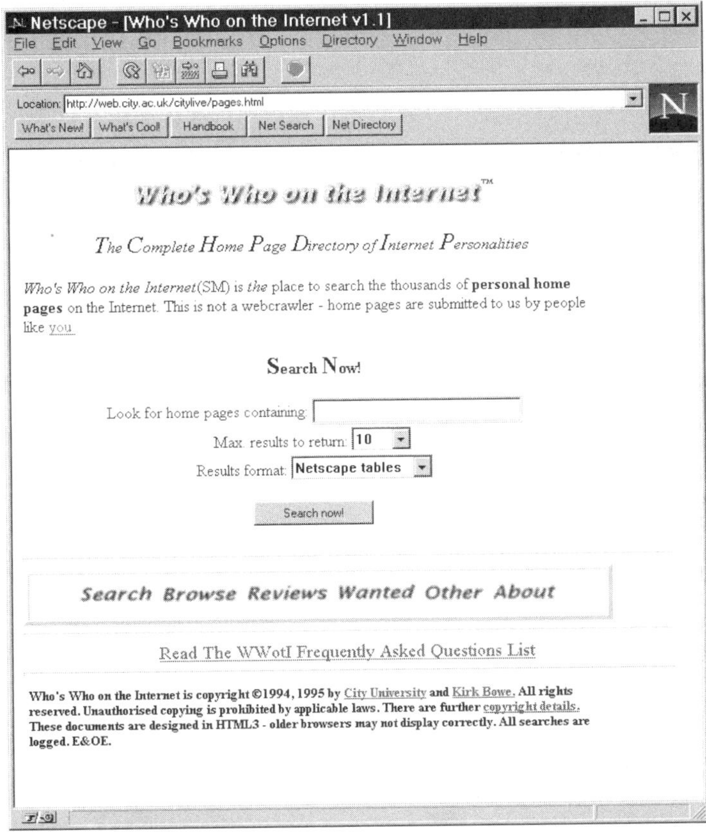

Figure 4.3 Who's Who on the Internet

- **Billy Boy's Home** Lots of goodies. This page is a gold mine of philosophy-related links: If you're interested in Aristotle, Kant, or any of the other biggies, you can download everything they wrote by following philosophy-related links from here. If physics is your bag, you can surf to all sorts of stuff on that topic from here. Also, you can download graphics of all sorts from my hard drive and link to graphics elsewhere.
- **Cliff Ecology Research Group** A page devoted to the study of cliff ecology and ancient cedars on cliffs [GIFS!].

- **Cynthia Marasco's Home Page** My personal page with lots of ways to waste time. It also includes tons of links to legal information.
- **Don't panic eat organic** An organic farmers' home page. May be of help to others interested in organic farming. A way organic farmers can network.
- **Expecting Rain** Bob Dylan information: the Dylan Atlas, Dylan Who's Who, Dylan pictures, Dylan links, and other links.
- **Mike's ARMY Home Page** Contains info on the Army, including weapons facts pages and GIFs of actual training.
- **Steve Rapport Photography** Steve Rapport's virtual portfolio of original rock 'n' roll photos: also stories, gossip, comedy (Young Ones, Monty Python, Simpsons), his kitties, West Ham United and Fortune's Always Hiding home pages, Counting Crows discography.
- **The Electronic Zoo** Vast collection of animal and veterinary Internet resources.

Using a Trailblazer Page as a Home Page

A trailblazer page is a Web document that attempts to sum up the URLs pertaining to a particular subject, such as astronomy or wine. If you're a student, teacher, or professional working in such an area, you may wish to find a trailblazer page and make it your home page, so that all these links are instantly available to you.

An excellent source of trailblazer pages is the Virtual Library, maintained at CERN (the Swiss birthplace of the World Wide Web). The Virtual Library is described as a distributed information system, and rightly so: The only page stored at CERN is the overview document, which lists the trailblazer page topics. Each trailblazer page is maintained by a volunteer and stored at the volunteer's Web site. Of course, this doesn't mean anything to you in practice; you just click away, and where you are—and where you wind up—doesn't really matter.

To access the Virtual Library's table of contents, use

http://info.cern.ch/hypertext/DataSources/bySubject/Overview.html

Table 4.1 lists the subject headings current at this book's writing.

If one of the Virtual Library pages (or some other page you see) looks like a good candidate for your home page, you can copy its URL and paste it into the Preferences dialog box. Here's how:

1. Display the page you want to use as your home page.
2. In the Location box, select the URL. To make sure you've selected all of it, click at the left edge of the box and drag all the way right.
3. Press Ctrl + C to copy the URL to the Clipboard.
4. From the Options menu, choose General Preferences.
5. Click the Appearances tab, if necessary.
6. Select the text that's currently in the Home Page Location box.

Table 4.1 Subject Headings in the Virtual Library

Aboriginal Studies
Aeronautics and Aeronautical
African Studies
Agencies
Agriculture
Animal Health, Well-being, and Rights
Anthropology
Applied Linguistics
Archaeology
Architecture
Art
Asian Studies
Astronomy and Astrophysics
Autos
Aviation
Beer and Brewing
Bio Sciences
Biotechnology
Chemistry
Climate Research
Cognitive Science
Collecting
Commercial Services
Community
Community Networks
Computing
Conferences
Cryptography, PGP, and Your Privacy
Crystallography
Culture
Dance
Demography and Population
Design
Earth Science
Education
Electronic Journals
Encyclopedia
Energy
Engineering
Engineering
Environment
Finance
Fish
Forestry
Fortune-telling
Furniture and Interior Design
Games
Geography
Geophysics
German Subject Catalogue
History
Home Pages
Human Computer Interaction

Table 4.1 *Continued*

Human Factors	Oceanography	Standards and Standardization Bodies
Human Rights	Paranormal Phenomena	Statistics
International Affairs	Philosophy	Sumeria
Italian General Subject Tree	Physics	Telecommunications
Landscape Architecture	Political Science	Tibetan Studies
Languages	Politics and Economics	Treasure
Latin American Studies	Psychology	U.S. Federal Government
Law	Publishers	U.S. Government
Libraries	Recipes	Information
Linguistics	Recreation	Unidentified Flying Objects (UFOs)
Literature	Reference	United Nations and Other International Organizations
Mathematics	Religion	Vision Science
Medicine	Russian and East European Studies	Whale Watching Web
Medieval Studies	Secular Issues	Wine
Meteorology	Social Sciences	World-Wide Web
Middle East Studies	Sociology	
Movies	Spirituality	
Museums	Sport	
Music		

7. Press CTRL + V to paste the URL from the Clipboard. This action deletes the current URL and places the new one into the box.
8. Click OK to confirm.
9. Click the Home button to test your new start page.

You can search the Web for trailblazer pages. There are thousands of them, in every conceivable subject area. To learn how, see Chapter 17.

FROM HERE

- Is Netscape too slow for your tastes? Speed up the program's performance considerably by following the tips and strategies in the following chapter.
- Learn how to save bookmarks—or better yet, use Netscape's new SmartMarks utility. See Chapters 6 and 7.

Chapter 5

Improving Netscape's Performance

By now, you've mastered the essentials of Netscape, and I'll bet you've had some fun exploring the Web. In this chapter, you go beyond the basics. You learn the time-saving tricks that Netscape mavens use to make Netscape run faster.

STOP! *PLEASE* STOP!

You just clicked a hyperlink. It looked interesting. But now you can see that it's going to be a pain. There are at least 50 pictures of the Brady Bunch. And it's taking forever to download. Stop the madness! Here's how:

- Click the Stop button

  or

For the Time-Challenged

- ♦ If you've inadvertently clicked a hyperlink and Netscape begins downloading a huge, unwanted file, click the Stop button.
- ♦ To speed document downloading considerably (a plus if you're using a slow SLIP/PPP connection), turn off the automatic display of in-line images. You can selectively display an individual graphic by right-clicking it and choosing Load This Image.
- ♦ Don't go nuts trying to get back to a document by clicking the Back button—use the Go menu and the history list instead. While you browse, Netscape keeps a record of the documents you've visited in the current lineage (a series of documents that are all linked outward from a single, beginning document). While you're still within the lineage, you can go back to any of these documents by choosing a document name from the Go menu. If you begin a new lineage, however, Netscape erases the previous lineage's history list and begins a new one.
- ♦ Because Netscape erases a lineage's history list when you start a new lineage, you should begin the new lineage in a new window. (Each window's history list is separate.)
- ♦ If Windows messes up Netscape's screen display, choose Refresh from the View menu. If you've redisplayed a previously accessed document and suspect that the original may have changed, click the Reload button.

- Press Esc

  or

- From the Go menu, choose Stop Loading.

After you stop downloading, you may see part of the document onscreen, but it may show signs of its brutal treatment (for example, in-line images that didn't download will be shown with placeholders, like the ones in Figure 5.1). Just click the Back button to abandon this battle scene. If you feel sorry for the document and would like to give it an opportunity to live once again, click the Reload button.

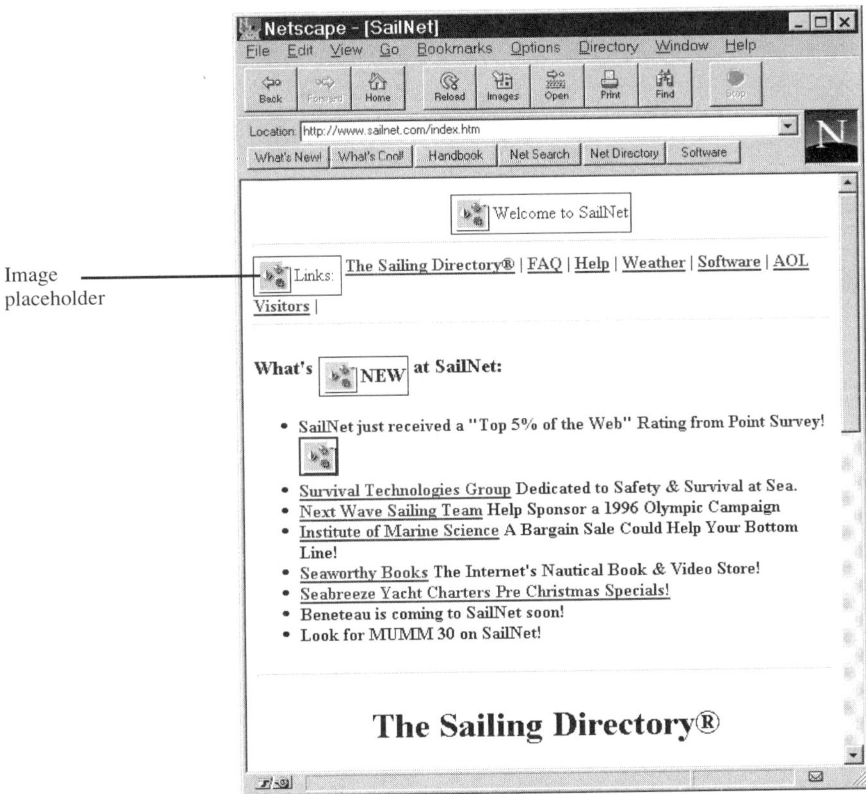

Figure 5.1 Document with image placeholders (produced by interrupted transfer)

THIS DOCUMENT'S TOO SLOW! (TOO MANY IMAGES)

If you're accessing the Web over a SLIP or PPP connection, documents stuffed with in-line images can take forever to download. That's OK, if you're really interested in the pictures; after all, why else would you access the *Playboy* Home Page? (Of course, I only read the interviews.) Often, though, you're

searching for some specific information, and the graphics—however pretty—serve only to delay your journey. For such Web ventures, you'll be wise to turn off the automatic downloading of in-line images. Here's how.

Using the Auto Load Images Toggle

In the Options menu, the Auto Load Images option is a *toggle command*. A toggle command has two states, on or off. When a toggle command is on, you see a check mark next to the command name. When a toggle command is off, there's no check mark. To change a toggle command, you choose the command. You can't really see what happens, because the menu disappears after you choose the command. If you open the menu again, though, you'll see that choosing the command did one of two things: It made the check mark appear (on), or it made the check mark disappear (off). It's simple, once you get the basic idea.

Let's assume that Netscape is automatically downloading in-line images, which is the default setting. That means there's a check mark next to Auto Load Images on the Options menu. You need to get rid of that check mark.

Turning Off Automatic Image Downloading

To turn off the automatic downloading of in-line images, do the following:

1. From the Options menu, choose Auto Load Images.
2. Just to make sure, click Options again, and look at the menu; there should be no check mark next to the Auto Load Images option. Press Esc to close the menu.
3. If you would like Netscape to save this option right now, click Options again, and choose Save Options. If you don't choose this option, the next time you launch Netscape you'll find that the program has reverted to the last options you saved.

Hey, I turned off images! Why do I still see some of them? After you turn off the automatic display of in-line images, you'll see placeholders wherever an image would appear. To some people, it looks like a little crying robot.

You've turned off automatic image downloading. Great! Documents load quickly, but they aren't much visual fun anymore, are they? Well, read on.

Selectively Loading In-Line Images

After you've turned off automatic image downloading, you can view any single in-line graphic, just as you please. This is very cool. The technique uses that sophisticated right-clicking maneuver that gives a certain distinguished body language to your computer usage.

To view an individual in-line graphic (when automatic image downloading has been turned off):

1. Point to the image's placeholder, and click the right mouse button.
2. From the pop-up menu, choose Load This Image (to display the image within the current document) or View This Image (to view the graphic in a new, separate document). Netscape will download the image you've clicked (Figure 5.2).

Downloading All the Images in a Document

You can also download all the images in a given document:

- From the View menu, choose Load Images

  or

- Press Ctrl + I (the letter "I," as in "me")

  or

- Click the Images button.

I don't care how long it takes to download the pictures! I want images on by default! No problem. From the Options menu, choose Auto Load Images again, so that the check mark reappears. By the way, you are a very patient person—or you have a very fast modem!

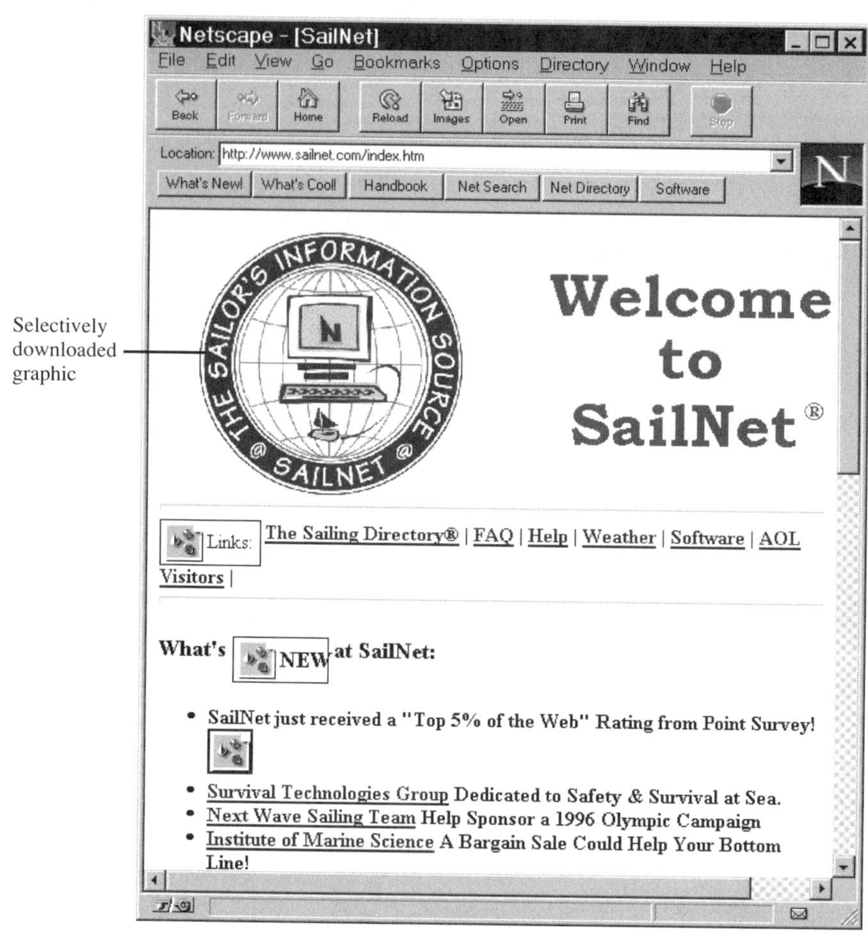

Figure 5.2 Image selectively downloaded

Increasing the Cache Size

A *cache* is a temporary storage location, like the ones thieves use to stash the loot until they get out of the pen. By the way, cache is pronounced "cash." Netscape uses cache memory to store recently accessed documents—and as you'll learn in this section, one of the best things you can do to increase Netscape's speed is to increase the size of the disk cache.

How the Cache Works

When you download a document, Netscape places the document in the cache. Should you wish to go back to a document you have viewed previously, Netscape locates and displays the document in the cache rather than retrieving it again from the network. Since cache retrievals are many times faster than network retrievals, this produces an impressive gain in Netscape's speed.

Where Does Netscape Store Cached Documents?

Netscape employs two caches, a memory cache and a disk cache.

- **The Memory Cache** This cache is a portion of your computer's random-access memory (RAM) that has been set aside for storing the most recently accessed documents. In comparison to network retrieval, retrieval from the memory cache is very fast; compare, for instance, how long it takes to download a new document and how long it takes to redisplay the same document by clicking the Back button. By default, Netscape sets aside 600 KB for the memory cache. Just how many documents the memory cache holds depends on the average size of the documents you've retrieved; a text-only document may require as little as 32 K, while a document loaded with in-line images may consume the entire cache. As you retrieve additional documents, older documents are flushed (removed) from the cache. At the end of your Netscape session, the memory cache is erased as you quit Netscape.
- **The Disk Cache** This cache is a portion of your computer's hard disk that, like the memory cache, has been set aside for storing the most recently accessed documents. By default, Netscape sets aside 5000 KB (roughly 5 megabytes) for this purpose. As you retrieve additional documents, older documents are flushed from the cache. Unlike the memory cache, the disk cache retains documents between Netscape sessions. Up to 5 megabytes of previously accessed Web documents are present on your disk, ready for fast retrieval should you access these documents again.

When Does Netscape Use the Caches?

The two caches come into play in the following situations:

- **When you access a visited hyperlink** As you know, Netscape keeps track of visited hyperlinks, hyperlinks to documents that you have previously accessed. These hyperlinks appear in a distinctive color. When you access a visited hyperlink by any means (choosing a bookmark, clicking a visited hyperlink, or typing the URL directly), Netscape contacts the server and attempts to verify whether the document has been altered since its last retrieval. If the document has been altered, Netscape retrieves a new copy. If not, Netscape retrieves the document from the disk cache. By default, Netscape verifies visited hyperlinks every time you access one.
- **When you click the Back button** If you click Back, you're returning to a document that you have accessed in the current Netscape session. For this reason, it's probable that the document has not been altered since its last retrieval, so Netscape does not contact the server to see whether the document has changed. Instead, the program retrieves the document from the memory cache or, if it has been flushed from the memory cache, from the disk cache.

Here's a tip that may improve Netscape's performance and reduce unnecessary load on the Internet. From the Options menu, choose Preferences, and select the Cache and Network preferences. In the Verify Documents area, click Once per Session (the default is Every Time). With this setting, Netscape will attempt only once per session to verify whether the document has been updated. Should you once again click this document's hyperlink or bookmark in the same session, or type its URL, Netscape will retrieve the cache copy immediately, without accessing the server. This saves you time and reduces network load.

Should You Increase the Size of the Caches?

If you can, yes. Take the following quick quizzes to find out whether increasing the size of the caches is for you.

- **Increasing the Size of the Memory Cache** Do you frequently find yourself clicking the Back button to go back to previously accessed documents? Do you run Netscape all by itself, with no other big programs running at the same time? Do you have 8 MB of RAM? If your answer to all these questions is "Yes," you can improve Netscape's performance dramatically by increasing the size of the memory cache. A cache that's 1000 KB will hold almost twice as many documents as the default 600 KB cache, but it will leave less memory for other applications. With a 1000 KB cache, there's a better chance that Netscape will be able to retrieve a redisplayed document from the memory cache, which is faster than the disk cache and much faster than network retrieval.

- **Increasing the Size of the Disk Cache** Do you have at least 50 MB of free hard disk space? Do you frequently access documents that have lots of in-line images, and redisplay them in subsequent sessions? If your answer to both these questions is "Yes," you may wish to increase the size of Netscape's disk cache. You won't notice any difference until you try to redisplay a document you accessed several weeks ago; the larger the cache, the less chance there is that this document has been flushed from the cache. If it's still in the cache, retrieval will be much faster than network retrieval, which is Netscape's only option if the document isn't present in either cache.

For information on modifying the size of the caches, see the next section.

Changing Cache Size Defaults

If you've decided to change the default size of the caches, follow these instructions:

1. From the Options menu, choose Network Preferences.
2. In the Preferences dialog box, click the Cache tab. You'll see the Cache options, shown in Figure 5.3.
3. To change the size of the memory cache, type a new number in the Memory Cache box. The default size is 600 K. If you have lots of free memory, change this to 1000 K or 2000 K.
4. To change the size of the disk cache, type a new number in the Disk Cache box. Don't type a number that exceeds half of your available disk space.
5. Click OK to confirm your preferences and exit.

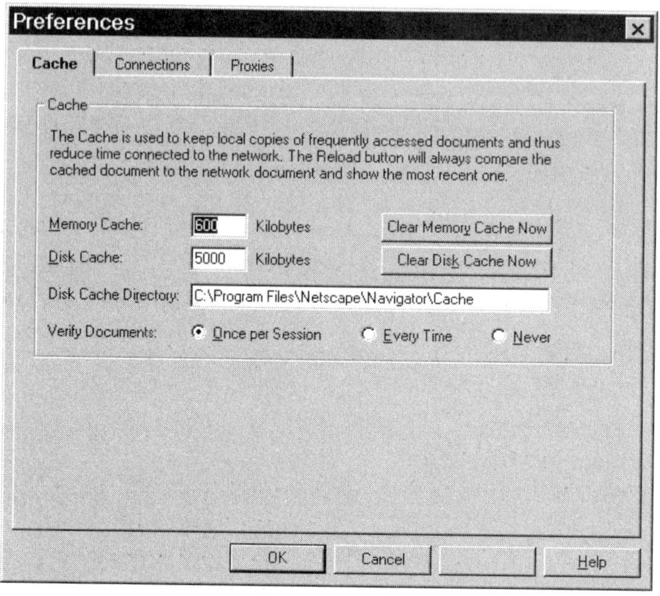

Figure 5.3 Cache options

I'm out of hard disk space! After you increase the size of your disk cache and use your system for a while, you may run out of hard disk space—believe me, it happens. Just bear in mind that you can free up space—maybe a lot of space—by reducing the size of Netscape's cache.

Changing the Verification Frequency

As you've just learned, Netscape stores a copy of visited documents in the disk cache. When you reaccess one of these documents, the program *verifies* the document. In brief, this means that the program contacts the original site to determine whether the document has changed since it was last downloaded. If the document has changed, Netscape downloads a new copy.

Verification is time-consuming—in fact, it cuts down the cache's performance considerably. Recognizing this fact, Netscape's designers set up the program so that it verifies documents only once per session. If you revisit the document later in the same session, the program loads it directly from the cache without verification—try it. As you can see, the second load is much faster. The speed is limited only by the data transfer rate of your hard disk drive.

So here's the super speed trick: You can change the verification setting so that Netscape *never* checks to see whether the document has changed. You can choose this setting in the Cache page of the Network Preferences dialog box—but before you do, consider whether you really want to do this.

What's the effect of changing the reload checking frequency to "never"? A super speed improvement—you won't believe it. When you access a document that's in the cache, it loads very quickly because Netscape does not have to send a message out over the network.

But here's the danger. If the document you're accessing really *has* changed, you won't know it. Netscape will show you the copy that's in the cache. There might be some important new information in the new version of the document, the one that's available out on theWeb—but you're in the dark. To be sure, you can manually initiate a check by clicking the Reload button (discussed later in this chapter), but you might forget to do so.

Because you might miss important new information by using the "Never" setting, you should think twice before changing the default setting (Once per Session). If you decide to go ahead and make the change, please put a big sign by your computer that says, "Remember to click Reload if you suspect the document has changed!"

To change the default verification setting:

1. From the Options menu, choose Network Preferences.
2. In the Preferences dialog box, click the Cache tab. You'll see the Cache options, shown in Figure 5.3
3. In the Verify Documents area, click Never.
4. Click OK to confirm your preferences and exit.

Should you use the "Always" verification option? Only if you're working with important, time-sensitive information, such as stock quotes. With this option, Netscape always verifies whether documents have changed before loading them from the cache. The result is sluggish operation, but you'll be certain that you'll never miss a change in an important document you're using.

When Should You Flush the Caches?

Netscape provides commands, found in the Preferences dialog box, that permit you to flush the memory cache and disk cache manually. There's no real reason to do this unless you suspect that, for some reason, the cache copy of a document has been corrupted by a transmission or storage error. I've never experienced this, personally, but should it happen to you, follow these steps:

1. From the Options menu, choose Network Preferences.
2. Click the Cache tab.
3. To flush the memory cache, click Clear Memory Cache Now.
4. To flush the disk cache, click Clear Disk Cache Now. Note: This operation may take a few minutes.
5. Click OK.

Here's another reason to flush the cache. If you're worried that somebody might snoop around in your system to find out where you've been browsing, you should be aware that Netscape has saved copies of all the hyperlinks you've recently visited. Anyone with a modicum of Netscape knowledge could browse around in the cache and find out what you've been doing with the program. If you're worried about this, flush the disk cache—but be aware that this precaution comes at the cost of reduced performance, since Netscape will have to retrieve the cached documents from the network now that you've erased them.

Finding a Document in the Cache

As you've just learned, Netscape downloads and saves a copy of the documents you've visited, up to the limits of the disk storage space that has been set aside for this purpose. Saved are every component of these documents, including the HTML text, GIF and JPEG graphics, and text files. And I do mean *every* component—every little button and rule, the cool icons and banners, the works.

Since these documents are stored in the cache, can't you go into the cache with File Manager (Windows 3.1) or Windows Explorer (Windows 95) and open them individually? Yes, but there's just one catch: Netscape renames all these files using a coding scheme that makes perfect sense to the browser (but no

sense at all to humans). The cache is full of files with names such as M0B8V1.gif and M0OB56LO.html. What's in 'em? Who knows? There are hundreds or even thousands of these files, and you'd go nuts going through all of them.

If you'd like to see one of these documents again, the easiest way is to use Netscape to locate the document on the Web, and let Netscape find and redisplay the cached version. Once you've done so, you can determine the cached file's name.

To determine the file name of a cached document:

1. Locate the document on the Web and display it using Netscape.

2. From the View menu, choose Document Info. You'll see the Document Info dialog box, shown in Figure 5.4

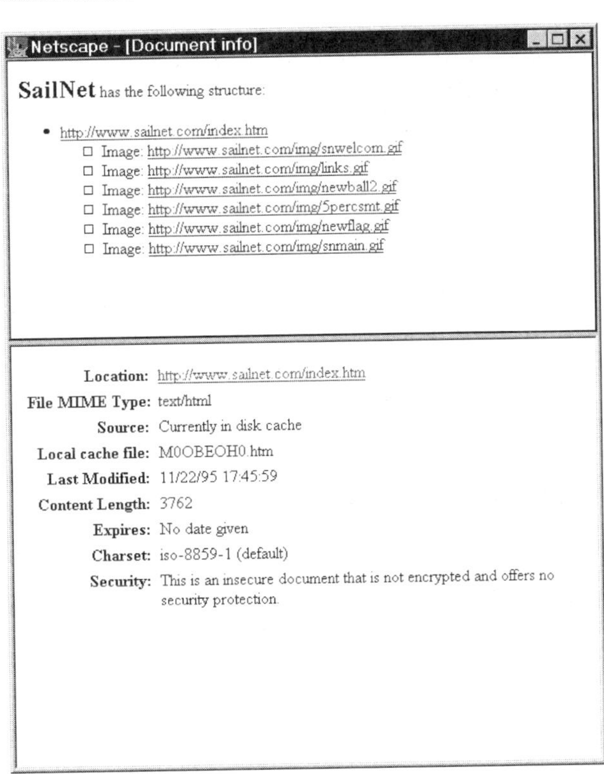

Figure 5.4 Document Info dialog box

The Document Info dialog box contains lots of interesting information about a document. Listed are not only the document's URL, but also the URLs of all the Web resources included in the document (hyperlinks, graphics, the works). You can access any of these by clicking the URL, which is an active hyperlink.

3. In the lower panel, look at the Local Cache File area and note the name of the file. That's it!
4. Close the window.

There's a History to This (The History List)

After a good, long Web surf, you'll be wondering, "Where am I?" And after spending five hours in biancaTroll's house, you'll be thinking, "How do I get back to that *useful* page I saw half an hour ago?" You've surfed so many sites, you'd have to click the Back button six zillion times. But there's a better way, maybe. You may be able to use the history list to go back quickly to previously accessed sites.

Unbeknownst to you, Netscape has been keeping a record of your travels. The program knows where you've been. Fortunately, it doesn't know whether you've been naughty (you didn't fumble around in biancaTroll's bedside drawer, did you?). It just keeps a record of the URLs you've visited, with certain important limitations, which I'll explain in a minute.

Using the Go Menu

You'll find a list of recently visited sites on the bottom portion of the Go menu (Figure 5.5). To go back to a document you've visited previously in the current Netscape session, do the following:

- From the Go menu, choose the title of the document to which you want to return.

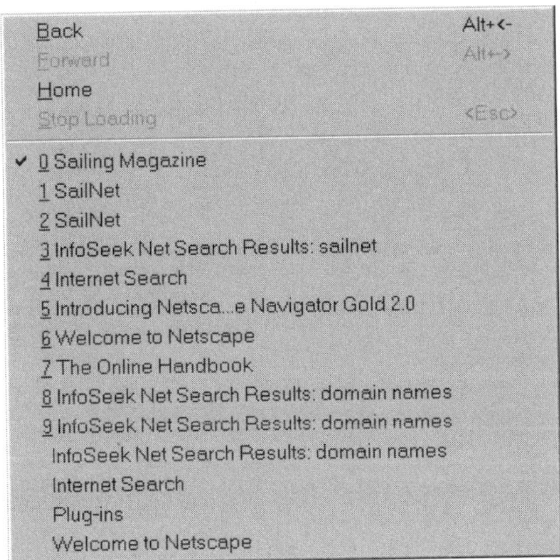

Figure 5.5 Recently visited sites on the Go menu

Using the History List

You can also go back to a document by using the History dialog box, as explained in the following:

1. From the Window menu, choose History, or use the Ctrl + H keyboard shortcut. You'll see the History dialog box, shown in Figure 5.6.
2. Highlight the document to which you want to return, and click Go To (or just press Enter).
3. Click Close.

Have you visited some interesting sites during this session? A quick way to add two or more bookmarks is to select the interesting sites in the History list, and click the Create Bookmark button (at the bottom of the History dialog box). To access the History dialog box, choose History from the Window menu or just press Ctrl + H.

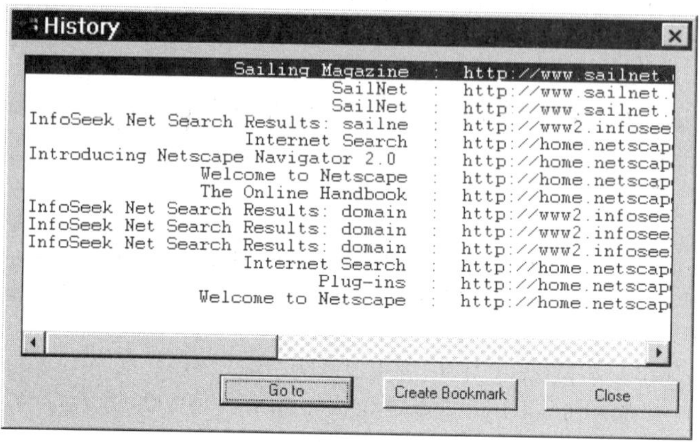

Figure 5.6 History dialog box

Why the History List Erases Some of the Sites You've Visited

Sooner or later, you'll look at the history list, hoping to return to a site you visited a few clicks ago—and it's gone. This is very frustrating, and you'll probably think it's a bug. But it isn't. There's a logic to it. That doesn't mean I like it, but at least there's an explanation—so here goes.

Netscape's history list records only a single lineage of sites. A *lineage* is a series of hyperlinks that all extend outward from a single, source document.

Here's an example of a lineage. Let's say you start with HOME.HTM, and click the Virtual Library link. From the Virtual Library, you select the Wine page. From the Wine page, you select Napa Valley. From the Napa Valley page, you select Napa Valley Wineries, and so on. For this lineage, Netscape keeps all the links.

But then you get tired of browsing in this area, and go back to HOME.HTM. You select Stock Quotes to check out how your stocks are doing. They're doing fine, but check out the history list (in the Go menu, or look at the History dialog box). Hmmm! All the previous links have been erased. That's because you're in a new lineage.

Don't trust the history list to keep an exact record of every site you've visited. If you see a Web page that you definitely

want to keep, choose Add Bookmark from the Bookmarks menu, and flip to Chapter 6 for more information.

When – and How – to Open a New Window

Now that you know how history lists work, there's another important thing to realize about Netscape: The program keeps a separate history list for each window.

Well, so what? Here's what: Whenever you start a new lineage, open a new window. If you do this, Netscape won't erase the history list in the last lineage's window, enabling you to go back to previously accessed documents (in case you get tired of the current lineage).

Just remember my motto: "New lineage, new window."

Working with a New Window

When you open a new window for Netscape, you see what appears to be a new, independent copy of the program—and as far as you are concerned, it is. In the new window, Netscape automatically displays the home page that you've chosen, just as if you were launching the program at the beginning of a new Netscape session.

The new window's history list is a copy of the previous window's list, but the window shows you the *oldest* document in this list—a veritable invitation to launch off in a new lineage, wouldn't you say?

Your subsequent actions in this window will not affect the history list in other Netscape windows.

To open a new window, do the following: From the File menu, choose New Web Browser.

Use this great trick to open a hyperlink in a new window. Point to the hyperlink, and click the right mouse button. From the pop-up menu, choose New Window with this Link. Netscape opens a new window. Instead of displaying the home page, the program displays the document you've chosen.

Here's another good reason to open a new window. If you suspect that you'll have trouble accessing a hyperlink, perhaps

because it's lengthy or the site is situated on a 56 Kbps network in Tasmania, use the pop-up menu to open the link in a new window. While the new window is stalled pending retrieval of the document, you can switch back to the original window and continue enjoying the Web.

Increasing the Number of Windows You Can Open

How many Netscape windows can you open? By default, a maximum of four. If you wish, you can increase this setting.

Be aware that each new window you open consumes system resources; you'll rarely feel a need for more than four windows.

If you really want to increase this number, open the Options menu and choose Network Preferences. In the Preferences dialog box, click the Connections tab, and type a new number in the Number of Connections box. Click OK to confirm your choice.

Managing Multiple Windows

When more than one Netscape window is open, you can switch between them as you please. When you're done with a window, you can close it without quitting Netscape, as long as at least one other Netscape window is open. The following instructions detail these procedures.

To switch from one Netscape window to another:

- Click on the window you want to activate. This shouldn't be difficult, since Netscape cascades new windows (each new window is slightly offset from the others, enabling you to read the title bar of each open window).

To close a Netscape window:

- From the File menu, choose Close

  or

- Press Ctrl + W

When more than one Netscape window is open, the window-closing procedures just described close the window without quitting the program. When you're down to the last window, these procedures quit the program.

When to Reload, When to Refresh

On the View menu, you'll find options called Reload, Reload Cell, and Refresh. Here's what they do:

Reload	When you choose this command, Netscape goes back to the network and determines whether the document you're viewing has changed—and if so, a new copy is downloaded.
New for 2 Reload Cell	This command works just like the Reload command, but it reloads only the frame that's currently selected.
Refresh	When you choose this command, Netscape retrieves a fresh copy of the current document from your computer's memory. The program doesn't check to see whether the document has changed.

When Should You Reload?

Only when you think there's a chance the document has changed since you last downloaded it. Here's why.

Netscape saves a copy of recently accessed documents in its *memory cache* (a special storage area designed for fast re-retrieval of documents). When you click a previously visited hyperlink, Netscape checks to see whether there's a copy of the document in the cache, and if there is, the program loads the cache's copy rather than retrieving the document from the network. In most cases, that's fine—the document appears much more quickly. But what happens if the original, network-based version of the document has changed? You wouldn't know this, because Netscape is showing you the old copy. If you suspect that the network version has changed,

choose Reload from the View menu, or press Ctrl + R, or just click the Reload button.

If you decided to select the "Never" verification frequency (see "Changing the Verification Frequency," earlier in this chapter), bear in mind that the document you're viewing may not be the most recent version. To find out, click Reload.

When Should You Use Refresh?

Sometimes your Microsoft Windows system will fail to update the screen properly. This isn't really Netscape's fault. Windows is notoriously susceptible to screen update problems attributable to low memory or system resources. For example, the fonts might not look right, or the background color may have changed in a weird way. If this happens, choose Refresh from the View menu.

From Here

- The next set of skills you'll need to master involves Netscape's somewhat quirky bookmarks features. Check them out in Chapter 6.
- The best way to keep track of your Netscape bookmarks is to download and install Netscape's SmartMarks plug-in. This utility is discussed in Chapter 7.
- Want to save or print a document or graphic? Find out how in Chapter 8.

Chapter 6

Creating and Using Bookmarks

Save That URL!

You've just found the most awesome Web site. It holds the key to your dreams—nay, your job. And then, following links, you surf off in a zillion directions—only to find, to your dismay, that you've started a new lineage, somehow, and the darned history list has erased that awesome site's URL. (For the lowdown on lineages and history lists, see Chapter 5.) No matter what you do, you can't find it again. You give up in frustration, and late that night you sob softly into your pillow.

Don't let this happen to you: Set bookmarks.

In Netscape, a *bookmark* is a document title that you've added to the Bookmarks menu. In addition to the document title, Netscape saves the URL. To return to the document, you just choose the bookmark name from the Bookmarks menu. Note: In other browsers, a bookmark is called a hotlist item, and the bookmark list is called a hotlist. Hotlist item, bookmark—same thing. The next time you run into some Mosaic user who says, "You ought to

see my cool hotlist," you can sniff disdainfully and say, "We Netscape users call them bookmarks." Then run.

This chapter presents indispensable Netscape skills. In particular, you'll learn what to do when your Bookmarks menu gets overstuffed—a malady, you will find, that befalls every Netscape user, including you. A plus: This chapter's tutorials will prove invaluable in learning how to reorganize bookmarks, a crucial Netscape skill.

New for 2

New to Netscape Version 2 is a completely reorganized bookmarks window. If you've used previous versions of Netscape and struggled with the poorly designed bookmarks dialog box, now thankfully extinct, you'll be glad to know that this feature is much easier to use.

Adding and Choosing Bookmarks

The simplest way to use bookmarks is to add them to the Bookmarks menu. To return to a bookmarked item, you simply choose it from the Bookmarks

For the Time-Challenged

- When you set a bookmark, the title of the Web page you've bookmarked appears on the Bookmarks menu.
- Very soon, your Bookmarks menu becomes too crowded. To alleviate this problem, you can create folders for your bookmarks. You do this within the Bookmarks window. After creating folders, you can organize your bookmarks by dragging them into the folders you've created.
- After you organize your bookmarks into folders, the folders appear on the menu and the bookmark items appear in pop-up submenus.
- By choosing What's New from the Bookmarks window's File menu, you can find out whether any of your bookmarked pages have changed since you last visisted them.
- To add new bookmarks to a specific folder, open the Bookmarks window, highlight the folder, open the Items menu, and choose Set to New Bookmarks Folder.

menu. The drawback of this technique, as you'll quickly discover, is an overly lengthy Bookmarks menu. When you get to that point, you'll want to organize your bookmarks, as discussed in the following section.

Adding a Bookmark to the Bookmarks Menu

You can add a Web document to your Bookmarks menu in two ways:

- **Right-clicking the URL** Point to the URL and click the *right* mouse button. From the pop-up menu, choose Add Bookmark for this Link.
- **Adding the bookmark after you download the document** From the Bookmarks menu, choose Add Bookmark, *or* press Ctrl + D.

Of the two methods for adding bookmarks, it's best to display the page and then use the Add Bookmark command (Bookmarks menu). This command places the page's title on the Bookmarks menu. If you right-click the page's hyperlink and use the pop-up menu, Netscape adds the URL to the Bookmarks menu. URLs are harder to read than document titles.

After you add a bookmark, the bookmark you've added appears on the lower portion of the Bookmarks menu (see Figure 6.1).

Choosing a Bookmark

After you've added a bookmark, you can choose it easily. Just click the Bookmarks menu, and click the bookmark you want. Netscape will download the document you've requested.

Introducing the Bookmarks Window

One of the most common complaints about Netscape, typically voiced by people who have been using the program for two weeks or so, is that the Bookmarks menu has become glutted with items. It's disorganized, out of order, too lengthy, and—for all these reasons—close to useless. The solution? Organize your bookmarks using the Bookmarks window.

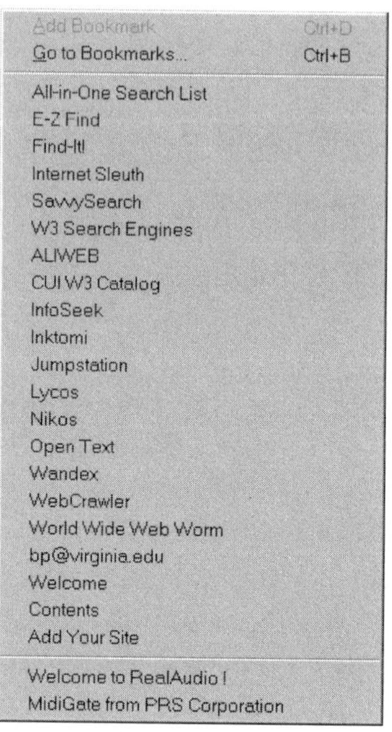

Figure 6.1 Bookmarks appearing on Bookmarks menu

New for 2

If you've used previous versions of Netscape, you'll be glad to know that the Bookmarks window has been completely redesigned. It's much easier to use and has some very nice new features.

Accessing the Bookmarks Window

To access this window, do one of the following

- From the Bookmarks menu, choose Go to Bookmarks

  or

- From the Window menu, choose Bookmarks

  or

- Press Ctrl + B.

What You Can Do in the Bookmarks Window

The Bookmarks window provides tools for doing the following:

- **Organizing bookmarks** When you create a folder, a new submenu shows up on Netscape's Bookmarks menu. To place bookmarks into a folder, just drag the bookmark into the folder. This bookmark will then appear on a pop-up submenu in the Bookmarks menu. In this way, you can quickly customize the Bookmarks menu so that it contains dozens or even hundreds of your favorite documents. Within a folder, you can sort your bookmarks so that they appear in alphabetical order. Additionally, you can change the title of a page to something that's more descriptive.
- **Accessing bookmark pages** Just double-click any Web page's title. Netscape will display the page. If you can't find the bookmark in a lengthy list, there's a Find command that helps you look.
- **Finding out whether source documents have changed** The What's New command (File menu) enables you to determine whether any of the Web documents in your bookmarks list have been altered since you last accessed them.
- **Adding new bookmark items to a folder you've created** After you've organized your bookmarks list, you can choose which of the folders you've created that you want to display on the Bookmarks menu, and you can also choose the folder to which you'd like Netscape to add new bookmark items.
- **Importing and exporting bookmarks** You can easily exchange bookmark lists with other Netscape users by exporting your list and importing lists that people give you.

The contents of the Bookmarks window are stored in a file called BOOKMARK.HTM, which you'll find in Netscape's directory. This file is actually a valid HTML document, which Netscape automatically creates. As you'll learn later in this chapter, you can open any valid HTML file using the File Open command in the Bookmarks window, and all the hyperlinks that this document contains will appear as bookmarks in this window. You can also give your bookmark file to anyone who uses Netscape or any other browser, so that others can open it and make use of the links you've found.

Organizing Your Bookmarks

Chances are that you have a lengthy, disorganized list of bookmarks, which you've saved directly to the Bookmarks menu. In the Bookmarks window, these appear in a list like the one shown in Figure 6.2. To organize your bookmarks, you'll want to create and name folders, and then drag the bookmarks into the appropriate folder. You may also wish to create *separators*, lines that appear on the Bookmarks menu, so that the menu looks neater. The following sections detail these procedures.

Creating Folders

To get your bookmarks organized, the first thing you need to do is to create and name folders. A folder is a storage place for your bookmarks.

Give some thought to how you want to organize your folders. Bear in mind that you can put folders within folders. Here's a plan that reflects my current interests and needs:

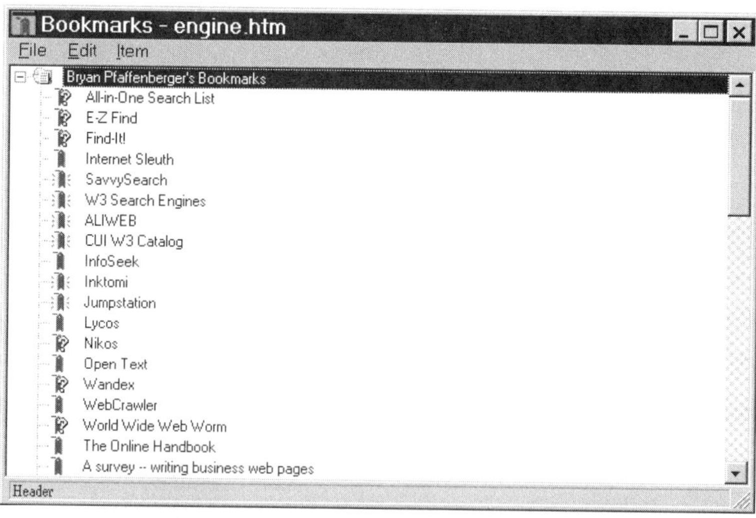

Figure 6.2 Bookmarks window with unorganized bookmarks

Backpacking Stuff
HTML Stuff
  HTML Documentation
  HTML Standards Docs
  HTML Tips and Tricks
Sailing Stuff
Search Tools
  Search Engines
  Subject Trees

Don't worry about getting your folder organization exactly right the first time around. It's easy to reorganize your list.

To create a folder, do the following:

1. In the Bookmarks window, select the top item ("[Your Name]'s Bookmarks").
2. From the Item menu, choose Insert Folder. You'll see the Bookmark Properties dialog box, shown in Figure 6.3.

Figure 6.3 Bookmark Properties dialog box

3. In the Name area, type the name for your new folder.
4. Click OK. You'll see the folder positioned beneath the selected item.

Adding Bookmarks to a Folder

It's easy to add bookmarks to a folder. Just select the bookmarks and drag them to the folder until the folder changes color, then release the mouse button.

Use these Windows shortcuts to select more than one bookmark item at a time. To select bookmarks individually, hold down the Ctrl key and click each of the items you want to select. To select a group of items, click the first one. Then hold down the Shift key and click the last one; Windows will select them all.

After you add bookmarks to a folder, you'll see that the Bookmarks window uses a tree-like diagram to show the list's logical organization (see Figure 6.4).

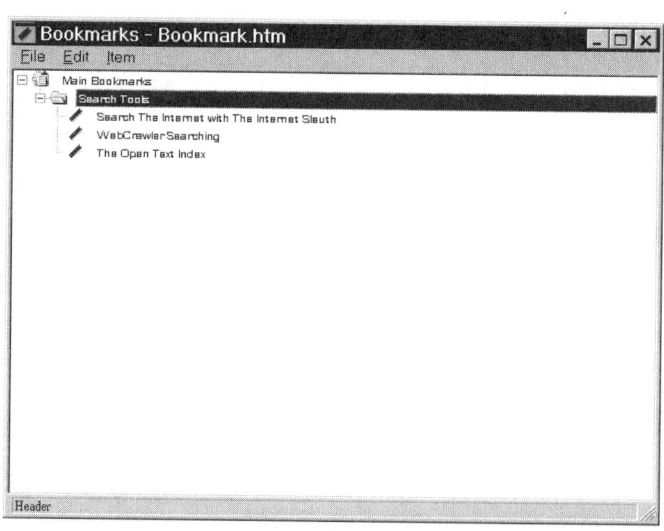

Figure 6.4 Tree structure of bookmarks list

Adding Folders within Folders

Add additional folders and subfolders to flesh out the list's organization, as shown in Figure 6.5. To add a folder within a folder, just select the folder into which you would like to insert a folder. Then choose Insert Folder from the Item menu, and name the folder as described in the previous section.

Alphabetizing Bookmark Items

By default, Netscape alphabetizes the folders at a given level, but bookmark items appear in the order you added them.

To sort the items in a folder, follow these steps:

1. Select the folder.
2. From the Item menu, choose Sort Bookmarks. The items will appear in alphabetical order.

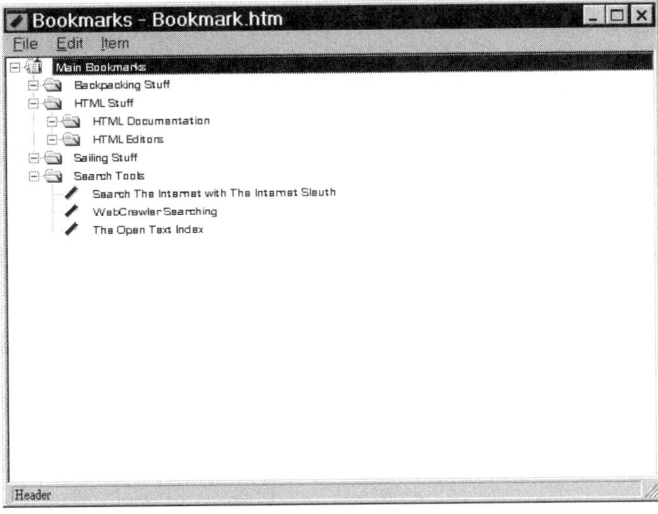

Figure 6.5 Bookmarks list after adding additional folders

Making an Alias

If you'd like a bookmark to appear in more than one folder, you can do so quickly by making an alias. To do so, follow these steps:

1. Select the bookmark item.
2. From the Item menu, choose Make Alias. You'll see a copy of the item in the same folder.
3. Drag the copy to its new location in another folder.

Deleting an Item

To delete a bookmark item, simply select it and press the Delete key. (This just deletes the bookmark, by the way—it doesn't delete the original document out there on the Web.)

Looking at the Bookmarks Menu

The changes you're making in the Bookmarks window will be reflected in the Bookmarks menu. Top-level folders appear as items on the menu; when you click one of them, you see a pop-up menu containing the items you've added (see Figure 6.6). If you've added folders within folders, you get pop-up menus within pop-up menus.

Adding Separators

To clarify the logical organization of your Bookmarks menu, you may wish to add separators (lines that appear on the menu).

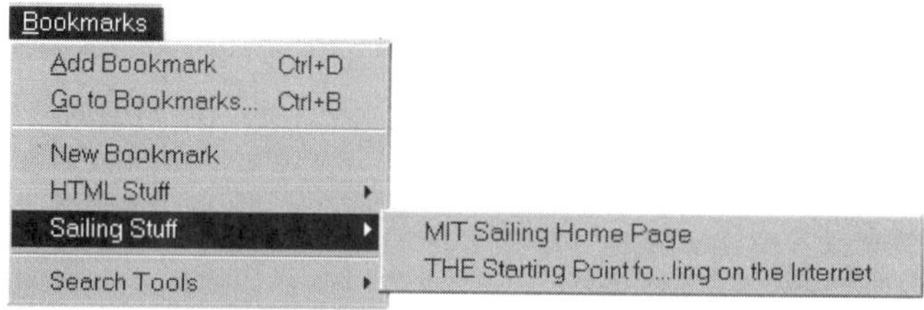

Figure 6.6 Pop-up menu containing added items

To add a separator, do the following:

1. Select the item above the place you want the separator to appear.
2. From the Item menu, choose Insert Separator.

If you don't like the placement of the separator, you can drag it to a new position within the Bookmarks window. To get rid of the separator entirely, select it and press Delete.

Reorganizing Folders

Once you've created your folders, you may wish to reorganize them. It's easy to do so. For example, suppose I've decided to create a new folder called Recreation, and I want to put Backpacking and Sailing Stuff into this new folder. To do so, I create the folder. Then I select the Backpacking and Sailing Stuff folders, and drag them into the new folder. Netscape includes the bookmark items, and any folders within folders, in the move.

Controlling the Bookmark List Display

Within the Bookmarks window, you can use the following techniques to control the way the list appears:

- To close a folder, so that only the folder name appears, double-click the folder icon. Alternatively, you can click the minus sign next to the folder. After the folder closes, you'll see a plus sign indicating that the folder contains items.
- To open a closed folder, double-click the folder icon. Alternatively, you can click the plus sign next to the folder.

Adding a Description

If you would like to make some notes about a bookmark item, you can do so in the Bookmark Properties dialog box (see Figure 6.3).

To add a description, do the following:

1. In the Bookmarks window, select the item to which you would like to add a description.
2. From the Item menu, choose Properties.

3. In the Description box, type a description.
4. Click OK to confirm your comments.

Accessing Bookmark Pages

You can use the Bookmarks window as well as the Bookmarks menu to access the bookmarks you've created.

To go to any bookmark listed in the Bookmarks window, just double-click it. The document appears in Netscape's window, not in the Bookmarks window. To see the document, switch back to Netscape's window.

Finding a Bookmark

In a lengthy bookmark list, you may have trouble finding a bookmark—especially if you've closed the folder in which it's stored. Let Netscape do the hunting for you.

To search for a bookmark item:

1. Select the folder where you want the search to begin (it proceeds downward from there). To search the entire bookmark file, select the top item.
2. From the Edit menu, choose Find. You'll see the Find Bookmark dialog box.
3. In the Find What area, type the text you want to find. Capitalization doesn't matter, unless you click Match Case. If a match is found, the program selects the item (if necessary, it opens the folder that contains the item).
4. To find the next matching item, click the Find Again button.

After you've exited the Find dialog box, you can still repeat the search with the same settings—just choose Find Again from the Edit menu.

Finding Out Whether Source Documents Have Changed

Chances are that the documents you've marked as bookmarks are pretty important to you—so naturally you'll want to know whether they've changed. Netscape can check the documents to find out whether they've changed. If any of them have, the Bookmarks menu will contain marks that indicate which of your bookmark items contain new material.

To determine whether source documents have changed:

1. Select one or more items.
2. From the File menu, choose What's New. You'll see the What's New dialog box, which enables you to look for changes in all the bookmark items or just the ones you selected.
3. Choose All Bookmarks to check out all the items, or Selected Bookmarks to check out just the ones you selected.
4. Click Start Checking. You'll see a dialog box that informs you how much time this operation will take. When it's finished, you'll see another dialog box informing how many documents, if any, contain changes.
5. Click OK to confirm, and look at the Bookmarks window. Documents that have changed are shown with a bright yellow flag.

Adding New Bookmarks to a Specified Folder

Once you've created folders for your bookmarks, you can select a new default folder to serve as the destination for new bookmark items. To do so, follow these steps:

1. In the Bookmarks window, select the folder you want to use as the destination for new bookmark items.
2. From the Item menu, choose Set to New Bookmarks Folder. In the bookmark item list, you'll see a check mark on this folder's icon.

Controlling the Menu Display

After you've added lots of folders and subfolders, your Bookmarks menu can seem cluttered again. If there's just one folder that you tend to use frequently,

you can restrict the Bookmarks menu so that just this folder appears. To do so, follow these steps:

1. In the Bookmarks window, select the folder that you would like to appear on the Bookmarks menu, to the exclusion of all others.
2. From the Item menu, choose Set to Bookmark Menu Folder. In the bookmarks item list, you'll see a little menu icon on top of this item's folder icon. Only the items in this folder will appear on your Bookmarks menu. You can access the other items by opening the Bookmarks window, however.

Note that your choice of a folder as the Bookmark menu folder does not affect into which folder Netscape inserts new bookmark items. That's controlled by the Set to New Bookmarks Folder command, discussed in the previous section.

Exporting Bookmarks

One of the nicer points of Netscape is the program's ability to export bookmarks to a bookmark file, which you can then give to friends and colleagues (or whomever). These fortunate persons can then import the bookmark file, and your bookmarks will magically appear on their Bookmarks menu. This has created a certain amount of Internet traffic in bookmark files.

Another reason to export your bookmark file is that this enables you to create and store more than one bookmark file on your system. For example, you could create one bookmark file for your research on Civil War memorabilia, and another for your collection of hot Web sites. To learn how to open one of the bookmark files you've created, see the next section.

To export your bookmarks to a bookmark file:

1. From the File menu in the Bookmarks window, choose Save As. You'll see the standard Windows Save As dialog box.
2. Type a name for the file (be sure to use the extension .htm), and click Save.

Don't try to edit a bookmark file directly. It contains lots of secret, weird codes and other information that enables Netscape to import the file properly.

Opening a Local Bookmark File

If you've saved a bookmark file as just described, or if someone has given you one, you can open it. The new bookmark file replaces the previous one, so you'll see different options on the Bookmarks menu.

To open a bookmark file, do the following:

1. From the File menu in the Bookmarks window, choose Open. You'll see a standard Open dialog box.
2. In the Files of Type box, choose Source.
3. Locate and select the file you want to open, and click Open. Netscape replaces the current bookmark file with the one you just opened.

I want my old bookmark list back! No problem. Just open it using the instructions just given.

Importing Links from an HTML File

Here's a cool trick: With the Import command on the Bookmarks window's File menu, you can import all the links from any HTML document that you've saved on your local disk. They'll appear as bookmark items. The document headings will appear as folder names. This is pretty cool—try it out.

To import the links in an HTML file, do the following:

1. From the File menu in the Bookmarks window, choose Import. You'll see the Import Bookmarks dialog box.
2. In the Files of Type box, choose Source.
3. Locate and select the file you want to open, and click Open.

Netscape imports all the headings as folders and all the links as bookmark items. Note that the organization may not be ideal; you may have to rearrange the folders to make the list useful.

Creating Internet Shortcuts

If you're using the Windows 95 version of Netscape, you can easily create shortcuts to your favorite Web documents. The shortcuts will appear on your Windows desktop, where you can access them quickly.

To create an Internet shortcut:

1. In the Bookmarks window, select the item that you want to become an Internet shortcut.
2. Drag the item to the desktop, and release the mouse button.

You'll see the shortcut icon on the desktop. To access this document quickly, just double-click the icon.

From Here

- The Bookmarks window is pretty neat, but wait 'til you see Smart-Marks, the subject of the next chapter.
- Want to print or save the documents you're downloading—and how about those neat graphics, too? Find out how in Chapter 8.

Chapter 7

Using SmartMarks

Netscape's SmartMarks add-on program greatly improves the bookmark-organizing capabilities of Netscape Navigator. Available for both the Windows 3.1 and Windows 95 versions of Netscape Navigator, SmartMarks starts automatically every time you launch Netscape.

Once active, SmartMarks modifies Netscape's Bookmarks menu, presenting you with several new options and capabilities, including the following:

- Enhanced bookmarking capabilities. Although you can still use the Bookmarks window, if you wish, SmartMarks provides an easier-to-use interface for creating, storing, and organizing bookmarks. In addition, SmartMarks comes with 300 predefined bookmarks, arranged into more than a dozen preconfigured folders (see Figure 7.1). You can add additional folders and bookmarks as you please.

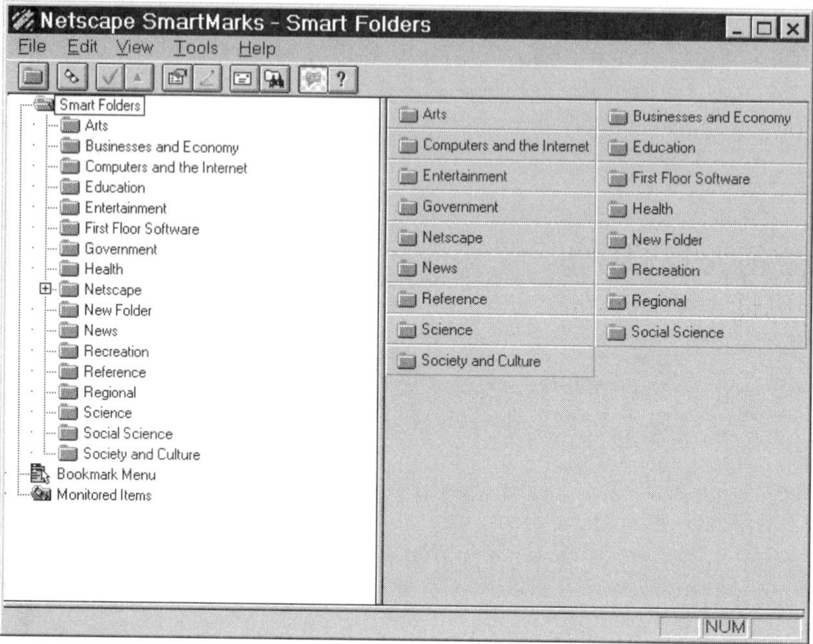

Figure 7.1 Preconfigured folders in SmartMarks

- Add extensive comments to your bookmarks. Unlike the descriptions you type in the Bookmarks window, these comemnts are fully searchable.
- Set up automatic notification of changes to existing bookmarks, including changed or added links on a monitored page.
- Automatically receive bulletins regarding changes to a monitored site. (The site must support this feature in order for these bulletins to be received.)
- Search the Internet using the most popular search engines, with a single, simple user interface.
- Save successful searches, and have them monitored so that you're automatically notified when new or changed links appear in the retrieval list.

These features add up to a significant improvement in Netscape's overall functionality. Unless you're not really interested in storing and organizing bookmarks, SmartMarks is a very wise choice. In this chapter, you'll learn how to get SmartMarks humming—and after you do, you'll have vastly increased your ability to keep track of fast-breaking information developments on the Web.

For the Time-Challenged

- SmartMarks is an add-on program that modifies Netscape's menus. To obtain the program, download it from Netscape's server or purchase the Netscape Power Pack.
- SmartMarks comes with more than a dozen predefined Smart Folders, containing the top 300 Web sites from Yahoo. To display these bookmark items, select a folder in the folder tree. The bookmark panel shows the bookmark items stored in the selected folder.
- Create your own Smart Folders by clicking the Smart Folder tool.
- The best way to add a bookmark item to a Smart Folder is to choose the File SmartMark option on the Bookmarks menu. This option enables you to choose the folder into which you would like to place the bookmark item. In addition, you can type a description and choose notification options.
- If you select a notification option for a bookmark item, Netscape will notify you when the page changes and, optionally, when the page contains new or altered links.
- You can select a notification frequency. By default, SmartMarks checks monitored sites only when you click the Update button. If you wish, you can have the program check monitored sites every time it starts, or at intervals you specify (in minutes, hours, or days). To select a notification frequency, open the Tool menu, choose Preferences, and click the Internet tab.
- To see which sites have changed, display the Web Monitor (choose Web Monitor from the View menu). To access a changed site, just double-click it.
- Smart Finder can search your folders to find items matching keywords that you specify. You can also use Smart Finder to search the Web with Lycos, Infoseek, Yahoo, and WebCrawler, as discussed in Chapter 17.

Obtaining SmartMarks

You can obtain SmartMarks in two ways:

- Download the software from Netscape's FTP server. For more information, see Appendix A.
- Purchase Netscape Power Pack. This package contains SmartMarks, Netscape Chat, and plug-ins developed by Apple Computer, Adobe, and Progressive Networks.

Importing Your Bookmarks File

After you've installed SmartMarks, the program starts automatically when you start Netscape. You'll want to import your current bookmarks file.

To import your current bookmarks file, do the following:

1. From the Tools menu, choose Import. You'll see the Select Import File dialog box.
2. Navigate to the location of your bookmark file (bookmark.htm).
3. Click OK. SmartMarks imports the existing bookmark file. Your bookmarks are named after you ("So-and-so's bookmarks").

Using the Enhanced Bookmarks Menu

After you install SmartMarks, the program replaces Netscape's Bookmarks menu with three SmartMarks options (Figure 7.2):

- **Add SmartMarks** Choose this command (or use the Ctrl + A shortcut) to create new bookmarks, just as you did prior to installing SmartMarks. You'll see your additions in the Bookmarks menu. Later, you can store these bookmarks in folders.

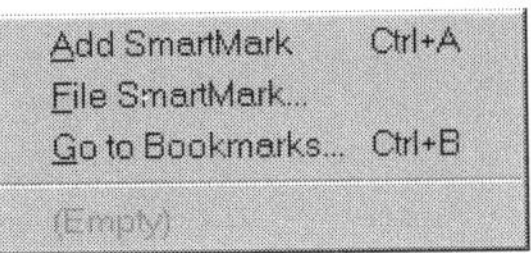

Figure 7.2 SmartMarks memu

- **File SmartMark** Use this command to store bookmarks with optional information, such as comments. You can modify the bookmark name, enter a description, and add keywords, which make it easier to find the bookmark. You can also choose the folder to which you would like to add the bookmark.
- **Go to Bookmarks** This command enables you to view and use the Netscape bookmarks you've previously saved (see Chapter 6).

Understanding the SmartMarks Window

The SmartMarks window (see Figure 7.1) consists of two panels, with the folder tree on the left. In the right panel, you see the bookmark panel. It contains bookmarks that have been added to that folder. To view the original document, just double-click the bookmark.

Below the menu bar you will find the following buttons:

New Folder Click here to create a new bookmark folder.

Monitor Changes Click here to have SmartMarks notify you when the selected document changes or contains added or changed links.

Clear Flags	Click here to clear the change flags from a selected item. A change flag signals that a monitored page has changed.
Update	Click here to run an update on items you've selected for monitoring.
Properties	Click here to display the property set for the selected item (including keywords, description, and monitoring options).
Comments and Bulletins	Click here to display the comments and bulletins for the selected site.
Send	Click here to send e-mail to another Internet user about the selected site.
Find	Search your folders or the entire Internet using keywords.
Smart Captions	Click here to display a pop-up balloon containing information about a bookmark on which you've placed the mouse pointer.
Help	Display SmartMark's help window.

You'll find that these buttons provide access to the SmartMarks tasks you'll undertake most frequently.

Using SmartMarks: An Overview

I recommend that you tackle SmartMarks in the following steps:

1. Begin by learning how SmartMarks' folder tree works. Since this tree already contains many preconfigured folders and the top 300 Web sites from Yahoo, this should be a lot of fun!

2. Create and organize your own bookmark folders. You'll use these to store your favorite Web sites.
3. Add new bookmarks to your SmartMarks folders. Add comments and keywords, if you wish.
4. Choose notification options for the sites that you want to monitor.
5. Look for icons informing you of changes in monitored sites. Use the Web Monitor, if you wish.
6. Search your folders matching keywords that you specify.

The following sections discuss these steps in detail.

Navigating the Folder Tree

SmartMark's folders are arranged in a tree structure (see Figure 7.1). You can do the following with the folder tree and bookmarks panel:

- To view the bookmarks stored in a folder, just click the folder. You'll see the bookmarks in the bookmark panel.
- To view more details about each item (including the first few characters of the description and the date of last modification), open the View menu and choose Details.
- To change the size of the bookmark tiles on the panel, open the Tools menu and choose Options. Click the Options tab. In the Display Options area, choose from the following three tile sizes: narrow, medium, and wide. You can also choose from one or two lines of tile text, and you can change the font.
- A plus mark indicates that a folder has hidden subfolders, which you can view if you wish. To view the subfolder names, click the plus sign.
- A minus sign indicates that the folder can be collapsed, hiding subfolders from view.
- The open folder's contents are on display in the bookmarks panel.
- To view the Web document linked with a bookmark, just double-click the bookmark. The document will appear in Netscape's window.

Creating New Bookmark Folders

To create a new folder, do the following:

1. Select the folder in which you want to place the new folder. To put the folder at the top-most level, select Smart Folders.
2. Click the New Folder tool, or choose New Folder from the File menu. You'll see the Smart Folder Assistant, shown in Figure 7.3.
3. In the Folder Name area, type the name of your new folder.
4. In the Description area, type a brief description (just a few words).
5. Click the Next button. You'll see the next page of the Smart Folder Assistant, which enables you to type keywords. These keywords can increase the chance that you'll find this folder in a search.
6. Type one or more keywords that describe the general subject area and specific contents of this folder.
7. Click Finish. SmartMarks creates the folder and automatically places it in alphabetical order among the other folders at the same level.

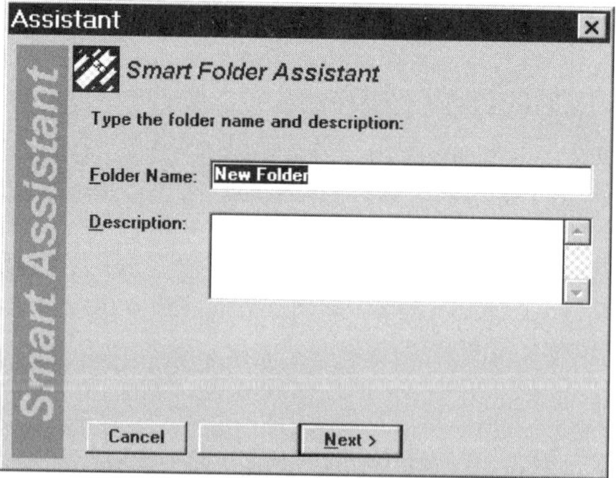

Figure 7.3 Smart Folder Assistant

Organizing Folders and Bookmarks

You can reorganize the folder tree by placing folders within folders, and you can also delete unwanted folders. Within the bookmark panel, you can sort bookmarks by name or by date, and you can move bookmarks from folder to folder.

Placing Folders within Folders

SmartMarks is a great utility, but here's one procedure that's not particularly obvious or easy: placing folders within folders. There's nary a word concerning this maneuver in the program's Help files, but your intrepid author has discovered the way.

To place a folder within another folder:

1. Make sure the destination folder is visible within the folder tree. If it isn't, click the plus sign so that it's visible.
2. Select the folder that's one level *above* the folder you want to move. For most of the existing folders, the folder that's one level above is the Smart Folders folder. After you select this folder, the folder you want to move will appear in the bookmarks panel.
3. Select the folder you want to move, and drag it from the Bookmarks folder to the destination folder. When the destination folder changes color, release the mouse button.

Deleting an Unwanted Folder

To delete an unwanted folder and all of its contents, just select the folder and press Delete. You'll see an alert box asking you to confirm the deletion of the folder and its contents. Click Yes to confirm the deletion.

Sorting Bookmark Items

Within the bookmarks panel, you can sort bookmark items by name or by date.

To sort bookmark items, follow these instructions:

1. Select the items you want to sort. To select all the items, open the Edit menu and choose Select All, or just press Ctrl + A.

2. From the View menu, choose Sort. You'll see a pop-up menu with two options, Name (the default sort option) and Date.
3. Choose Name or Date to initiate the sort.

Moving Bookmark Items

To move a bookmark item to a different folder, display the item in the bookmarks panel and select it. Then drag the bookmark tile to the destination folder and release the mouse button.

Adding Bookmarks to SmartMarks Folders

When you've found a site that you want to add to SmartMarks, you have two options:

- You can add the SmartMark to the Bookmarks menu. SmartMarks places the bookmark item into the Bookmark Menu folder. (Note: This is not the same thing as the Bookmarks window, discussed in the previous chapter.) Later, you can drag the bookmark to a Smart Folder.
- You can choose the folder to which you would like to add the bookmark. This option is best because you don't have to worry about adding the new bookmark to a Smart Folder later.

Adding a Bookmark to the Bookmark Menu Folder

To add a bookmark item to the Bookmarks menu and the Bookmark Menu folder (one of the folders in the SmartMarks folder tree), open the Bookmarks menu and choose Add Bookmark (or just press Ctrl + D). Netscape adds the bookmark to the Bookmarks menu, and it also places a bookmark tile in the Bookmark Menu folder, which you'll find at the bottom of the folder tree. Later, you can move this item to a Smart Folder by selecting it and dragging it to a destination folder.

Adding a Bookmark to a Smart Folder

The best way to add new bookmarks to your SmartMarks menus is to use the File SmartMarks command, one of the three new commands you'll find

on the SmartMarks (Bookmarks) menu. This command enables you to choose the folder in which you would like the bookmark to be stored. You can also type a description and choose notification options.

To store a bookmark in a Smart Folder:

1. In the Bookmarks menu, choose File SmartMark. You'll see the Add SmartMark dialog box, shown in Figure 7.4.
2. In the Document Title area, change the document title to something more descriptive, if you wish.
3. In the Description area, type a short, informative description.
4. In the File Into Folder area, select the folder in which you want the bookmark item to be stored.
5. Select a notification option, if you wish. You can choose to be notified concerning any changes to the page or only to its hyperlinks.
6. Click OK to add the bookmark to the selected folder.

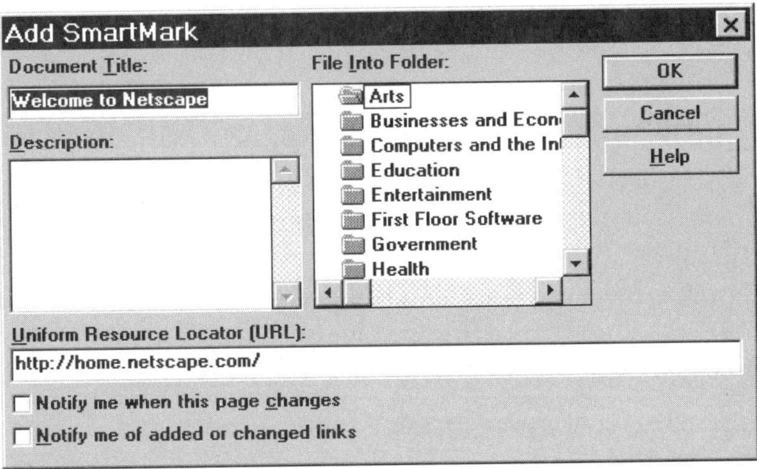

Figure 7.4 Add SmartMark dialog box

Choosing Notification Options

One of the most innovative characteristics of SmartMarks is the programs' ability to update sites. You'll receive notification if the site or its links change. To initiate notification, select notification options for one or more sites. Then select how you want SmartMarks to monitor the items.

Selecting Notification Options for Bookmark Items

Notification isn't automatic—you have to choose it when you create the SmartMark, as described above. If you didn't choose a notification option when you created a bookmark, you can do so in any of the following ways:

- Click the Monitor Changes button.
- Drag the bookmark item into the Monitored Items folder.
- From the File menu, choose Monitor Changes.

You'll see the Monitor Page dialog box, which enables you to choose notification when the page changes (the default choice) and notification when links are changed or added. Click OK to confirm your notification choices.

After you choose one or more notification options for bookmark items, SmartMarks places a copy of the bookmark tile into the Monitored Items folder.

Choosing How SmartMarks Updates the Monitored Items

Once you've selected some items for monitoring, you can choose how SmartMarks updates the monitored items. By default, the program updates manually—you must select the item and click the Update tool. If you wish, you can instruct SmartMarks to update the items at specified intervals.

To change the updating method, follow these steps:

1. From the Tool menu, choose Preferences. you'll see the Preferences dialog box.
2. Click the Internet tab. You'll see the Internet Preferences panel, shown in Figure 7.5. In this panel, you can choose to update sites

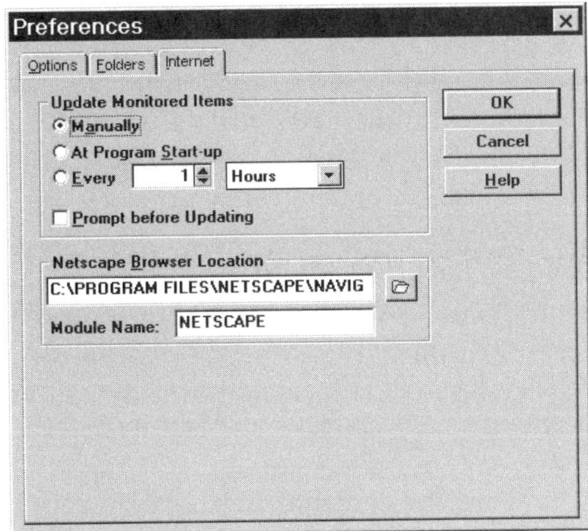

Figure 7.5 Preferences dialog box (Internet tab)

at program startup, or at intervals you specify (in minutes, hours, and days).

3. If you would like SmartMarks to prompt for an OK before updating, click the Prompt before Updating option.
4. Click OK to confirm your options.

Updating Bookmark Items

If you've chosen automatic updating, SmartMarks will automatically detect changes in your monitored items, and you'll receive notification by means of the Web Monitor, discussed in the next section. If you chose manual updating, you'll have to initiate the update yourself. You can do so in two ways:

- To update an item that isn't monitored, select the item. Then open the File menu and choose Update, or just click the Update button.
- To update all the monitored items, choose Refresh from the View menu, or just press F5.

Viewing Changed Bookmarks

When SmartMarks determines that a monitored site has changed, the program flags the altered site with a vertical bar. If the bookmark item is buried within a folder, though, you might not run across the flag. For this reason, it's preferable to work with the Web Monitor. The Web Monitor automatically lists all the sites that have changed since the last update.

To view the Web Monitor, open the Tools menu and choose Web Monitor. The Web Monitor appears at the bottom of the SmartMarks window (see Figure 7.6), but you can detach Web Monitor so that it functions as a separate window, if you wish. To detach Web Monitor, click the magnet icon. To reattach the window, click the magnet icon again.

If you see an item in the Web Monitor window, you know that it has changed since you last accessed the page. To view the page, just double-click the item's name. You'll see the changed page in Netscape's window.

To clear the flags, select one or more items and click the Clear Flags button.

Performing a Search

SmartMarks includes unusually powerful features for searching not only the contents of your Smart Folders, but the entire Internet. The program's Find command enables you to search the Web's top subject trees and search engines (Yahoo, Lycos, WebCrawler, and Infoseek), which are discussed more fully in Chapter 17. Most useful of all is a feature that enables you to save a search and repeat it at intervals you specify—if the search turns up any new documents in your area of interest, SmartMarks lets you know. Here's a great way to keep on top of fast-breaking Web developments!

Searching Smart Folders

After you've added hundreds or thousands of sites to your Smart Folders, you may find that it's getting difficult to find a particular bookmark item—now, which folder was it that you stored it in? If you find yourself hunting around for a lost item, let SmartMarks do the work for you.

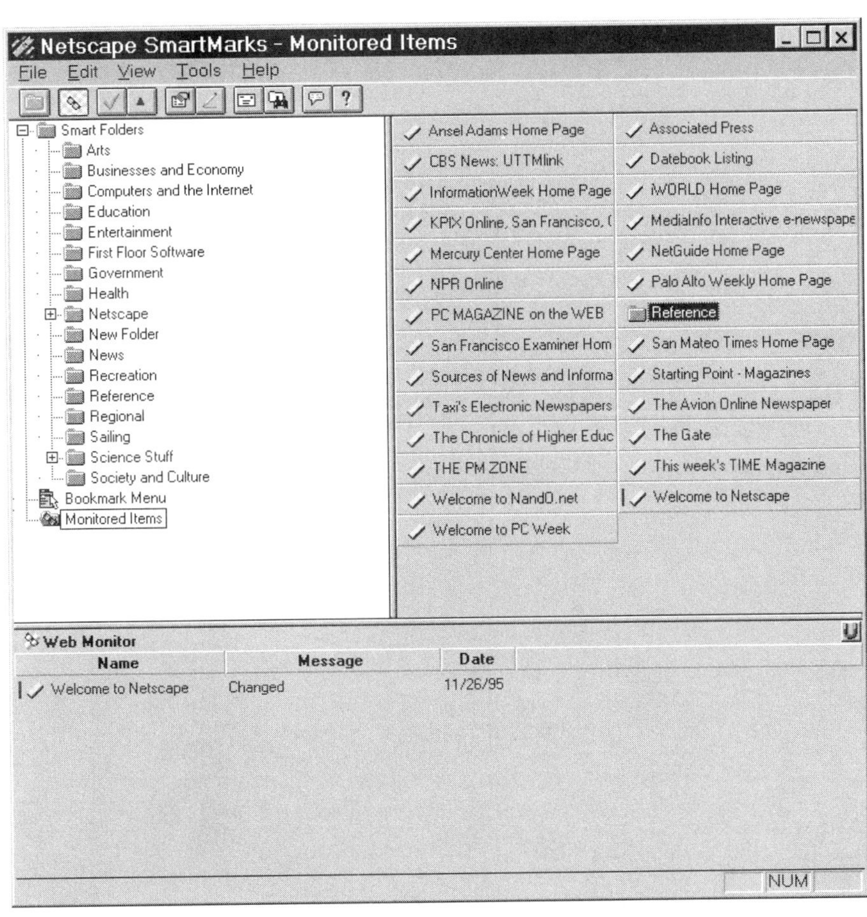

Figure 7.6 Web Monitor

To search for a bookmark item, do the following:

1. From the Tools menu, choose Find, or just use the Ctrl-F keyboard shortcut. You'll see the Smart Finder, shown in Figure 7.7.
2. In the Search box, choose All Folders.

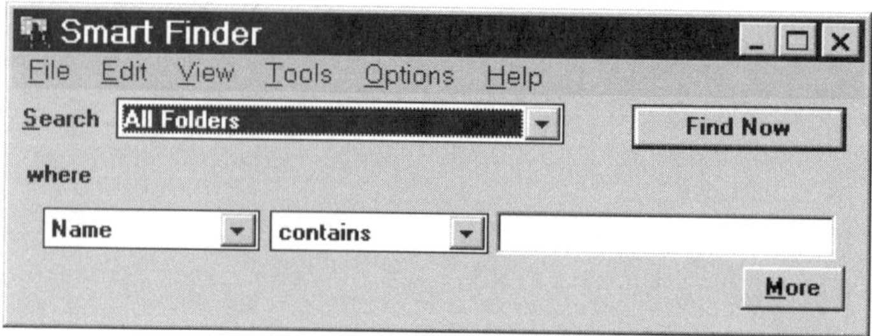

Figure 7.7 Smart Finder dialog box

3. In the first text box below Where, choose the portion of the bookmark item that you want to search. You can choose from Name, Description, Comments and Bulletin, or keywords.
4. In the second text box, choose a matching option. You can choose contains, does not contain, starts with, or ends with.
5. In the third text box, type a keyword that you want to match.
6. If you would like to add an additional keyword, click the More button. You'll see an additional row of three text boxes; choose the part of the item to search, select a matching option, and type another keyword. Note that Smart Finder won't retrieve an item unless an item matches *both* keywords. To add additional keywords, click More again. You can specify up to five keywords this way.
7. When you are finished choosing options, click Find Now. If the search succeeds, you'll see the matching items in a panel that appears at the bottom of the Smart Finder window. To access an item, just double-click it.

If the search fails, you may have typed too many keywords. To broaden the search, try clicking the Fewer button and removing some of the keywords.

Searching the Web

A powerful feature of Smart Finder is its ability to search Yahoo, WebCrawler, Lycos, and Infoseek. What's more, you can save searches and repeat them at intervals that you specify, and SmartMarks will inform you of changes. These powerful features are discussed in Chapter 17.

Importing and Exporting Catalogs

In SmartMarks, a *catalog* is a list of hyperlinks that is formatted and stored in a way that optimizes SmartMark's functions. But these catalogs are not insulated from the Web. You can import any HTML file into SmartMarks so that it becomes a new Smart Folder, and you can also export one or more SmartMark catalogs to an HTML file.

Importing an HTML File into SmartMarks

You can import any HTML file containing hyperlinks into SmartMarks so that it becomes a new Smart Folder in your folder tree. SmartMarks ignores the text; it only stores the hyperlinks.

To import an HTML file into SmartMarks so that its hyperlinks appear in a new folder:

1. Display the HTML file with Netscape.
2. From Netscape's File menu, choose Save, and save the file as a Source (*.htm) file.
3. In SmartMarks, open the Tools menu and choose Import.
4. Use the Import dialog box to open the HTML file you just saved. You'll see a new SmartMarks folder containing the hyperlinks in the file you imported.

Like to find some cool bookmark files to import? Check out http://www.firstfloor.COM/catalogs/. You'll find a number of new and interesting catalogs to import, including Health & Fitness, Music, and Windows 95 resources. All these pages can be monitored with bulletins, if you wish.

Exporting Folders to an HTML File

Would you like to share your Web discoveries with others? You can do so by exporting one or more Smart Folders to HTML files. You can then mail the file to others, or give it to them on a disk.

To export one or more Smart Folders to an HTML file:

1. Unless you want to export everything in your SmartMarks catalog, select the bookmark items or the folders you want to export.
2. From the Tools menu, choose Export. You'll see the Export dialog box, shown in Figure 7.8.
3. In the Which Things to Export area, choose Selection to export the selected bookmark items, Folders to export the selected folders, or All Folders to export everything.
4. In the What Data to Export area, choose the items you want to include with the exported hyperlinks. By default, SmartMarks exports keywords and subfolders.
5. In the Filename area, choose a file name for the exported file.
6. Click OK to export the file.

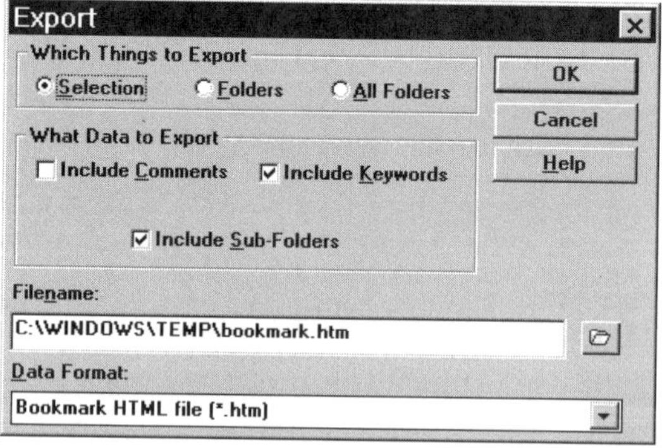

Figure 7.8 Export dialog box

From Here

- Learn how to save and print the documents you're viewing with Netscape. You'll find the lowdown in Chapter 8.
- Chapter 9 shows you how to use Netscape customization options, so that the program looks and works the way you want.

Chapter 8

Managing Documents

While you're viewing Web documents with Netscape, you can select and copy text from the screen to the Clipboard, search for text, save the document to your hard drive (in HTML or plain text), save in-line images to your hard drive, print documents, and view the source HTML. This chapter fully discusses these document-handling aspects of Netscape Navigator.

Copying Text or Graphics to the Clipboard

You can easily select and copy any text or in-line graphic image that you see on-screen in Netscape Navigator. The copied text goes to the Clipboard, where you can paste it using other applications.

For the Time-Challenged

- You can copy text and graphics from any document that Netscape displays. The copied text or graphic goes to the Clipboard, where you can paste it using other applications.
- If you need to find text within a document you're displaying, click the Find button, type some search text, and click OK.
- To open a local document, use the Open File command.
- To save an in-line image to your hard drive, right-click it and choose Save This Image As.
- To print the document you're currently displaying, click the Print button.
- To view information about a document, choose Document Info from the View menu.
- To view the source HTML, choose Document Source from the View menu.

To copy text to the Clipboard, follow these steps:

1. Using the mouse, select the text on-screen.
2. From the Edit menu, choose Copy, or just use the Ctrl + C keyboard shortcut.
3. To paste the text using another application, use that program's Edit Paste command, or press Ctrl + V.

I tried to copy the darned text but I clicked a hyperlink instead! If the text you're copying contains a hyperlink, the copy operation can sometimes inadvertently turn into a hyperlink click. If this happens, click the Back button to return to the document. Try selecting the text again, but start by clicking *just outside* the text you want to copy, and carefully drag all the way over the text and release the mouse button just beyond the edge of the text.

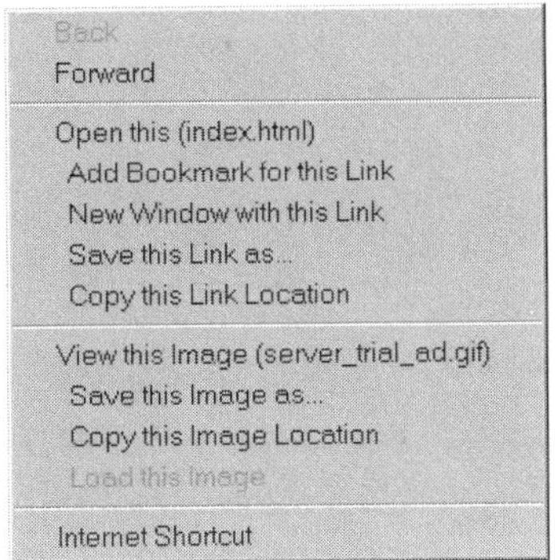

Figure 8.1 Pop-up menu (right-click)

To copy graphics to the Clipboard:

1. Point to the graphic with the mouse, and click the right mouse button. You'll see the pop-up menu shown in Figure 8.1.
2. Click Copy this Image Location.
3. To paste the text using another application, use that program's Edit Paste command, or press Ctrl + V.

Finding Text in a Document

You've just downloaded a humongous document, and you know it contains something of interest to you . . . somewhere. Don't wear out your eyes searching the text manually; use the Find button.

To search for text in the document that's currently displayed:

1. Click the Find button. Alternatively, open the Edit menu and choose Find, or press Ctrl + F. You'll see the Find dialog box, shown in Figure 8.2.

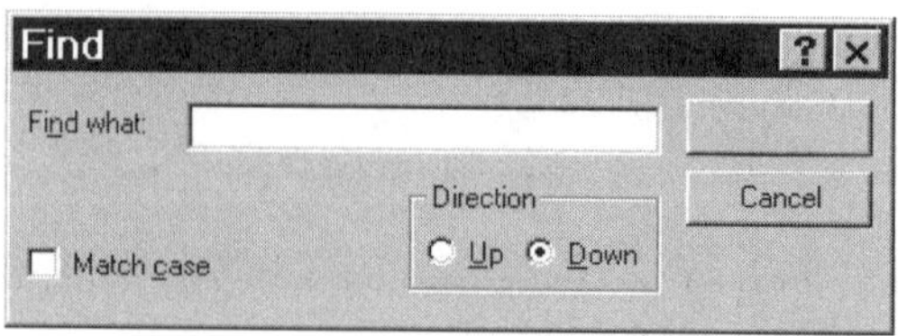

Figure 8.2 Find dialog box

2. By default, Netscape searches down in the document and ignores capitalization. To search up, click the Up button. To match a capitalization pattern (for example, to find "Robert Frost" but not "morning frost"), click Match Case.
3. In the Find What box, type the text that you want to match.
4. Click Find Next. Netscape tries to find the text you've matched. If the program finds a match, it scrolls to the text's location and highlights it. The Find dialog box remains on-screen.
5. To find another match, click Find Next. To close the Find dialog box, click Cancel.

After you close the Find dialog box, you can still repeat the search with the same settings—just press the F3 key, or open the Edit menu and choose Find Again.

Saving Documents

You can save any document that Netscape can display. It's easy to save documents in native HTML or plain text. But be aware that Netscape doesn't automatically save in-line images. To save a document with in-line images, you're in for some work, as the following sections explain.

Saving Documents in Plain Text

If you've downloaded a document that contains lots of interesting text that you'd like to save for future reference or use, you can save the document as plain text. With this option, Netscape removes all the HTML codes and hyperlinks.

If you just want a clean printout of the document, print it instead of saving it as plain text. Netscape's Print command produces an attractive-looking printout of the document, just as you see it on-screen—no ugly HTML codes.

To save a document as plain text:

1. From the File menu, choose Save As, or press Ctrl + S. You'll see the Save As dialog box (Figure 8.3).
2. In the Save as Type box, choose Plain Text (*.txt).
3. In the Directories list, choose the directory to which you would like to save the document.
4. In the File Name box, type a name for the document. Netscape suggests a name using the document's current title. Be sure to use the extension .txt.
5. Click Save.

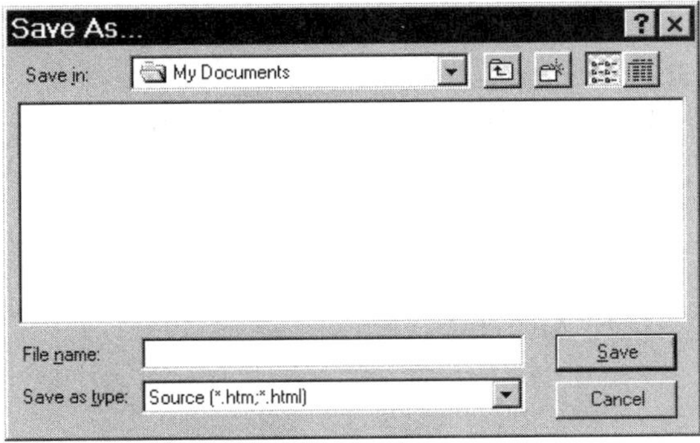

Figure 8.3 Save As dialog box

Saving Documents in HTML

The Web documents that Netscape displays are written in HTML, as you know. If you save a document in HTML format, you can reopen the document using Netscape's Open File command (File menu), and you'll see all the text formatting and hyperlinks that the document contains. But you may not see the in-line graphics, as explained below.

When should you save HTML documents? There's really only one good reason: You're learning HTML, and you want to study the HTML coding. Don't make disk copies of documents in an attempt to cut down on network retrieval delays; Netscape already does this job for you automatically (see Chapter 5).

To save the document in HTML format:

1. From the File menu, choose Save As, or press Ctrl + S. You'll see the Save As dialog box, shown in Figure 8.3.
2. In the Save as Type box, choose Source (*.htm).
3. In the Directories list, choose the directory to which you would like to save the document.
4. In the File Name box, type a name for the document. Netscape suggests a name using the document's current title.
5. Click Save.

Why don't you see in-line images when you open an HTML file you've saved? To understand, you need to know the difference between a relative link and an absolute link.

- A *relative link* displays a graphic or document that's stored in the same directory as the document; it doesn't contain any path information other than, in effect, "Look in the same directory for this."
- An *absolute link* displays a graphic or document that's stored on some other computer, and contains complete instructions on where it should be obtained.

Now let's say you download an HTML file to your \docs directory, and open the file. Almost certainly, all of the in-line images were created with relative links. Netscape goes hunting for the graphics in the \docs directory, but they're not there, so you see lots of placeholders. Web authors are loathe to use absolute links for in-line images and for good reason: If you link to

an image on somebody else's computer, what happens if that someone else decides to erase the image? Since you can't control this, it's easier and safer to use relative links for in-line images.

Viewing and Saving In-Line Graphics

Netscape's pop-up menu enables you to save graphics to your hard disk.

To save an in-line graphic:

1. Point to the graphic.
2. Click the right mouse button. You'll see the pop-up menu shown in Figure 8.1, earlier in this chapter.
3. Choose Save this Image as. You'll see the Save As dialog box. Netscape has automatically placed the graphic's name in the File Name box.
4. In the directories list, select the directory where you want to save the graphic.
5. Click Save.

I can't save the background graphic! That's right. Click as hard as you might, you can't download the background graphic. If you're dead-set on getting your hands on one of these, you'll find most of them at

http://home.netscape.com/home/bg/index.html

You can right-click the versions of the background that you'll find in this document.

Opening Local Documents

With Netscape, you can open any HTML or text file that's present on a disk in your computer. To do so, follow these instructions:

1. From the File menu, choose Open File, or just press Ctrl + O (the letter). You'll see the standard Open dialog box.
2. Use the folder tree commands to locate the disk and directory containing the file that you want to open.
3. In the Files of Type box, choose the type of file you want to open.

Printing Documents

By far the best way to produce a permanent record of a Netscape-accessed document is to print it. Netscape prints all the fonts and graphics just as you see them on-screen.

Choosing Page Setup Options

The Page Setup command on the File menu enables you to choose a number of print output options, including margins. To use the Page Setup dialog box, open the File menu and choose Page Setup. You'll see the Page Setup dialog box, shown in Figure 8.4.

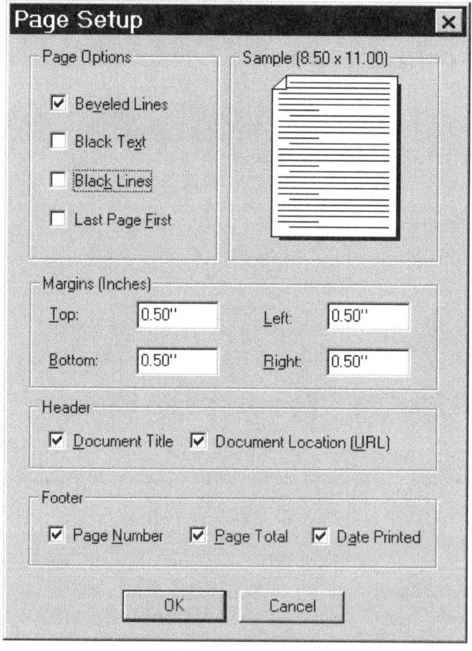

Figure 8.4 Page Setup dialog box

In the Page Options area, you can make the following choices:

Beveled Lines	Click here to print the beveled rules you see on-screen.
Black Text	If you have a color printer, click here to suppress color printing of hyperlinks.
Black Lines	Click here to print rules as a solid black line.
Last Page First	Click here if you need this option to avoid having to hand-collate the printed output.

In the Margins area, you can change the margins by typing new measurements in inches.

In the Header area, you can choose to print the document title and the URL. It's a great idea to leave both of these selected—they're on by default—so that you can return to the Web location of a page you've printed.

In the Footer area, you can control page numbers, the printing of a total number of pages with the page numbers, and the date printed.

Previewing Print Output

To see what your document's printed output will look like, you can use the Print Preview command (File menu):

1. From the File menu, choose Print Preview. You see the Print Preview window, shown in Figure 8.5.
2. To see the next page, click Next Page. To return to the previous page, click Previous Page.
3. To view two pages in the same window, click Two Page.
4. To zoom in for a closer look, click Zoom In once or twice. Click Zoom Out once or twice to return to full-page view.
5. To exit Print Preview, click Close. If you would like to print, click Print, and see the next section for printing instructions.

Choosing Print Options and Printing Your Document

Depending on your printer's capabilities, you can choose from a variety of printing options before printing. Options found in most printers include

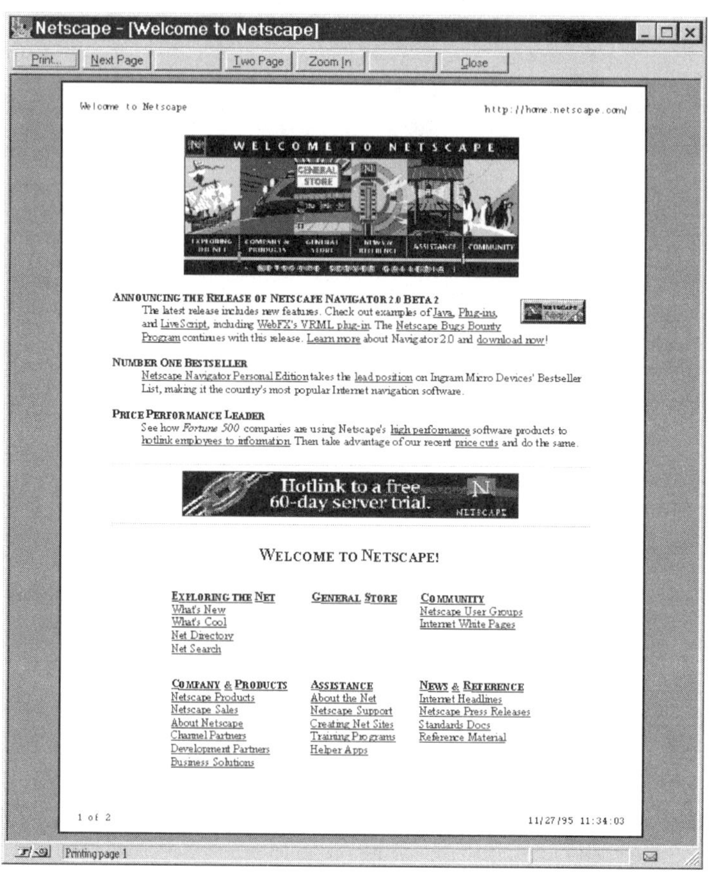

Figure 8.5 Print Preview window

selecting the page range and the number of copies to print. After you choose your options, Netscape prints your document.

To choose print options and print your document:

1. Do one of the following:

   In the Print Preview window, click the Print button
   or
   Click the Print button on the toolbar
   or

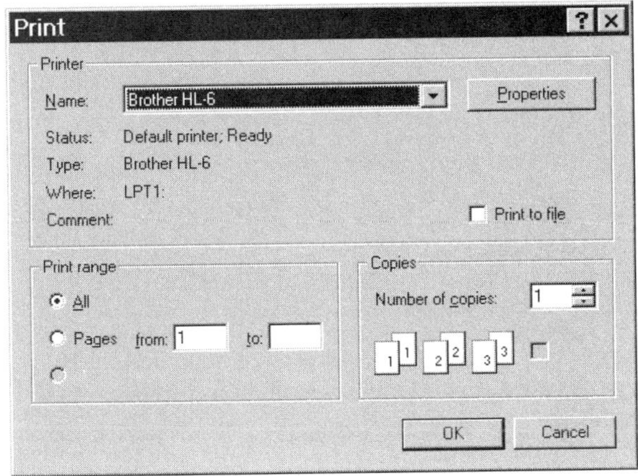

Figure 8.6 Print dialog box

From the File menu, choose Print
or
Press Ctrl + P.

2. You'll see the Print dialog box, shown in Figure 8.6.
3. If you would like to print just some of the pages in the document, select Pages in the Print Range area, and type the beginning page number in the From box and the ending page number in the To box.
4. To make more than one copy, type the number of copies you want to make in the Copies box.
5. Choose OK to initiate printing.

Viewing Document Information

New for 2

If you'd like to know more about the document you're viewing, open the View menu and choose Document Info. You'll see the Document Info about the document you're currently viewing, as shown in Figure 8.7. You'll find

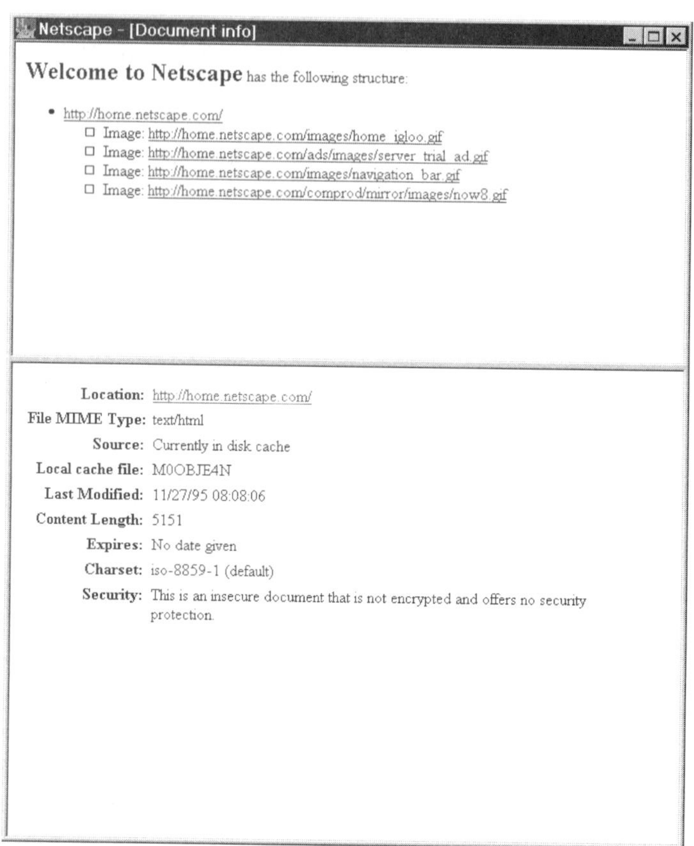

Figure 8.7 Document Info

information that may prove helpful in certain situations; for example, you can find out from this window which file name Netscape has used to store the document in the disk cache.

Note that the Document Info page contains a list of all the hyperlinks in a document, including links to graphics. You can click any of these links to access the links and graphics referenced in the document. If you'd like to access and save all the graphics referenced in a document, this is the most convenient way to do so.

VIEWING THE SOURCE HTML

If you're learning HTML, the language used to code Web documents, you'll sooner or later access a particularly cool site and exclaim, "How did they *do* that!" Here's how you can find out. From the View menu, choose Document Source, and you'll see a colorful view of the underlying HTML code (Figure 8.8). The colors help the eye to separate the code from the text.

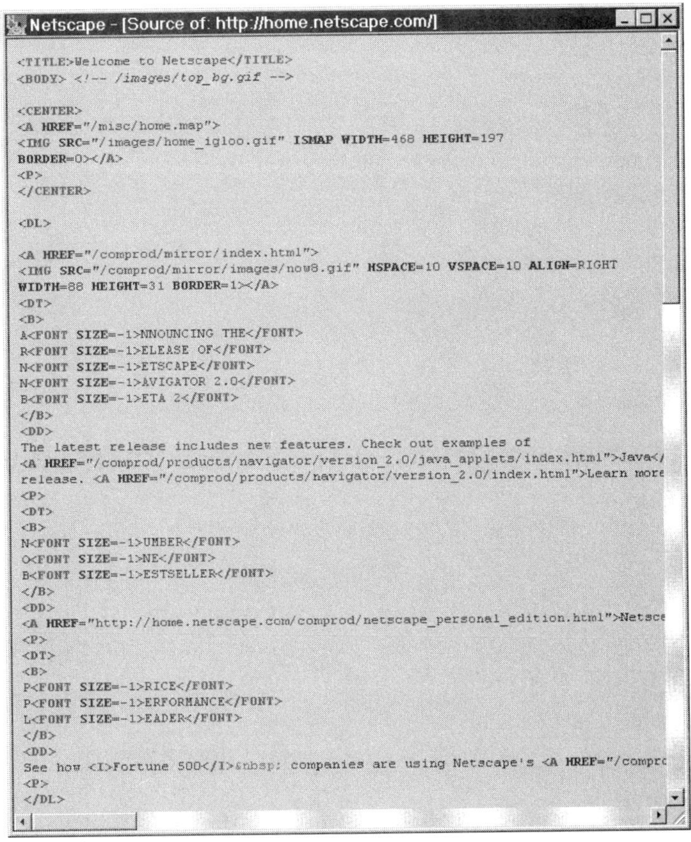

Figure 8.8 Web page displayed using Document Source

From this screen you can select and copy snippets of HTML code verbatim, and paste them into HTML documents with which you're experimenting. Try varying some of the attributes to see what effect the variations have on the result.

From Here

- Customize Netscape in Chapter 9.
- Master the helper applications and plug-ins in Chapters 10 through 15.

Chapter 9

Customizing and Configuring Netscape

Netscape is more fun when it works the way you want. You can choose the fonts you like, and you can also paint the screen with colors and even graphic backgrounds. On the Options menu and the Preferences dialog boxes, you'll find many more options that will make Netscape run your way. In addition, you'll find many essential configuration options.

New for 2 New with Netscape release 2 is a much-improved method of organizing the Preferences options. There are now four Preferences commands (General Preferences, Mail and News Preferences, Network Preferences, and Security Preferences).

For the Time-Challenged

- Netscape doesn't give you much control over fonts; in the Fonts page of the General Preferences dialog box, you can select the base font and font size for the proportionally spaced font (which applies to most of the text on the screen) and fixed fonts (plain text documents and computer code). For the proportionally spaced font, choose one that you find highly readable.
- You can mess around with colors all you like, but I'll bet you get sick of seeing pink text on a chartreuse background and want the defaults back. Save yourself the trouble.
- In the Options menu, leave all the options on except Show Directory Buttons (which you can access in the Directory menu anyway).
- In the Images page of General Preferences, choose After Loading if you want the text to appear more quickly in downloaded documents.

This chapter discusses all the configuration options available in the Options menu, but you'll find more detailed discussions of some of them elsewhere in this book:

- For an in-depth discussion of cache configuration options, see Chapter 5, "Improving Netscape's Performance."
- For specific information on installing the helper applications that come with this book, see Appendices B and E.

Using the Options Menu

You'll find Netscape's most frequently chosen options on the Options menu. Some of these options are duplicated within the sea of Preferences dialog box options, but it's easier and quicker to choose them from the Options menu.

I can't figure out how these options work! To use the customization options on the Options menu, you need to understand that they're *toggles*. On a Windows menu, a toggle is an option that you can turn on or off using the same command. When the option is turned on (activated), you see a check mark next to the item's name. When the option is turned off, the check mark disappears. To turn off the Toolbar, for example, open the Options menu and look at the Show Toolbar option—since the Toolbar is visible, this option has a check mark. To turn off the Toolbar, choose this option. Open the menu again—you'll see that the check mark has disappeared. Believe me, this is a *lot* simpler than it sounds and you'll get used to it quickly enough.

Options Accessible on the Options Menu

Here's a quick overview of the customization options you can choose on the Options menu:

- **Show Toolbar** (default: on) Choose this command to hide or display the Toolbar.
- **Show Location** (default: on) Choose this command to hide or display the Location box.
- **Show Directory Buttons** (default: on) Choose this command to hide or display those nice big Directory buttons.
- **Show Java Console** (default: off) Choose this command to display or hide the Java console, which displays the Java code that Netscape is currently executing (if any).
- **Auto Load Images** (default: on) Choose this command to hide the automatic downloading of in-line images (you'll see placeholders instead); choose it again to redisplay the images.
- **Document Encoding** (default: Latin1) Choose this command to select the character set that Netscape uses to display the text onscreen. This option is useful if you're trying to read Web pages written in foreign languages, such as Japanese.

Which options are right for you? I'd recommend that you work with the Toolbar and Location boxes displayed, but you can skip the Directory buttons—they're accessible from the Directory menu.

Saving Your Options Choices

When you quit Netscape, the program automatically saves the choices you've made on the Options menu, and the program uses these options the next time you start it. If you would like to save the options right away, choose Save Options from the Options menu.

Choosing Options in the Preferences Dialog Box

As just mentioned, the most frequently chosen options are available on the Options menu—but there are loads more on the several pages of the General Preferences dialog box. This dialog box has the following tabbed pages:

Appearance In this page, you can choose options for the Toolbar, startup, and link styles.

Fonts In this page, you can choose a character set encoding (for displaying foreign languages), and you can choose fonts for each of these character sets.

Colors In this page, you can choose distinctive colors for links, followed links, text, and backgrounds.

Images In this page, you can choose the method Netscape uses to display the colors in downloaded in-line images, and you can also select options for the timing of image display.

Apps In this page, you can identify the helper applications Netscape uses to deal with Telnet and 3270 sessions. These options are discussed in Appendix B, "Configuring Support and Helper Applications."

Helpers	In this page, you choose the helper applications Netscape uses to display multimedia files, such as MPEG movies and Real Audio sounds. These options are discussed in Appendix B, "Configuring Support and Helper Applications."
Language	In this page, you choose the languages that Netscape tells a server it can accept. Very few servers are set up to work with this message presently.

The following sections detail the choices you can make in the Appearance, Fonts, Colors, and Images pages. You'll find detailed discussion of the Apps and Helpers pages in Appendix B.

Controlling Netscape's Appearance

You can change Netscape's on-screen appearance by choosing Toolbar options, startup options, and link styles.

To choose appearance options, open the Options menu and choose General Preferences. In the Preferences dialog box, click the Appearance tab. You'll see the Appearance options, shown in Figure 9.1.

Choosing Toolbar Options

Netscape's Toolbar is preset to display *pictures* (the cute little drawing of the house, for example, on the Home button) and *text* (the button's name). If you prefer, you can display only the pictures, or only the text. To choose one of these options, click the appropriate option button in the Toolbars area.

To hide the Toolbar entirely, open the Options menu and deselect Show Toolbar so that this item's check mark disappears.

Choosing Startup Options

By default, Netscape starts with a browser page that shows Netscape's home page. You can change the page that Netscape displays when the program

Figure 9.1 Appearance page (General Preferences)

starts. If you prefer, the program will start with a mail or news window instead of the browser window.

To change the default start page, type the URL you want to use in the Home Page Location box.

Want a faster startup? Choose Blank Page in the Start With area. Netscape will start much faster, but you'll see a plain gray screen until you access a Web site somewhere.

To start the program with a mail or news window, choose Netscape Mail or Netscape News in the On Startup Launch area. The default option is Netscape Browser.

You can start more than one window automatically. If you want Netscape to start with three windows—one each for mail, news, and browsing—just click all three options.

Choosing Link Styles

By default, Netscape displays links with a distinctive color and underlining. If you'd like to get rid of the underlining, deselect the Underlined option in the Link Styles area.

In this area, you can also control how long Netscape keeps track of the links you've visited. The hyperlinks you've visited appear in a distinctive color on-screen. By default, the program keeps track of these links for 30 days. You have the following options for visited links:

- If you would like Netscape to keep track of visited links forever, click Never Expire.
- To change the number of days that Netscape keeps track of links, type the number of days next to Expire After.
- To cause all your links to expire immediately, click the Expire Now button.

Choosing Fonts

Netscape is designed to work with a number of standardized character set encodings. These encodings enable Netscape to display foreign languages. For each chararacter set, you can choose the following fonts:

- **Proportionally Spaced Base Font** This is the font used for almost all of the text you'll see on-screen. In a proportionally spaced font, each character is given a width proportional to its size ("m" gets more space than "l"). The default proportionally spaced font is Times Roman.
- **Fixed (Monospace) Base Font** This is the font used for plain-text documents (such as README files in FTP file archives) and text marked with the <CODE> tag in HTML. (The <CODE> tag is used to give examples of computer programming code.) In a monospace font, each character gets the same amount of space, producing the effect of a typewriter. The default monospace font is Courier.

Don't change the monospace base font to a font that uses proportional characters—if you do, some of the text you're viewing won't align correctly on-screen. But do consider changing

the proportionally spaced base font. Times Roman is a beautiful font, but it's designed to fit as many characters as possible in a given space (after all, it was designed for use by newspapers). For this reason, it's hard to read on-screen. Try choosing a less compact font such as Bookman or Book Antiqua.

To change the base fonts:

1. From the Options menu, choose General Preferences. You'll see the Preferences dialog box, with the Appearance page displayed.
2. Click the Fonts tab. You'll see the Fonts page, shown in Figure 9.2.
3. In the For the Encoding box, the current setting is Latin1, which is the correct choice for English or European languages. If you would like to choose fonts for another character set, choose the character set from the list box.

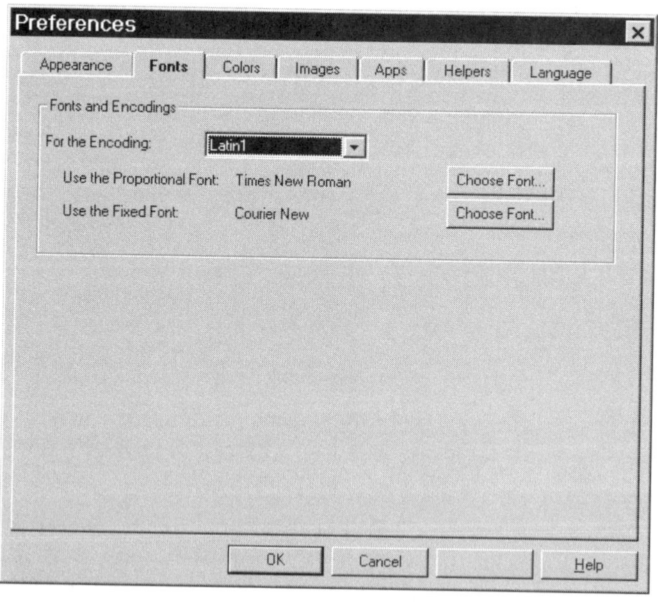

Figure 9.2 Fonts page (General Preferences)

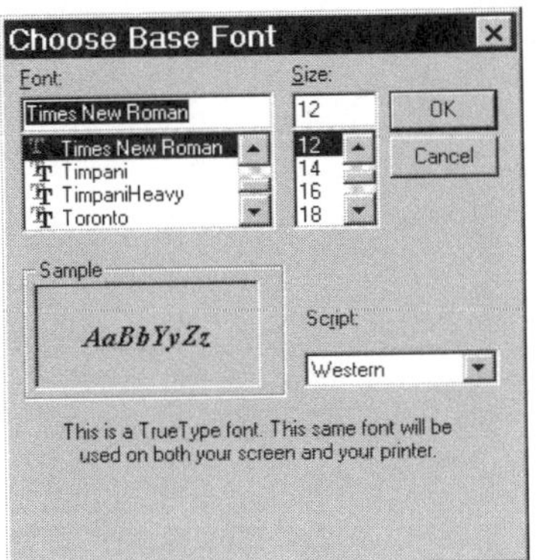

Figure 9.3 Choose Base Font dialog box

4. Next to the proportional font setting, click the Choose Font button. You'll see the Choose Base Font dialog box, shown in Figure 9.3
5. Beneath the Font box, scroll until you see the font you want, and then click it. The highlighted font appears in the Sample box.
6. In the Size box, use the scroll bar to choose the size you want, or type a font size (in points) in the box.
7. Click OK to choose your proportionally spaced font.
8. Click OK to close the Preferences dialog box.

Choosing Colors

Netscape provides several options for choosing colors:

Links Hyperlinks you haven't visited appear in this color. By default, they're blue.

Followed (Visited) Links Hyperlinks you've already visited. By default, they appear in lavender.

Text All other document text. By default, it's in black.

Background The default background is battleship gray. You can choose colors or, to make things even more visually confusing, a background graphic.

New for 2 New to this version of Netscape is the ability to override Web authors' background and color choices—choices that were made possible by Netscape's own innovations (the Netscape extensions to HTML). Unfortunately, some Web authors choose colors and backgrounds that make their pages nearly illegible. By default, Netscape shows you the color and background choices made by the author of the page you're viewing. If you're trying to read a page with overly wild colors, you can hide them by clicking the Always Use My Colors box.

To change the default colors:

1. From the Options menu, choose General Preferences.
2. Click the Colors tab in the Preferences dialog box. You'll see the Colors preferences, shown in Figure 9.4

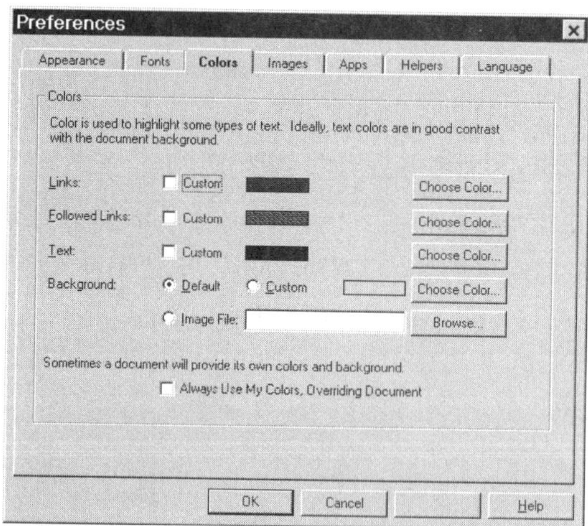

Figure 9.4 Colors page (General Preferences)

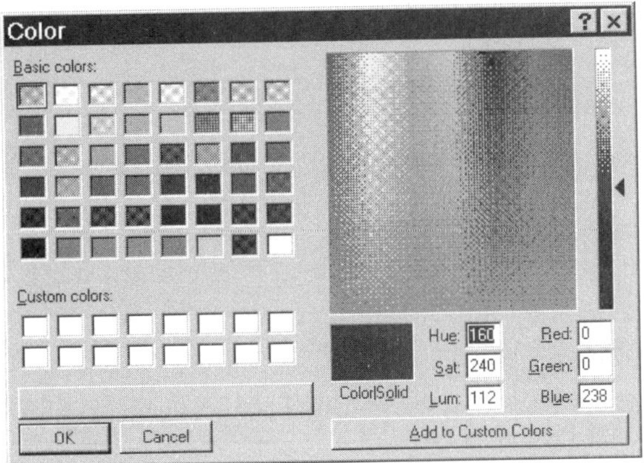

Figure 9.5 Choose Color dialog box

3. To choose a color for Links, click the top Choose Color button. You'll see the Choose Color dialog box (Figure 9.5).
4. Click the color you want, or click Define Custom Colors to see the color model (right side of Figure 9.5). Move the pointer until you've defined the color you want, and click Add to Custom Colors. Then click the color you just created.
5. Click OK to confirm your color choice.
6. Repeat steps 3 through 5 for Followed Links and Text, clicking the appropriate Choose Color box.
7. To set the background, click Custom and choose a color, or click Image File and use the Browse button to select a JPEG or GIF graphic.
8. Click Always Use My Colors if you really want Netscape to override incoming documents' color choices. I'd suggest leaving this option off.
9. Click OK to confirm your choices.

For a super collection of background patterns, check out http://home.netscape.com/home/bg/index.html. You can download any of the patterns by right-clicking the pattern you want and then choosing Save this Image As.

I'm sick of this! I want the defaults back! No problemo. Just open the Colors preferences again, deselect all the Custom check boxes, and click Default in the Background area. Click OK to confirm, and you're back to boring-old-gray background with boring-old-black text. Want your colors back again? Sheesh, make up your mind! Well, you can get them; the Preferences dialog box retains your color choices. Open the Colors preferences again, select the Custom boxes, and restore your background by clicking Image File.

Controlling Image Options

Netscape provides a variety of options for downloading images. You can use the Options menu to specify whether Netscape downloads images automatically. In the Preferences dialog box, you can choose how Netscape interprets image colors, and you can also select the timing of image display. To display the image options, open the Options menu, choose General Preferences, and click the Images tab. You'll see the Images page, shown in Figure 9.6.

Choosing Color Display Options

By default, Netscape automatically determines the most appropriate method of color display for your color monitor. If you would like to change the image display options, choose one of the following:

Dithered In a dithered image, Netscape simulates a color that your monitor can't actually display. It does this by grouping tiny dots of colors that are within your monitor's capabilities, so that this area appears to have the correct color. Dithered images are closer to the original's true colors, but they take much longer to download.

Substitute Colors Choose this option if you would like Netscape to use your monitor's closest color in place of the image's true color. If you choose this option, some colors may not look quite right but images will download faster.

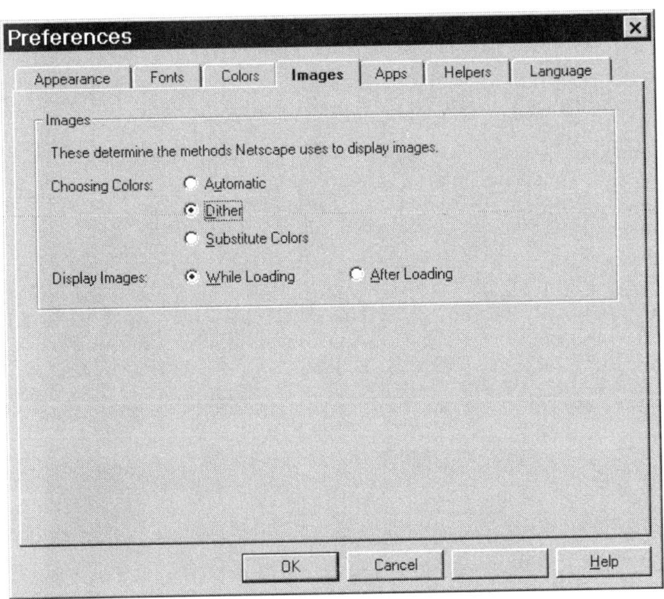

Figure 9.6 Images page (General Preferences)

From Here

- For an in-depth discussion of cache configuration options, see Chapter 5, "Improving Netscape's Performance."
- Choosing mail preferences? See Chapter 18.
- For information on choosing news (Usenet) preferences, see Chapter 22.
- For specific information on installing the helper applications that come with this book, see Appendices B and E.

Part III

Grooving on Multimedia

Chapter 10

Understanding Helper Apps and Plug-Ins

Netscape can't handle all the types of data out there on the Web—at least, not without help. Sure, Netscape can read HTML, and the program can handle GIF and JPEG graphics natively. (By *natively*, I mean on its own, without any outside help.) It can also decode Java instructions (see Chapter 13 for more information about Java). But there's much more out there—so much, in fact, that Netscape couldn't possibly include enough program code to handle everything the Web is capable of slinging at a browser. Linked to Web pages are sounds, movies, animations, live radio broadcasts, live TV broadcasts, spreadsheets, virtual reality worlds, and even a model railroad (I am not making this up—check out http://rr-vs.informatik.uni-ulm.de/rr/).

For the Time-Challenged

- Netscape needs help to deal with the huge variety of data types available on the Web. This help is needed to play sounds, videos, animations, and other multimedia resources, as well as to cope with spreadsheets, virtual reality worlds, and other neat things that are popping up on Web pages.
- To deal with these data types, Netscape has always been able to work with helper applications. Netscape Version 2 can work with plug-in programs.
- When Netscape is properly configured, a helper application starts after Netscape has downloaded some data that it can't deal with directly, such as a sound. The helper application runs in its own window.
- Plug-in programs work differently. They actually extend Netscape's capabilities so that the program can display multimedia data within Netscape's window.
- Streaming audio and video technologies enable you to start listening or watching without waiting for the whole file to download. There's some sacrifice of quality, though.

Here's something fun: A collection of links to pages that connect bizarre devices to the Web, including clocks, coffee machines, pets (!), robots, spy cameras, and more. Check out

http://www.yahoo.com/Computers_and_Internet/Internet/Interesting_Devices_Connected_to_the_Net/

In order to deal with all the data that's accessible on the Web, Netscape needs two kinds of help:

- **Helper Applications** These are programs that Netscape starts when it encounters a type of data that it can't handle directly. All versions of Netscape can work with helper applications. You'll find lots of them on the disc included with this book. Appendix B shows you how to install these helper applications.

- **Plug-Ins** These are programs that modify Netscape so that it can deal directly with data of a certain type. For example, after you install the Live3D plug-in, Netscape can directly display virtual worlds—and you can navigate inside of them in three dimensions!

This chapter introduces helper applications and plug-ins. The rest of the chapters in Part III show you how to use these programs after they're installed.

Please remember that you must install helper apps and plug-ins before you can do most of the things described in this chapter and the remaining chapters of Part III. For more information on installing the helper apps and plug-ins included with this book, see Appendices B and E.

Help Me, Helper Apps

In brief, a helper application is a program that's designed to start automatically when data of a certain type is encountered.

For example, suppose you click on the name of a file that was compressed by PKZip, a popular compression utility. Your browser looks for PKZip—and if the program is present on your disk, the browser starts PKZip and the file downloads and decompresses automatically.

When you've configured your browser to work with helper applications and they work correctly, it's cool. Here's an example. Suppose you click on a hyperlink for an MPEG video. If everything's working smoothly on your system, your browser starts an MPEG helper application, downloads the video, and you see it on-screen (Figure 10.1).

What Types of Helper Apps Are Available?

To deal with all the types of data you'll encounter on the Web, you'll need to equip your system with the following helper apps:

- **Sound Players** Sounds are stored in a variety of file formats. When you click a hyperlink that accesses a sound, Netscape determines the

Figure 10.1 MPEG video played by helper application (NET TOOB)

format in which the sound file is stored and starts the appropriate sound player. You'll need to install several sound players if you wish to hear all the sounds available on the Web. The Windows version of Netscape comes with a sound player already installed, configured, and ready to go—but it can only play some of the sounds you'll encounter on the Web. **Please note**: In order to play sounds on your Windows system, you'll need a sound card and speakers.

- **Video Players** Videos, animations, and movies are stored in several formats. You'll need several players if you wish to see the movies available on the Web.
- **File Decompression Software** Many of the files you can obtain with Netscape have been compressed. This cuts down on disk space usage as well as bandwidth usage when the files are transferred. After you configure Netscape to use WinZip, the file decompression software included with this book, Netscape will start WinZip automatically after you download a compressed file.
- **File Viewers** Netscape displays HTML documents beautifully, but many authors find that HTML does not meet their formatting needs. For this reason, they sometimes save their documents in formats that

require special reading software. In increasing use among Web authors is Adobe Acrobat.

- **VRML Viewers** VRML is short for Virtual Reality Modeling Language. If you've got a VRML viewer, you can access and explore three-dimensional worlds on the Web. (If you've ever played the popular game Doom, you've explored a three-dimensional world.)
- **Telnet Viewer** To access Telnet sessions, you need special software that can communicate with large mainframe computers. Included with this book is the National Center for Supercomputing Application's (NCSA) Telnet for Windows.

Where do I get all this stuff? You've already got it. The CD-ROM disc packaged with this book contains all the helper software you need.

How Does a Helper Application Work?

Here's an illustration. Suppose you click a link to a sound. When Netscape accesses the sound, the program realizes that it doesn't have the capability of dealing with this data. But it downloads the data anyway. Then it looks for, and launches, the appropriate helper application. The helper application appears in a new, separate window and plays the sound.

Hey–How Did Netscape Know Which Program to Launch?

Netscape may be a great program, but it's not all-knowing. Like other browsers, Netscape relies on *MIME extensions* to determine which kind of data the program is accessing.

What's a MIME extension? MIME is short for Multipurpose Internet Mail Extension. Originally, MIME was a standard for enabling Internet e-mail users to exchange graphics, sound, and video files. Since its creation more than a dozen years ago, MIME has been adapted for use with the Web. The valuable thing about MIME is that it provides a standardized way of associating *file extensions* with certain types of data.

If you've used MS-DOS, you're familiar with file extensions, those three-letter additions to file names that come after the period. When Netscape encounters a sound, the program looks at the extension (such as "beep.au").

It then consults a table and finds out which program—if any—is associated with the "au" MIME type.

What the heck does "*.mpg" mean? You're looking at a DOS or UNIX wild card. It means, basically, "any file with the extension .mpg." The computer nerd types on the Web love to write MIME types this way; don't let it put you off.

To get your helper applications to work, you must associate each of the MIME types with the specific helper app you've installed. Appendix B tells you how to do this. Your helper apps won't work until you've configured them by following these instructions!

What's on the CD-ROM Disc for Windows 3.x Users?

The CD-ROM disc packaged with this book contains a very impressive suite of helper applications, ready for installation on your system (see Appendix E).

Here's a list of the programs for Windows 3.x systems (they'll also run on Windows 95 systems):

- **Adobe Acrobat Reader for Windows 3.x (Version 2.1)** Using this program, you can display and print documents with rich formatting and graphics. It's copyrighted but freely distributable.
- **Autodesk Animation Player for Windows 1.00** This program enables you to play movies recorded in the Autodesk (*.fli) format. There aren't too many of these, but if you run into one, you've got the player you need. The program is freeware (copyrighted but freely distributed without charge).
- **MidiGate 5.C.2** This program enables Netscape to play MIDI files. In brief, MIDI files are text files containing coded instructions to a MIDI playback device. Most sound cards are able to play MIDI instructions, although the sound isn't very impressive unless you have a pricey wave-table synthesis sound card. (A wave-table synthesis sound card contains recordings of actual musical instruments, which are used to synthesize the musical sounds from MIDI files.) A share-

ware program, MidiGate costs only $10. The program may be used free of charge for an evaluation period of 30 days; subsequently, you'll need to send the registration fee to PRS Corporation, 502 Kinwick Centre, 32 Hollywood Road, Hong Kong. *Tip:* Check out the Classical MIDI Archive, which I'll discuss in the next chapter. *Note:* Because MidiGate is a Visual Basic application, you'll need the file VBRUN300.dll to be installed on your computer system.

- **NCSA Telnet for Windows** This program enables you to access the resources available at Telnet sites, which are widely accessible through the Web and through Gopher.

- **NET TOOB** Unlike MPEG Play and most other movie players, this player is capable of dealing with almost all the video formats you encounter on the Web: MPEG, QuickTime, and AVI (Windows). It's a shareware program that will run only for two weeks after you first install it. The registration fee is $14.95. For more information on NET TOOB, see http://www.duplex.com/. To pay the registration fee, call (508) 741-5500 between 9 and 5 Eastern Standard Time. Alternatively, you can send the registration fee by check or credit by writing to Duplexx Software, 35 Congress St., Salem, MA 01970.

- **QuickTime for Windows 2.03** This program, included courtesy of Apple Computer, plays videos and animations created in Apple's QuickTime format. It's freeware (copyrighted but distributed without charge).

- **RealAudio 1.0** This helper application plays RealAudio sounds. Although the quality is similar to a rather tinny AM radio, RealAudio sounds start playing very soon after you access them. For voice recordings, the convenience makes up for the poor sound. The RealAudio 1.0 player is designed for users of 14.4 Kbps dialup lines.

- **WHAM (Waveform Hold and Modify) Version 1.33** This versatile sound player can handle Soundblaster (*.voc), Silicon Graphics/Apple (*.aiff), and Sun/NeXT (*.au) sounds and provides many features for modifying the sounds you download. It's shareware. If you find WHAM useful, please send a check of $25–30 to Andrew Bulhak, 21 The Crescent, Ferntree Gully, VIC 3156, Australia.

- **WinZip 6.0a** This Windows program enables you to decompress files that were compressed using a variety of formats, including PKZIP and GNUzip. You can use WinZip for a 30-day evaluation period free of charge; subsequently, you need to register the program ($29). Please send a check to Nico Mak Computing, Inc., P.O. Box 919, Bristol, CT 06011. You can also register the program by calling PsL, a credit-card ordering service (800-242-4775).

- **XingSound Freely Redistributable Audio Player** This sound player enables you to listen to sounds recorded in the MPEG audio format. The version of XingSound included with this book (and widely available on the Web) is a monoaural program that employs the Windows audio driver, producing acceptable (but not spectacular) results. For high-quality stereo playback, you can purchase the retail version of XingSound from Xing Technology Corporation, 1540 West Branch Street, Arroyo Grande, CA 93420 (info@xingtech.com).

What's on the CD-ROM Disc for Windows 95 Users?

If you're using Windows 95, you can run most of the Windows 3.x applications just discussed. In addition, the following Windows 95 native application is included on the CD-ROM disc packaged with this book:

- **WinZip for Windows 95** This Windows 95 program enables you to decompress files that were compressed using a variety of formats, including PKZIP and GNUzip. You can use WinZip for Windows 95 for a 30-day evaluation period free of charge; subsequently, you need to register the program ($29). Please send a check to Nico Mak Computing, Inc., P.O. Box 919, Bristol, CT 06011. You can also register the program by calling PsL, a credit-card ordering service (800-242-4775).

If this list looks a little thin—after all, there's only one item on it—remember that you can run most of the Windows 3.x programs just mentioned. What's more, you'll find lots of very cool Windows 95 plug-ins, as described later in this chapter.

Helper Programs You Already Have

You don't need a helper application to display GIF and JPEG graphics, which Netscape can handle on its own. In addition, you will find the following helper applications on your system already:

- **Windows Media Player** This program, included with Microsoft Windows, enables you to play Windows-compatible sounds (*.wav files) as well as Video for Windows movies and animations (*.avi files). After you install QuickTime for windows, you can also use Media Player to view QuickTime videos.
- **Netscape Audio Player** This program can play a variety of the sound files you'll encounter on the Internet, including Sun/NeXT sounds (*.snd files) and Apple IFF (*.aiff) sounds. It's included with Netscape Navigator; you'll find it in Netscape's directory. Netscape is already configured to start Netscape Audio Player when it encounters these files.

When Helper Applications Don't Help

Lots of people have trouble with helper applications. Here are two things that can go wrong:

- **Installation** Before you can run the helper program, you must obtain it and install it on your hard drive. This is often a major pain because these programs aren't included with most browsers. You have to find them and download them yourself.
- **Configuration** You have to configure your browser to work with helper applications. This is done by associating an *extension* (a three-letter addition to a file name) with a specific program. For example, you can associate .zip files with WinZip, the Windows version of the popular PKZIP compression utility.

Installing and configuring helper applications takes time and a modicum of computer smarts. I'll bet that at least half of the people browsing the Web haven't configured their browsers to work with the most common data types, such as videos, animations, and sounds. And as a result, their Web isn't very lively.

Even if you can get helper applications running correctly, there are two additional reasons why they're not very satisfactory. First, helper applications run in their own window. Although this isn't a serious problem, it takes your attention away from the Web page you were viewing, which remains static. Wouldn't it be cool to see the action and hear the sounds without having to leave the page you're viewing? That's why Netscape Version 2.0 features plug-ins, which are described in the next section.

Installing Helper Apps

For information on installing helper applications, see Appendix B.

Plug In to This!

New for 2

New with Version 2.0 of Netscape Navigator is a new program architecture, which enables *plug-ins*. A plug-in is a program that, after installation, extends Netscape's capabilities. What's really cool about plug-ins is that, unlike helper apps, there's no separate program to fuss with—the plug-in becomes part of Netscape, seamlessly extending its capabilities. With most plug-ins, you view the data right on the Web page you're accessing!

Compared to a helper application, a plug-in program is a pleasure to use. To be sure, you still have to obtain and install the plug-in, but after that it's a piece of cake. There's no configuration, and the plug-in operates automatically. Best of all, the action takes place right on the Web page you're viewing, not in a secondary window such as the ones that helper applications use. In Figure 10.2, you see the very impressive results you'll get after installing a virtual reality plug-in. Such a program enables Netscape to display three-dimensional spaces, which you can explore using the special controls that the program adds to Netscape. Included on this book's CD-ROM disc is VR Scout, Chaco Communication's highly rated virtual reality plug-in for the Windows 95 version of Netscape. (For more information on virtual reality, see Chapter 15.)

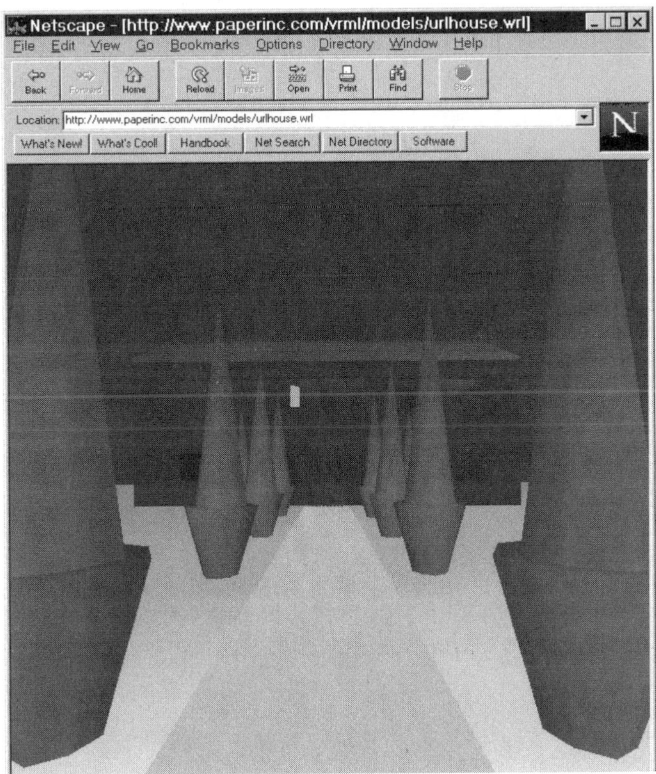

Figure 10.2 Data display within Netscape's window via plug-ins

Plug-Ins

Here's what you'll find on the CD-ROM disc:

- **Shockwave Plug-In for Windows 3.x** This amazing plug-in enables you to display Macromedia Director animations in-line—right on the Web page you're viewing.

- **Formula One/NET Plug-In for Windows 3.x** Here's something really amazing. After you install this plug-in, you'll be able to access Web pages that contain Excel-compatible spreadsheets—and you'll be able to interact with them right on-screen!
- **Shockwave Plug-In for Windows 95** This is the Windows 95 version of the Shockwave plug-in.
- **Formula One/NET Plug-In for Windows 95** This is the Windows 95 version of the Formula One/NET spreadsheet plug-in described above.
- **VR Scout** This is an incredible virtual reality plug-in program that lets you explore VRML worlds.

Also included on the CD-ROM is Chaco Communication's amazing Pueblo client, which enables you to join three-dimensional MUD games. Pueblo requires Windows 95.

Installing Plug-Ins

For information on installing the plug-ins included with this book, see Appendix E, or just access the file WELCOME.HTM, which you'll find on the CD-ROM disc.

Getting into the Stream of Things

The latest wrinkle in Web multimedia is *streaming* data. With streaming audio and video, the sound or movie arrives as a data stream, which the plug-in starts playing immediately. For example, when you click a RealAudio sound, the player kicks in and starts playing the sound almost immediately. The wonderful thing about streaming data is simply this: You don't have to wait for the whole darned file to download before things start happening. (That's probably the biggest drawback of helper applications.)

What's sacrificed with streaming audio and video? Quality, mainly. With RealAudio Version 2, the sound can approach the quality of an FM radio station, as long as the Internet isn't too busy. In other words, if you're accessing a RealAudio sound at about 3 AM, you'll probably get good results. At peak usage times, the signal may fade in and out, as if you were trying to listen to a car radio at the fringes of the reception area.

Despite the reduction in quality, you'll probably like streaming audio and video—it's neat to have the multimedia start right away. I'll admit that I like streaming audio (especially for voice) more than streaming video, which—at best—gives you herky-jerky motion in a postage-stamp-sized window. You'll need a very fast Internet connection to make streaming video look good.

From Here

- Have you installed and configured your helper apps yet? If not, please go directly to Appendix B. Do not collect $200, and most of all, don't go to the next chapter—the stuff that's described there won't work until you've installed the helper apps.
- You did install the helper apps? OK. Check out Chapter 11 for the lowdown on sounds, movies, and animations.
- In Chapter 12, you'll find a thorough discussion of Adobe Acrobat, including the use of the new Amber reader.
- Macromedia's way-cool Shockwave receives a similar, full-chapter treatment in Chapter 14.
- Explore three-dimensional virtual worlds! Check out Chapter 15.

Chapter 11

Playing Sounds and Watching Movies

It's hypermedia time! Assuming you've installed and configured the helper applications and plug-ins you want to use (please see Appendix B), you can click links to sounds, movies, and animations—and things start to happen. In this chapter, you'll learn how to work with the many types of sounds, videos, and animations you'll encounter on the Web.

This chapter assumes that you've installed the helper applications included on this book's CD-ROM disc and configured Netscape to start them automatically. For information on installing these programs, see Appendix B.

For the Time-Challenged

- After Netscape downloads a sound, you'll see the sound player. Look for a VCR-type Play button to initiate the sound, unless it starts playing automatically. You can use the VCR-type controls to pause, stop, "rewind," or "fast-forward" the sound. When you're finished listening to the sound, exit the sound player.
- After Netscape downloads a movie, you'll see the movie player. Look for a VCR-type Play button to start viewing the movie. When you're finished watching the movie, exit the movie player.

Listening to Sounds

To listen to sounds on your Microsoft Windows system, you must equip your computer with a sound card and speakers. The applications discussed in this section won't play through your computer's tinny little standard speaker.

After you configure Netscape to work with helper apps and plug-ins as described in Appendix B, the program automatically detects the type of sound file you are downloading and starts the appropriate player.

Understanding Sound File Formats

Here's a list of the sound file formats that you're most likely to encounter on the Web; each is followed by the MIME type that's associated with the sound, the name of the program that Netscape launches when you access a file of this type, and brief description of what to expect in terms of sound quality. Note that Netscape launches these programs only if you've configured Netscape according to the instructions in Appendix B.

- **Silicon Graphics/Apple sound (audio/x-aiff)** These sound files have the extension *.aif, *.aiff, or *aifc. When you access one of these sounds, Netscape starts the Netscape Audio Player. You don't often encounter these sounds.

- **Sun/NeXT sound (audio/basic)** This is a Sun/NeXT (*.au or *.snd) sound. When you access one of these sounds, Netscape starts the Netscape Audio Player. *.au sounds are fairly compact, and generally of low quality; they're often used, though, to provide a small-size "sampler" of a much bigger MPEG sound file.
- **WAV sound (audio/x-wav)** This is a standard Microsoft Windows sound, which you can play using the Windows Media Player. The sound quality depends on how the recording was done—there are a number of options, ranging from low-quality monoaural to high-quality stereo—but it's probably going to be very good.
- **MPEG sound (audio/x-mpeg)** This may prove to be of very high quality—at best, near-CD quality in stereo. When you click an MPEG sound, Netscape starts Xingplay (Windows 3.x systems) or the Media Player (Windows 95 systems).
- **MIDI sound (audio/midi)** MIDI sound files are compact—they consists only of ASCII text. When you click a MIDI sound, Netscape starts the remarkable MidiGate. What you hear depends on the quality of your sound card. If you've got a wave-table synthesis card, the sound might actually be pleasing to the ear. If your sound card uses FM synthesis, it will sound like some kid playing a $29 electronic organ.
- **RealAudio sound (audio/x-pn-realaudio)** When you access a RealAudio sound, Netscape starts the RealAudio player. RealAudio sounds begin playing almost immediately after you access them, but don't expect good sound quality—it's OK for voice but barely acceptable for music.

The following sections discuss the techniques you use to play each of these sounds.

When Netscape downloads a sound or any other multimedia resource, the program places a copy of the file in the current temporary directory. To find out where this directory is located, open the Options menu, choose General Preferences, and click the Apps tab. Look in the Temporary Directory box to see the current temporary directory setting. I recommend that you create a directory called Temp to store downloaded files; this ensures that the downloaded files

don't clutter up Netscape's directory. After you create this directory, type C:\temp in the Temporary Directory box and click OK.

Using the Netscape Audio Player

When you access a Sun/NeXT (*.au) or Silicon Graphics/Apple (*.aiff) sound, Netscape downloads the sound to the current temporary directory and launches the Netscape Audio Player (Figure 11.1).

To play the sound, you don't do anything: The player starts, plays the sound, finishes, and decamps from the scene.

I want to hear that sound again, but Netscape Audio Player quit! Yes, the player quits when you stop playing the sound. To play it again, use the File Manager (Windows 3.x) or Windows Explorer (Windows 95) to locate the Netscape Audio Player file (naplayer.exe), which you'll find in Netscape's directory. Double-click the file to start the audio player. Switch to Netscape, and open the Preferences dialog box (from the Options menu, choose General Preferences). Click the Apps tab, and look at the current setting for the Temporary Directory. This is where Netscape downloads the files. In Netscape Audio Player, choose Open from the File menu, and use the Open dialog box to open the sound you want to play.

If you're quick on the draw while the player is playing a sound, you can use the VCR-like controls to stop, rewind, and replay the sound—but you'll have to click the Stop button before the sound stops playing.

Figure 11.1 Netscape Audio Player

Here's a quick guide to the controls you'll find on Netscape Audio Player's control panel:

Go to the beginning

Seek back (rewind)

Play

Stop

Seek forward (fast forward)

End

Netscape Audio Player is a pretty simple affair—it's OK for playing sounds, but not much good for replaying them or saving them with different file names. If you'd like to play around with *.au and *.aiff sounds more than the Player allows, I suggest that you configure Netscape to run WHAM (Waveform Hold and Modify), a sound helper app that's included on this book's CD-ROM disc. WHAM enables you to replay, save, and modify the sound in all kinds of interesting ways.

Using the Microsoft Windows Media Player

When you access a *.wav sound, Netscape downloads the sound to the current temporary directory and launches the Media Player (Figure 11.2). The Media Player is a versatile application that is capable of playing movies, audio CDs, and a variety of sounds. If you're using Windows 95, this is the player you'll use to play MPEG (*.mpg) sounds.

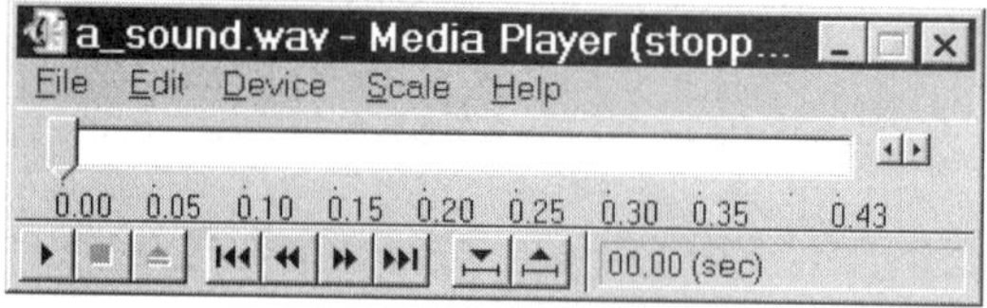

Figure 11.2 Microsoft Windows Media Player

To start playing the sound, click the Play button. Here's a quick guide to the controls you'll see on the Media Player's control panel:

Play

Stop

Eject (this works only if you're playing a CD)

Rewinds the sound to the beginning of the file, or to the previous mark (if any have been set)

Steps backward through the sound in 10 percent increments

Steps forward through the sound in 10 percent increments

Fast forwards to the end of the file, or to the next mark (if any have been set)

Marks the beginning of a selection using the current location of the slider

Marks the end of a selection using the current location of the slider

In addition, you can drag the slider to the place where you want the sound to start playing.

Using the XingSound Player

When you access an MPEG (*.mp2) sound with the 16-bit (Windows 3.x) version of Netscape, Netscape downloads the sound to the temporary directory and launches the XingSound Player (Figure 11.3).

Here's a quick guide to the controls you'll see on XingSound's simple control panel:

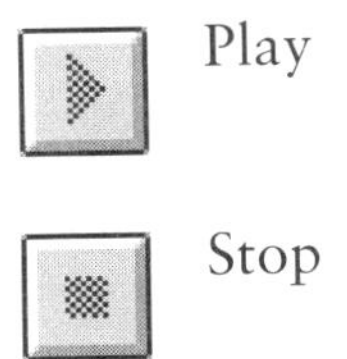

Play

Stop

In addition, you can drag the slider to the place where you want the sound to start playing.

Like to find some cool sounds on the Web? Check out the "Sites With Audio Clips" metapage at

http://www.eecs.nwu.edu/~jmyers/other-sounds.html

The creation of Jennifer Myers, it's an awesome collection of aural resources that's sure to keep you busy for hours.

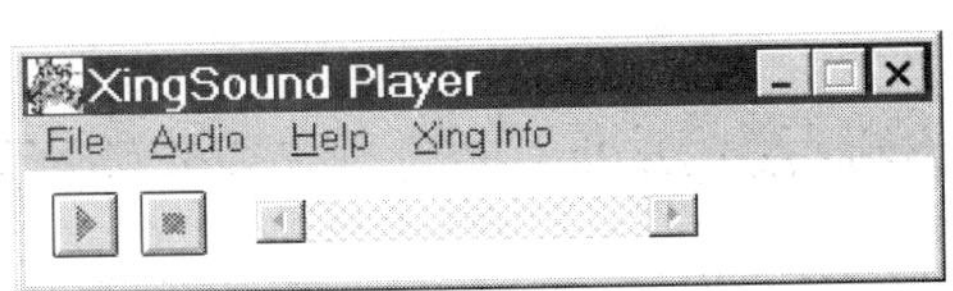

Figure 11.3 XingSound Player

Using MidiGate

Perhaps the coolest helper app that's included on this book's CD-ROM disc is MidiGate, which plays MIDI files. A MIDI file, in case you don't know, is an ASCII text file that contains a representation of musical tones and effects.

When compared to other sound file formats, MIDI has a huge advantage in that it's very compact—a 10-minute harpsichord sonata, for example, requires only about 10K of disk storage space and downloads very quickly.

The down side of MIDI is that your computer's sound card will probably play the MIDI file with quality reminiscent of a cheap electronic organ.

When you access a MIDI sound file, Netscape downloads the file to the temporary directory and launches MidiGate (Figure 11.4). The sound starts playing immediately.

There's quite a lot to MidiGate, especially if you're a MIDI hobbyist. Our concern here is just to play the sounds you'll encounter on the Web, so we'll keep it simple.

Here's a quick guide to the controls you'll find on the MidiGate control panel:

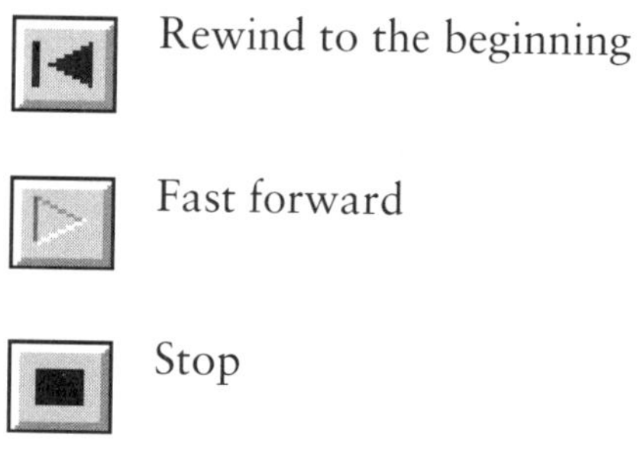

Figure 11.4 MidiGate

Exit

Exit

Position of current selection in queue, if more than one sound has been loaded

Displays Queue dialog box, which enables you to open more than one sound for continous playing

Select File

Open a MIDI sound file on disk

Save As...

Saves the current sound with a different file name

There's no slider control on MidiGate's control panel, but you can still click the sound progress bar to indicate where you'd like the sound to start playing.

You'll find some stunning repositories of classical MIDI sound files on the Web. Check out the Classical MIDI Connection

http://206.96.214.4/~raborn/index.html

and the astonishing Classical MIDI Archives

http://www.prs.net/midi.html

which contains more than 1,500 MIDI files. Cool!

Using the RealAudio Player

You'll find two kinds of RealAudio sound files on the Web:

- **RealAudio Version 1** You can download and listen to these files using a 14.4 Kbps modem.
- **RealAudio Version 2** To listen to these files, you'll need a Pentium computer and a 28.8 Kbps modem. These files are often flagged with a RealAudio 28.8 icon. To play them, you'll need to install the RealAudio plug-in.

When you access a RealAudio sound file (*.ra), Netscape starts the RealAudio sound player, shown in Figure 11.5, and you hear the sound almost

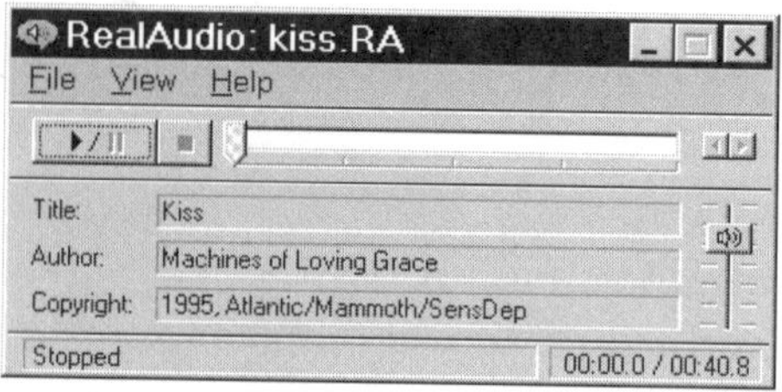

Figure 11.5 RealAudio player

immediately. The RealAudio dialog box shows the title of the sound being played, the author, and the copyright holder, if any. You'll also find the following controls:

 Play/Pause

 Stop and return to beginning of sound

 Rewind

Fast Forward

Adjust the volume using the slider control.

It sounds really garbled! If you've heard some good sound, but all of a sudden the quality goes way down, chances are the data stream has run into a roadblock on the Internet. (It happens.) Just be patient—the quality will probably come back up in a few moments. If not, you'll see a dialog box informing you that the quality is unacceptable. Try accessing the site later, when the Internet's not so busy.

One of the most valuable resources to be found anywhere on the Internet is accessible from the RealAudio home page (http://www.prognet.com/index.html): full-length audio files of National Public Radio (NPR) news programs, including All Things Considered and Morning Edition. If you heard a story on an NPR broadcast and you'd like to hear it again, you can do so by accessing RealAudio's home page and clicking the NPR button. At this writing, RealAudio required that you register and obtain a password—there's no fee or obligation for this, however. You'll also find links to RealAudio versions of ABC news broadcasts.

Viewing Movies

You'll find thousands of movies on the Web, but don't expect too much in terms of quality. Every movie, digital or otherwise, is simply a succession of still images (called *frames*); in a high-quality movie, the frames go by quickly enough that the brain is tricked into seeing smooth motion. To keep file sizes down, the creators of most of the digital movies you'll find on the Web kept the number of frames per second to a minimum, which results in a very jerky presentation that won't trick your eye, your brain, or anything else.

It's taking a half hour to download this movie! Unfortunately, movie files tend to be big and bigger—the one I'm downloading right now is about 2.5 MB. On a 14.4 Kbps modem line, a file that large will take many minutes to download. If it's taking too long, remember that you can switch back to Netscape and browse elsewhere while the file's downloading—or you can cancel the download, skip the whole thing, and go down to your video store and rent a real movie.

The best movie formats offer sound as well as video. As with the digital sound just discussed, you'll need to equip your Windows system with a sound card and speakers if you wish to hear these sounds.

Understanding Movie File Formats

Like sounds, the digital movies you'll find on the Web are stored in a variety of file formats, so you'll need more than one movie viewer. Here's a quick

overview of the movie file formats you're most likely to find on the Web. Also indicated here is the MIME type, the file extension that's used with the type, and the application that Netscape will launch when you've access one of these movies (assuming you've installed the software according to the instructions in Appendix B).

- **MPEG (video/mpeg)** MPEG is short for the Motion Picture Experts Group, an industry consortium that meets periodically to define digital video standards. At present the MPEG-1 standard defines a relatively low-quality video standard. MPEG movies, stored in *.mpg files, aren't much to write home about, you'll find, and they require huge files. When you access an MPEG file, Netscape will start NET TOOB. If you're using Windows 95, you can also play MPEG movies with the Windows Media Player.
- **QuickTime (video/quicktime)** Originally created by Apple Computer, the QuickTime format is now an international standard, and it's better than MPEG. In addition to offering good compression and performance, QuickTime offers near-CD-quality digital stereo sound. Stored in *.mov and *.qt files, QuickTime movies are played by NET TOOB, which is modified by QuickTime for Windows so that it can play *.mov files. If you don't want to register NET TOOB, you can watch QuickTime movies with Apple's free QuickTime viewer, PLAYER.EXE (located in the Windows directory).
- **Video for Windows (video/x-msvideo)** The Windows movie format (*.avi) offers another high-quality movie standard with digital stereo sound. Not as efficiently compressed as QuickTime movies, the files are very large but the quality is good. You can play *.avi movies with the Windows Media Player, but NET TOOB can also play them.

In addition to these movie formats, you can also display streaming video with the VDOLive plug-in.

I just downloaded an 8 megabyte movie, and it plays for only three minutes! And the picture's the size of a postage stamp! Don't say I didn't warn you. Is network video here yet? Use your own judgment, but I'd say no. Right now, it's an amusing diversion at best. Movies aren't going to become a significant attraction on the Web until better compression techniques are developed and people have much faster Net connections.

Using NET TOOB

The shareware program NET TOOB, included on this book's CD-ROM disc, is a versatile movie player that can handle MPEGs, QuickTime movies, and Video for Windows movies. (In order to view QuickTime movies with NET TOOB, you must first install QuickTime for Windows) I recommend that you use NET TOOB for viewing all three types of movies.

When you've configured NET TOOB to play the movies you download, the program will start automatically after downloading is complete. You'll see the NET TOOB video player (Figure 11.6). Here's a quick rundown of the controls you'll find in this window:

 Rewind

 Play/pause

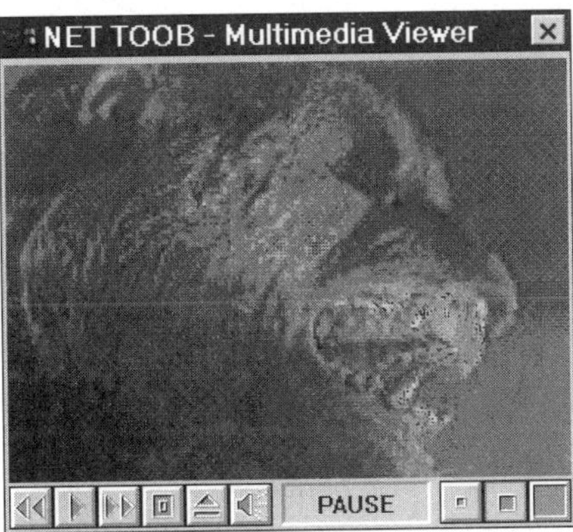

Figure 11.6 NET TOOB display window

 Fast forward

 Stop

 Close video player

 Turn sound on/off

 Small video size

 Medium video size

 Full-screen video

NET TOOB plays the video with continuous looping. Try experimenting with the different sizes; at the smallest size, your computer can display the video with sufficient numbers of frames per second to trick your eye into seeing continuous motion. This effect collapses with larger sizes. When you're finished playing the video, click the Close Video Player button.

Can I see that video again? Sure. Netscape wrote the downloaded file to the temporary directory. From Program Manager (Windows 3.x) or the Start menu (Windows 95), choose NET TOOB. You'll see the NET TOOB control panel, shown in Figure 11.7. To open a video file, click Select Video File and open the temporary directory. Use List Files of Type to select the type of video file you're opening—Video for Windows (choose AVI video), QuickTime (choose QTW video), or MPEG (choose All Files).

Using VDOLive

Thanks to Netscape's new plug-in capabilities and some key technical advances, streaming video is now possible. With streaming video, you get two impressive capabilities:

- **In-Line Video** A live-action video can appear within a Web page, just as in-line graphics now appear. When you click an in-line video, the video starts playing almost immediately—with stereo sound.
- **Dynamic Adjustment** Some users are accessing the Internet by means of slow, 14.4 Kbps means, while others have faster modems, and still others have very fast network-based connections. A one-size-fits-all approach would saddle modem users with jerky, unconvincing videos, or unnecessarily punish users of fast connections by depriving them of the quality that their systems can support. With dynamic adjustment, the plug-in detects the speed of the connection and adjusts the quality automatically (lower for slow connections, higher for better connections).

Streaming video has come to the Web today, thanks to VDOLive, a plug-in for Netscape Version 2. Created by VDOnet, a small Israeli company, the plug-in enables Web authors to embed streaming video within their Web pages. At 14.4 Kbps, the quality isn't anything to write home about—the audio's fuzzy, the picture's the size of a postage stamp, and the action's herky-jerky—but quality improves markedly at 28.8 Kbps.

After you've installed the VDOLive plug-in, you don't need to do anything special to view a VDOLive movie—just access a site that's offering a VDOLive movie. At some sites, you'll see in-line video; at others, you'll see the video in a separate Web page. But all the action's within Netscape.

You can get a good idea of streaming video's potential by taking a look at KPIX's VDO Video Library. The San Francisco-based TV station offers videos on earthquake preparedness, hidden hikes in the Bay Area, Hawaii's innovative health plan, and much more. If you're viewing the videos with a 28.8 Kbps modem, it's a lot of fun. Check it out at http://www.kpix.com/video/.

From Here

- Learn how to view Adobe Acrobat documents in Chapter 12.
- Try out some Java sites in Chapter 13.
- Take a look at Shockwave animations in Chapter 14.
- Explore three-dimensional virtual worlds in Chapter 15.

Chapter 12

Viewing Adobe Acrobat Documents

When you view HTML documents with Netscape, you'll see Netscape's interpretation of the underlying HTML tags. The formatting is simple and effective. Unfortunately, HTML does not include tags needed for more complex document formats, such as multiple-column text or footnotes.

To provide richer document formatting, some document authors prefer to encode their documents using a proprietary document format. One such format is the PostScript page description language, familiar to users of laser printers. PostScript can also generate richly formatted screen displays, but this requires a reader capable of decoding the PostScript commands. Such readers exist—GhostScript is an example—but Adobe, the originators of PostScript, have developed a set of extensions to PostScript, called Adobe Acrobat, that produce superior results on-screen. You will encounter growing numbers of Acrobat documents on the Web (for an example, see Figure 12.1), and you

Acrobat Reader - [TIMES.PDF]

File Edit View Tools Window Help

Friday
January 12, 1996

Internet Edition

Eight pages
© 1996 The New York Times

TimesFax
FROM
The New York Times

FROM THE FRONT PAGE

Budget Battle Turns To Campaign Fodder

WASHINGTON — There was little mourning among political consultants when the budget talks were suspended this week. The strategists were already planning Congressional campaigns that revolved around the great, unresolved differences between the two parties on balancing and reconfiguring the Federal budget; the lack of a deal just makes those differences sharper.

"I haven't lost a lot of sleep over it," said Stan Greenberg, who polls for the Democratic National Committee. After weeks of surveys and voter research, Democrats are convinced that their party can prosper mightily if it presents itself as the last line of defense against Republican cuts in Medicare, education and environmental protection.

As Democratic consultants see it, Republican incumbents enter the 1996 campaign with a crippling record of votes on those issues, and the lack of a budget deal means they have no overarching accomplishment to outweigh those votes.

Republican strategists counter with a very simple theme that takes into account the lack of a budget deal, (or, perhaps someday, a less-than-perfect budget deal) as well as the stalling of other high-profile parts of their legislative agenda: Their party tried to bring about the fundamental change the voters demanded in 1994, but the Democrats blocked them.

By ROBIN TONER

Gingrich Hits Clinton on Budget Plan

WASHINGTON — Insisting that a balanced budget plan was "within our grasp," President Clinton called on Congressional Republican leaders to renew the drive for an agreement Thursday. But he was instantly rebuffed by Speaker Newt Gingrich, who accused him of misleading the public in "a political game."

The deep difference between the two sides in the drawn-out budget battle was made starkly clear when the President held a televised news conference to declare his own optimism that a deal can be reached "if we set aside partisanship and work to seize this moment."

"We shouldn't let our fundamental agreement on a balanced budget," Mr. Clinton declared, "be held hostage to a narrower agenda that seeks to prevent America from giving Medicare to senior citizens or quality nursing home care or educational opportunity for young people or environmental protection to all of us."

Mr. Clinton was soon castigated by Mr. Gingrich for accusing the Republicans of seeking excessive "cuts" in Medicare, Medicaid and other social welfare spending when the financing of these programs, Mr. Gingrich said, would actually be increasing.

"It was a very disappointing press conference," Mr. Gingrich commented in Seattle after watching the President on television during a West Coast fund-raising trip. "It does not give me much encouragement."

By FRANCIS X. CLINES

Peru Convicts American Woman of Treason

LIMA, Peru — Lori Helene Berenson of New York was convicted of treason Thursday by a secret Peruvian military court and sentenced to life in prison for aiding Marxist guerrillas who prosecutors said were planning to seize the Peruvian Congress and abduct lawmakers.

The widely expected verdict was announced six weeks after Ms. Berenson was arrested in an anti-terrorist police operation that also led to the capture of 22 other people after an all-night shootout in a Lima suburb. But the sentence came as a surprise, especially since prosecutors had requested a 30-year prison term, the minimum penalty for treason in Peru, and reflects the Government's tough policy toward insurgent groups.

Ms. Berenson is expected to be moved soon to Yanamaygo Prison in Puno, a special prison for terrorists situated in the Andes. Lawyers for Ms. Berenson, 26, said a treaty between the United States and Peru allows her to serve her sentence in the United States after all judicial appeals have been completed. But the lawyers said their client had indicated no desire to serve her time in the United States.

By CALVIN SIMS

Fear of Diseases Drives Britons From Beef

LONDON — For centuries, beef has held pride of place at the British table. All that may change. Despite pledges by Government ministers that British beef is safe, consumers by the droves are giving it up for fear that meat from diseased cattle could cause a degenerative brain disease.

The Government emphasizes that no link has been established between bovine spongiform encephalopathy, commonly known as mad-cow disease, and Creutzfeldt-Jakob Disease, a rare brain disease fatal to humans.

Since November, when the scare erupted, the Ministry of Agriculture, Fisheries and Food has trotted out scientists and reports suggesting that it is unlikely for a disease to cross the "species barrier" and that even if it did, regulations are in place to keep the diseased portions of cow carcasses out of the human food chain. But the scare refuses to go away. For every scientist who says beef is safe, there is one who says it may not be. The debate over a possible link rages in British medical journals.

The public is voting with its fork. According to a research organization, 1.4 million households have stopped buying beef.

The decline began in November and by mid-December, sales were down 25 percent.

By JOHN DARNTON

1 of 8 | 100% | 8.50 x 11.00 in

Figure 12.1 New York Times (TimesFax) displayed by Adobe Acrobat

For the Time-Challenged

- Acrobat enables you to download and view richly formatted documents, no matter on which brand of computer they were created.
- Once you've downloaded a document, you can easily navigate through it by using the Acrobat toolbar.
- The Amber plug-in for Netscape 2 enables you to view Acrobat presentations in-line (that is, within Netscape's window) and to download just one page at a time.

can read them with the Adobe Acrobat Reader software included with this book.

In Adobe's nomenclature, Acrobat documents are *portable documents*—and it's a great term. Unlike richly formatted documents created with word processing programs such as Microsoft Word, Acrobat documents can be viewed and read on any computer system for which an Acrobat reader has been provided (and there are Acrobat readers for almost all commonly used types of computers). Acrobat is a major plus for large organizations, in which people using many different types of computers must be able to exchange richly formatted documents and don't have time to translate them. And it's a natural for publishing on the Web.

Adobe has added lots of new features to the basic Acrobat design, by means of plug-ins. The coolest of the lot is Weblink (included in the version of Acrobat on this book's CD-ROM disc), which enables Acrobat authors to incorporate Web links into their Acrobat documents. And with Weblink installed in the Reader, you can access Web documents by clicking links, just as you would within Netscape.

New for 2

If you're using the Windows 95 version of Netscape, you can take advantage of the amazing new Acrobat Amber plug-in, which enables you to view Acrobat presentations within Netscape's window. What's more, you can view one page at a time—there's no need to wait for the whole presentation to download before you can start viewing.

This chapter begins by discussing the Adobe Acrobat helper application, which runs in a separate window. If you're using Windows 95, you can take advantage of the Amber plug-in, which is discussed later in this chapter.

Downloading an Acrobat Document

Adobe Acrobat documents are stored in *.pdf files (the "pdf" is short for Portable Document Format).

When you click a link to an Adobe Acrobat document, Netscape downloads the document and starts the Acrobat Reader. When the downloading is complete, the Acrobat Reader starts and appears in its own window. You use the Acrobat Reader's controls to page through the document.

Understanding the Acrobat Reader Window

The Acrobat Reader window has its own toolbar, which offers the controls discussed in the following sections. You'll rarely use the menu commands.

Choosing a Display Mode

Acrobat enables you to view the document three different ways. The default mode is the Page Only display mode, and it's the one you'll probably want to use most often.

Page Only Display Mode In this mode, the default mode shown in Figure 12.1, the Adobe Acrobat document fills the window.

Bookmarks and Page Mode In this mode, you'll see a vertical list of bookmarks in the left panel of the page, with the document displayed in the right panel. These bookmarks are like hyperlinks. You can click them to display a page other than the one you are viewing. You may encounter some Acrobat documents that take advantage of this feature.

Thumbnails and Page In this mode, you see a vertical list of thumbnail (postage-stamp-sized) images of the document's pages in the left panel, while the document is displayed in the right panel (Figure 12.2). To go to one of the pages, click the thumbnail image.

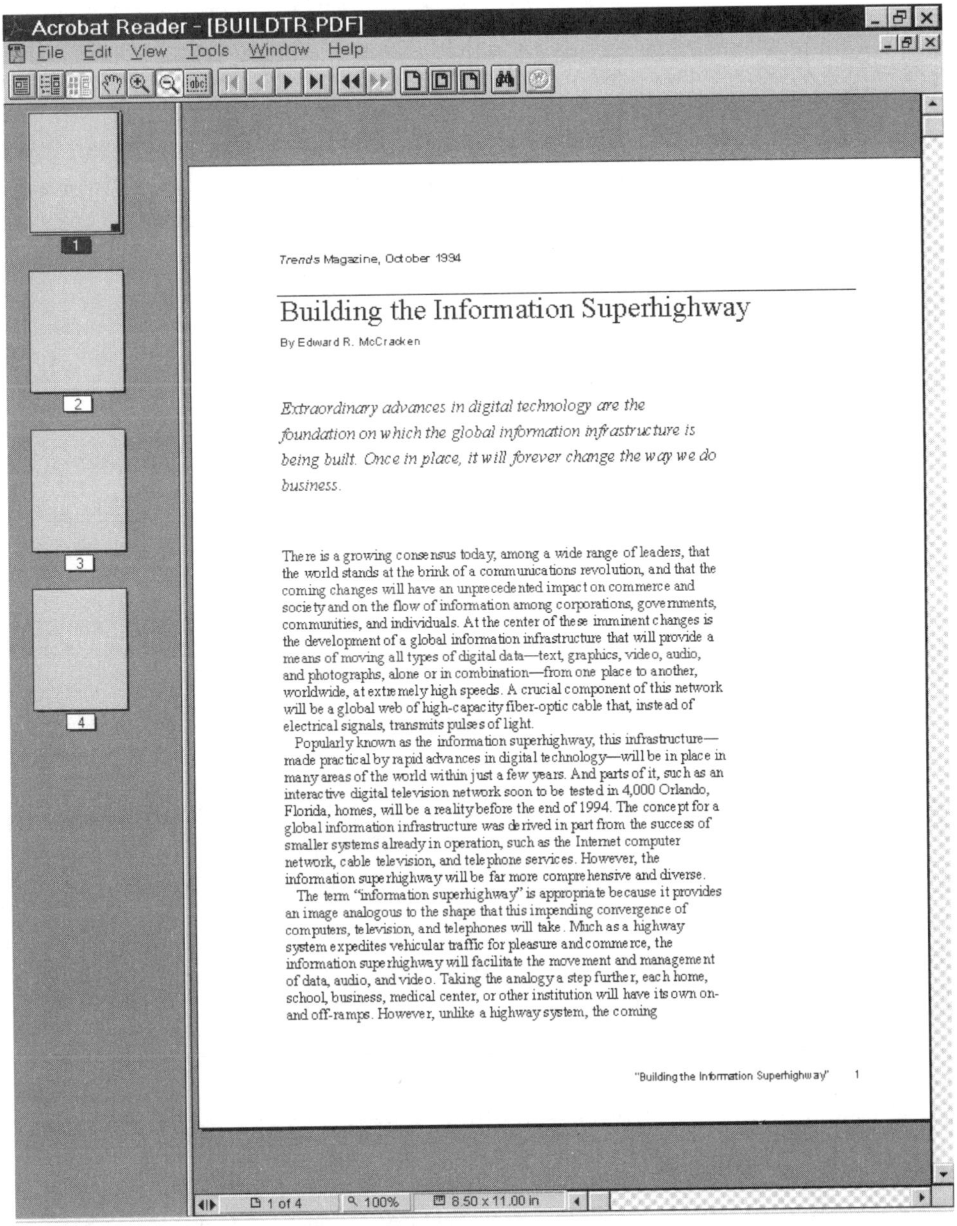

Acrobat Reader - [BUILDTR.PDF]

File Edit View Tools Window Help

1 2 3 4

Trends Magazine, October 1994

Building the Information Superhighway

By Edward R. McCracken

Extraordinary advances in digital technology are the foundation on which the global information infrastructure is being built. Once in place, it will forever change the way we do business.

There is a growing consensus today, among a wide range of leaders, that the world stands at the brink of a communications revolution, and that the coming changes will have an unprecedented impact on commerce and society and on the flow of information among corporations, governments, communities, and individuals. At the center of these imminent changes is the development of a global information infrastructure that will provide a means of moving all types of digital data—text, graphics, video, audio, and photographs, alone or in combination—from one place to another, worldwide, at extremely high speeds. A crucial component of this network will be a global web of high-capacity fiber-optic cable that, instead of electrical signals, transmits pulses of light.

Popularly known as the information superhighway, this infrastructure—made practical by rapid advances in digital technology—will be in place in many areas of the world within just a few years. And parts of it, such as an interactive digital television network soon to be tested in 4,000 Orlando, Florida, homes, will be a reality before the end of 1994. The concept for a global information infrastructure was derived in part from the success of smaller systems already in operation, such as the Internet computer network, cable television, and telephone services. However, the information superhighway will be far more comprehensive and diverse.

The term "information superhighway" is appropriate because it provides an image analogous to the shape that this impending convergence of computers, television, and telephones will take. Much as a highway system expedites vehicular traffic for pleasure and commerce, the information superhighway will facilitate the movement and management of data, audio, and video. Taking the analogy a step further, each home, school, business, medical center, or other institution will have its own on- and off-ramps. However, unlike a highway system, the coming

"Building the Information Superhighway" 1

1 of 4 100% 8.50 x 11.00 in

Figure 12.2 Thumbnails and Page mode

Navigating Through the Document

Use the following buttons to navigate through the Acrobat document:

Click this button to display the next page.

Click this button to display the previous page.

Click this button to display the last page.

Click this button to display the first page.

Click this button to go back to the previously displayed page.

Click this button to redisplay the page you were just viewing.

Sizing the Document On-Screen

To get a closer look at a portion of the page, use one of the following tools:

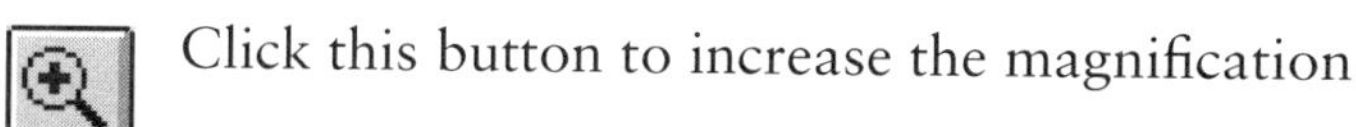

Click this button to increase the magnification.

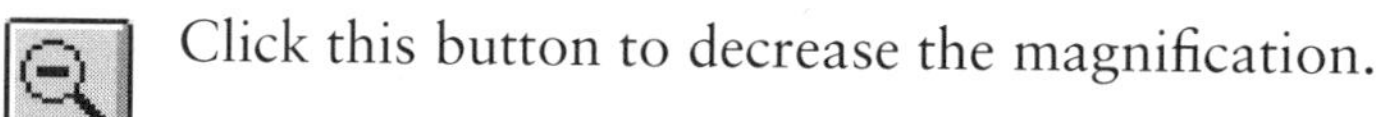

Click this button to decrease the magnification.

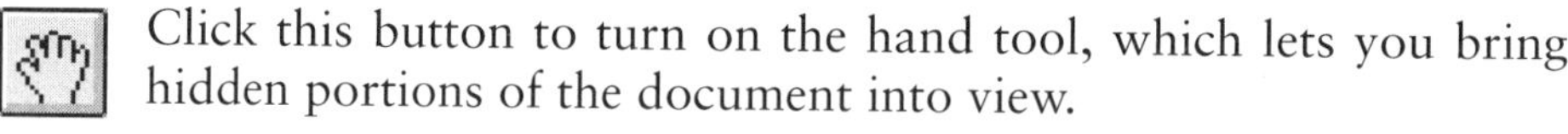

Click this button to turn on the hand tool, which lets you bring hidden portions of the document into view.

Note that some Acrobat documents contain author-defined articles, which are designed so that you can page through them almost automatically. To find out whether the document has articles, open the View menu and choose Articles. You'll see a list of the articles the document contains, if any. To read an article, select it and click OK. The Reader will display the beginning of the article. Just click the mouse button to page through the article automatically.

You can also size the document by clicking one of the three page size buttons, which are situated near the right end of the toolbar:

Click this button to display the page at 100% magnification.

Click this button to fit the page to the window.

Click this button to fit the width of the page to the window.

Reading the Document in Full-Screen Mode

You can also read Acrobat documents in full-screen mode, in which the page takes up the whole screen. From the View menu, choose Full Screen. To view the next page, press Enter, the right arrow key, or the down arrow key. You can also click the left mouse button. To view the previous page, press the left arrow or up arrow key. When you are finished paging through the document, the program switches back to the normal display mode (you see the Adobe Acrobat Reader in a window).

Finding Text in an Acrobat Document

If you would like to search for text in an Acrobat document, click the Find tool (the button with binoculars). In the Find dialog box, type the text for which you want to search. Click the Whole Word option to avoid retrieving embedded strings, and click Match Case, if desired, to match the capitalization pattern you have typed. To search backwards, click the Find Backwards option. Click Find to initiate the search. If the program finds a match, it highlights the matched text on-screen. Press F3 to find the next occurrence of the same text.

If no match is found, you'll see a dialog box asking whether you want to continue searching from the beginning of the document. If you click OK, the program continues the search. Should this search fail to retrieve a match, you'll see an alert box informing you that the text could not be found.

Copying Text and Graphics to the Clipboard

If you find text in an Adobe Acrobat document that you would like to copy to another document, click the Select button (the one with "abc" on the button face), and select the text. Then open the Edit menu and choose Copy, or press Ctrl + C.

You can also select and copy graphics. To do so, open the Tools menu and choose Select Graphics. Then drag a selection box around the graphic you want to copy. From the Edit menu, choose Copy, or just press Ctrl + C.

Printing the Document

To print the Adobe Acrobat document you are viewing, follow these steps:

1. From the File menu, choose Print.
2. In the Print dialog box, choose printing options, if you wish. You can print all the pages (the default setting), the current page, or a range of pages. You can also choose to print more than one copy. Additional options may be available, depending on your printer's capabilities.
3. Click OK to start printing.

I can't save this document! You're right—there's no Save option on the Reader's File menu. What gives? Simple—there's no need. Netscape has already downloaded the Acrobat document to the directory listed in the Temporary Directory box (Apps page of the General Preferences menu item). Unless you deliberately erase it, there it will stay. Even after you quit Netscape, you can open the Adobe Acrobat Reader and load this document using the Open command in the File menu.

For an introduction to the extremely cool things that can be done with Adobe Acrobat and the Web, check out the following URL:

http://www.adobe.com:80/Acrobat/PDFsamples.html

You'll find Acrobat versions of Shakespeare's plays and sonnets, the Declaration of Independence and other historical documents, Aesop's fairy tales, and lots of other very interesting things. Don't miss Sun Tzu, *The Art of War.*

Using the Amber Acrobat Reader

New for 2

If you're using Windows 95, you can take advantage of the Amber plug-in for Netscape.

This plug-in enables Netscape to view Acrobat files within Netscape's window, and what's more, only one page downloads at a time—you don't have to wait for the whole presentation to download before reading.

There's more! Like the progressively displayed JPEGs you're used to viewing with Netscape, Amber progressively displays a page, beginning with the text first. And to speed things even more, Amber uses *font blitting*—which means that fast substitution fonts are used first, followed by the true fonts only after everything's finished downloading.

Amber is a major step forward in making Acrobat documents more accessible on the Web.

From Here

- Take a look at the most exciting thing to hit the Internet since Netscape itself—Java. You'll find a complete introduction in Chapter 13.
- Like to see in-line animations? You can, with Macromedia's Shockwave plug-in. There's a copy on the CD-ROM disc packaged with this book. See Chapter 14 for details.
- Explore three-dimensional worlds with Netscape's Live3D plug-in. Find out how to use it in Chapter 15.

Chapter 13

Taking a Sip of Java

Java is many things—a programming language, a key innovation in the history of computing, even a step into a new technological world. For Netscape users, though, it's fun, most of all. With Java, those static Web pages come alive with action, which can include sound, animation, and video. And these pages also provide *inter*action, enabling you to make choices or input data and see the results immediately, right on the page you're viewing.

In this chapter, you'll take a tour of some of today's best Java sites, and you'll learn more about what lies behind Java—and why some people think that Java will change the face of computing forever.

For the Time-Challenged

- Helper programs aren't a very good solution for Web multimedia. They run in a separate window. Worse, if you don't have the helper software, you're out of luck—you can't use the multimedia file. Java solves both problems by downloading the needed software (called an *applet*) along with the multimedia material. You then see the multimedia presentation within Netscape's window.
- Netscape 2 contains a built-in Java interpreter, so you don't need to do anything special to run Java programs. When Netscape accesses a Web page containing a Java applet, Netscape downloads the code and runs it.
- Java is a new programming language that's beautifully suited to the Web environment. Unlike other programming languages, a Java program generates a *byte code*, which is expressed in plain ASCII characters that any computer can read. A Java interpreter, designed for a particular computer, transforms the byte code into instructions designed for a particular computer. Security precautions are built in so that you don't have to worry about computer viruses.
- JavaScript is a subset of Java that enables amateur programmers to bring rich, interactive features to their Web pages.

Java – What's the Big Deal?

You've done some serious surfing now, and I'll bet you've run into this problem: You've clicked on something, but Netscape tells you that it doesn't recognize the file you're trying to access. What's going on? The problem: You don't have the right helper program. So you've got two choices, neither of which is terribly satisfactory: You can skip the file, or you can download it and then try to find a helper program that will run it.

What's so cool about Java is that, when a Web page includes Java code, Netscape automatically downloads the program, called an *applet,* that is needed to make things happen. Your computer than executes (runs) the applet, producing action—and interaction—right on the Web page you're viewing.

Helper programs aren't about to go away, though. Java's very useful, but it works best when the programs being downloaded are relatively small. As you'll see in the next section, where you'll take a look at some excellent Java sites, these programs do simple things, such as displaying an interactive crossword puzzle or a real-time clock. For now, you'll still need helper programs to play sounds, watch movies, and run animations.

A Tour of Java Sites

You don't need to do anything special to run Java programs—with Netscape, it's all automatic. When you access a site that contains Java code, you'll know it—there are placeholders where the Java action will take place, and it takes a while for the code to download and execute. Once it does, things start happening!

Note that Java is so new (at this writing) that relatively few Web sites incorporate Java code. That's going to change quickly, especially since Netscape incorporates a Java interpreter! By the time this book reaches you, many Java sites will have appeared besides the ones listed here, which have a "demo" flavor to them. But it won't be long before some of the Web's top sites begin incorporating useful Java applets.

EarthWeb

The name makes this site sound as if it's an environmental trailblazer page, but it's not—it's the headquarters for a Java development team. And what a team! EarthWeb is a New York-based company that specializes in Web site development using Java. When you access EarthWeb (http://www.earthweb.com/java/, shown in Figure 13.1), you'll find a series of demonstration applications. They'll give you a pretty good idea of what Java can do.

Here's a sampler of what's on the site at this writing (on the Web, things change, so you can be sure this page will have been updated when you access it):

3-D-Netris The popular game takes on new meaning in a rotatable 3-D display.

Jigsaw Puzzle Drag the pieces to the squarc, and see if you can win.

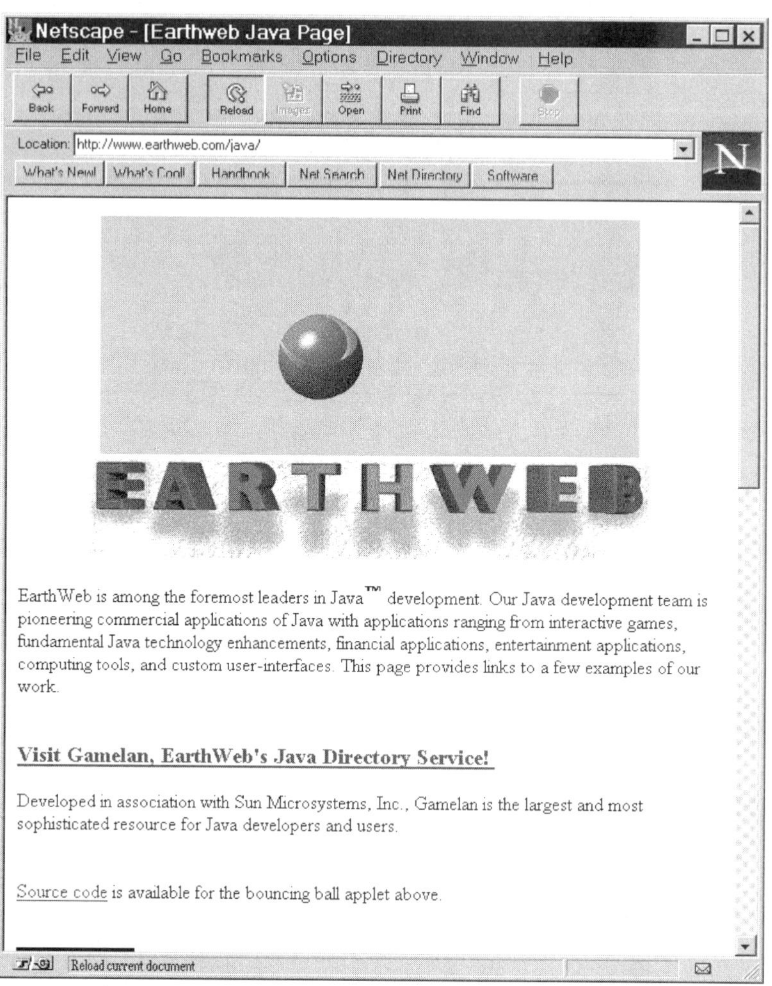

Figure 13.1 EarthWeb

Maze	This will a-maze you! This fascinating program generates and solves its own maze. To start it, just click within the maze.
Throw the Ball	Catch the ball by clicking and dragging. Release the button while moving the mouse to throw the ball!

Don't miss Gamelan (http://www.gamelan.com/about.html), an EarthWeb project that summarizes tons of Web-based information about Java. Included are dozens of Java applets that you can try. Don't miss The Impressionist! Incidentally, in case you're curious, *gamelan* is the name of the traditional gong orchestral ensemble of the Indonesian archipelagos of Java and Bali.

Robert's Online Loan Pricer

Like to know how much that new sailboat is going to cost you every month? Here's a great demonstration of Java's ability to create interactive pages: It's a loan payment calculator, but with a twist—You type in any four of the five needed lines of information, and the Java applet does the rest (Figure 13.2). To access this site, use http://www.ripley.org/~robert/option-pricer.html.

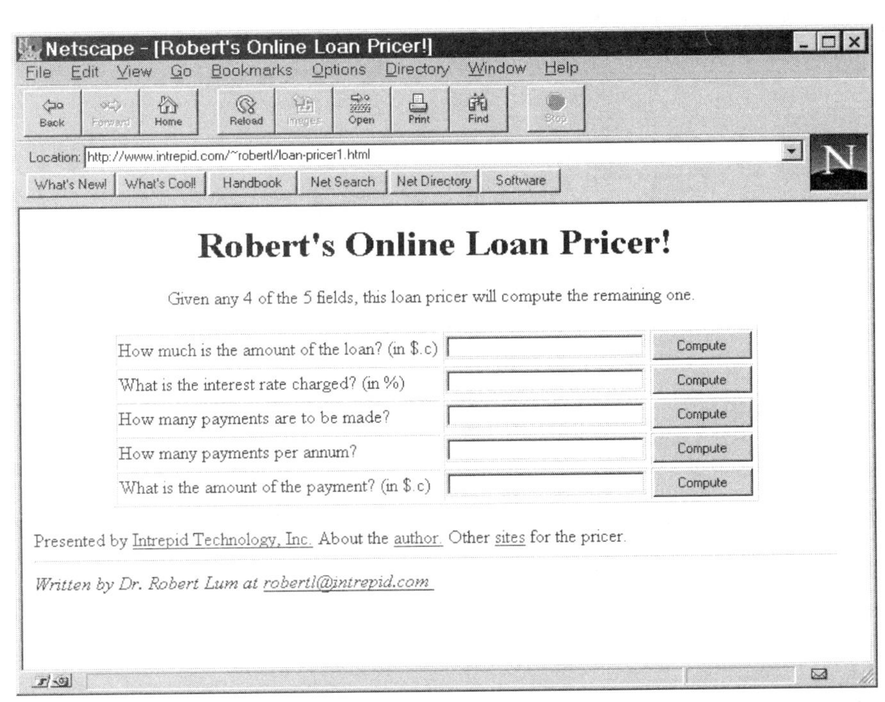

Figure 13.2 Robert's Online Loan Pricer

Solitaire

If you're wondering whether Java applets can have enough functionality to really *do* something, check out Solitaire (http://w3.gwis.com/~thorn/Beta-Sol.html). Shown in Figure 13.3, this site displays an impressive Solitaire game, which is bound to keep you busy for a while!

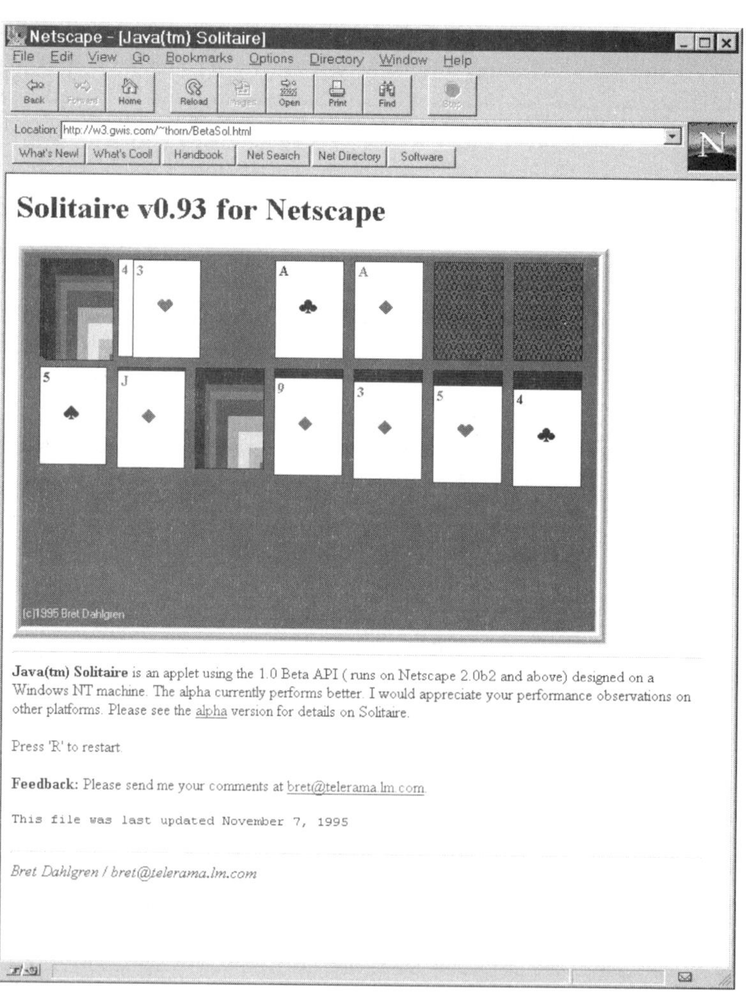

Figure 13.3 Solitaire

Where Did Java Come From?

You may be surprised to learn that Java got its start before the Web did. Java creator James Gosling, a programmer at Sun Microsystems, conceived of Java in early 1991—and at that time, Gosling thought that Java would be used to program consumer electronic devices. Specifically, Java would be used to create programs for TV set-top devices which, from the early 1990s and pre-Web perspective, were a sure bet to bring the Information Age into the home.

As Gosling initially conceived Java, the language would have to work with any kind of computer processing unit, since consumer electronic devices would surely have lots of different processors installed. Thus Java was intended to be *platform-independent* from the beginning, meaning that it would work with just about any processor made. As you'll see, that's one of the reasons it works so well with the Web—but we're getting ahead of the story.

The TV set box idea didn't work out—it seems that interactive television is always about to happen, but never quite makes it—but Java didn't die. Looking at the rapid growth of the World Wide Web, Gosling and his colleagues quickly realized that the Web, not interactive television, provided the perfect vehicle for disseminating Java applets. They created the first Java-enabled browser, called HotJava, to demonstrate what Java could do in tandem with the Web. Then Netscape Communications Corporation announced that the next version of their browser would include a Java interpreter—and the rest, as they say, is history!

Ironically, something like the TV set-top box is appearing in stores right now—but it's not designed for interactive television. On the contrary, it's a small computer (sans disk drives), priced at about $500, that enables you to access the Web!

What's JavaScript?

One of the most wonderful things about the World Wide Web is that just about anyone can learn HTML and put up a Web page. Java's great, but many Web enthusiasts fear that Java will raise the technology bar, preventing nonprogrammers from creating interactive Web sites. Thanks to JavaScript, a subset of Java designed for use by nonprogrammers, this pessimistic scenario may not occur.

Gosling and his team started with a programming language called C++, but quickly found that it was too quirky to serve their purposes. Taking the best ideas from C++ and other programming languages, they devised a new language from the ground up. Java would have the following characteristics:

- **Simplicity** Reacting against the oddly named key words and other deficiencies of previous programming languages, Java's developers wanted the language to be easy to learn and use.
- **Object-Oriented** In an *object-oriented* programming language, programmers create and polish small program modules, each of which accomplishes a certain task, such as displaying a dialog box on the screen. Once this module (called an *object*) is tested, it can be copied and used in any program. As an object-oriented language matures, programmers create hundreds and even thousands of objects, which can be put together to construct new applications in short order.
- **Robustness** Java eliminates some of the programming traps that bedevil users of C++ and other programming languages. By encouraging good programming habits, Java helps to ensure that the Java programs you run will be bug-free.
- **Architecture Neutral** This is probably the most amazing thing about Java—its ability to run on any kind of computer ever made. Unlike all previous programming languages, a compiled Java program doesn't generate binary code, which is tied to the instruction set of a particular processor. Instead, it generates a *byte code*, a list of intermediary instructions that can be expressed in ASCII characters that any computer can deal with.
- **Interpreted** To translate the byte code into instructions that a specific computer can read, you need a Java interpreter. Netscape has its own, built-in Java interpreter, so you're ready to go!
- **High Performance** All these innovations wouldn't add up to much if Java performed sluggishly. To ensure high performance, Java introduces a number of important innovations. Among them is the Java *garbage collector*, a program that runs in the background, cleaning up disused memory so that a program always has the maximum amount of memory to run.

- **Multithreading** A good program can do two or more tasks at once, so Java incorporates multithreading. In multithreading, two or more separate program processes, called *threads*, can execute at the same time.
- **Security** Programs bandied about over the network pose security problems, but Java incorporates a number of advanced protection measures to safeguard your system.

JavaScript enables anyone who's able to learn HTML to create rich, interactive sites. The cool thing about JavaScript is that it enables you to become the master of ceremonies for the events on a Web page. For example, when a user clicks a button, a portion of the script jumps into action and performs a function, such as searching a database for information or running a prepackaged Java applet.

From Here

- Your excursion into the incredible new capabilities of Netscape 2 is just beginning. For the next step, take a look at Chapter 14, which explores the new Macromedia Shockwave plug-in.
- In Chapter 15, you'll experience your first taste of virtual reality, thanks to the Live3D plug-in.

Chapter 14

How Shocking!

Viewing Animations with Shockwave

Macromedia Director is the program of choice for professional animators, artists, educators, publishers, corporate presentation specialists, and more—roughly 100,000 of them, in fact. Using Director, animators can combine text, graphics, animations, sound, digital video, and interactivity to create dynamic multimedia presentations.

New for 2 With the Shockwave plug-in for Netscape 2, Macromedia Director presentations can now be made available on the Web. If you think that's shocking, that's exactly what Macromedia intended—in fact, professional animators are said to *shock* a Macromedia presentation to transform it into a Shockwave presentation. You'll run into lots of references to "shocked" versions of a page, and if you do, by all means access them—you'll see all kinds of interesting things happening on-screen.

For the Time-Challenged

- Shockwave is a plug-in program for Netscape that enables the browser to play Macromedia Director animations (called movies). Macromedia movies can include text, sound, animation, and graphics.
- This one's simple: After you install Shockwave, you don't need to do anything special to access Shockwave presentations. When you access a page containing a Shockwave movie, Netscape will download it and begin playing it—that's it.

Ultimately, the coolest thing about Shockwave is that you'll see the Macromedia presentation within the Netscape window—this isn't a helper application, folks, it's a *plug-in.* After installing the plug-in, Netscape seamlessly takes on Macromedia capabilities. Whenever you access a site containing a Macromedia presentation, Netscape automatically detects the presentation. Suddenly, the Web becomes capable of interactive multimedia!

For information on obtaining and installing Shockwave, see Appendix B.

Like Java, Shockwave brings a welcome dimension of interactivity to the Web. But it also signals a trend away from the Web's "do-it-yourself" technical level, in which amateurs could put up pages that were fully the equal of the best efforts of Corporate America. It's expensive and time-consuming to develop Macromedia skills (not to mention full-bore multimedia presentations), so it's hardly surprising that Macromedia's Shockwave demo page (located at http://www.macromedia.com/Tools/Shockwave/Vanguard/index.html) is top-heavy with corporate presences, including the likes of MTV, C|NET, USA Today, Times-Warner, United Airlines, and Sony Music Entertainment.

How Shockwave Works

To create a Shockwave presentation, professional animators begin by creating a Macromedia Director movie. Next, they run Afterburner, a Macromedia post-processing program that transforms the movie into the Shockwave format. (Along the way, it also compresses the movie by 60%, making it small enough to be transmitted via slow SLIP/PPP connections.) Web authors can then incorporate the presentation into their Web pages.

What about you, the Netscape user? Is it difficult to run a Shockwave presentation? It couldn't be easier. It's automatic!

After installing the Shockwave plug-in, you won't notice any immediate change in Netscape. When you access a site that contains a Macromedia presentation, you'll see a Macromedia placeholder (with lots of Ms) that stays in place while Netscape downloads the presentation. And then things start to happen! For a sampler, see the next section.

Will I have to download 5 MB of data to see a Shockwave presentation? Nope. You'd be surprised how compact most Shockwave presentations are. Most fall in the 350 KB range, which download pretty snappily on a 28.8 Kbps modem.

How much does Shockwave cost? It's free. Why? It's to Macromedia's advantage to distribute this plug-in as widely as possible. That will encourage Web designers to incorporate animations into their pages, and to do this, they'll need Macromedia Director—well, you get the idea.

Ultra-Cool Shockwave Sites

Just about every one of the hottest Web sites is experimenting with Shockwave versions of their home pages. Here's a sampler.

The Active Marquee

One of the most obvious uses of Macromedia Director animations is to make a Web site's *marquee* come alive. A marquee is the portion of the page that contains the site's name and often its navigation buttons.

Many sites are experimenting with Shockwave marquees at this writing, and no doubt you'll find plenty more by the time this book reaches you. One of the most impressive experiments is Apple's, located at http://www2.apple.com/sw/. When you access the site, you'll see the usual Macromedia placeholder—but then things really start to happen. Piece by piece, the marquee shown in Figure 14.1 arrives on-screen, replete with a

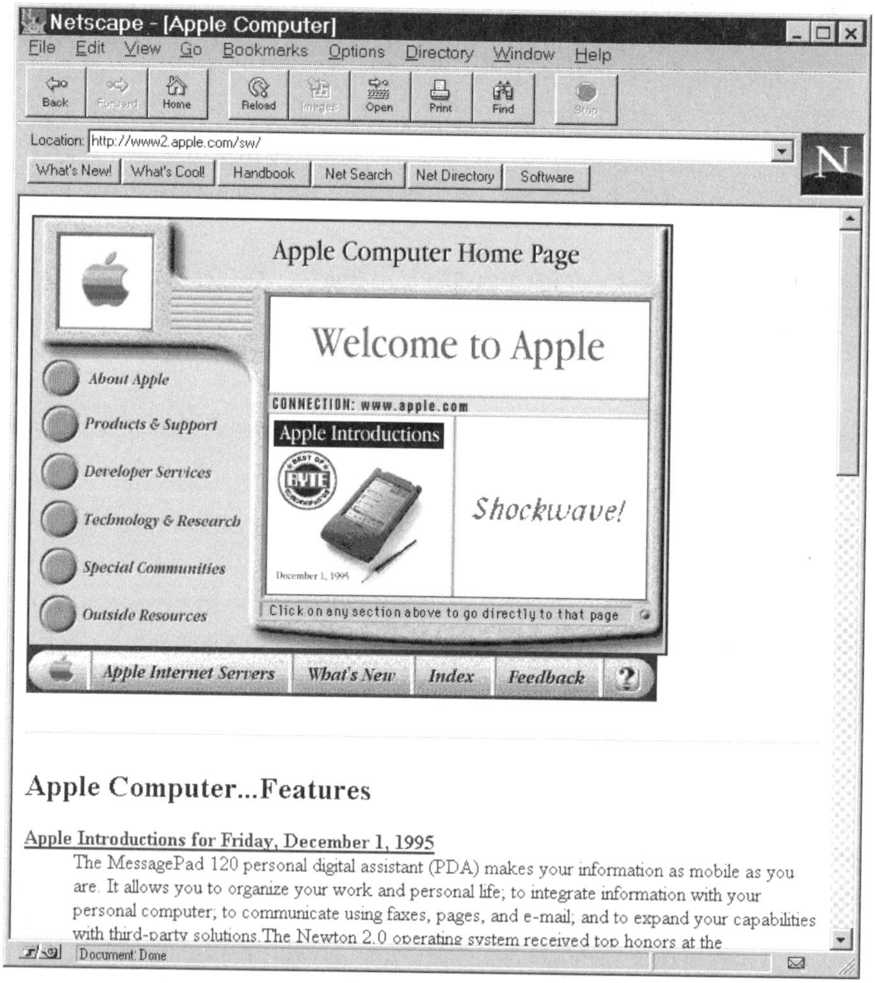

Figure 14.1 Shockwave version of Apple home page

rearrangement of the design elements, serving to illustrate their various functions. The last element to appear is the bank of navigation buttons, which smoothly arrive on the scene, one by one.

Take a look at these active marquees, too:

- **Yahoo** (http://shock.yahoo.com/shock/) Just what you'd expect from the Yahoo folks. Those cute Yahoo letters dance around as if they're sounding off.
- **Netscape** (http://www.netscape.com/comprod/product/navigator/version_2.0/plugins/director_example/director_example1.html) Not to be outdone, Netscape has created a cool animated version of its home page, too. You'll see the familiar Netscape marquee and navigation buttons—but only after they've done an amusing pirouette.
- **Epicurious** (http://www.epicurious.com/epicurious/ba/shock/shock1.html) Watch red peppers fly at you from all directions (Figure 14.2).
- **MTV** (http://www.mtv.com/shock/tube/) A darkly weird marquee (Figure 14.3), with pulsating globes. A cool feature: when you move the pointer to a hyperlink, the TV screen lights up with an animation that's relevant to the link.

Beyond Glitz

What you've seen thus far testifies to the extremes businesses will go to get and hold your attention—after all, we're all part of the TV generation, right? But there's much more potential to Web-based interactive multimedia, particularly in the fields of education and training.

My Computerized House

Can you find examples of educational multimedia on the Web? The big corporate players were the first to dive in, but there's a wonderful exception. Alone among the demonstration sites in Shockwave's home page is the sole amateur effort, My Computerized House, by Wulia Beakoi, all of 9 years old. (I think Wulia might have had a little help with the Macromedia coding.) It's a story about a very computerized house, replete with a robot that keeps a little girl's room clean (now I could use one of THOSE!).

Netscape - [text]

File Edit View Go Bookmarks Options Directory Window Help

Back Forward Home Reload Images Open Print Find Stop

Location: http://www.epicurious.com/epicurious/ba/shock/shock1.html

What's New! What's Cool! Handbook Net Search Net Directory Software

BON APPETIT

To start class click here

Cooking Class

DECORATING CHRISTMAS COOKIES

If this page isn't doing what it should (you'll know), use these links to get the latest version of Netscape Navigator 2.0 and the Shockwave plug-in from Macromedia.

FRUITCAKE, RUM BALLS AND MINCEMEAT PIE are all well and good, but Christmas wouldn't be Christmas without decorated cookies. This year, take a lesson from Sarah Tenaglia, associate food editor of *Bon Appetit,* and turn out plates filled with pretty, festive treats. Both the citrus sugar cookies and the gingerbread cookies are easy to make and even easier to decorate, thanks to our step-by-step instructions for glazing, piping and drizzling. With the ideas and tips on the following pages, you will have lots of beautiful cookies for holiday guests--including old Saint Nick.

Figure 14.2 Shocked version of Epicurious home page

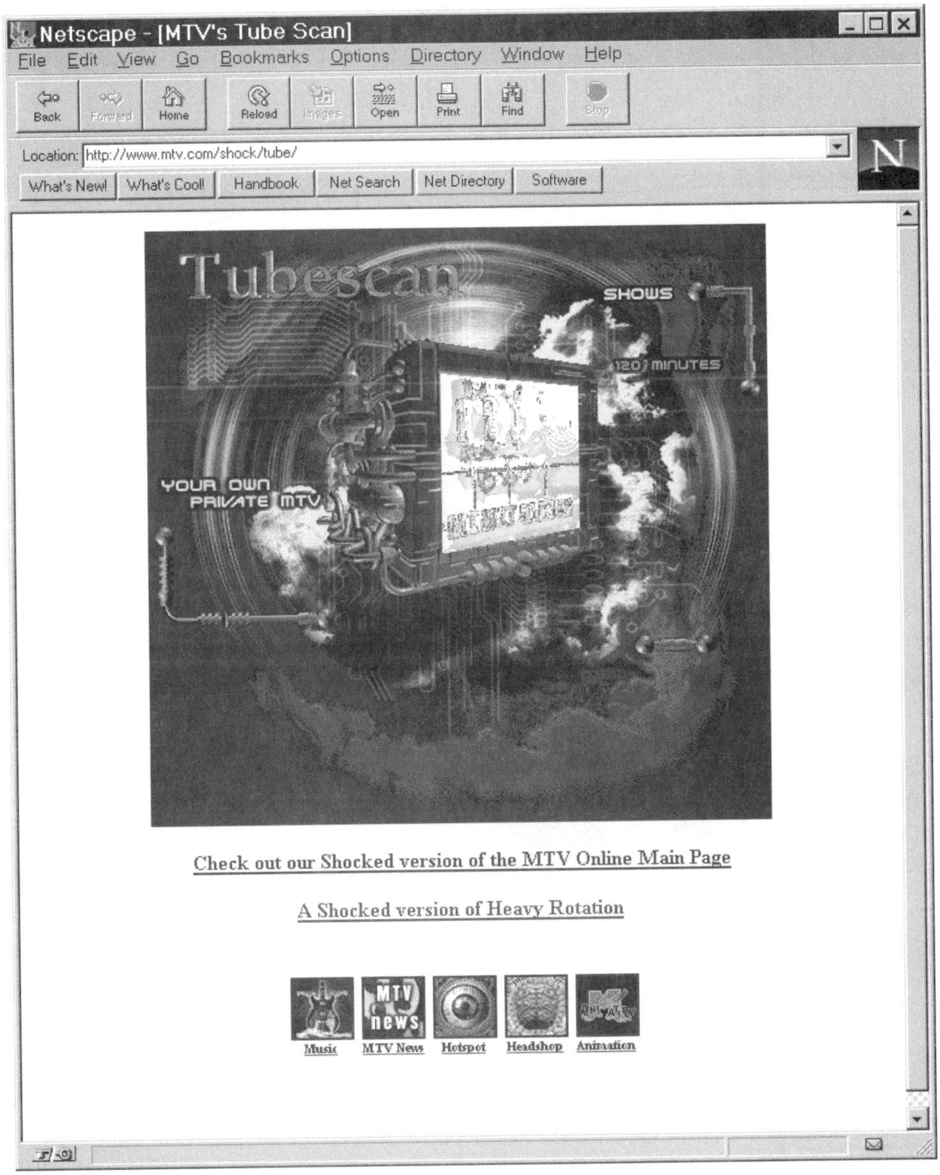

Figure 14.3 Shocked version of MTV home page

To access the shocked version of My Computerized House, use

http://orchidweb.woodwind.com:443/mtl/sw/MCH/mch1.html

You'll see the first page of the story, in which the protagonist pushes a button on her watch to open the front door (Figure 14.4). You're asked to find

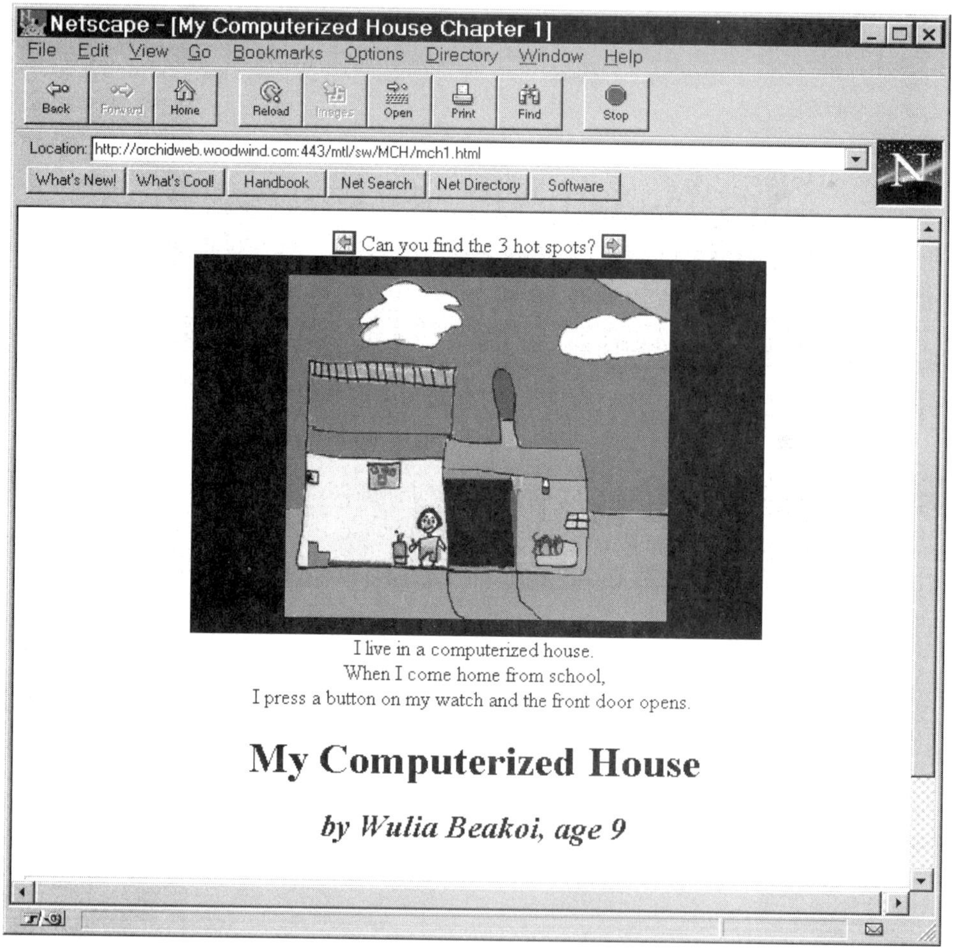

Figure 14.4 Shocked version of My Computerized House, by Wulia Beakoi

Figure 14.5 Newton's Cradle (@radical.media)

the three hot spots with the mouse pointer, and when you do, you're rewarded with action—touch the sleeping cat, for instance, and you'll scare him out of his wits. It's a fun page for beginning readers and adults alike, although adults will spend some time pondering how Wulia's computers seem to take on some of the attributes we'd associate with magic.

Shockwave Showcase

For an in-depth exploration of what Shockwave can do, check out @radical.media's Shockwave Showcase. @radical.media is a New York City- and Los Angeles-based multimedia development firm that's doing some pretty impressive work. To access the Shockwave Showcase, use

http://www.radicalmedia.com/~shockwave/

You'll find lots of proto-corporate glitz on the Showcase, but there's one demo—Newton's Cradle—that illustrates the educational potential of Shockwave (Figure 14.5). Newton's Cradle illustrates the classic physical principle of inertia When you drag one of the four suspended balls and release it, the two middle balls remain stationary, and the one on the end pops out. Unintentionally, though, the page also illustrates the non-physical principle of perpetual motion, because the balls keep swinging until you click the animation again. (Apparently, there's no friction in cyberspace.)

From Here

- Experience the ultimate plug-in: Live3D, which enables you to explore three-dimensional virtual worlds! Read all about it in the next chapter.

Chapter 15

Exploring Virtual Worlds with Live3D

By now, you're probably impressed with what the new Web can do, thanks to the impressive capabilities of plug-in programs and Netscape Version 2. In this chapter, you'll learn how to view virtual reality presentations, which are the most amazing things to hit the Web yet—or the most useless, depending on your point of view.

What's virtual reality? Different people define it in different ways—cyberpunk author William Gibson calls it a "shared consensual hallucination," while others, perhaps more down to earth, prefer to term it an "experience in three-dimensional computer graphics." However you define virtual reality, it's best experienced first-hand. Thanks to Live3D, a plug-in developed for Netscape Navigator Version 2, you can.

New for 2

This chapter provides an in-depth introduction to virtual reality and Live3D, beginning with the scripting language, VRML, that makes it all happen. You'll learn how to work with Live3D's navigation commands—yes, they differ from Netscape's—and you'll take a tour of some of the Web's hottest virtual reality sites. You can obtain Live3D by downloading the program from Netscape's home page.

Introducing VRML

Short for Virtual Reality Modeling Language, VRML got its start at Silicon Graphics, a California-based firm that had developed Open Inventor, a three-dimensional programming language. In 1994, computer programmers Mark Pesce and Tony Parisi started thinking about a "virtual reality markup language" for the Web, along the lines of HTML, the markup language that's used to create Web pages. Mark and Tony shared a belief that the Web is too "flat." To be as intoxicating and enchanting as possible, they argued, the Web should reveal three-dimensional spaces, which you could explore as if you were walking into a huge castle.

After a vigorous discussion on Usenet, Pesce and Parisi settled on a subset of the ASCII version of Open Inventor as the basis for VRML. Silicon Graphics graciously agreed to place this language in the public domain so that VRML could proceed. By early 1995, a draft specification of VRML 1.0 had been produced.

As currently specified, VRML provides the tools needed to describe a scene in three-dimensional detail. The scene consists of objects (such as cones, cubes, or rectangles), which can be nested within other objects. Like HTML, VRML includes the ability to embed hyperlinks within the objects that a programmer creates. In South of Market (SoMa), a VRML world created to navigate the streets south of San Francisco's main thoroughfare, you may find your way to the offices of *Wired* magazine—and when you click the front door, you'll wind up at Hotwired's home page.

Virtual reality is best explored while wearing a stereovision headset, which tricks you into believing that you're physically inside the computer-created space. Viewed from Netscape's perspective, the three-dimensional worlds created by VRML are inviting, but don't produce the exclamations of wonder often heard from those donning headsets for the first time. Still, VRML offers something that headset-based systems don't: the possibility of creating vast hyperlinked worlds that one could explore endlessly, just as one can now explore the Web via ordinary hyperlinks.

For the Time-Challenged

- The Virtual Reality Modeling Language (VRML) was developed by Silicon Graphics, Inc., and released into the public domain. Currently standardized in Version 1.0, VRML enables programmers to create three-dimensional virtual worlds. These worlds can contain hyperlinks.
- To explore virtual worlds, you can use Live3D, a plug-in program for Netscape Version 2. When Netscape encounters a VRML world, the program automatically starts Live3D.
- Live3D has three modes: walking, flying, and pointing. The easiest is pointing. If you get lost, just click the reset button on Live3D's toolbar to begin at the entry point.

The newest wrinkle on the VRML scene is the Moving Worlds specification (VRML 2.0), which is backed by 56 leading Internet companies. Backed by Mark Pesce, Moving Worlds enables VRML designers to integrate Java applets, leading to some interesting possibilities for interactive VRML worlds. And that's not all. Moving Worlds scenes can incorporate animations, sounds, videos, high-resolution graphics, and text.

Using Live3D

A product of Netscape Communications Corporation, Live3D functions as a plug-in program for Netscape 2. It transforms Netscape into a program capable of exploring three dimensions, instead of the usual two.

When Netscape encounters a VRML world, the program automatically starts Live3D, and you'll see the Live3D command bar in the lower portion of the window (Figure 15.1). If you click the question mark (?), you'll see tips on mouse techniques on-screen. There are three navigation modes in Live3D: walking, flying, and pointing, which are described in the following sections.

To get started with Live3D, you'll need to access a VRML site. Here's a great place to start: Intel Inside (http://www.intel.com/procs/ppro/intro/vrml/nav.wrl). You're inside an Intel microprocessor. Very professionally

done. Walk up to the processor, and you'll find hyperlinks to additional segments of the world.

Ooooh, is this slow! In a virtual world that has lots of hyperlinks, don't count on rapid navigation—every new "world" requires downloading at least 50 KB of information, and maybe as much as 300 KB. All this is going to work much better when we all have 10 MB/sec connections, huh?

Have you ever played Doom? If so, you've got a real advantage, because most of Live3D's commands duplicate the popular (if violent) shoot-'em-upper. Don't count on seeing anything quite as responsive as Doom's three-dimensional world; the worlds you're about to enter have to be downloaded from the Net, which is considerably slower than your computer's hard disk.

Walking

When you walk with Live3D, you move within the virtual world at a manageable pace. Start with walking until you've mastered the basic maneuvers.

Here's a rundown of the basic walking commands:

- To start walking, click "walk" on the Live3D control panel (at the bottom of Netscape's window).
- To move ahead, press the Up arrow or hold down the left mouse button and drag up. To go back, press the Down arrow, or hold down the left mouse button and drag down.
- To turn right, press the Right arrow key, or hold down the left mouse button and drag right. To turn left, press the Left arrow key, or hold down the left mouse button and drag left.
- To slide (move right or left without turning in either direction), hold down the Alt key and drag the mouse right or left.
- To move faster, hold down the Shift key.
- To get to something quickly, hold down the Ctrl key and left-click the object.
- As you move, you can tilt your head up by pressing the Z key, or down by pressing the A key.

Figure 15.1 Live3D command bar

- If you come to a doorway, it might be openable—to find out, get close to it and press the Spacebar.
- To orbit around the entire scene (you'll have to try this to see what this means), hold down the right mouse button and drag.

Flying

Flying is a lot like walking, but it's faster and you need thrust (which is provided by the A and Z keys). To enable flying, click the "fly" button on the command bar.

When you fly, you bank, like you're flying on an aircraft. Here's a rundown of the flying commands:

- To point yourself up, down, left, or right, use the corresponding arrow keys, or just hold down the left mouse button and point to where you would like to be headed.
- To give yourself some thrust, press the A key. To reverse the thrust, presss the Z key.
- To revolve counterclockwise, click the Q key. To revolve clockwise, click the E key. To stop spinning, press the W key.
- To automatically fly to an object, hold down the Ctrl key and click the object with the left mouse button.
- To fly faster, hold down the Shift key.
- As with walking, you can open doors or manipulate objects by pressing the Spacebar.

Pointing

Probably the easiest way to get around a virtual world, pointing enables you to go quickly to a point that you click with the mouse. To enable pointing, click the "point" button on the command bar.

When you move by pointing, Live3D initiates an animation sequence that moves you to the point you've clicked. If you drag the mouse, you get the same results that you'd get if you were walking.

I'm lost! Happens fast, doesn't it? To get back quickly to the point where you entered the virtual world, click the Reset button on the command bar.

Using the Pop-Up Menu

If you click the right mouse button anywhere within a virtual world, you'll see Live3D's pop-up menu (Figure 15.2). On this menu you can make additional choices about the way Live3D operates. Here's a quick rundown:

- Click ViewPoints to see whether this virtual world offers predefined viewpoints. Most worlds have an Entry view, which is the same as clicking reset on the command bar.
- Click Navigation to see navigation options. You can choose from Walk, Fly, or Point, which are the same as clicking the corresponding options on the command bar. Additional options on this submenu toggle on such features as playing an animation when you go to a viewpoint, bank when flying, detect collisions with objects or walls, add momentum effects, or add gravitational effects.
- Click Lights to toggle the Headlight on or off (by default, it's on). You can also choose shading and intensity options.
- Click Detail to see image detail options. You can display the image as a solid (the slowest setting), a wireframe, or a point cloud (the fastest setting).
- Click Heads up Display to turn on various navigation aids. You can turn on cross hairs that show where you've clicked and enable navigation help (this is the same as clicking the Help question mark on the command bar).

Figure 15.2 Live3D's pop-up menu

The Best VRML Sites

To see what people are doing with VRML, check out Live3D's What's Cool site, located at http://www.paperinc.com/wrls.html. My favorites:

- **Intel Inside** (http://www.intel.com/procs/ppro/intro/vrml/nav.wrl) Fly into a Pentium Pro microprocessor. When you get right up to the processor's case, you'll see hyperlinks appearing on the wall. Click any of these to see more information on the Pentium Pro microprocessor.
- **ORC's Fractal Landscape** (http://www.ocnus.com/cgi-bin/fracland.wrl.gz) You'll want to fly over this one (Figure 15.3).
- **SoMa** (http://www.hyperion.com/planet9/worlds/vrsoma.wrl) Here's an incredible world that simulates Multimedia Gulch, an area dense with multimedia- and graphics-related firms situated along Howard Street, just south of Market Street (San Francisco's main drag).

Is Virtual Reality Good for Anything?

Good question, and one you well might ask after exploring some of the early virtual worlds on the Web. All in all, they're pretty crude, and downright slow over a SLIP/PPP line. But there are plenty of ways virtual reality in general, and VRML on the Web in particular, may prove of value. Consider these:

- An engineer could design a part and view it from all angles prior to making a physical prototype—and then share the design with engineers located elsewhere in the world.
- An architect could create an interior plan of a major construction project, and make it accessible on the Web so that clients from all over the country could see it.
- A physician could visualize a portion of a patient's body prior to surgery and go deeply within the simulated physique, exploring organs and other structures.

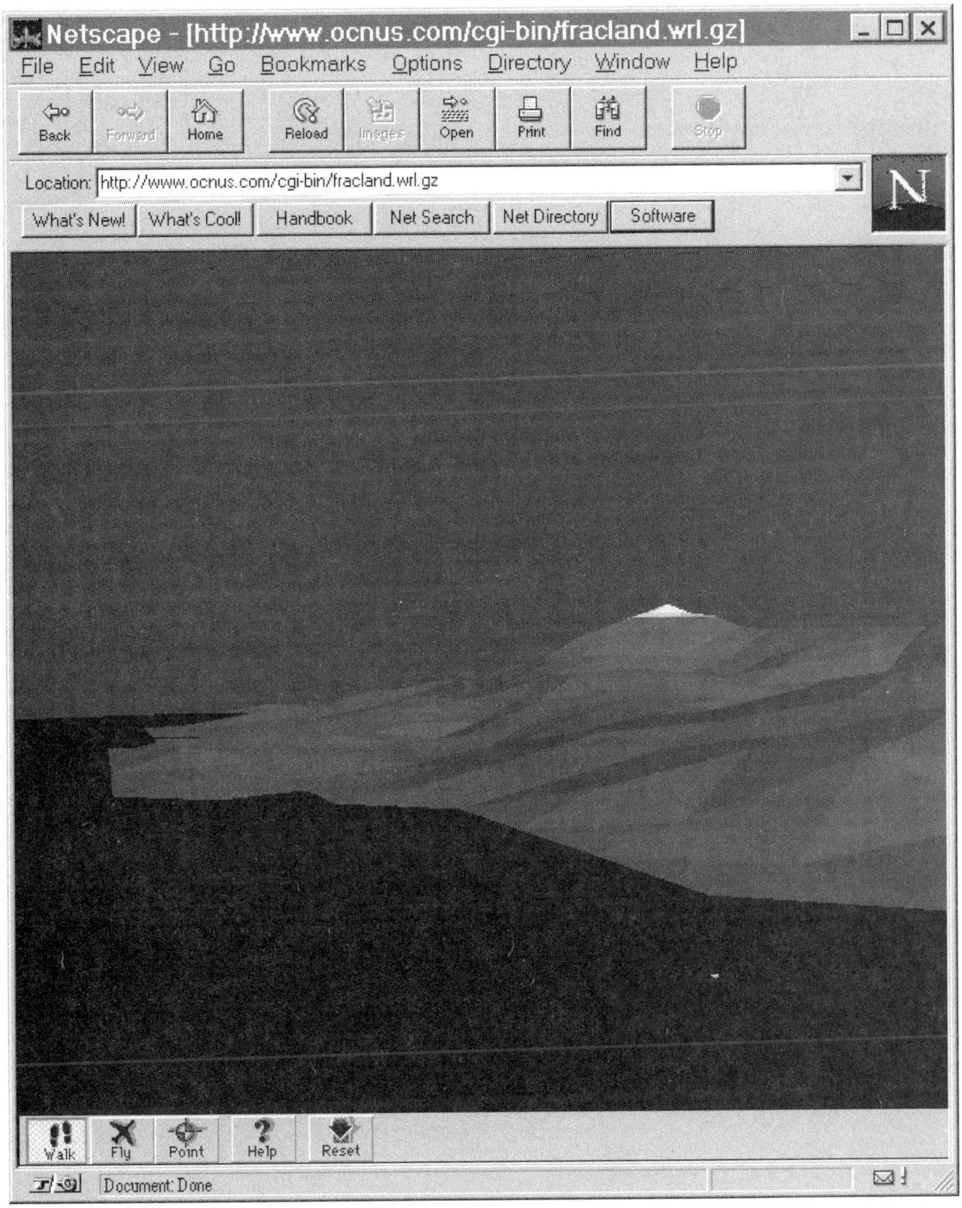

Figure 15.3 ORC's Fractal Landscape

When placed on the Web, virtual worlds experience precisely the same multiplication effects that other Web resources do—that is, they become accessible to far more people, and benefit proportionally from the vastly increased feedback, than applications based on a single, non-networked computer system. If there's really a practical dimension to virtual reality, it will happen on the Web.

From Here

- This chapter concludes this book's survey of Web multimedia. In Part IV, you'll learn how to make full use of the Web's search tools.

Part IV

It's Out There Somewhere!

Finding It on the Web

Chapter 16

Explore the Web!

It's a big Web out there, with several hundred million documents. One thing's for certain: You're going to need help finding information. Surfing alone won't do it.

Fortunately, there are plenty of people who are trying to help. In this chapter and the next, you'll learn how to make full use of Web documents that people have created in an attempt to help you find your way. I call these *trailblazer pages*. They don't attempt to be complete, up to date, or even 100% accurate—those URLs come and go—but they can be invaluable. Chapter 17, on subject trees and search engines, covers Web information resources that *do* try to be comprehensive. But for now, you're looking for good places to launch your exploration of the Web, and this chapter points the way to some very useful resources.

For the Time-Challenged

- Trailblazer pages point the way toward Web information resources.
- Use starting points pages to begin your exploration of the Web.
- Locate metapages in your areas of interest.
- Check out "Best of the Web" pages to see what's cool.
- Use "What's New" pages to keep up with new Web developments.

Don't know how to access the pages discussed in this chapter? Check out HOME.HTM, the home page provided on this book's CD-ROM. It contains all the hyperlinks mentioned in this chapter. Please note that some of the URLs mentioned in this chapter may have joined the dead byte heap of history by the time you read this. Still, I've chosen most of these documents because they appear to be more or less stable, so most of them should be up and running when you read this book.

Introducing Trailblazer Pages

Pioneers, explorers, adventurers, helpful souls—whatever you want to call them, they're the saints of the hour. Often on a purely voluntary basis, they've gathered the best of the Web (and sometimes the weirdest of the Web) into collections of hyperlinks. I divide this fast-evolving class of documents into the following categories:

Starting Points These are Web documents that are intended to help neophytes get started with the World Wide Web. Some are created and maintained by organizations, but the better ones are voluntary efforts by individuals.

Metapages These pages attempt to summarize all the links in a particular subject area. If you can find one in your area of interest, you will find it very helpful.

Most Popular Links	What everyone is accessing, largely because people read pages like this to find out what everyone is accessing.
Best of the Web	What some people (or more likely, one person) think the best sites are—a cyberspace Top Ten.
Cool Links	I'm not sure what the difference between "Best" and "Cool" is, but see for yourself by checking out these pages. Be prepared to waste at least five hours.
Worst of the Web	A relatively new and praiseworthy development, these pages list sites singled out for wasting Internet bandwidth with unnecessary junk (such as a list of some guy's T-shirts).
Weird Links	Compilations of links to the Web underground. Forget sex, incidentally; there are too many dateless geeks out there looking for sex sites. When one appears, it gets inundated with several million accesses per day, which overloads the server and brings the computer to a halt. The service provider screams bloody murder, and the site gets shut down. A Sports Illustrated swimsuit site made a brief appearance, but after getting 7.2 million accesses in the space of 48 hours, it was withdrawn.
What's New	These resources try to keep track of the deluge of new Web documents.

Starting Points Pages

Starting points pages stem from the ancient past (maybe two years ago) when the Web was completely unfamiliar to people. Created by organizations such as the European Center for Particle Physics (CERN) and the National Center for Supercomputing Applications (NCSA), they provide a good point of entry for people accessing the Web for the first time. They include lots of links that introduce you to fundamental Web concepts, such as "What is a browser?" You'll also find links to subject trees, search

engines, Usenet FAQs (Frequently Asked Questions), Internet documents of all kinds, and What's New documents.

The World Wide Web Home Page

Does the Web have a home? Yes—according to CERN, it's located in Geneva, Switzerland. (The acronym CERN, incidentally, stands for the Center's name in French.) This isn't mere arrogance; CERN is actually the birthplace of the Web, which got its start in 1989 as an information system for physics researchers. To access the General Overview of the Web page (Figure 16.1), use this URL:

http://www.w3.org/hypertext/DataSources/Top.html

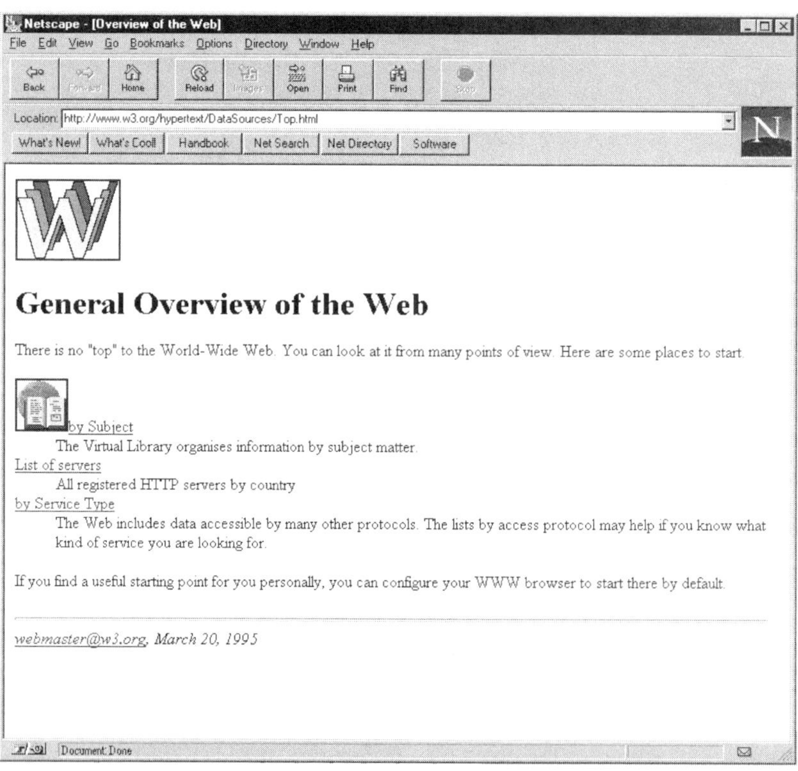

Figure 16.1 The CERN General Overview of the Web page

The CERN home page's main claim to fame is the link to the Virtual Library, discussed in the next chapter. Apart from that, it's a bit of a yawner, although the By Service Type link takes you to a useful list of Internet resources accessible throughout the Web.

National Center for Supercomputing Applications Starting Points Page

The National Center for Supercomputing Applications, located in Urbana-Champaign, Illinois, is the birthplace of Mosaic, the graphical browser that launched the Web into the big time. Its starting points document (Figure 16.2) is still one of the best. What's available here? You'll find a lot of information

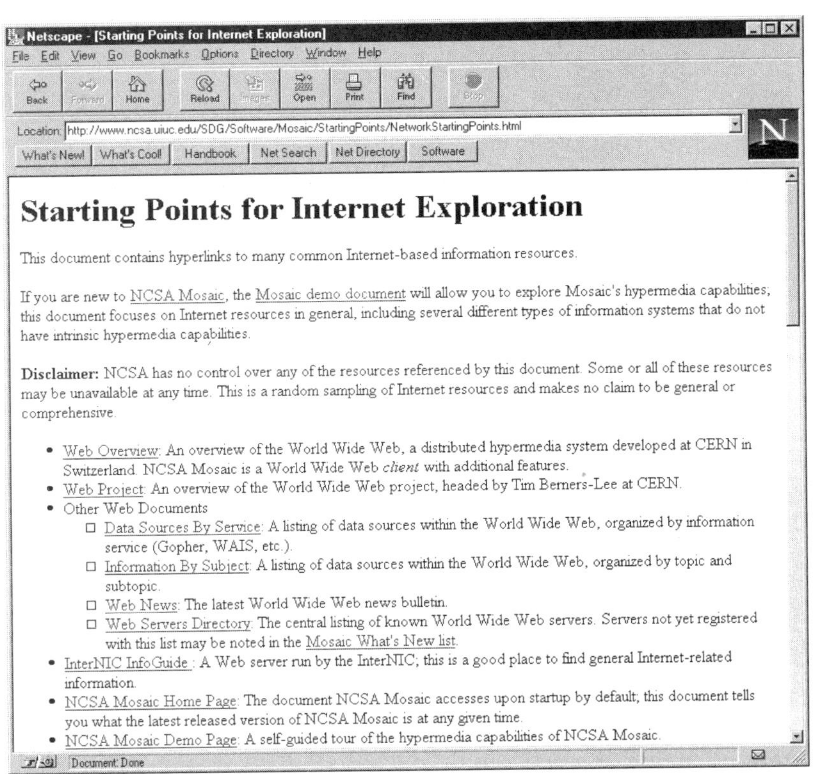

Figure 16.2 The NCSA Starting Points page

Figure 16.3 The Planet Earth Home Page

about the World Wide Web—its history, development, and future. Here's the URL:

> http://www.ncsa.uiuc.edu/SDG/Software/Mosaic/StartingPoints/NetworkStartingPoints.html

The Planet Earth Home Page

The Planet Earth Home Page (PEHP; Figure 16.3) is arguably the Web's best starting point. It's loaded with basic information about the Web and the

Internet, pointers to information resources, and much, much more. Here's the URL:

http://www.nosc.mil/planet_earth/info.html

PEHP is the work of Richard P. Bocker, a physicist at the Naval Command, Control and Ocean Surveillance Center in San Diego, California. PEHP doesn't attempt to provide a comprehensive subject tree, like the ones discussed in thc next chapter. It's just a wonderful place to start your exploration of the Web.

PEHP's offerings are organized into categories, which you select by clicking one of the on-screen buttons. After you do, you'll see additional pages crammed with graphics, URLs, and links to other resource-crammed pages. Explore—and have fun!

When you click one of PEHP's hyperlinks, you may see additional PEHP pages, or you may be transported directly to a distant site. You can also search PEHP by typing one or more words in the Search box and clicking the Search button. If PEHP finds any matches, you'll see a new page listing the documents that contain the words you typed.

John S. Makulowich's Awesome Lists

An Internet trainer, John Makulowich has assembled lists of what he calls "the glory and grandeur of the Internet, the sine qua non of Cyberspace, the main characters in the evolving drama . . .," with special focus on the needs of journalists, trainers, and first-time Web users. Distilled down to the best of the Web, it's an excellent starting points document (Figure 16.4). Here's the URL:

http://www.clark.net/pub/journalism/awesome.html

The Awesome Lists contain lots of very useful URLs, and I'll bet they keep you busy for a while. For a quick tour of the Web, check out the Truly Awesome sites listed at the top of the document.

John's Monster Hotlist

John's Monster Hotlist (Figure 16.5) incorporates an unusual, innovative interface: You click on one of the uppercase headings located at the bottom of the screen, and the pertinent hotlist items appear at the top (in the figure, you're looking at the PERL items). The verdict? Not very artsy, but easy to

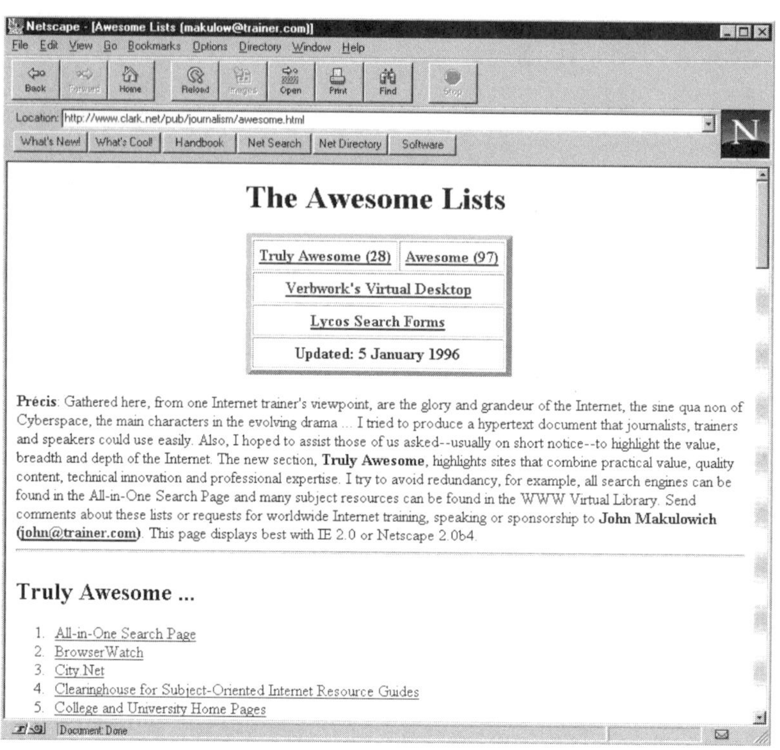

Figure 16.4 John S. Makulowich's Awesome Lists

use and packed with great information, especially about weather and computer networking. Here's the URL:

http://ns.uoregon.edu/~kemp/hotlist/

Internet Points-of-Interest

Maintained by Tony Sanders, this page (Figure 16.6) is what NCSA and CERN should be offering. It's an excellent list of essential introductory hyperlinks, including navigation catalogs, guides, general interest sites (including reference sources, on-line magazines, and Web storefronts), and Internet documentation resources. Here's the URL:

http://www.bsdi.com/points-of-interest.html

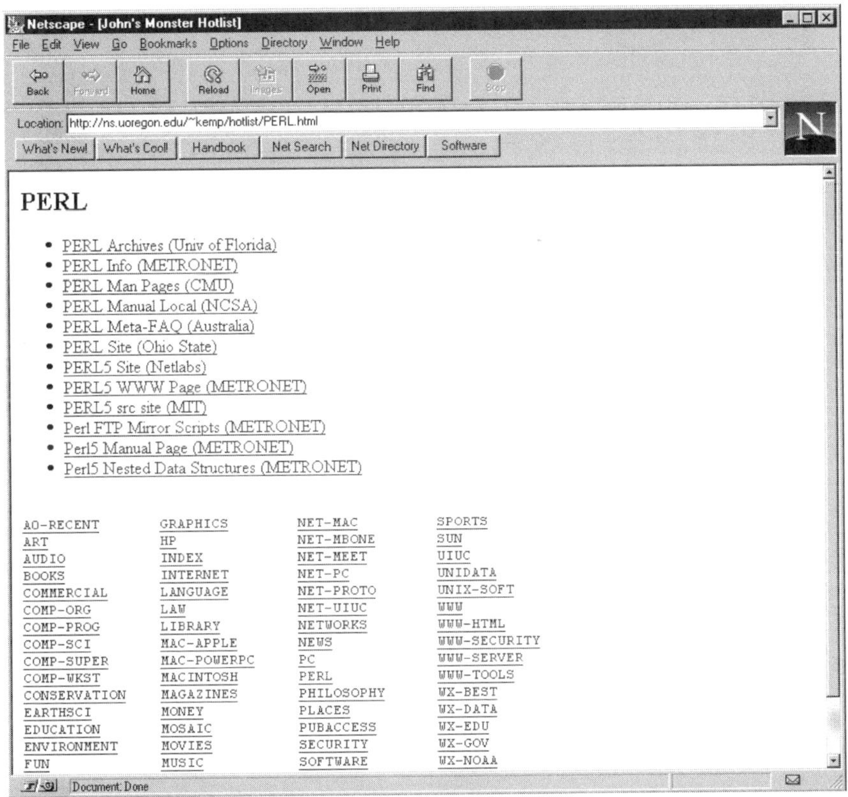

Figure 16.5 John's Monster Hotlist

More Starting Points Documents

Still looking for the perfect starting points document? Here are a few to try:

- **Spry's General Internet Page** (http://www.spry.com:80/internet.html) The home page of Spry, Inc., the makers of Air Mosaic. Lots of links to Internet guides and tutorials, and archives of connectivity software.
- **John December's Internet Index** (http://www.rpi.edu/~decemj/index.html) Lots of useful Internet information focusing on the

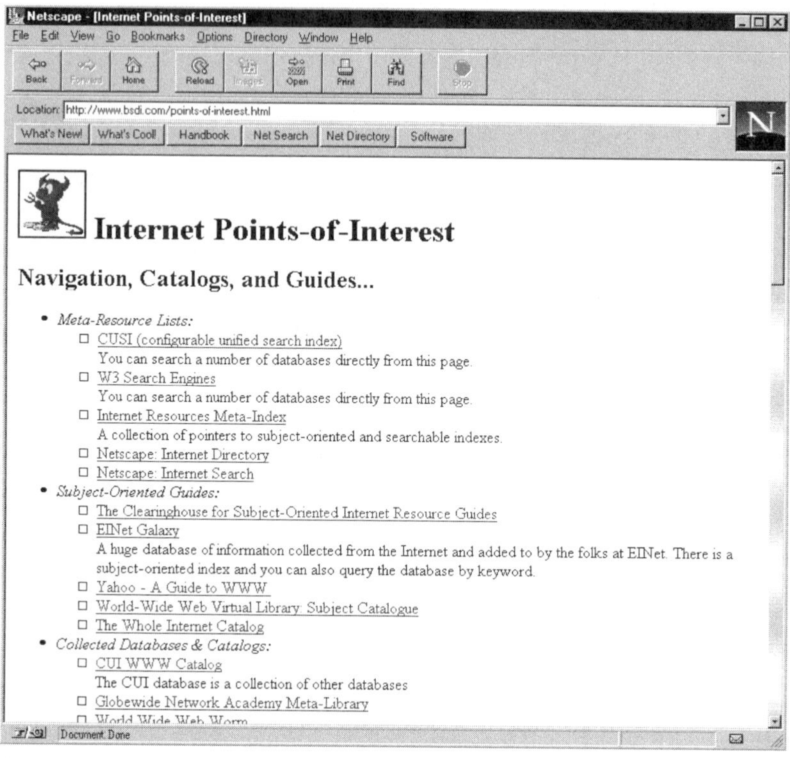

Figure 16.6 Internet Points-of-Interest

analysis of computer-mediated communication. Lots of stuff focusing on John, too.

- **Internet Services List** (http://www.uwm.edu/Mirror/inet.services.html) Scott Yanoff's excellent subject tree listing links for every subject from geophysics to women's issues.
- **WWW Power Index** (http://www.webcom.com/power/index.html) A nice starting points selection: WWW information, pointers to search tools and subject indexes, and links to great sites in fields such as art, government, and education.

As a source of good starting points, don't forget personal home pages, which were introduced in Chapter 4. These are essentially hotlists (bookmark lists) that certain individuals

have made accessible to the public. Here are some more great personal home pages:

- **Bazik** (http://www.cs.brown.edu/people/jsb/hotlist.html) Lots of stuff on commercial sites, random cool things, government sites, and lots, lots more.
- **Cybergrrl** (http://www.cybergrrl.com/title.html) Music, people, good causes, and a link to Grrls on the Web; some great women's/feminist links.
- **Karen** (http://www.cs.cmu.edu/afs/cs.cmu.edu/user/kcf/www/me/newhot.html) Very good entertainment links, plus a collection of cool home pages.
- **Lorrie** (http://dworkin.wustl.edu/pub/lorracks/home.html) Some good stuff on social issues facing the Internet.
- **Meng** (http://www.seas.upenn.edu/~mengwong/meng.html) The single most substantive page on the Web, if she does say so herself.
- **Ranjit** (http://moonmilk.volcano.org/playground.html) Toys for the amusement of travelers on the Information Superhighway.

You clown! You referred me to a home page—you said it was great—and it's not there anymore! That's the chance you take with personal home pages. Unlike companies, which tend to establish permanent Web presences, people move around, establishing pages on one server, then another, then disappearing from the Web altogether. This is especially true of college students, who still have a higher per capita home page count than any other demographic group. You can try using a search engine to search for the person's name, but, odds are, you're out of luck. Sorry.

Metapages

Metapages seek to sum up all the hyperlinks pertaining to a particular subject. Put together by volunteers who have personal interests in the area, they

are gold mines of information. The following list provides some examples of useful metapages. Unfortunately, there's no real index of them; nobody's even sure what to call them (some people call them "home pages," while others call them "pointers pages," and still others call them "indexes"). You can try to discover a metapage in your area of interest by using the search techniques introduced in the next chapter.

- **Backcountry Home Page** (http://io.datasys.swri.edu/Overview.html) Fishing, hiking, backpacking, climbing—and the "distilled wisdom" of the experts.
- **Chronic Fatigue Syndrome** (http://metro.turnpike.net/C/cfs-news/) Tons of information about this disabling disease.
- **FedWorld** (http://www.fedworld.gov/) A very impressive list of U.S. government Web resources.
- **Games Domain** (http://www.gamesdomain.co.uk/) Everything you would ever want to know about computer games.
- **Human Languages Page** (http://www.willamette.edu/~tjones/Language-Page.html) A treasure trove of information about human languages, past and present.
- **Legal Links on the Internet** (http://ssnet.com/~james5/business.html) Emphasizing federal law and litigation.
- **Rockhounds Information Page** (http://www.rahul.net/infodyn/rockhounds/rockhounds.html) Everything on the Internet pertaining to rock collecting, including links to rock shops and photos of cool rock formations.
- **Science Fiction Links** (http://www.abdn.ac.uk/~u01rpr/sci-fi.html) Tons of links to *Star Trek*, *Star Wars*, and science fiction sites.
- **Television Sites** (http://www.gu.edu.au/gwis/cinemedia/CineMedia.tv.html) Grand Central Station for TV-related hyperlinks on the Web.
- **The Froggy Page** (http://www.cs.yale.edu/HTML/YALE/CS/HyPlans/loosemore-sandra/froggy.html) An unbelievable assortment of frog-related items: pictures, songs, sounds, links to scientific studies, lists of famous frogs. Wow!

- **The Web as a Learning Tool** (http://www.cs.uidaho.edu/~connie/interests.html) A very nice effort to bring together Web resources for K–12 education.
- **Ultimate Band List** (http://american.recordings.com/wwwofmusic/) Links to all the rock bands—over 1200 of them, from the 3D House of Beef and Cling to Trendy Wednesday and Weeping Tile—represented on the Web. There are some bands you've heard of here, too, somewhere.
- **Wine Home Page** (http://www.speakeasy.org/~winepage/wine.html) Dozens of links concerning wines, wineries, wine collecting, and wine accessories.
- **WWW Tennis Server** (http://www.cs.utoronto.ca/~cwong/tennis/tennis.html) Get the pun? Everything for the tennis fan, including ATP and WTA rankings, the code of tennis, and lots of tennis-related hyperlinks.

By far the best resource for subject-oriented metapages is the Virtual Library, a subject tree that is actually a compilation of volunteers' metapages. For more information on the Virtual Library, check out the next chapter.

What's Popular

Want to know what everyone else is doing with their Web browsers? Here's how to find out:

- **Most Popular Links at EINet Galaxy** (http://galaxy.einet.net/most-popular.html) EINet Galaxy is a subject tree/search engine hybrid. This page links the most popular sites directly accessed from Galaxy.
- **The WebCrawler Top 25** (http://webcrawler.com/WebCrawler/Top25.html) The top 25 most popular pages accessed by means of the WebCrawler search engine, discussed in Chapter 17.
- **The Whole Internet Catalog Top 25** (http://gnn.com/wic/wics/top.new.html) The most popular sites in the Whole Internet Catalog's subject tree (discussed in Chapter 17).

- **Yahoo What's Popular** (http://www.yahoo.com/popular.html) The most popular sites accessed from the Yahoo subject tree, also discussed in Chapter 17.

Best of the Web

What are the best sites available on the Web? Everyone has an opinion, but some have pages:

- **High Five** (http://www.highfive.com/index2.html) "The Carnegie Hall of Web Sites."
- **Best of the British Web Page** (http://www.vnu.co.uk/hc/pcw/bob.htm) Best sites in the U.K.
- **Best Webs of the World** (http://www.sct.fr/net/ubest.html) A French view, and a nice, succinct list.

Cool Links

Frankly, I'm not sure what differentiates a "best" site from a "cool" site. You figure it out, and e-mail me (bp@virginia.edu), and I'll give you credit in the next edition. In the meantime, you're going to enjoy these pages:

- **Cool Site of the Day** (http://cool.infi.net/) Glenn Davis selects a new site every day for this coveted distinction. You can browse a voluminous list of previous cool sites.
- **What's Cool** (http://home.netscape.com/home/whats-cool.html) At least according to Netscape. I think this is verging on the "Best of the Web" territory. Or maybe it's a gallery of Netscape's business partners?
- **Yahoo Cool Links** (http://www.yahoo.com/Entertainment/COOL_links/) Definitely cool.
- **What's Hot and Cool on the Web** (http://kzsu.stanford.edu/uwi/reviews-l.html) A collection of cool sites, organized in a somewhat hard-to-figure-out table.

Worst of the Web

It had to happen. With all those "Best of the Web" pages, somebody, somewhere, would have had to come up with this idea.

- **Mirsky's Worst of the Web** (http://turnpike.net/metro/mirsky/Worst.html) This is the *worst* worst Web site.
- **Useless Web Pages** (http://www.primus.com/staff/paulp/useless.html) This is actually onc of the Web's best sites. With additions made on a daily basis, you'll find plenty of hysterically funny stuff here. Latest editions: A penis length chart, a dissertation on barbecue potato chips, and a shocking exposé of the lesbian Barbie doll scene.
- **Enhanced for Netscape Hall of Shame** (http://www.meat.com/netscape_hos.html) Too many blinks spoil the broth.

Weird Links

It's the fringe. The edge. And if you're looking for it, here are the starting points:

- **Anders' Weird Page** (http://www.nada.kth.se/~nv91-asa/weird.html) Discordiana, very substantial collection of links to the Church of the Subgenius, Geek-related mysteries, and more; you figure it out, you let me know, OK?
- **The Web's Edge** (http://kzsu.stanford.edu/uwi.html) This is apparently the leading edge of some kind of worldwide conspiracy.

What's New Pages

As if there weren't enough stuff on the Web to wade through, there are dozens—possibly hundreds—of new Web documents created daily. Here's how you can find out what's new:

- **Automatic News HREFs** (http://www.cs.cmu.edu/afs/cs.cmu.edu/user/bsy/www/auto_news/auto_news.0.html) URLs culled automatically from Usenet postings.

- **Global Network Navigator What's New** (http://gnn.com/wic/wics/nunu.new.html) GNN is a subject tree, to be discussed in the next chapter; this page lists the links that have been added recently to the subject index.
- **NCSA's What's New** (http://www.ncsa.uiuc.edu/SDG/Software/Mosaic/Docs/whats-new.html) Probably the best What's New resource. Includes a Pick of the Week.
- **What's New** (http://home.netscape.com/home/whats-new.html) Netscape's own list. Just click the "What's New" button on Netscape's button bar.

From Here

- Take advantage of subject trees and search engines to find information on the Web. Both subjects are covered in Chapter 17.
- Manage those Web documents—print 'em, save 'em, and cache 'em. Find out how (and what cache means) in Chapter 8.
- Put those helper applications to work! Chapter 10 documents all the multimedia helper applications included with this book.

Chapter 17

Find It on the Web!

Search Engines and Subject Trees

Looking for information on the Web? Let's start with the bad news. No single, up-to-date catalog of Web documents has ever been created. To do so would require a staff of hundreds of subject indexers working 'round the clock. Perhaps we'll see a Web Library someday, a service that would exhaustively catalog everything that's on the Web, but nothing like it exists right now.

Now here's the good news. To find information on the Web, you can make use of the following tools:

- **Subject Trees** A subject tree is an alphabetically organized list of selected Web resources that is usually organized with major headings such as Arts and Humanities, Business, Economy, Government, and the like. Within each category are found subheadings, which in turn

display pages listing specific hyperlinks. Because subject trees are manually updated, they cannot hope to cover all of the Web—these services aren't the Web Library, or anything close. But they are very useful because they are selective; they list only those documents that would likely prove useful to you.

- **Search Engines** A search engine enables you to search a database of Web documents using keywords (such as "frogs" or "wine"). The search engine ransacks a database of Web documents. Where does this database come from? In most cases, the databases are created by Web-roaming programs called *spiders*. These programs seek out new URLs and add them to the database. Searching one of these search engines will very likely produce a lot of useless, junk URLs, but you may find some gold amidst the gravel.

This chapter shows you how to construct an effective Web search using Netscape, subject trees, and search engines. If it's out there, you'll know how to find it after reading this chapter. You should use the information in this chapter with that in Chapter 16, which discusses trailblazer pages, metapages, and other subject-specific Web resources.

Understanding Search Techniques

In both subject trees and search engines, you can make use of keyword searches. In subject trees, you search the subject tree entries. In search engines, you search a huge database of URLs. In either case, you will find it helpful to understand a few basic concepts:

- **Choosing Keywords** Try to think of one or more words that best describe the subject you're searching for. The more general the term, the more likely it is that you'll find something useful.
- **Choosing Portions of the Document to Search** Some of the search tools discussed in this chapter let you specify which part of the document to search. For example, Yahoo enables you to search the document title, the URL, and the document description. It searches all three by default. You can perform a more focused search by restricting the search to the document title. This will eliminate irrelevant documents that just happen to include the keyword in their descriptions.

For the Time-Challenged

- ♦ Subject trees try to classify Web documents according to subject. You can browse the subject tree. You can also search the subject headings and document titles. But bear in mind that subject trees classify only a small percentage of the total number of documents available on the Web.
- ♦ Search engines compile huge databases of Web documents, and you can search the databases using keywords. The trouble is, you'll retrieve a lot of junk amidst the useful documents.
- ♦ A good search strategy uses both subject trees and search engines. To make sure you've found all the useful documents in a given subject area, you should repeat your search in several subject trees and search engines.

- **Case Sensitivity** Most of the search tools discussed in this chapter are case-insensitive, which means that they ignore the capitalization pattern you type. However, some offer the option of case-sensitive searching. If you choose this option, the search tool will match only those documents containing keywords with the capitalization pattern you typed (if you type "MRI," the software will match "MRI" but not "mri").
- **AND Operator** Most of the search tools you use will use the Boolean AND operator by default. If you type more than one key word, the software will not retrieve a document unless it contains all of the words you type. This is a very restrictive search and may not produce good results. However, it's a good approach when your initial search produces too many documents.
- **OR Operator** Some search tools enable you to use the Boolean OR operator. If you type more than one keyword, the software will retrieve documents that contain any of the words you typed.
- **Contiguous Strings** A few search tools let you specify that the software should match the keywords you type only if they occur in the precise order you typed them, with no other words in between. For example, if you type "Mesoamerican archaeology," the software

will retrieve only those documents that contain these two words in this exact order, without any other words between them.

- **Substrings and Whole-Word Searches** By default, most of the search tools discussed in this chapter search for substrings. A substring is a series of characters that might be embedded in a longer word. For example, if you search with the substring *very*, the software will retrieve documents that contain *every* as well as *very*. To restrict the search to whole words only (*very* only), you can sometimes choose a "whole word" or "complete word" option. If you choose this option, the search software will not retrieve documents in which the keyword appears as a substring.

If the search doesn't produce any results, click the Back button to redisplay the search page, and check your spelling! This is the most common cause of search errors. If the search retrieves too many documents, try using more specific keywords—and be sure to use the AND rather than the OR operator. To cut down on false drops, use whole-word searches instead of substring searches.

A Guide to the Web's Subject Trees

There are several excellent subject trees available on the World Wide Web. Each has its own plusses and minuses, as you'll see in the pages to follow. We'll survey the top three: Yahoo, the Virtual Library, and the Whole Internet Catalog.

Yahoo

Yahoo—short for Yet Another Hierarchically Odiferous Oracle—is the work of David Filo and Jerry Yang, two Stanford University graduate students who abandoned their Ph.D. work to make their subject tree the centerpiece of a private company. It's the best place to start your quest for Web information.

To access Yahoo, just click the Net Directory button and click the Yahoo hyperlink, or enter the URL (http://www.yahoo.com/) directly. You'll see the Yahoo page, shown in Figure 17.1. Listed are Yahoo's main subject classifications, followed by the number of hyperlinks in each category. The word "new" signals categories to which new hyperlinks have been added.

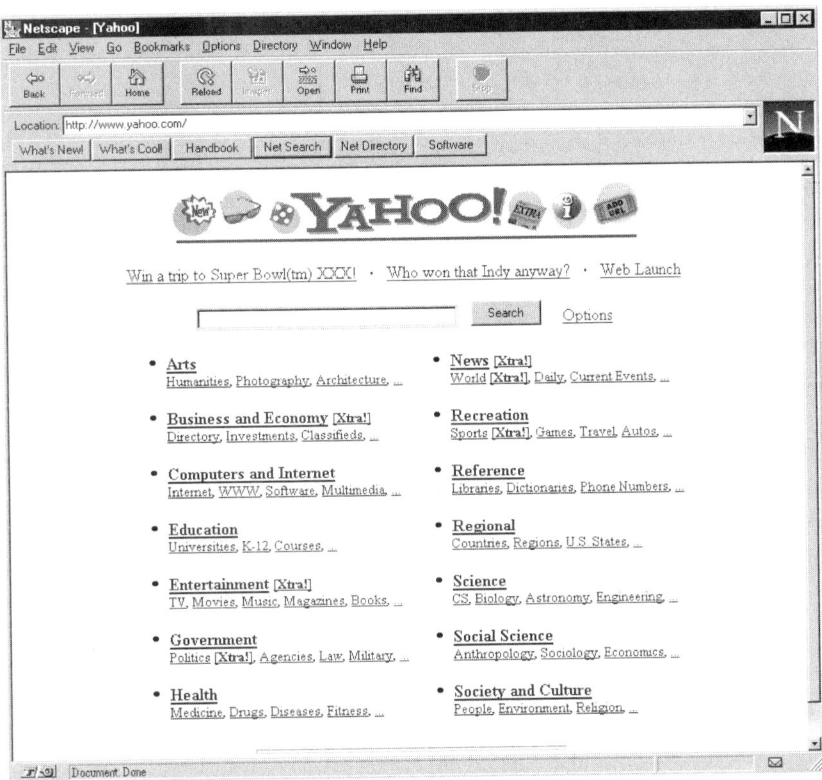

Figure 17.1 The main Yahoo page

What's up with all these academic sites becoming private companies? The Web started as an academic phenomenon—and then the general public caught on. It makes sense that the best academic resources break free of their academic incubators and make a go at it in the private sector, and that's what's happening. All the major academic search tools, including Lycos and WebCrawler, have "gone .com," and other resources are doing the same with regularity. It's part of the trend toward privatization on the Web.

Listing over 34,000 documents (at this writing), Yahoo offers a rich library of hyperlinks. To explore them, you can use two techniques, exploring the tree and searching.

Exploring the Tree The first way to use Yahoo is to navigate the subject tree by clicking on hyperlinks. To do so, just click on one of the subject classifications, such as "News." You'll see an additional page of hyperlinks, such as the one shown in Figure 17.2. If you keep clicking, you'll eventually reach a page that includes hyperlinks to Web documents. Unlike Yahoo's internal links, hyperlinks to Web documents aren't followed by a number, and many of them include descriptions (see Figure 17.3). To access a hyperlink to a Web document, just click it.

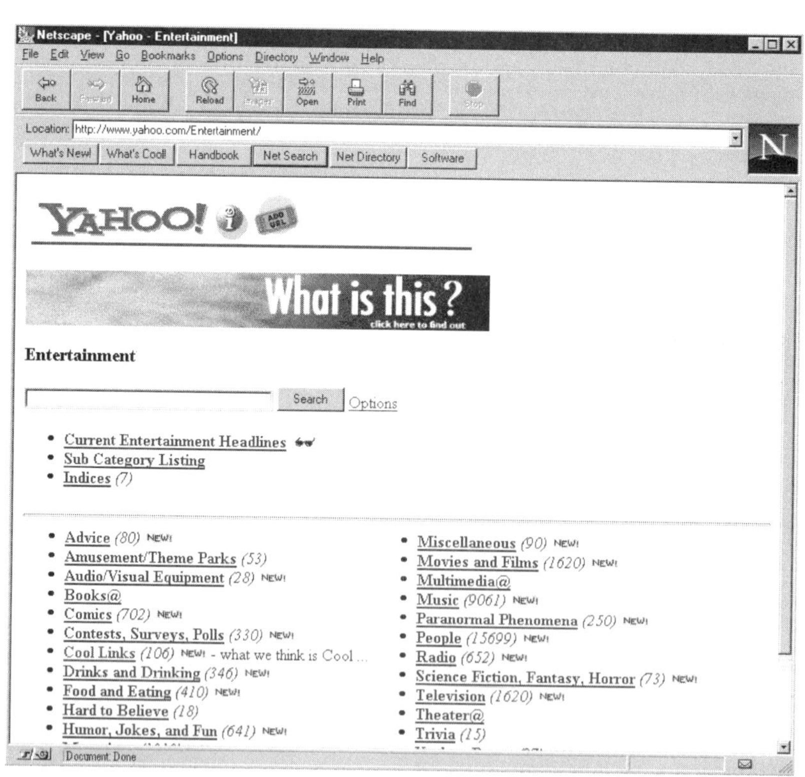

Figure 17.2 A page of hyperlinks in Yahoo

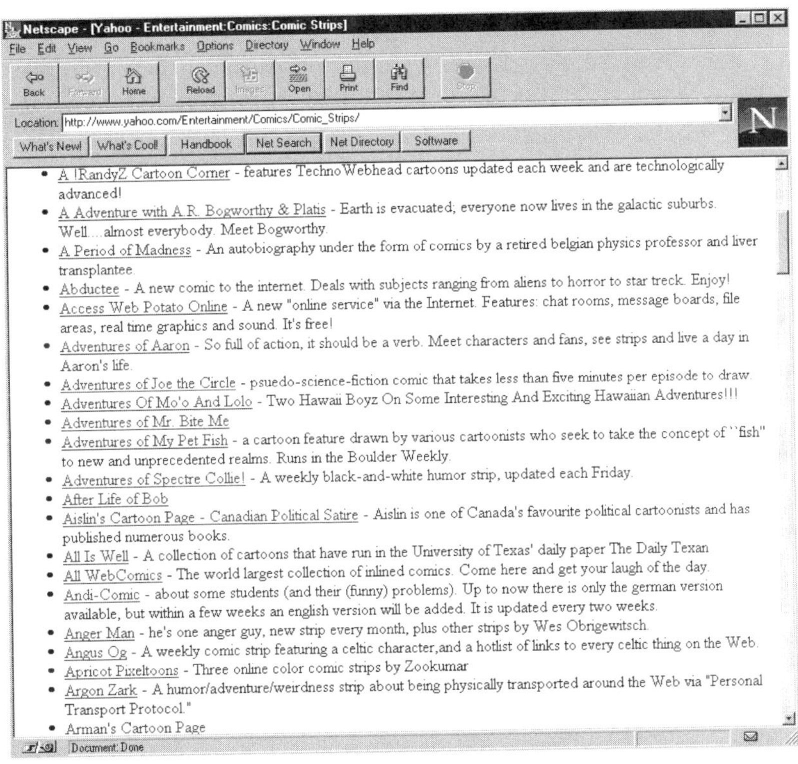

Figure 17.3 Descriptions of sites in Yahoo

Look for hyperlinks that have a picture of a little pair of sunglasses next to them. These are the cool links—the ones that Yahoo recommends!

Yahoo's toolbar, positioned near the top of the screen, provides handy navigational aids. Here's what the options do:

YAHOO! Displays Yahoo's opening (top-level) page.

Displays the What's New At Yahoo page—the most recently added links.

 Takes you to The Cool Links page.

 Takes you to a random Web site—I ended up at the University of Toledo.

 Brings up Yahoo's Reuters news feed.

 Displays the Yahoo Information and Help page.

 Lets you suggest a URL to add to Yahoo.

Searching for Information Another way to access the information in Yahoo is to perform a keyword search. To do so, go back to the Yahoo welcome page. You'll see a text box for entering keywords at the top of the page. That's a pretty basic search. If you need a more flexible search, click the Options hyperlink to the right of the search box. You'll see a complete search page, as shown in Figure 17.4. The instructions explain how to use the expanded search page you see after clicking the options hyperlink.

Yahoo offers excellent search capabilities, allowing all of the search options discussed in "Understanding Search Techniques," earlier in this chapter. To search Yahoo, follow these steps:

1. You should see the Yahoo search box on every Yahoo index page. If you don't see it—if, for example, you're looking at the Information page—click the large "Yahoo" at the top of your screen. To the right of the search box is the Options hyperlink. Click it to bring up the complete search page.
2. In the text box, type one or more keywords. Check your typing and spelling carefully.
3. If you would like to restrict the search to the area of Yahoo from which you entered the search facility, click the lower radio button. By default, Yahoo searches its entire subject tree.
4. To perform a Boolean search, click the OR or AND button.
5. To perform a contiguous string search, click Substrings.

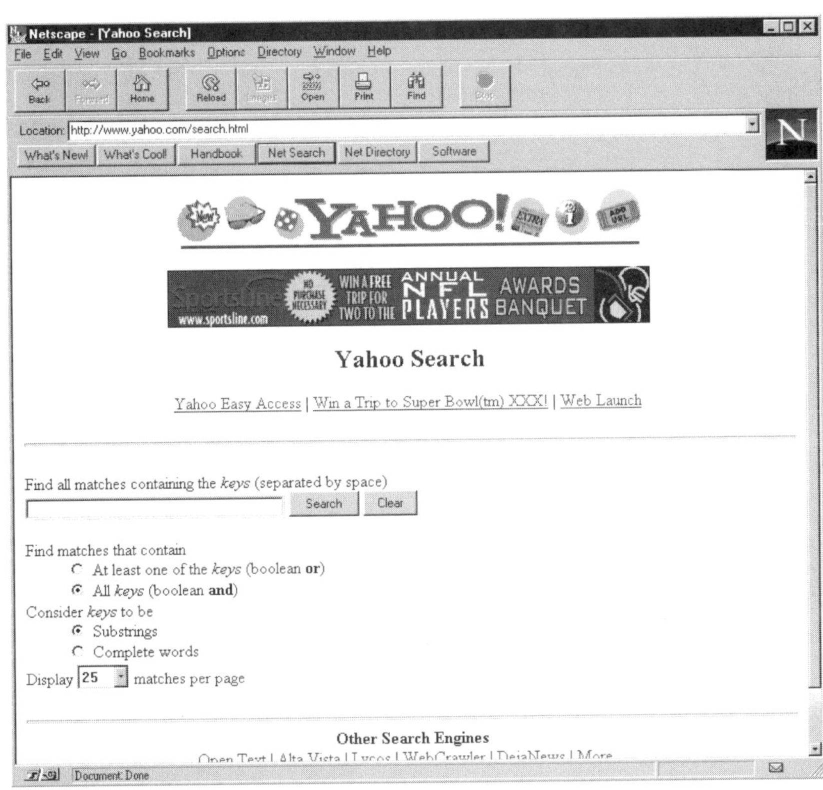

Figure 17.4 The Yahoo search page

6. To perform a whole-word search, click Complete words.
7. To specify the number of matches, choose a number next to Limit the number of matches.
8. To start the search, click Search.

The result of a Yahoo search is a list of Yahoo entries that match your keywords (Figure 17.5)—or, if there aren't any matches, a message that no match was found. You can browse the list and click the links as you please. To redo the search, click the Back button. Click the Clear button to clear the previous search and try again.

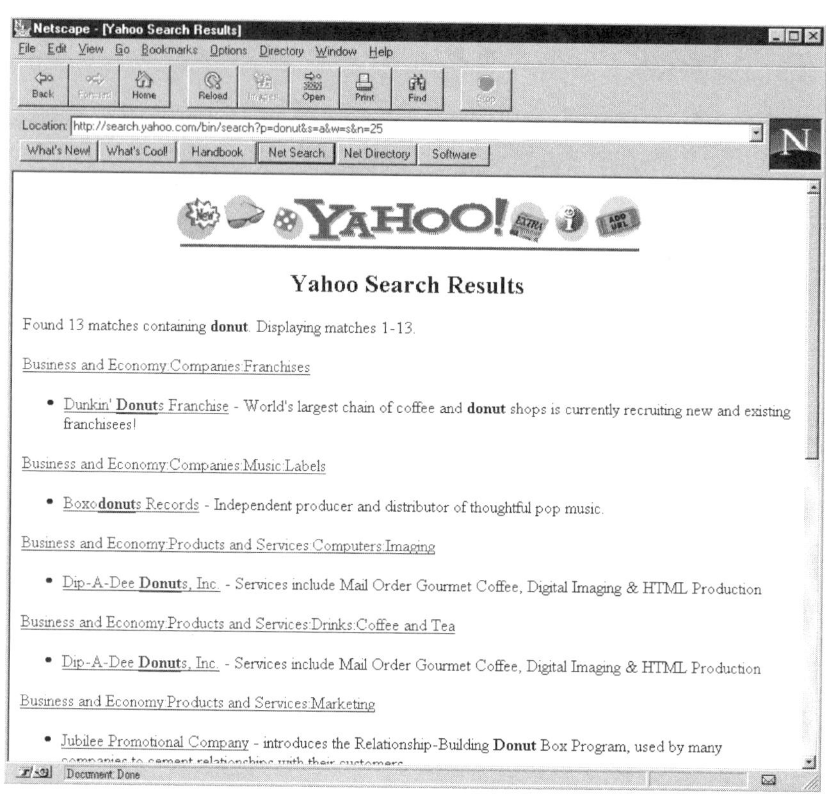

Figure 17.5 The results of a Yahoo search

The Virtual Library

CERN, a center for particle physics research located in Geneva, Switzerland, is the birthplace of the Web. Among its many contributions to the Web is the Virtual Library, one of the first subject trees to be developed and still one of the most useful and comprehensive. The Virtual Library, in order to allow CERN to focus on high-energy physics, is now maintained by the W3 Consortium.

Unlike Yahoo, whose administrators take upon themselves the arduous task of adding new URLs to the subject tree, the Virtual Library is a *distributed subject tree*. This means that the responsibility for maintaining the pages is distributed among individuals, each of whom possesses expertise in their area.

The Virtual Library's links (Figure 17.6) point to pages maintained by these individuals, who have been chosen to maintain only the page for which they are responsible.

Many of the Virtual Library's pages got their start as metapages. They were incorporated into the Virtual Library after it became obvious that they had succeeded in achieving the most comprehensive collection of links in a given area.

You can browse the list of subject headings in numerous ways. The default list is more compact and somewhat easier to browse. If you click the Category Subtree hyperlink, you see a lengthier list of subject headings and subheadings. The Category Subtree gives you more of a sense of the riches stored within the Virtual Library's hyperlinks. In addition, you can display the subject headings according to Library of Congress subject classifications

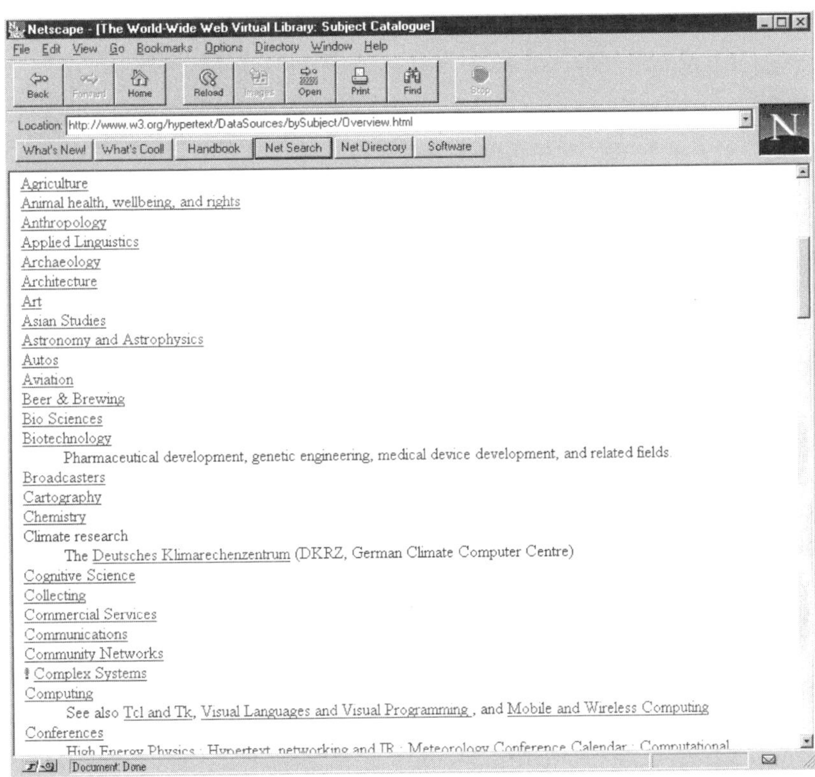

Figure 17.6 Virtual Library links

(to do so, click the Library of Congress Classification hyperlink). Alternative listings include Statistics, which orders subject fields according to their popularity, and Service Type, which orders the Library's resources by type of service (Web servers, Gopher, WAIS databases, etc.).

To access the Virtual Library, just click the Virtual Library icon in this book's home page (HOME.HTM), or use the following URL:

http://www.w3.org/hypertext/DataSources/bySubject/Overview.html

To access one of the pages in the Virtual Library, just click one of the subject hyperlinks. Figure 17.7 shows the African Studies page, which is maintained by the Schomburg Center for Research in Black Culture at the New York Public Library.

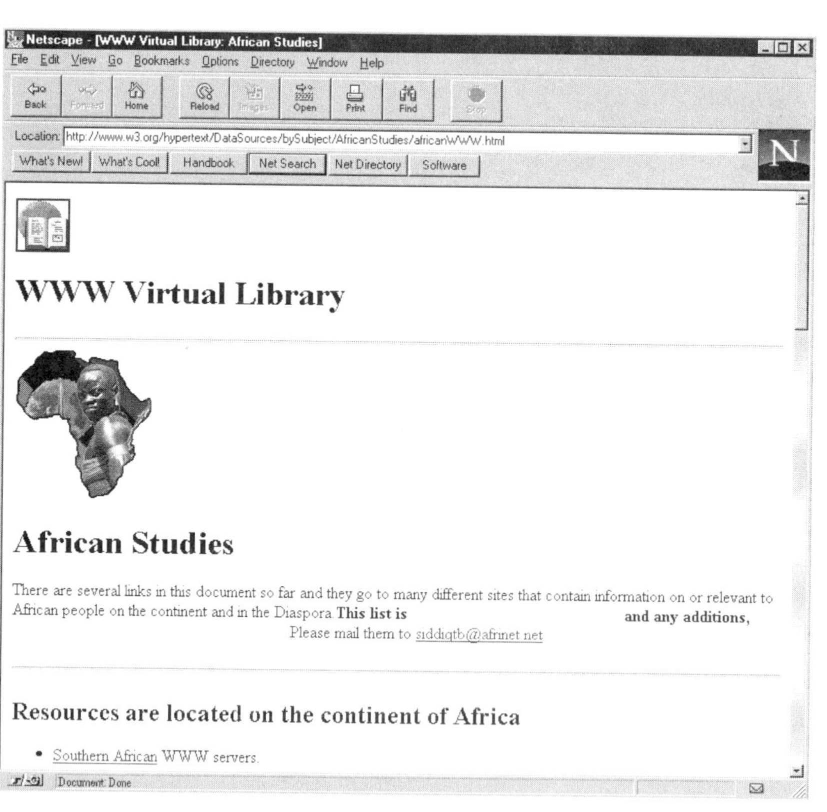

Figure 17.7 The Virtual Library African Studies page

Like Yahoo, the Virtual Library can be searched, but the search is far more comprehensive: It searches not only the Virtual Library but also the entire CUI W3 Catalog, a huge database that is automatically compiled by searching a number of What's New pages (see Chapter 16).

To search the Virtual Library, follow these steps:

1. From the Virtual Library top-level page, click the Index hyperlink. You'll see the CUI W3 Catalog search page, shown in Figure 17.8.
2. In the text box, type the keyword or words to search for. By default, this search page is case-insensitive. If you enter more than

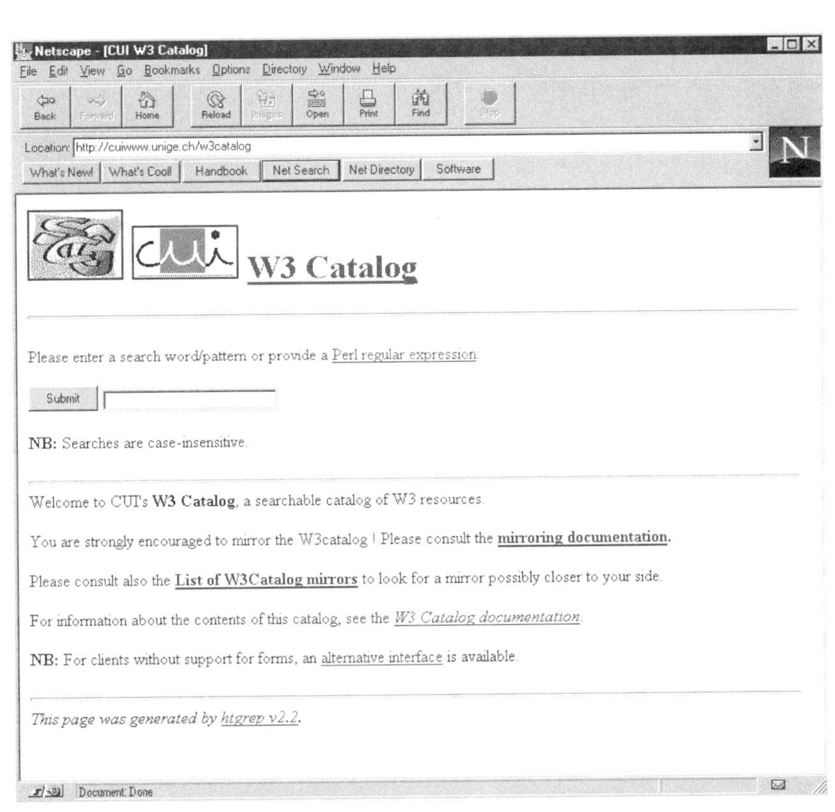

Figure 17.8 The CUI W3 Catalog search page

one word, the search employs a Boolean AND (no document will be retrieved unless it contains all of the words you typed).

3. Click the Search button. You'll see a list containing What's New and other items (see Figure 17.9 for the results of a search for "UNIX").

It says, "Enter a Perl regular expression!" What's Perl? You will frequently see this prompt when you are about to type keywords for searching. Perl is short for Practical Extraction

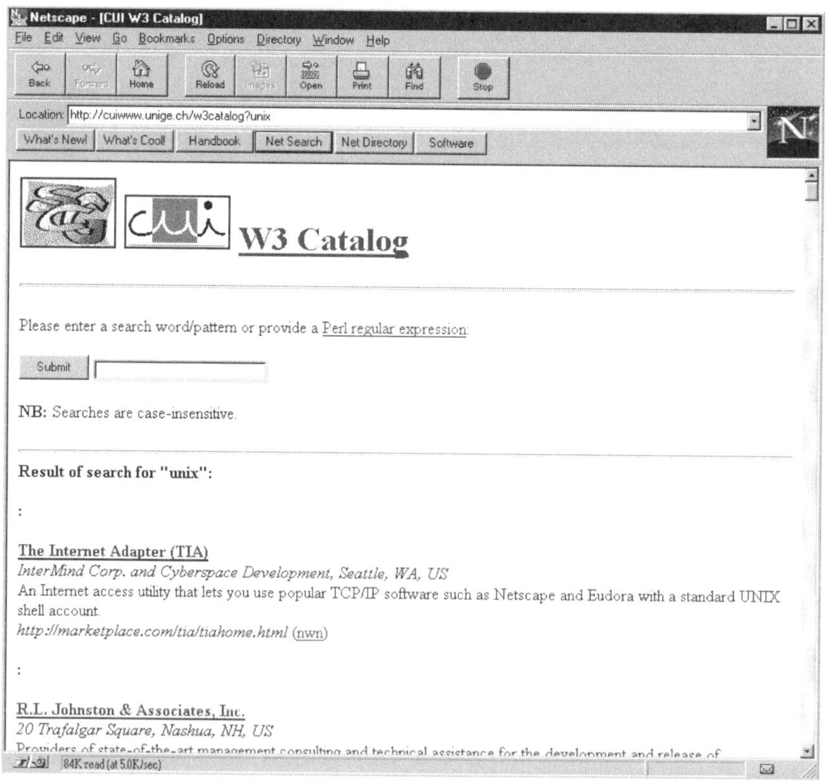

Figure 17.9 The results of a Virtual Library search

and Report Language. Developed by Larry Wall of Netlabs, it is a freely available scripting language for use on many different kinds of computers. When you see this message, you can just type a search word, as you would normally. But Perl also enables you to perform powerful searches by entering a valid Perl expression. For more information, see

http://www.lpac.ac.uk/SEL-HPC/Articles/PerlRegexp.html

The Whole Internet Catalog

One of the most impressive publishing phenomena of the 1990s was the success of Ed Krol's *The Whole Internet*, published by O'Reilly & Associates. Formerly a sleepy, strictly low-volume publisher of obscure books on obscure UNIX topics, O'Reilly hit the jackpot with Krol's excellent book. The revenue led to all sorts of ventures, and the Whole Internet Catalog—based on the useful appendix included in Krol's book—is one of them (Table 17.1). Now there's an on-line version (Figure 17.10), and you'll certainly want to make it part of your document-hunting strategy.

Like Yahoo, the Whole Internet Catalog is maintained manually, but the Catalog's staff doesn't even try to put in thousands of links. On the boundary between a starting points resource and a subject tree, the Catalog offers only about 2,000 links—but they're good links.

To access the Whole Internet Catalog, just click the hyperlink in HOME.HTM, or use this URL:

http://nearnet.gnn.com/gnn/wic/wics/

Table 17.1 Whole Internet Catalog Subject Classifications

Arts & Entertainment	Humanities & Social Sciences
Business	Internet
Computers	Life & Culture
Daily News	Personal Finance
Education	Recreation & Sports
Government & Politics	Science & Technology
Health & Medicine	Travel

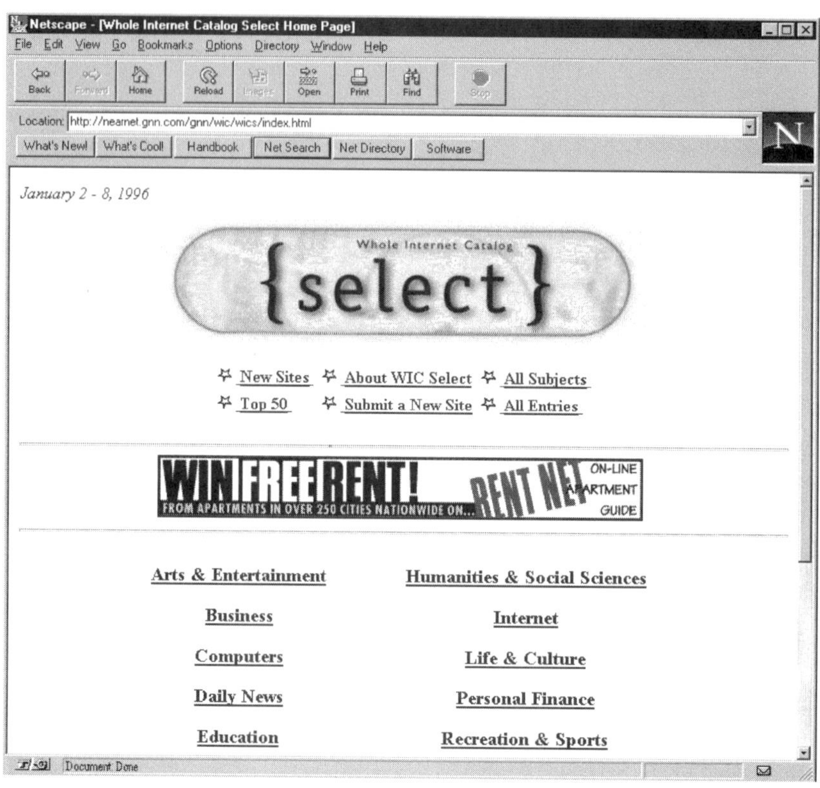

Figure 17.10 The Whole Internet Catalog welcome page

To access one of the Catalog's subject pages, just click the hyperlink. You'll see a page such as the one shown in Figure 17.11.

Watch out for those "INDEX" tags next to items in the Catalog's lists. They're what we call metapages—comprehensive collections of hyperlinks on a subject. You'll find these metapages incredibly useful for finding high-quality documents!

Search Engines

With more than two million documents on the Web and hundreds more arriving daily, there's no chance that Yahoo, the Virtual Library, or the

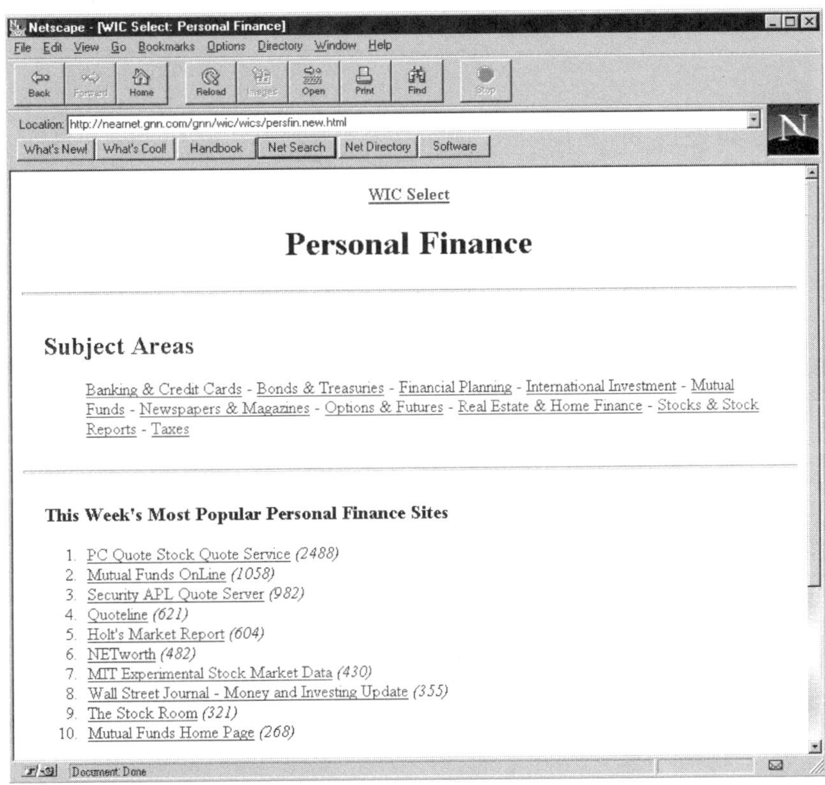

Figure 17.11 A Whole Internet Catalog subject page

Whole Internet Catalog can keep up. That's why your search strategy should include search engines.

Most search engines are based on robot-like programs called spiders (also called worms), which roam the Web looking for new URLs. Most of them do little more than catalog the words in the URL and the document's title and move on. Some spiders index the first few dozen words in the document itself, and a few index all the words in the entire document.

There's a tradeoff here. If the spider indexes only the title and words in the URL, it can index a lot of documents—the search goes quickly. But don't expect good results from your search. Web authors don't give much thought to their document titles, unfortunately, and URL words may have little or nothing to do with the document's content. Searching the database

created by such a spider is sure to produce a lot of false drops, documents that aren't relevant to your interests. On the other hand, if the spider indexes the full text of the document, don't expect the database to include more than a few hundred thousand documents—the search takes a long time. However, searching the database produces better results. Now that you know about this tradeoff, you can make a more informed choice among the various search engines that are available.

Alta Vista

A service of Digital Equipment Corporation, Alta Vista indexes the full text of more than 16 million Web pages at this writing. It's the newest major-league Web search engine, and it's one of the best, too.

To access Alta Vista, click the hyperlink on HOME.HTM, or use this URL:

http://altavista.digital.com/

Alta Vista offers one of the most customizable search interfaces out there. Here are some useful tips for Alta Vista searches:

- Putting words in quotes requires that the search engine find those words together, in sequence. A search for "scientific calculator," for example, would not return a site containing the words "scientific graphing calculator."
- The plus symbol means AND; the minus sign means AND NOT. For example, a search for "cleveland+ohio-columbus" (without the quotes) would return sites containing "cleveland" and "ohio," but not "columbus."
- Use the asterisk as a wildcard. A search for "fly" would return sites containing that word by itself; a search for "*fly*" would return "flypaper," "flygirl," and "barfly."
- Use the modifier "title:" to specify words that must appear in a document's title. "title:Jones" would return sites with "Jones" in the title.

You'll see the Alta Vista welcome page and search form, shown in Figure 17.12.

To search Alta Vista:

1. In the large text box at the top of the page, type your search terms.
2. Tell Alta Vista to search either Web documents or Usenet news by selecting an option from the list box.
3. Opt for Standard, Compact, or Detailed (long) site descriptions.
4. Click the Search button.

Figure 17.12 The Alta Vista search form

You'll see the results of your search on a new page, like the one shown in Figure 17.13. If you selected Standard output, the title of the site, hyperlinked to the site itself, appears at the top of its description. The URL, also hyperlinked to the site, appears at the bottom.

There's an advanced search form at Alta Vista, too. Access it by clicking the Advanced Query button on the toolbar on the Alta Vista welcome page. The Advanced Query form appears in Figure 17.14.

The advanced search form lets you construct searches with the Boolean operators AND, OR, NOT, and NEAR. NEAR specifics that one word must be within 10 words of another.

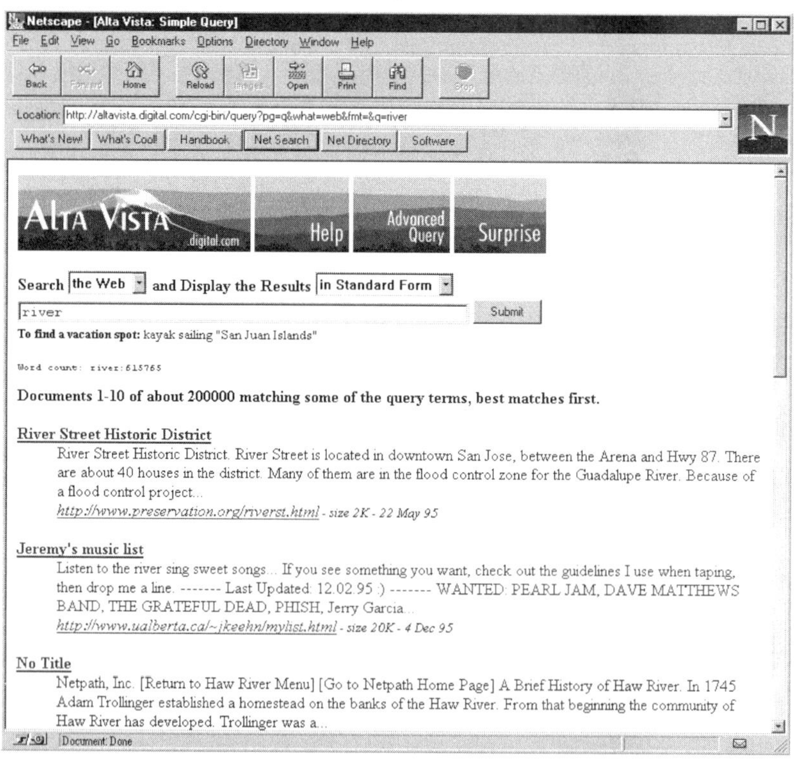

Figure 17.13 Results of an Alta Vista search

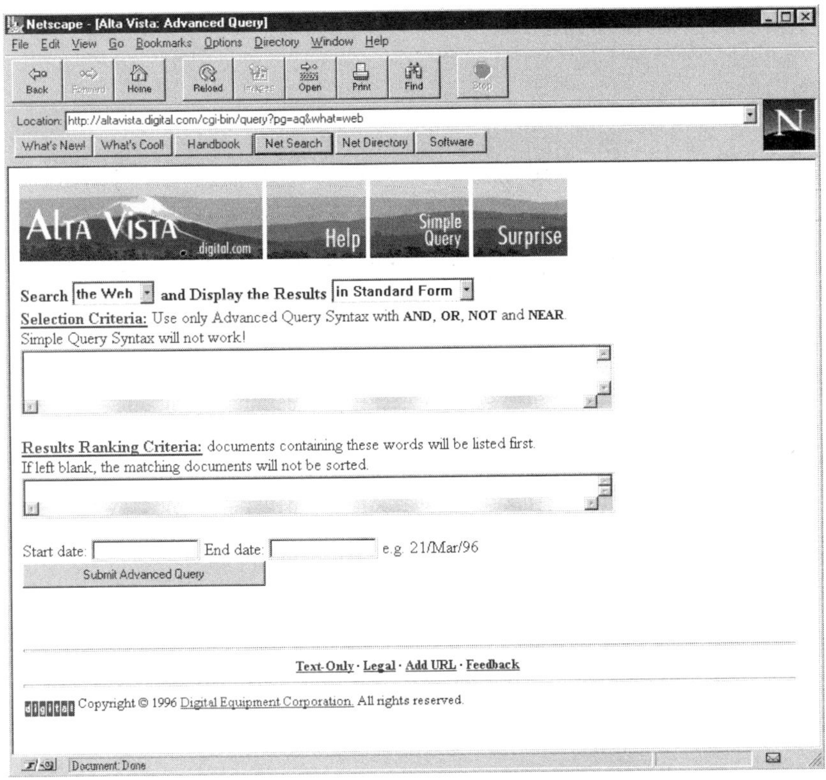

Figure 17.14 The Alta Vista Advanced Query form

For example, an advanced search for the following:

grapes AND raisins AND NOT walnuts

would return a document containing the phrase, "How to make raisins from grapes," but would ignore one that contained the phrase "Grape-Raisin-Walnut Salad."

The NEAR operator is useful in searching for someone's name. The search

richard NEAR jones

would return references to "Richard Jones," "Richard A. Jones," and "Richard Allison Jones, M.D." Unfortunately, that search would also return hits on documents containing phrases like, "Richard Krinklemeyer and

Joyce Jones are pleased to announce..." since "Richard" and "Jones" are within 10 words of each other in that phrase, too.

The advanced search form also lets you specify the order in which your search results appear. Enter the most important words in your search in the second text box. Alta Vista will rank documents containing these words ahead of documents that satisfy the search criteria but do not contain the words you put in the second box.

Infoseek Guide

In an effort to interest you in its for-a-fee services, Infoseek Corporation puts a basic version of its search engine on the Web for everyone's use. Infoseek Guide, as the service is called, isn't as exhaustive as Alta Vista, and you can't perform flexible searches there, but Infoseek Guide is a good way to get a fast idea of what's on the Web on a certain topic. The Infoseek Guide page appears in Figure 17.15.

To access Infoseek, click the hyperlink on HOME.HTM or type its URL:

http://guide.infoseek.com/

To search Infoseek Guide:

1. Type your search terms in the text box.
2. Specify, using the radio buttons under the text box, whether you want to search Web pages, Usenet newsgroups, Usenet FAQs, or whatever.
3. Click the Search button.

Infoseek Guide will display the results of your query on a page like the one shown in Figure 17.16. Click the heading for a page's listing to see that page. Click the "Similar Pages" hyperlink after an entry that you like to search for pages that match that page's profile.

What a lame interface! That's what they want you to think, so you'll consider signing up for their for-a-fee service. Visit http://www.infoseek.com/ for information.

Lycos

The Web search engine that started it all, Lycos left Carnegie-Mellon University in 1995 to form the centerpiece of a private company. Though it competes with such wonderful search engines as Infoseek and Alta Vista, Lycos still offers excellent capabilities and belongs in everyone's search repertoire.

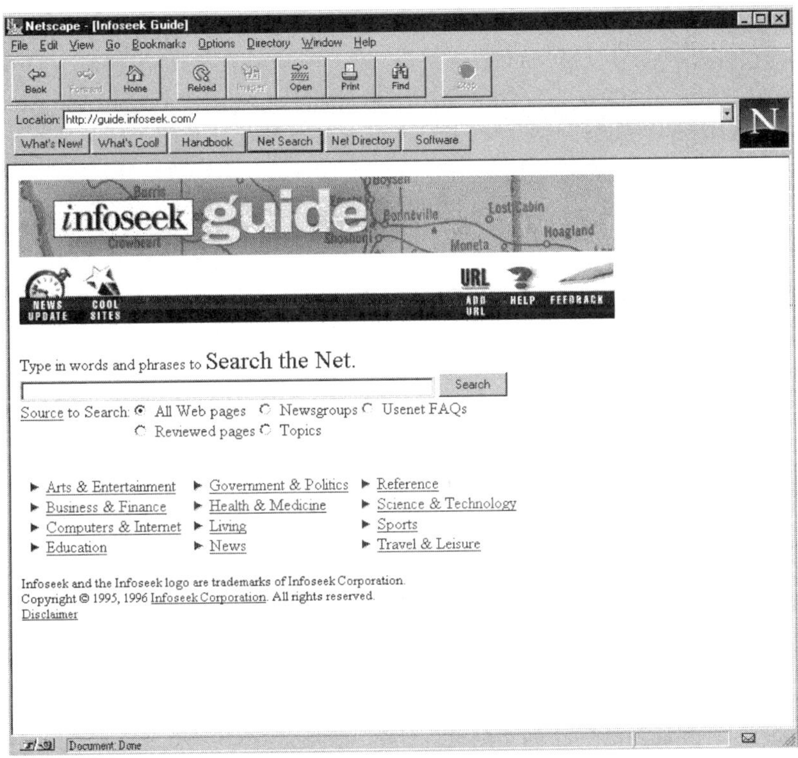

Figure 17.15 Infoseek Guide

To access Lycos, just click the hyperlink on HOME.HTM, or use this URL:

http://www.lycos.com/

You can work with that simple form, or click the Search Options hyperlink to see a search form like the one shown in Figure 17.17. These instructions deal with using the advanced form.

To search Lycos:

1. Next to "Query," type one or more keywords.
2. If you wish, search with one of these options:
    - To exclude documents containing an unwanted word, type a minus sign followed by the word. For example, suppose you're

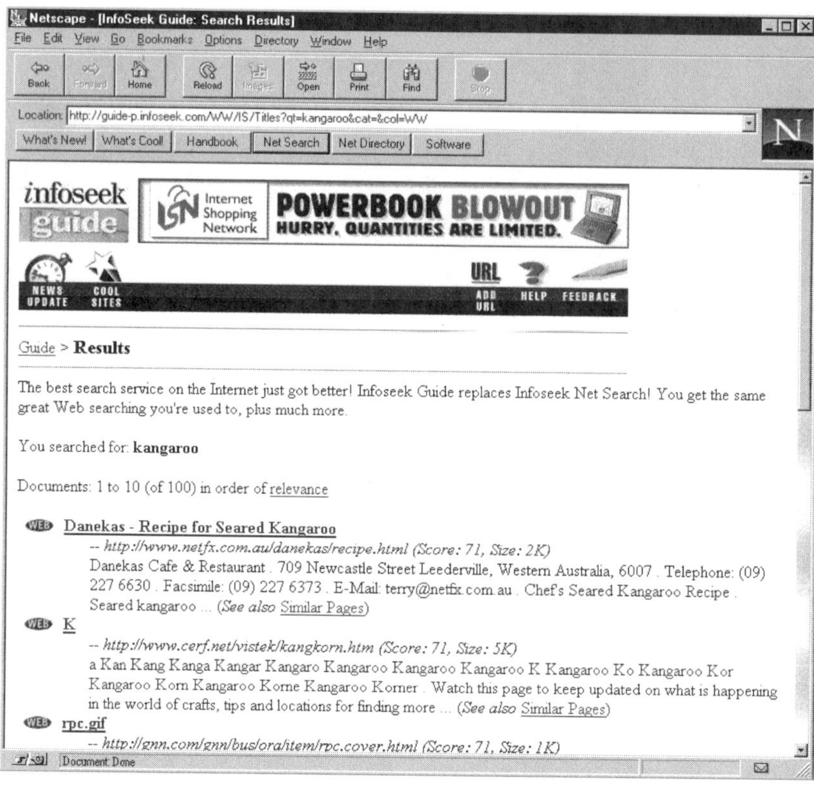

Figure 17.16 Results of an Infoseek Guide search

interested in X Window software and you don't want to see documents about Microsoft Windows. Type the following key words: X Window – Microsoft.

- To perform a whole-word search, type a period after the key word (for example, "cat." retrieves "cat" but not "caterpillar," etc.).

3. Set options in the list boxes below the Query box. You can link all your search terms with AND or OR, or specify the number of search terms the engine must match. You can also specify the number of hits that appear on a results page, and specify the amount of detail about each hit.

4. To initiate the search, click the Search button.

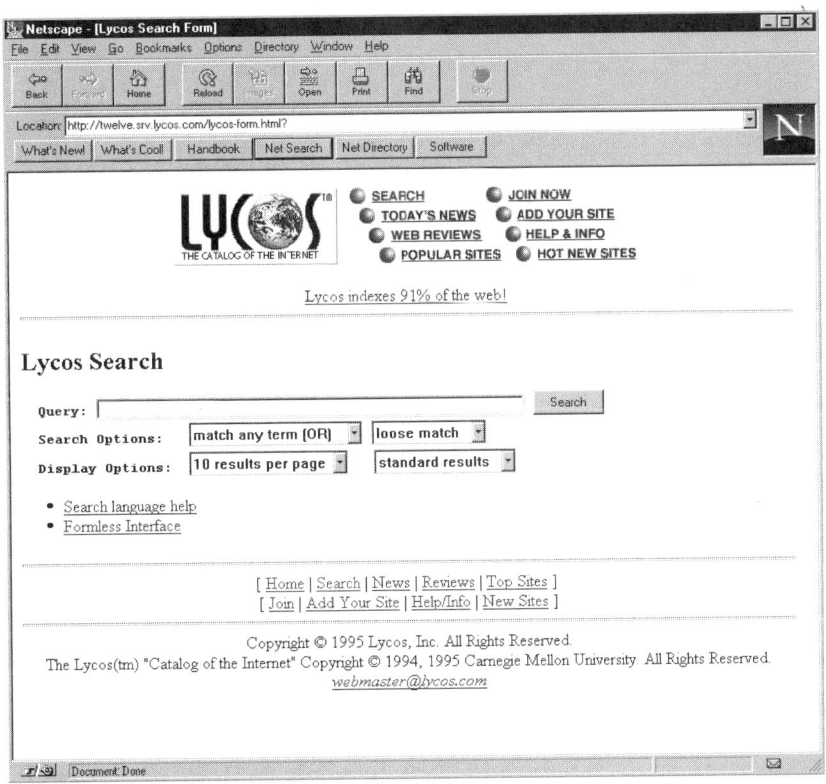

Figure 17.17 The Lycos search form

The results of your Lycos search appear in a new window (Figure 17.18), unless the server is too busy (an all-too-frequent result, I fear). You see your keywords, plus a list of the words in Lycos' database that match the keywords you typed. Following are the hyperlinks that Lycos retrieved, if any. If you find an interesting hyperlink, click it—or click the Back button to revise your search strategy.

This document's score is 1.000, but it isn't relevant to my interests! Just because a document scores 1.000—Lycos assigns all its results a numerical ranking from 0 to 1—doesn't mean that it's going to contain material of interest to you. This calculation is done by mindless computers,

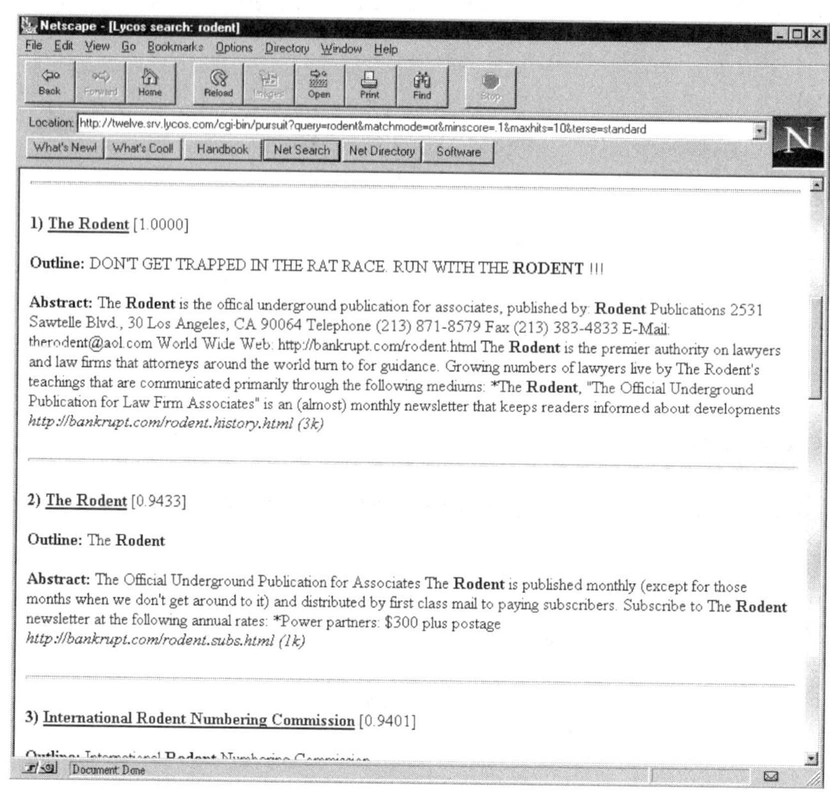

Figure 17.18 The results of a Lycos search

blindly following their programming. They can't read the documents or understand the content—they can just match characters. Sometimes the result is laughably off the mark.

WebCrawler

Owned by America Online, the spider-based WebCrawler doesn't have a very large database, but it amply compensates by indexing the full text of the documents it analyzes. As such, WebCrawler is much more likely to retrieve that valuable document in which the keywords appear only at the end of the document, buried deeply within the document's text. Even though its database isn't very big, you should still include WebCrawler in your search. To access WebCrawler, click the hyperlink in HOME.HTM, or use the following URL:

http://www.webcrawler.com/

You'll see the WebCrawler page, shown in Figure 17.19.

To search WebCrawler, follow these steps:

1. Type one or more keywords in the text box.
2. If you would like to perform a Boolean OR search, select ANY from the "Find pages with" list box. If you want a Boolean AND search, select All.

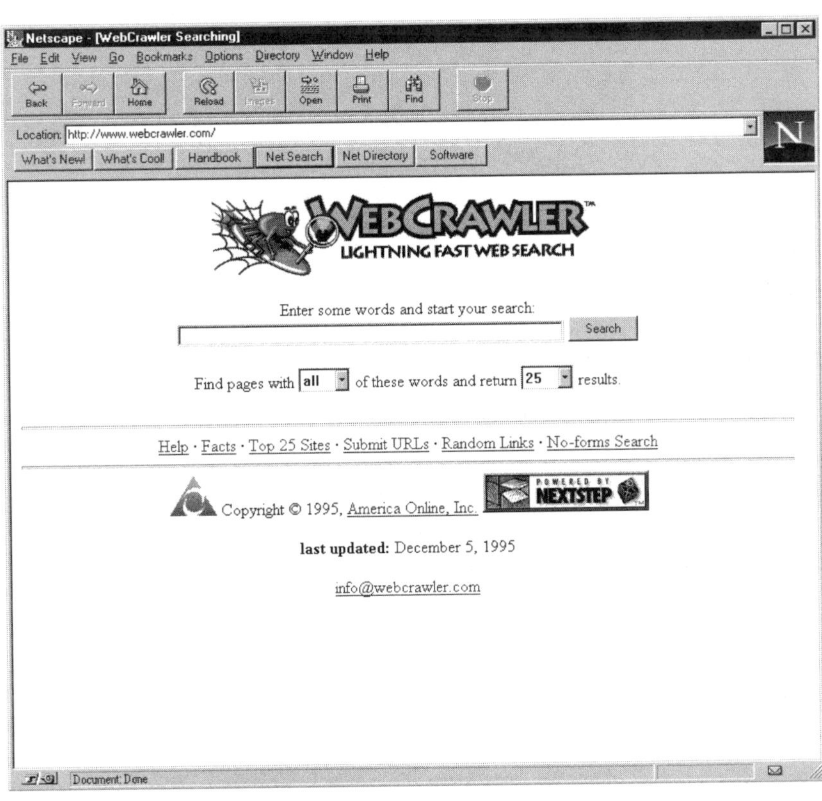

Figure 17.19 The WebCrawler welcome page

3. If you would like to see more than 25 documents, choose a larger number next to "return."
4. Click Search to initiate the search.

The result of your WebCrawler search is a page of hyperlinks, such as the one shown in Figure 17.20. Like the results of a Lycos search, the documents are ranked numerically in order of relevance, with the top-scoring document (score: 100) at the top.

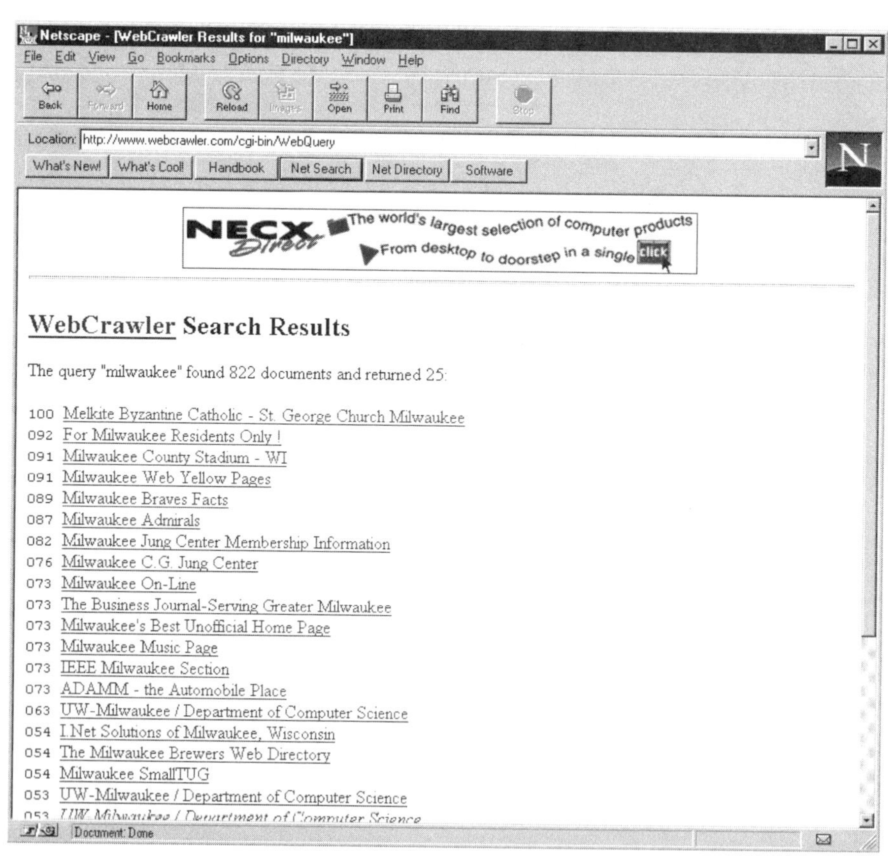

Figure 17.20 The results of a WebCrawler search

From Here

- If you've gotten this far in this book, congratulations! You're a darned good Netscapist by now, and what's more, you know how to retrieve information in an orderly way. You'll be getting tons of useful documents, so you'd better learn how to share them with others by electronic mail, the subject of Chapter 18.
- What, electronic mail isn't fast enough for you? Learn about real-time chat with IRC in Chapter 19.
- The information you want isn't on the Web yet? Learn how to access Gopher resources in Chapter 20.

Part V

Exploring the Internet with Netscape

Chapter 18

Sending and Receiving E-mail

New for 2

Netscape is fast becoming the only tool you'll need to access just about everything on the Internet. With Version 2.0, you can use Netscape to send and receive electronic mail.

Introducing E-mail

When you establish an account with an Internet service provider (ISP), you'll get an electronic mailbox. This mailbox is stored on the ISP's *mail server*, an Internet-connected computer with special mail software and a very large hard disk. The mail server stores your mail temporarily until you log into the system. At that time, Netscape looks for new mail—if there's any waiting for

you, you'll see an envelope on the status bar. (This envelope shows up in the browser as well as the Mail and News windows.) Think of the mail server as a temporary parking place for your mail.

When you compose and send e-mail to others, what happens is the reverse of the above process: Netscape sends your mail to the server, which relays it on to its Internet destination.

How do I know whether someone's read my message? Some e-mail programs enable you to send messages with receipt notification, but Netscape doesn't include this feature. If you don't get a reply from somebody, don't assume you're being ignored—the person may not have logged on! If you want others to have confidence in sending mail to you, be sure to log on to your server frequently and check your mail.

About E-mail Addresses

To exchange e-mail with someone, you'll need your own e-mail address, as well as the e-mail address of the person with whom you'd like to correspond. You'll receive your e-mail address when you establish an account with an Internet service provider.

For the Time-Challenged

- Netscape's e-mail capabilities are excellent and convenient. You'll need to configure the Mail window using information supplied by your Internet service provider.
- Create a signature containing your name, address, and phone numbers. Netscape will append your signature to the messages you send.
- Click To: Mail to compose a message.
- Click Re: Mail to reply to a message.
- Add e-mail addresses to the Address Book for convenient entry.

Internet e-mail addresses have three parts:

- **User name** The first part of the e-mail address identifies your personal mailbox. For example, if your name is David Smith, you may be assigned a mailbox name of *dsmith*.
- **At sign (@)** The second part of the e-mail address is a separator: It separates the first part from the third part, so those dumb computers can tell the difference.
- **Mail server's domain name** The third part of the e-mail address gives the domain name of your e-mail server.

A complete, correct e-mail address looks like the following fictitious one:

dsmith@asteroid.chv.va.us

Please note that you can't place any spaces in an e-mail address.

If you're familiar with electronic mail, you're probably wondering how Netscape compares to other e-mail programs. If you're using Windows 95, you'll be pleased to know that Netscape's e-mail beats the default Windows e-mail client, Microsoft Exchange, hands down. However, Netscape has one drawback for a serious e-mail user: There's no provision for filtering messages automatically. With message filtering, you set up filters using keywords, such as a person's name or message text (such as "test" or "ignore"); when the program detects an incoming message that contains the specified text, it diverts the message to a folder of your choice—including the trash can, if you wish! With filtering, you're not bombarded with dozens of unwanted or low-priority messages. Instead, they're parked into folders where you can read them later, if you wish. Aside from this shortcoming, though, Netscape has some cool features—including the ability to thread mail messages, so you can see the relationship between the mail you've sent and the mail you've received.

E-mail addresses aren't case-sensitive, the way URLs are. Most people use lowercase letters for e-mail addresses, though, and it's a good practice because it prevents confusion (if you type part of your address in capital letters, people might think they need to do so).

Configuring E-mail

To get started with Netscape's e-mail, you need to configure your copy of Netscape so that it knows where your mail server is located. Before you do this, call your ISP and ask the following questions:

- What is the address of the SMTP server for outgoing mail?
- What is the address of the POP-3 server for incoming mail?
- What is my user name?
- What is my mail password?

Often, the addresses for the outgoing and incoming mail are the same. Be sure to write all this information down, but keep your password from prying eyes.

To configure Netscape's e-mail:

1. From the Options menu in any Netscape window, choose Mail and News Preferences. You'll see the Preferences dialog box, shown in Figure 18.1.
2. Click the Servers tab. Figure 18.1 shows the Servers options.
3. In the Outgoing Mail (SMTP Server) box, type the Internet address of the computer that handles your outgoing mail.
4. In the Incoming Mail (POP) Server box, type the Internet address of the computer that handles your incoming mail.
5. In the Pop User Name box, type the user name that your ISP gave you.
6. The other options can be left as is, but consider whether you want to leave your messages on the server or have Netscape delete them when they're downloaded. The best option is to have Netscape

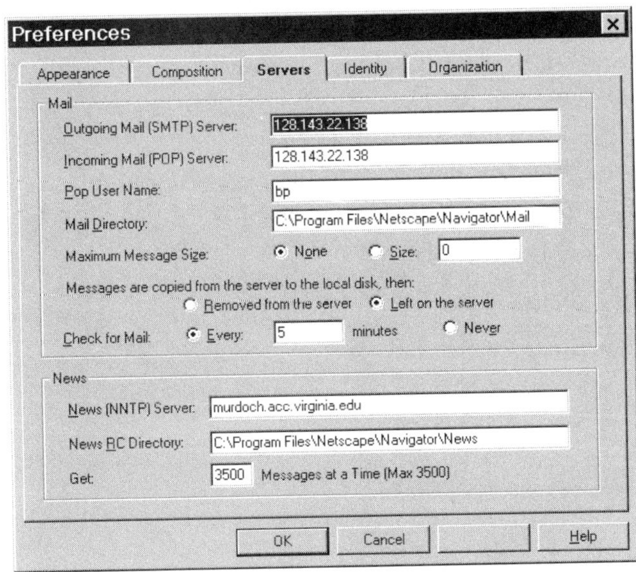

Figure 18.1 Mail and News Preferences dialog box (Servers page)

delete them. This preserves disk space on the server. To choose this option, which I recommend, click the option button next to "Removed from the server."

7. You may also wish to have Netscape check your mail automatically at intervals you specify. To do so, click the Every option and type the interval, in minutes, at which you want Netscape to check for mail. I recommend 10 minutes.
8. Click the Identity tab. You'll see the Identity page, shown in Figure 18.2.
9. In the Your Name box, type your name as you wish it to appear in other people's inboxes.
10. In the Your Email box, type your e-mail address exactly the way your ISP gave it to you.
11. Leave the Reply-To box blank, unless you want people to reply to an e-mail address other than your own.

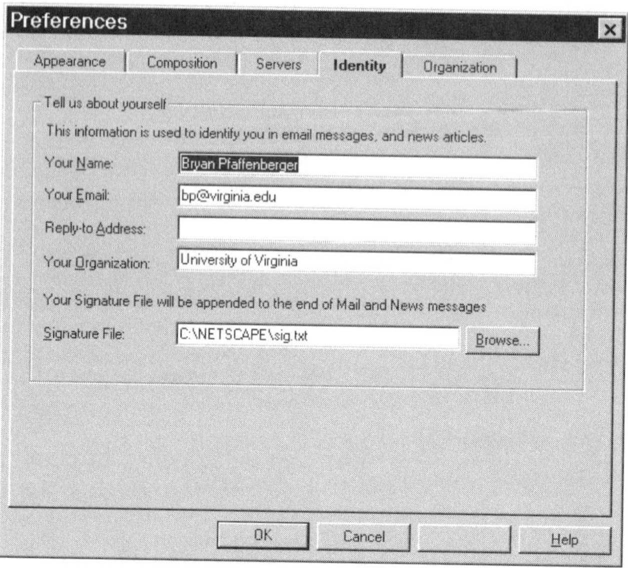

Figure 18.2 Mail and News Preferences dialog box (Identity page)

12. In the Your Organization box, type the name of your organization (school or company), if you wish (this is optional).
13. Click the Organization tab. You'll see the Organization page, shown in Figure 18.3.
14. In the General area, click Remember Mail Password if you would like Netscape to remember the password that accesses your mail server. However, you should not do this if anyone besides yourself has access to your computer.
15. Netscape can "thread" e-mail messages the same way it organizes Usenet messages: replies are shown beneath the original message, so that you can see the "thread" of discussion. This is a very cool feature and I recommend that you enable it. To do so, click Thread Mail Messages.
16. In the Sorting area, you'll see that Netscape sorts e-mail by date, by default. With this sort order, you'll see the most recent messages first, which is the best way to sort your e-mail. As you'll see

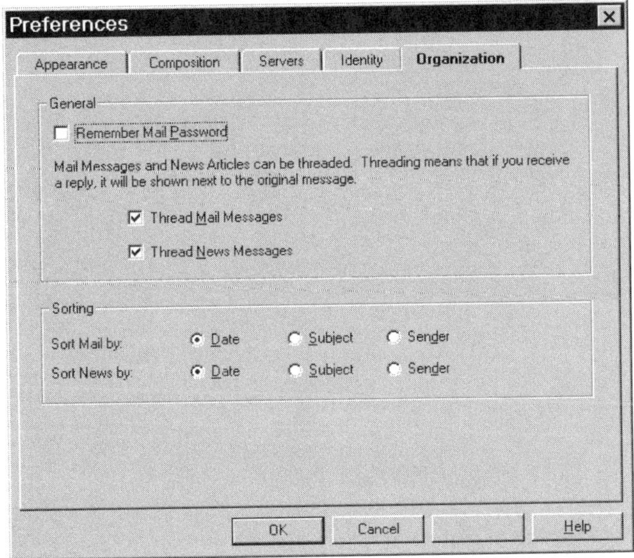

Figure 18.3 Mail and News Preferences dialog box (Organization page)

later on, you can re-sort the messages by name or subject, if you wish, without changing the default sort order. This comes in handy for finding a message that you received some time ago.

17. Click the Appearance tab. You'll see the Appearance page, shown in Figure 18.4.
18. In the Message Styles area, you can choose to display messages with a fixed width font or a variable (proportional) width font. The fixed width option is actually better; many people send e-mail messages with spacing options that assume you're viewing the message with a fixed width font.
19. In the Text beginning with (quoted text) area, choose a text style for quoted text, if you wish. The default is italic, which is fine. This shows up only in the copy of the message you're viewing with Netscape; your recipients won't see it.
20. In the Text Size area, choose a text size for quoted text, if you wish. The default is plain; you can choose a bigger or smaller font

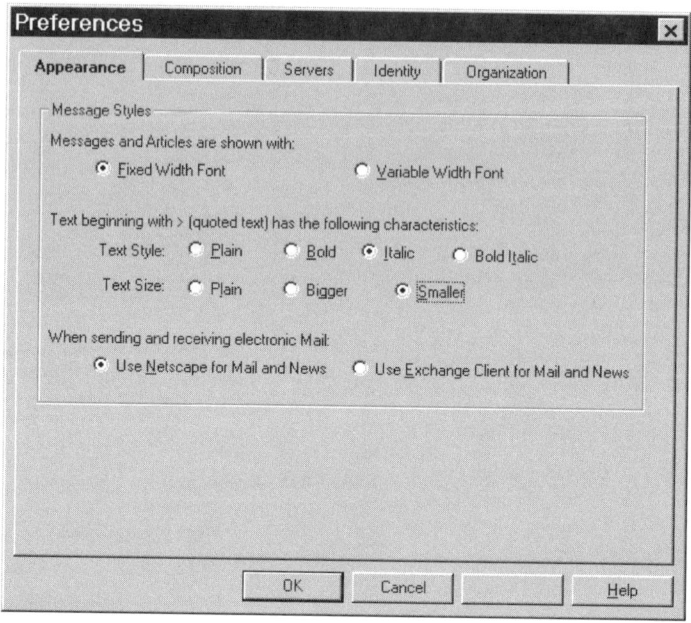

Figure 18.4 Mail and News Preferences dialog box (Appearance page)

size. This shows up only in the copy of the message you're viewing with Netscape (your recipients won't see it).

21. **Important**: Under the heading "When sending and receiving electronic mail," choose Use Netscape for Mail and News.

22. Click the Composition tab. The default options are fine in this page (Figure 18.5). You need to fill in these areas only if you would like to copy all of your outgoing news and mail messages to someone. One option you may wish to consider is the quotation option on the bottom of the dialog box; if you click this, Netscape will automatically quote the text of every message to which you're replying. This is convenient, but it's not advisable: Not every reply message needs to contain a verbatim quotation of the original. If you leave

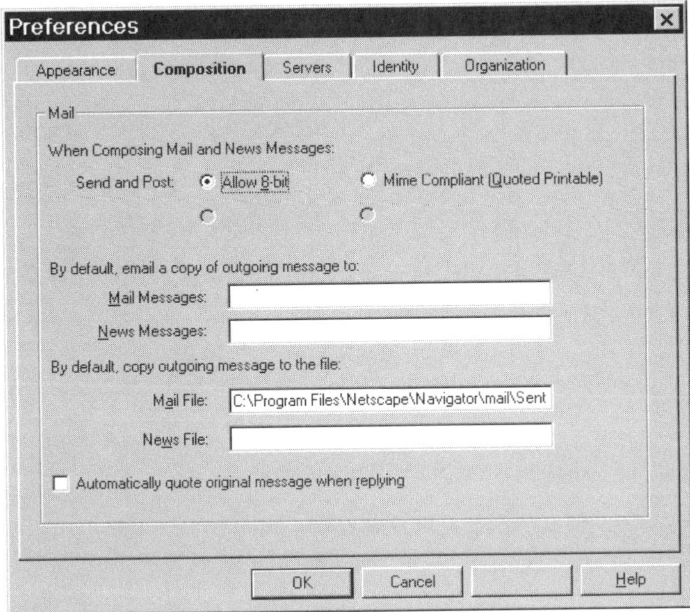

Figure 18.5 Mail and News Preferences dialog box (Composition page)

this option blank, you can quote text in replies by clicking the Quote button—and that's what I'd advise you to do.

23. Click OK to confirm your options and return to Netscape.

Understanding the E-mail Window

Now that you've configured Netscape for your e-mail account, it's time to open the e-mail window and log on to your server. Ask someone to send you some mail, so you'll have something to work with! In the meantime, you can get to know Netscape's Mail window.

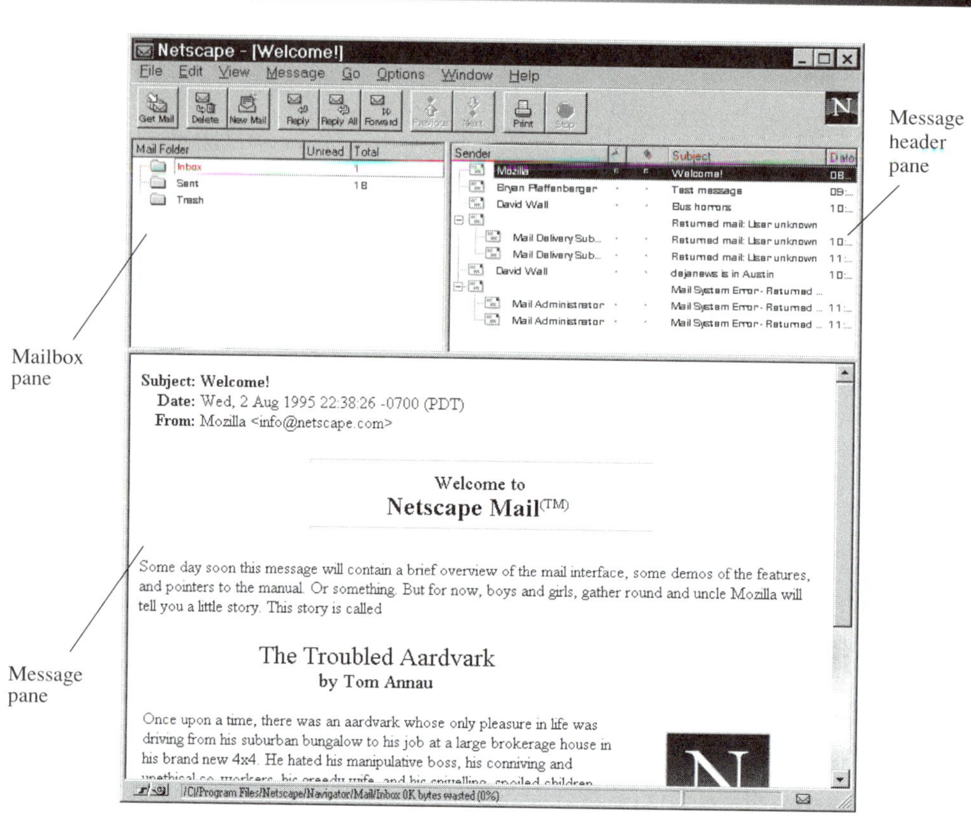

Figure 18.6 Mail window

Opening the E-mail Window

To open Netscape's e-mail window, open the Window menu and choose Netscape Mail. You'll see the Mail window, shown in Figure 18.6.

The Parts of the Mail Window

The Mail window has its own menu and button bar, which we'll examine in a moment. For now, note that the window is divided into three panes:

- **Mailbox Pane** Here you see Netscape's default folders (mailboxes). The Inbox holds your incoming messages, while the Sent folder holds the messages you've sent. The Trash folder holds messages that you've deleted. (You can recover messages from the Trash until you've emptied it.)

- **Message Header Pane** Here you'll see the messages that you've received. You'll see the sender's name, the subject of the message, and the date received. You can also see whether you've flagged the message (if so, you'll see a red flag in the second column) and whether you've read the message (unread messages are shown in boldface and there's a tiny icon in the third column).
- **Message Pane** Here you see the text of the message that's currently selected in the message header pane.

With the mouse, you can adjust the size of the window panes. Just drag on the borders to do so. You might try decreasing the size of the mailbox pane—it doesn't need so much room—so that there's more room to display the message header pane.

The Mail Window's Menu Bar

The Mail window's menu bar differs slightly from the one you're used to seeing in the browser window. Missing are the Bookmarks and Directory menus; in their place, you'll find a Message menu. In addition, the menus contain many new options. You'll learn about them later in this chapter. For now, note that the commands and options you'll choose most often are accessible using the button bar, described in the next section.

The Mail Window's Button Bar

The Mail window's button bar enables you to choose frequently used options quickly. Here's a quick rundown of what these buttons do; you'll learn more about them later.

Click here to see if there are any new messages waiting for you on the server.

Click here to delete the message you're currently viewing.

Click here to compose a new message.

Click here to write a reply to the sender.

Click here to write a reply to everyone included in the message header, including people who receive "carbon copies" of the original message.

Click here to forward the message to someone.

Click here to display the previous unread message.

Click here to display the next unread message.

Click here to print the message.

Click here to stop downloading a lengthy, unwanted message.

Logging on to Your Server

To log on to your mail server, open the File menu and choose Get New Mail. Alternatively, press Ctrl + T or just click the Get Mail button.

If this is the first time you've logged on, you'll see a dialog box asking you to type your password. Do so, and click OK.

If nobody else uses your computer, and you're sure it's secure, you can avoid having to type your password every time you log on. Netscape will remember your password and supply it automatically. From the Options menu, choose Mail and News Preferences, and then click the Organization tab. Activate the Remember Mail Password option, and click OK. *Note*: Some ISPs regard this to be a security violation, since this setting would enable anyone who could gain access to your computer to log on to your account and send e-mail under your name. Don't choose this option unless you're sure that your system is secure and that it's OK with your ISP.

After you log on to the mail server, Netscape checks to see whether you've received any mail. If there's no mail for you—and at this point, there probably isn't—you'll see a dialog box informing you that no mail is waiting for you. Click OK to proceed.

If there is some mail for you, you'll see a new message header in the message header pane. To learn how to read and reply to your mail, see "Reading and Replying to Mail," after the next section.

Composing and Sending a Message

Now that you've configured Netscape Mail and logged on to your server, it's time to send a message! You've probably got somebody's e-mail address—but if not, you can send a message to yourself. Either way, try it out!

Creating a Signature

A signature (abbreviated "sig") is a brief return address (no more than four lines in length) that contains your name, e-mail address, and other information. Signatures are optional, but it's good manners to include it: Doing so makes it easier for people to reply to you.

Compose your signature using a text editor, such as the Windows Notepad utility. Make it brief and simple. Here's an example:

```
Suzanne Smith, M.S.
Environmental Engineering, Green Valley College
Green Valley, VA 22876
ssmith@speedy.greenv.edu
```

Save your signature. Now tell Netscape where your sig file is located:

1. From the Options menu, choose Mail and News Preferences.
2. Click the Identity tab.
3. In the Signature File box, type the location of your sig file, or use the Browse button to locate this file.
4. Click OK.

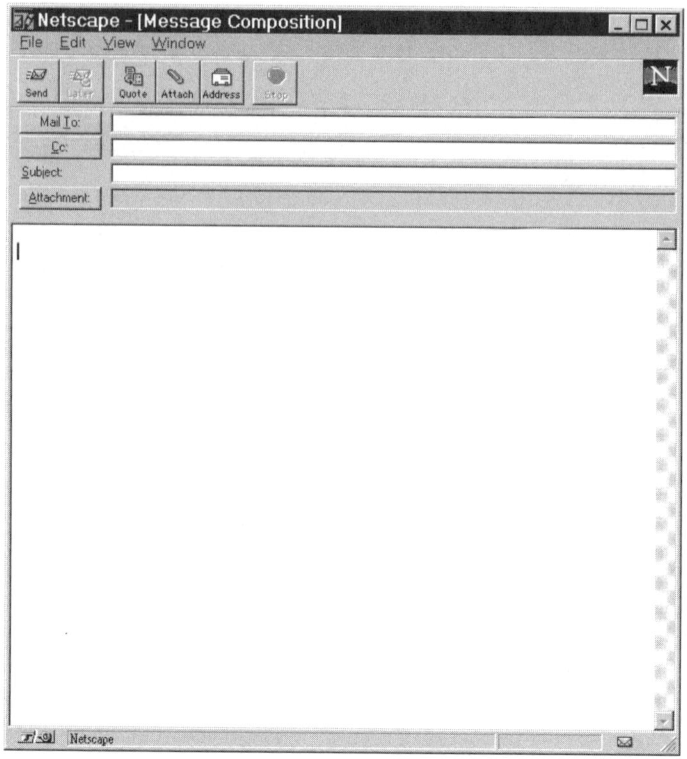

Figure 18.7 Message Composition window

Composing Your Message

To compose your message, open the File menu and choose New Mail Message. Alternatively, use the Ctrl + M shortcut, or just click the To: Mail button. You'll see the Message Composition window, shown in Figure 18.7. If you've added a signature, as explained in the previous section, you'll see the sig text at the bottom of the message area.

To compose your message:

1. In the Mail To box, type the e-mail address of the person to whom you're sending the message. If you would like to send the message to more than one person, type additional e-mail addresses, separated by semicolons (as in this example: jn@snoopy.virginia.edu; rm683e@grumpy.green.edu).

2. In the Cc: box, you can optionally type the e-mail address or addresses of anyone whom you'd like to receive a copy of this message.
3. In the Subject box, type a subject line for your message. *Note*: Don't forget to do this. People get annoyed when they see messages without subjects.
4. In the message body area, type your message.

Would you like to send a blind carbon copy? (A *blind carbon copy* is a copy of your message that's sent to a third party without your recipient knowing that this person has also received the message.) To send a blind carbon copy, choose Mail Bcc in the View menu. In the Blind Cc box, type the e-mail address of the person to whom you'd like to send the blind carbon copy.

Adding an Attachment

Using established Internet standards, Netscape enables you to include an attachment with your e-mail message. An *attachment* is a file that's carried along with your message. The standards that support sending and receiving attachments are called the Multipurpose Internet Multimedia Extensions (MIME). Thanks to these standards, you can send just about any computer file your system can create—formatted word processing files, graphics files (including bitmaps, JPEG, and GIF images), compressed files of any type, and even computer programs.

Will your recipient be able to receive the attachment? That depends. To receive a message that contains an attachment, your recipient must be using a computer that's directly connected to the Internet. In general, people using on-line services (such as America Online) can't receive attachments, although they can receive Internet mail. In addition, the person must be using a MIME-compliant mail program, such as Netscape Mail. Most decent mail programs are MIME-compliant.

To add an attachment, do the following:

1. In the Message Composition (New Mail) window, click the Attach button. You'll see the Attachments dialog box.
2. To attach a Web document, click Attach URL. You'll see a dialog box asking you to specify the location to attach. Type the URL that you want to attach. Click OK to confirm.

3. To attach a file, click Attach File. You'll see a dialog box asking you to enter the file to attach. Use this dialog box's navigation controls to locate and select the file you want to attach, and click Open.
4. In the Attachments dialog box, you'll see a list of the attachments you've added to your message. If you would like to delete one of them, select it and click the Delete button. For each attachment, you should make sure that the As Is option is selected; don't select Convert to Plain Text unless you really want Netscape to do this.
5. Click OK to confirm your attachment. You'll see the attachments you've added listed in the Attachment box of the Message Composition window.

If you're thinking about sending an attachment, bear in mind the capabilities of your recipient's system. Generally, it's pretty easy to send an attachment successfully to somebody who's using the same type of system and the same software you're using; problems occur, though, when Windows users send files to Mac users, and vice-versa. A little advance planning can solve these problems. For example, if you're sending a Word for Windows document to somebody using a Macintosh and Microsoft Word 5.1, it might be wise to convert the file to the file format used by the Macintosh version of Word (Word for Windows can do this). The person to whom you send the file will then be able to open it with no problems.

Sending the Message

Before you send your message, check it carefully for grammatical and spelling mistakes. When you're sure that it's ready to go, think again!

I shouldn't have sent that message! Can I cancel it? Nope, you're out of luck. That's why we say Think first!

Lots of people get themselves into trouble—sometimes serious trouble, liking losing jobs or Internet privileges—by sending threatening or abusive e-mail. Remember that e-mail isn't secure—it can be easily intercepted and read en-route by anyone with a modicum of Internet knowledge.

Please carefully consider the following before you click the Send button:

- Would you want your letter to wind up on your boss's desk the next morning?
- Would you want your mother to read it?
- Would you want it published in your home-town newspaper?
- Would you like to receive such a letter?

If your answer to any of these questions is "no," then *don't send the letter!* To abandon your letter, just click the close box; you'll see a dialog box informing you that the message has not been sent. To abandon the message, click No.

When you're sure that the message is OK, click the Send button.

Reading and Replying to Mail

Have you received some mail from someone? You'll know if you do. After you log on to your mail server, Netscape automatically begins downloading any messages you've received, and they'll be shown in bold in the message header area. In addition, you'll see icons in the Read column, indicating that the messages haven't yet been read.

If you've set up Netscape Mail as I suggested earlier, the program will automatically check for new mail at intervals you specify, such as every 10 minutes. You can also check for new mail whenever you wish. When you've got some new mail, you can read it, view the attachments (if any), reply to the mail you've received, forward the mail to others, flag messages for later attention, and print messages. The following sections discuss each of these procedures in detail.

If you switch to another Netscape window, Mail lets you know if a new message has arrived at your server. On the status bar, you'll see a mail envelope preceded by an exclamation point. If you see an envelope without an exclamation point, Mail is telling you that there's a previously downloaded message that you haven't yet read.

Checking for New Mail

To check for new mail, open the File menu and choose Get New Mail. Alternatively, use the Ctrl + T shortcut, or just click the Get Mail button.

Reading Your Mail

If you've received a new message, select the new message in the message header pane. You'll see the message text in the message pane.

Did you receive more than one message? To read the next message, click the Next button. To redisplay the previous message, click Previous.

You'll soon find that your mailbox is filled with messages that you've already read. However, very few of them are worth keeping. Do yourself a favor and delete worthless messages right after you've finished reading them. To do so, click the Delete button. Note that this button doesn't actually delete the message—instead, it moves the message to the Trash folder, where you can recover it should you later decide that it wasn't so worthless after all.

Viewing Attachments

If you've received a message with one or more attachments, you can view the attachment in-line (you actually see the attachment within the mail message, if Netscape can figure out how to display it) or as a link (to see the attachment, you click the link). Unless the attachment is very small, it's much more convenient to view the attachment as a link.

To control the way attachments are viewed, open the View menu and choose one of the following: Attachments Inline (to view attachments in the same window as the message) and Attachments as Links (to view the attachment as a link).

Replying to Your Mail

To reply to a message, select the message in the message header pane, and click Re: Mail. You'll see a composition window. Netscape automatically filled in the sender's e-mail address (look at the Mail To box), and the pro-

gram has proposed a subject (using Re: followed by the original message's subject line). You can change the subject, if you wish.

If you set up Netscape Mail to quote the original message's text automatically, you'll see the text in the window. If not, and if you'd like to quote the text, click the Quote button. You'll see the quoted text in the window. Note that each line is preceded by a greater than sign (>), and that's desirable: To experienced Internet users, these characters immediately convey that the following text is quoted.

Note that you don't have to use all the quoted text. If you prefer, you can edit the text down to just a line or two that you want to discuss.

To finish the reply, type your message, and proofread it carefully. As always, ponder the "think before you send" rules before you click that Send button!

Replying to All Senders

If you've received a letter from more than one sender, Netscape automatically sends the reply to the first sender only. If you would like to reply to all senders, begin your reply by clicking the Re: All button. Create and send your reply as described in the preceding section.

Forwarding Mail

To forward a message to someone, highlight the message in the message header panel, and click the Forward button. You'll see a message composition window. Note that Netscape has automatically included the message as an attachment.

Type text that explains why you're forwarding the message, and click Send.

If you're forwarding mail to somebody whose system can't handle attachments, you can forward the mail as quoted text. To do so, start the forwarding process by opening the Message window, and choosing Forward as Quoted Text. This command automatically quotes the message you're forwarding instead of adding it as an attachment.

While you're working in the message pane, you can use the right mouse key to display a pop-up menu. From this menu, you can reply, reply to all, forward, forward quoted, and delete messages.

Marking and Flagging Messages

When you're reading your mail, you'll often say to yourself, "I don't want to answer this right now" or "I better remember to look at this again, later, and do something about it." With many e-mail programs, the messages you've read disappear into a long, lengthy list of read messages, and you forget about them. With Netscape, though, you can mark messages as unread (even if you've read them). The message then shows up in bold in the message header pane, encouraging you to look at it again. If that's not enough, you can also put a red flag next to a message.

To mark a message as unread (even though you've read it), highlight the message in the message header pane. Then open the Message menu and choose Mark as Unread. If you change your mind, open the same menu again and choose Mark as Read.

To flag a message, highlight the message in the message header pane. Then open the Message menu and choose Flag message. You'll see a red flag next to the message. To unflag the message, open the Message menu again and choose Unflag message.

To mark or flag items quickly, or to unmark or unflag them, click on the mark or flag column next to the item's name.

Printing Messages

You can easily produce hard copy (printed output) of one or more messages.

To print the message you're currently viewing, just click the Print button.

To print more than one message, hold down the Ctrl key; in the message header pane, select all the messages you want to print. Then open the File menu and choose Print Message(s).

Creating an Address Book

As you'll surely agree after typing a few e-mail address, it's tedious to type all those funny characters, obscure user names, and funny computer names—and what's worse, your message won't reach its destination if you make a typing mistake. For these reasons, it's a great idea to build an Address Book. The Address Book will contain the e-mail addresses of the people with whom you frequently correspond. From the Address Book, you can quickly and accurately enter a recipient's e-mail address. The following sections show you how to take full advantage of this neat capability.

Adding Addresses to Your Address Book

The easiest way to add an address to your Address Book is to display a message that somebody has sent you. Point to the message within the message pane, and click the right mouse button—you'll see a pop-up menu with lots of reply and forwarding options. But what you're after is Add to Address Book. When you select this option, you'll see the Address Book dialog box, shown in Figure 18.8.

To add an address to your Address Book:

1. In the Nick Name box, type a nickname for this person, if you'd like to use one. For example, if you type "ken," you can simply type "Ken" when you wish to address mail to this person, and

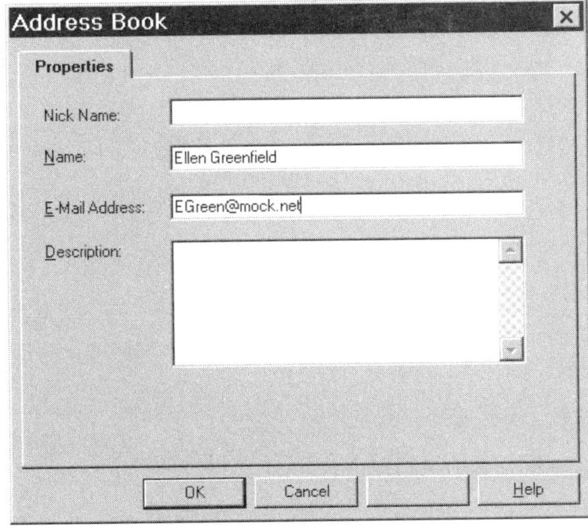

Figure 18.8 Address Book dialog box

Netscape will automatically fill in the full e-mail address. Note that nicknames must be one word and must contain nothing but lowercase letters.

2. Note that Netscape has automatically entered the person's name (if available) and e-mail address in the Name and E-Mail Address boxes. If you wish, type a short description.
3. Click OK to confirm the addition to your Address Book.

This guy's address has changed! How do I edit his entry? Simple. In the Address Book window, select the person's name. From the File menu, choose Properties. You'll see the Address Book dialog box with the person's current information. Edit this information, and then choose OK.

If you would like to add an address to your Address Book without right-clicking an existing address, choose Address Book from the Options menu. From the Item menu, choose Add User. You'll see the Address Book dialog box. You'll have to type the name and e-mail address manually.

Pasting an Address from Your Address Book

After you've added names to your Address Book, you can paste them into e-mail messages you're composing. To add an address to a message, click the Mail To button in the Message Composition window. You'll see the Select Addresses dialog box, shown in Figure 18.9. Select the address you want to add, and then click one of the following buttons:

To:	Click this button if you want to send the message to this person.
Cc:	Click this button if you want to send a copy of this message to this person.
Bcc:	Click this button if you would like to send a copy of this message to this person without the main recipient knowing.

Click the close box to close this dialog box.

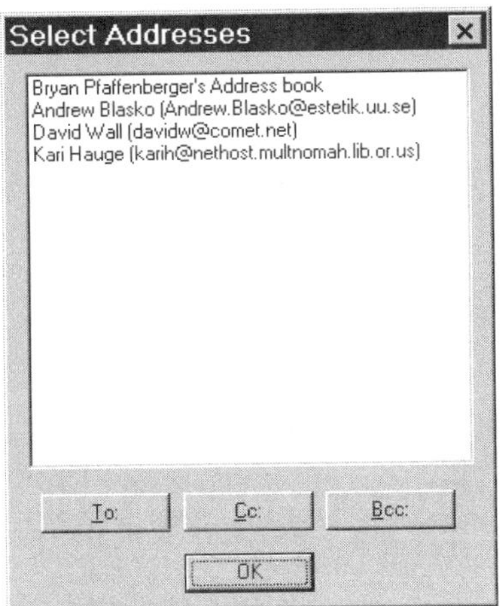

Figure 18.9 Select Addresses dialog box

You can add addresses in other ways, too. To start a new message from the Address Book window, select the person to whom you want to send a message, and choose Send New Message from the File menu (or just use the Ctrl + M shortcut). But the simplest way to add an address to your message is to type the person's nickname in the Mail To box (Message Composition window). If you didn't define a nickname for a person, you can do so by opening the Address Book window, selecting the person's name, choosing Properties from the File menu, and adding a nickname in the Nick Name box.

Creating a List of E-mail Addresses

Sometimes you will wish to send frequent e-mail messages to more than one person, such as a group of co-workers. To do so, you can use the Address Book to create a list of e-mail addresses all grouped under a single name. This greatly simplifies the task of sending e-mail messages to two or more people. You need only type the nickname of the list, or enter the list's name from the Address Book—Netscape takes care of the rest.

To create a list of e-mail addresses:

1. In the Address Book window, choose Add List from the Item menu. You'll see an Address Book window, but the e-mail address box is dimmed.
2. In the Nick Name box, type a lowercase, one-word nickname. You can enter this name in the Mail To box (Message Composition window) to send a message to all the people in the list.
3. In the Name box, type the name you want to use for this list.
4. In the Description box, type a description, if you wish.
5. To add e-mail addresses to the list, select the name of the list in the Address Book window.
6. Click Add User. You'll see an Address Book dialog box.
7. Add the information for this recipient.
8. Click OK.
9. Repeat steps 5 through 9 to add additional people to your mailing list.

I can't find so-and-so's e-mail address! Added a lot of names, huh? To search your Address Book, choose Find from the Address Book's Edit menu, or just press Ctrl + F within Address Book. You'll see a Search Headers dialog box. Type all or part of the person's name, and click OK. Netscape will find and select the person's name, if it's able to find it. If not, check your spelling and try again.

Organizing Your Messages

Before long, you'll have a lengthy list of e-mail messages. Searching for a message by hand can become a time-consuming process. However, Netscape has tools that enable you to search the messages, sort them in a variety of ways, delete unwanted messages, and move messages to folders. To save disk space, you can compress the folders—or just delete them.

Finding a Message

To find a message, choose Find from the Edit menu, or just press Ctrl + F. You'll see the Find dialog box, shown in Figure 18.10. This box enables you to search for text in the message headers (which include the sender's name, e-mail address, and subject). In addition, you can search the full text of the message that's currently selected in the Mail window.

To use the Find dialog box:

1. In the Find box, type the text for which you want to search.
2. In the Find In area, click Message Headers in This Folder if you want to search the message headers. If you want to search the full text of the currently selected message, click Body of This Message.
3. If you selected Body of Message, choose whether you want to search Up or Down by clicking the appropriate option button in the Direction area.
4. If you would like Netscape to match the case of the text you've typed, click Match Case. The program will ignore case if you leave this check box blank.
5. Click Find Next.

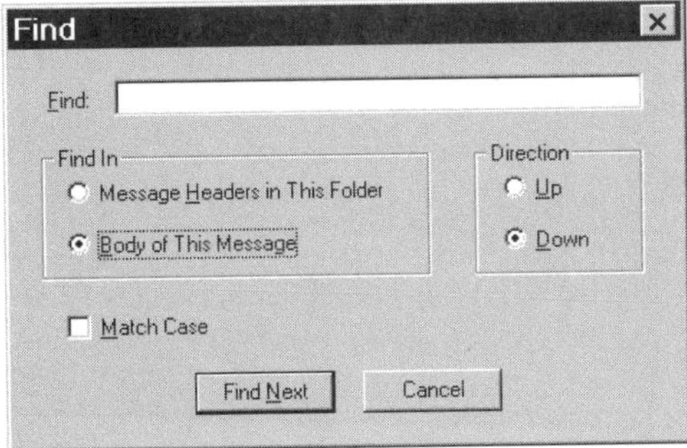

Figure 18.10 Find dialog box

If Netscape finds a match, the program displays the message. If not, you'll see a dialog box informing you that the search string was not found. Try again, and check your spelling.

Sorting Messages

Netscape enables you to sort the messages in a number of ways. First, you choose the sort criterion (Date, Subject, Sender, or Message Number). For example, if you choose to sort the messages by Sender, the program will organize the messages in alphabetical order sorted by the sender's name. To choose a sort criterion, choose Sort from the View menu, and then choose a sort criterion from the pop-up menu.

You can also choose whether you would like Netscape to thread the messages. This unique feature groups messages that share the same subject. For example, suppose you've received a message with the subject "Catalina sailboats." You reply, and then you receive another message entitled "Re: Catalina sailboats." With this option, Netscape will group these two letters together, rather than separating them. This makes it much easier to follow the "thread' of discussion that you've been having with somebody. This is the best sort option for most purposes. You can turn threading on or off independently of other sort options. To turn threading on or off, choose Sort from the View menu, and then choose Thread Messages from the pop-up menu.

You can also choose whether you'd like Netscape to sort the messages in ascending order. This doesn't make much sense, in my humble opinion, if you're sorting by Name or Subject, unless you really like reading lists in reverse alphabetical order. It's a great choice, though, if you'd like to sort by Date. With the Ascending option, you see your most recent messages at the top of the mail window.

To sort your list quickly, just click the Sender, Subject, or Date buttons at the top of the message header pane.

Deleting Messages

If you don't want to keep a letter, delete it so that it doesn't clutter up your message header panel. To delete the message you're viewing, just press the Delete key.

To delete more than one message, hold down the Ctrl key and click the headers of all the messages you'd like to delete. Then press the Delete key.

Oh no! I just deleted a really important letter! Don't worry—you're saved. Netscape didn't really delete the letter—it just moved the letter to the Trash folder. To open the Trash folder, click Trash in the folder panel. To restore the letter, drag its header back to the Inbox folder.

To really delete unwanted letters, you must empty the Trash folder. To do so, choose Empty Trash Folder from the File menu.

Creating New Folders

Once you've got an Inbox full of letters that you really want to keep, you may experience problems navigating through the list and finding letters (despite all of Netscape's neat finding and sorting tools). To keep your Inbox to a minimum, you should create additional folders for storing your messages. For example, I've got folders for messages pertaining to Sailing, Backpacking, Wine, and other hobbies of mine, and then of course I've got one (down at the bottom of the list) called Work.

To create a folder, choose Create New Folder from the File menu. You'll see a dialog box prompting you to type the new folder's name. Type the name, and click OK.

To add messages to the new folder, select the messages in the Inbox window and drag the messages to your new folder.

To delete a folder and all the messages it contains, select the folder and choose Delete Folder from the Edit menu.

Compressing Folders

The storage technique that Netscape uses for your mail is very inefficient, but it maximizes retrieval speed. That's great for the messages you're reading right now. If a folder contains a lot of messages that you don't plan to read very often, but want to store indefinitely, you can compress the folder. You'll still be able to acces the messages, but they'll open a little more sluggishly.

To compress a folder, select a folder and choose Compress Folder from the File menu.

From Here

- Don't like the time delay in e-mail? Talk to other Internetters in real time with Chat, discussed in the next chapter.
- Get into the swing of things on Usenet, and you'll get lots more electronic mail—not all of it friendly! Check out Chapter 22.

Chapter 19

Chat It Up!

Internet Relay Chat. It's the coolest thing on the Net—or the biggest waste of time, depending on your perspective. Tales are rife of the positive role played by eyewitness IRC reports of the downfall of the Soviet Union, the devastation of the Los Angeles earthquake, and the defeat of the Cleveland Indians. Tales are equally rife of idiotic, expletive-laden conversation, in which the overall maturity quotient seems to be in the early adolescent phase. You should be aware, too, that the IRC is a sort of playground for some of the most malicious computer hackers you'll ever run across.

Decide for yourself, and to do so, take a look at Internet Relay Chat, which usually goes by its acronym IRC. It's a real-time chat system of global scope, made possible by the Internet. And thanks to Netscape's Chat accessory, IRC takes on a new level of user-friendliness and functionality: As

For the Time-Challenged

- Netscape Chat enables you to join IRC conversations.
- After you join an IRC group, you can type messages that the whole group will see, or "whisper" to just one person.
- If you'd like, you can invite someone to join you in a private conversation.
- You can create your own IRC channel, if you wish.

you'll see, Chat enables you to send and display Web pages while you're chatting it up with other denizens of IRC.

This chapter introduces IRC and fully explores the Chat accessory, which transforms the rather quirky IRC interface into something that's actually a pleasure to use. You'll learn how to join conversations, whisper to individuals without anyone hearing, and how to start your own conversations. And throughout, you'll learn how to bring all of Netscape's functionality to your chat sessions. As you'll see, it's fun to send people the URL to your home page and to see other peoples' pages displayed while you're chatting to them!

My, what filthy language! Let's get this straight: IRC is strictly an *adult* pastime: There's a lot of discussion of every conceivable aspect of human sexuality, and many of the groups are frankly erotic in intent. It's definitely not for kids. Don't install Netscape Chat on a Net-connected computer that your kids are using! That said, there are plenty of non-erotic conversations to join, so don't write off IRC as another Internet playground for perverts. As with anything on the Internet, there's dross and there's gold.

What Is IRC?

IRC is an Internet-based chat network that enables you to engage in live conversations with real people—who might be located just about anywhere in the world. At any one given time, there are hundreds of distinct conversations going on in IRC, each with its own title. Within each conversation, you'll find one to dozens of people, chatting it up.

Looking at a Conversation

"Conversation" is a misnomer, since what's going on, really, is that you're typing and sending lines of text, and you see on-screen what you've typed and what others have typed. A conversation might look something like this:

```
<El Viejo> So where did you-all go to school?

<Furrmonger> Berserkely—degree in late Sixties

<Ju-ju> U of Texas

<Inconnubula> I dropped out
```

Starting a Private Conversation (Whispering)

If there are too many people in the conversation, you'll find it difficult to carry on a meaningful dialogue with a person. For this reason, it's possible to engage any single individual in a private conversation that the others can't "hear," as in the following example:

```
<El Viejo whispers to Furrmonger> I went there too! What was
your major?

<Furrmonger whispers to El Viejo> Biology. I'm a vet now.
What was yours?
```

Starting Your Own Conversation

After browsing around IRC for a while, you'll get the idea—correctly—that many conversations are private clubs, set up in advance by friends scattered hither and yon. Some are ongoing affairs, with regulars who know each other well and in these conversations, you'll need a lot of patience and time to feel that you're accepted into the clique. At the extreme, you might even get kicked out of a conversation that turns out to be a purely private affair (yes, it's possible to kick people out—if this happens to you, don't whine to your system administrator; just find a new conversation).

If you find the current conversations alienating or unfriendly, there's a ready cure: Start your own. Of course, there's no guarantee that anyone will show up, but I'll tell you this: There are a *lot* of lonely people out there!

As you'll see in the pages to follow, Netscape Chat makes it easy to perform all these actions. Before you know it, you'll be chatting away on IRC—who knows, maybe you'll get hooked.

Getting Started with Netscape Chat

Netscape Chat is downloadable from Netscape's FTP server, which you can access by clicking the Netscape Now! button on Netscape's home page. Once you've downloaded and installed Netscape Chat (see Appendix A), you'll need to configure it for your copy of Netscape, the IRC server you're going to use, and your personal information. All these topics are explored in the sections to follow.

Starting Netscape Chat

To start Netscape Chat with Windows 3.1, open the Netscape Chat program group and double-click the Netscape Chat icon.

To start Netscape Chat with Windows 95, open the Start menu, click Programs, and click Netscape Chat.

Configuring Netscape Chat

The first time you start Netscape Chat, you'll see the Server Connection dialog box (Figure 19.1), which enables you to supply some needed information, including the name of the IRC server you want to use. An IRC server is a program that enables you to connect with other IRC users worldwide. Without accessing an IRC server, you can't use IRC.

Unfortunately, the number of IRC servers seems to be shrinking rather than growing, for the simple reason that IRC is perceived by most system administrators as a waste of Internet resources.

For a list of publicly accessible IRC servers, see http://benso.com/irchjelp.servers.txt

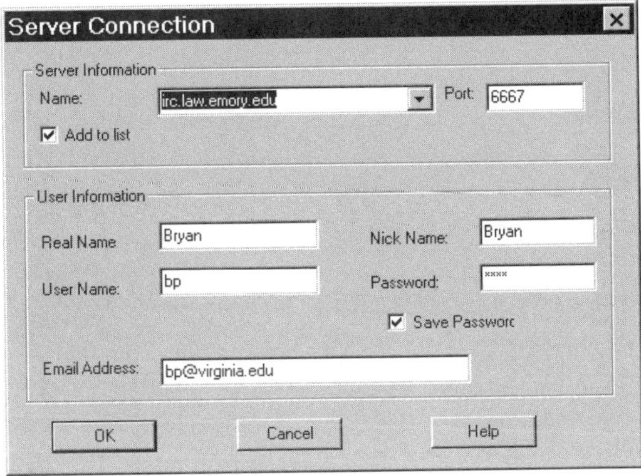

Figure 19.1 Server Connection dialog box

To configure Netscape Chat, follow these instructions:

1. In the Server Information area's Name box, type the name of the IRC server you want to use. Chat is already configured to use the Netscape Chat server (iapp.netscape.com, on port 6667), but this server has many restrictions (for example, you can't create your own conversations). It's OK for demonstrating Chat's basic capabilities, but you'll want to change to a real IRC server at some point.

   Note the Add to List check box. With this box activated (checked), Netscape Chat will add every server's name you type to a list, which you can access later. This is a good thing. If for some reason you don't want the server's name to be added to the list box, deselect this item.

2. In the Real Name box, type a name. *Note*: This name is accessible to IRC users. If you don't want your real name to be known, type a pseudonym here—many people do.

3. In the Nick Name box, type the nickname that you want to use. This name will appear in conversations. If you're female, I'd suggest using a gender-neutral name—unless you really like being bombarded with tasteless come-ons. You can use up to nine characters, with no spaces.

4. The user name, password, and e-mail address fields are optional. Fill them in only if the IRC server you're using requires these.
5. To initiate the connection, click OK.

Assuming Netscape Chat is able to make a connection with the server you chose, you'll see a message in the Console area of the Chat window (see Figure 19.2). This message welcomes you to the server and explains the server's rules, if any. Please read these carefully.

It says "No bots!" What's a bot? A bot, short for robot, is an automated program that pretends to be a person. Bots aren't welcome on most IRC servers. Although some bots perform useful functions, such as welcoming people to a conversation and explaining the ground rules, many more

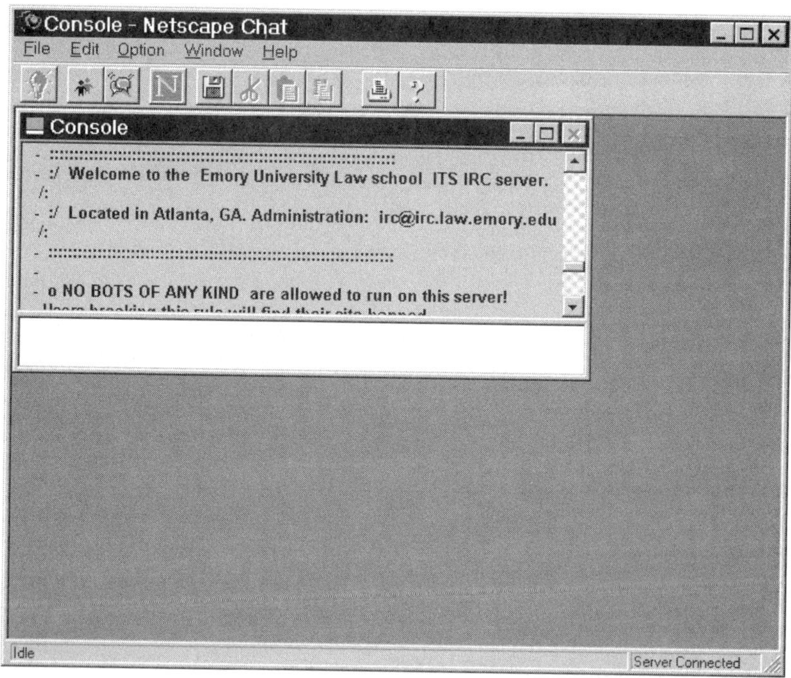

Figure 19.2 Console window with welcome message

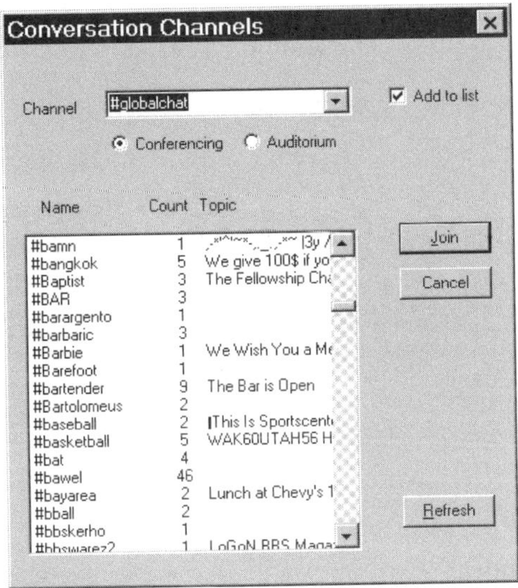

Figure 19.3 Conversation Channels dialog box

are downright nasty. The nasty ones are the playthings of the socially maladjusted types who are all too commonly encountered on IRC.

As you're using Chat, the Console window keeps a running record of your transactions with the server, and it also shows who's joined—and who's left—the conversation you will join (as described in the next section). You can ignore this information, unless you're insatiably curious to know what's going on behind the scenes.

Joining a Conversation

After you've successfully connected to a server, you'll see the Conversation Channels dialog box (shown in Figure 19.3). This window lists all the chat channels that are currently operating. A *chat channel* is a named "chat room" that you can join.

You may need to scroll down a bit to get past the initial garbage—lots of people think it's cute to set up groups named with garbage characters.

In the Count column, you'll see how many people are currently enrolled in a given chat channel. As you'll see, there are lots of channels with one person, while others have as many as several dozen. Try to find a channel that's got from three to seven participants—you'll find some lively action, but not so much that it becomes overwhelming.

There are some really nice folks on IRC—you just have to know where to look. Try starting with a group called #irchelp or #ircnewbies; chances are you'll meet other newcomers like yourself, chatting away with some helpful IRC vets. Another suggestion: Try some of the age-grouped conversations (such as #40+), or those focused on an interest (such as a musical group or hobby). Stay away from groups that have sex-related or incomprehensible names.

To join a conversation, just highlight the conversation's name and click Join. You'll see a new Conferencing window, as shown in Figure 19.4.

After you've used Chat a few times, you'll find that the program has kept a list of the channels you frequently visit. To join one of these channels quickly, open the Edit menu and choose Frequent Channels. In the Fequent Channels dialog box, highlight the name of the channel you want to join, and click OK. If you would like to remove a channel's name, highlight the name and click Remove Selection.

When you enter a conversation, the person who set it up will probably say hello. It's polite to answer—see "Sending a Message," later in this chapter—but you *don't* need to say hello to everyone who's present. Doing so is a considered a waste of IRC bandwidth and could even get you kicked out of a conversation.

Understanding the Conferencing Window

The Conferencing (Chat Channel) window displays what's going on in the chat channel you're currently using. It contains the following sections (see Figure 19.4):

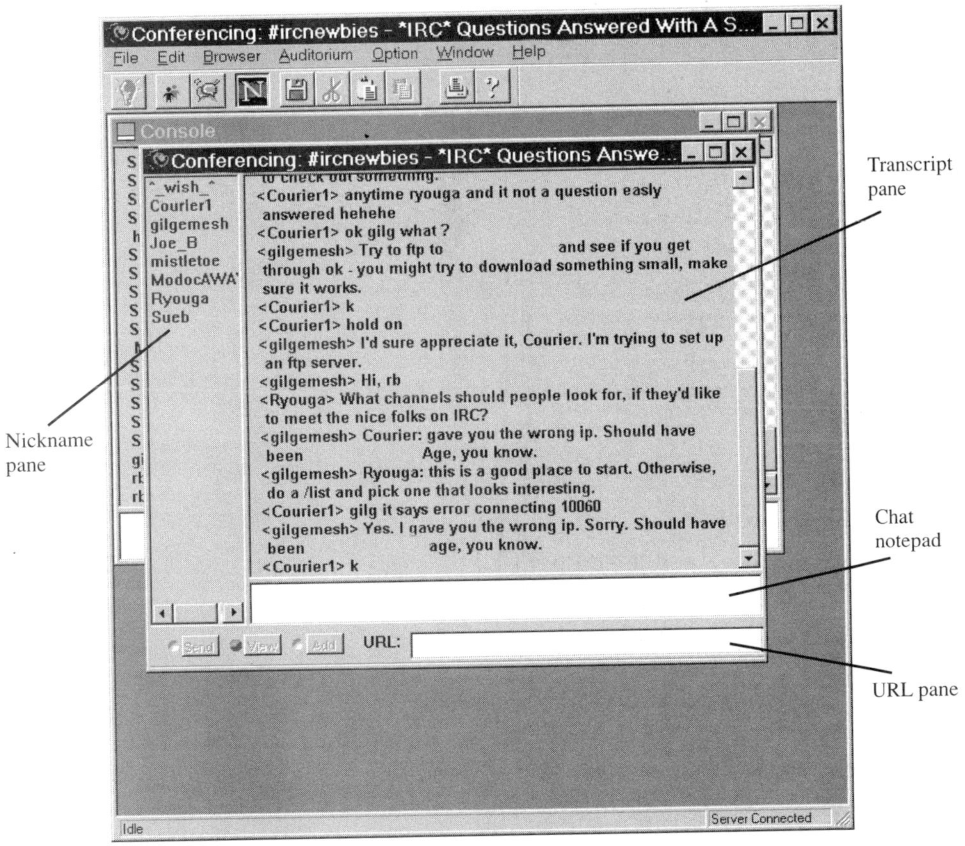

Figure 19.4 Conferencing window

Nickname Pane This pane shows a list of the people currently enrolled in this conversation.

Transcript Pane Here's where you see a running transcript of the conversation you've joined. When you type a message and press Enter, you'll see your message in this pane. You also see the messages other people have sent. When you exit the conversation, you'll have an opportunity to save the transcript, if you wish.

Chat Notepad	Here's where you type your messages and describe your actions, as described in the following section.
URL Pane	This pane displays a URL list. When you display a Web page in the Navigator window, you'll see the URL in this pane. Additional pages are added to a list, with the most recently added page shown first.

You'll soon become familiar with the Conferencing window, once you've worked with it a while.

Chatting It Up

After you've joined a conversation, it's time to chat! You should begin by reading the dialog for a while. Then you can send your own messages and get involved in the swim of things. You can whisper to someone, describe actions you're performing (virtually, of course), send Web pages, view Web pages, compile a list of Web pages to linked partners, and much more. The following sections describe all the actions you can perform during the time you're engaged in a conversation.

Reading the Dialog

When you first join a channel, you'll start seeing the messages that others are typing. In the Nickname pane, you'll see a list of the people currently enrolled in the conversation. Follow the conversation for a while until you grasp what's going on.

Sending a Message

If you've joined a friendly group, somebody will say "hi" to you. Here's your chance to type your first message. To send a message, simply type your message in the Chat Notepad, and press Enter.

While you're working in the Chat Notepad, you can use all the standard Windows editing commands (Undo, Copy, Cut, and Paste) to create and perfect the text you're writing.

As you'll soon find, IRC users employ abbreviations to cut down on the amount of text they type. Here's a quick rundown on the abbreviations you'll commonly find on IRC:

2	to	k	OK
bbiaf	Be back in a few minutes	lol	Laughing out loud
bbl	Be back later	m	male
brb	Be right back	r	are
c	see	re	Hi again ("repeat hi")
f	female	ttyl	Talk to you later
imho	In my (not-so) humble opinion	u	you
		y	why

I was just trying to be friendly, and they got mad! Don't say "hi" to everyone in the group, one by one. This is considered a waste of IRC bandwidth. Just say "Hi all."

Once you've got an idea of what's being discussed in the channel you've selected, you'll soon find yourself in the swim of things.

If you're having a one-to-one conversation with somebody in the channel, you may wish to converse privately, so that others don't see the exchange. For more information, see the section entitled "Whispering to Someone."

Whispering to Someone

If you're getting into a one-on-one conversation with somebody, you may prefer to *whisper* to the person. When you whisper, only the person to whom you're whispering can read your message. For this reason, it doesn't interfere with the group's ongoing dialog.

To whisper to someone, select the person's nickname in the Nickname List. Then type and send your message. Your message will be seen only by the person whose name you've highlighted.

To stop whispering to the person, deselect the person's name. Now your messages will be seen by everyone in the group.

If a whispering session starts going great guns, consider starting a private conversation, as described later in this section. You'll have a one-on-one chat window without the distractions of the group's conversation. You can leave the group channel open while you're doing this, too.

Finding Out More about Someone

Like to know more about one of the people you're conversing with? From the File menu, click Personal Conversation. You'll see the Show People dialog box (Figure 19.5). Scroll down and highlight the person's name, and click Info. You'll see the Personal Info box for that person, showing the information that the person has chosen to make public. This may include the person's real name and e-mail address—but more than likely, it won't. Knowing that one can run into some pretty malicious people on IRC, most people like to keep their personal information private.

Starting a Private Conversation

If you find that you'd rather talk one-to-one with an individual rather than join in the channel's conversation, you can whisper, as described above. But it's difficult to track the conversation when so many other messages intervene. Happily, there's a solution: You can start a private conversation with someone.

To start a private conversation, follow these steps:

1. From the File menu, choose Personal Conversation. You'll see the Show People dialog box, shown in Figure 19.5.
2. Scroll down the list to find the name of the person to whom you'd like to chat privately.
3. Select the person's name.
4. Click Talk. Chat sends out an invitation to this person to join you in a private conversation. If he or she accepts, you'll see a new Chat window, and you can begin the one-to-one conversation (Figure 19.6).

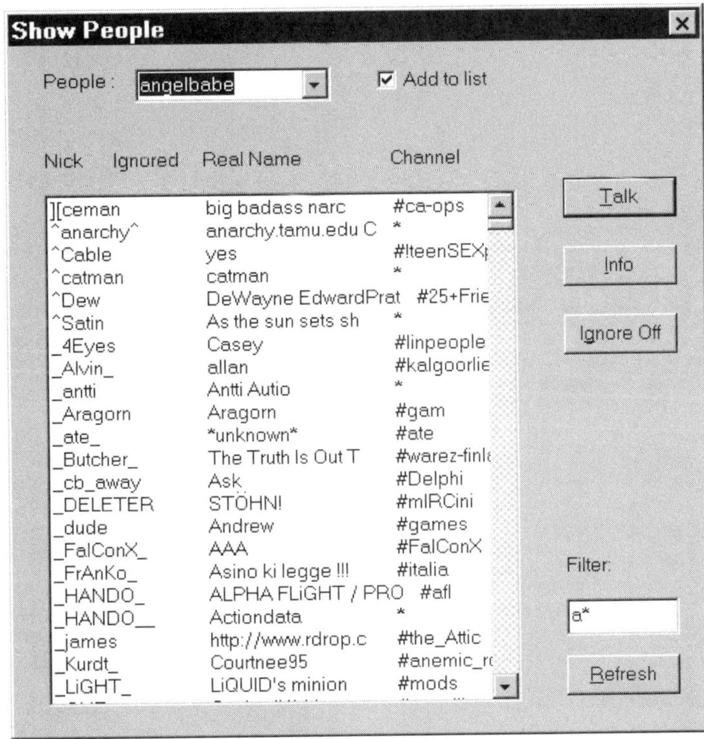

Figure 19.5 Show People dialog box

When you successfully initiate a personal conversation with somebody, Chat automatically adds that person's nickname to your Personal Phone Book. To talk to this person again, open the Edit menu and choose Personal Phone Book. Highlight the person's name and click OK.

Performing an Action

You'll often see *actions*, which are written descriptions of somebody doing something:

```
<Lacy1> Lacy sidles up to the bar, and orders a glass of
chilled Chardonnay
```

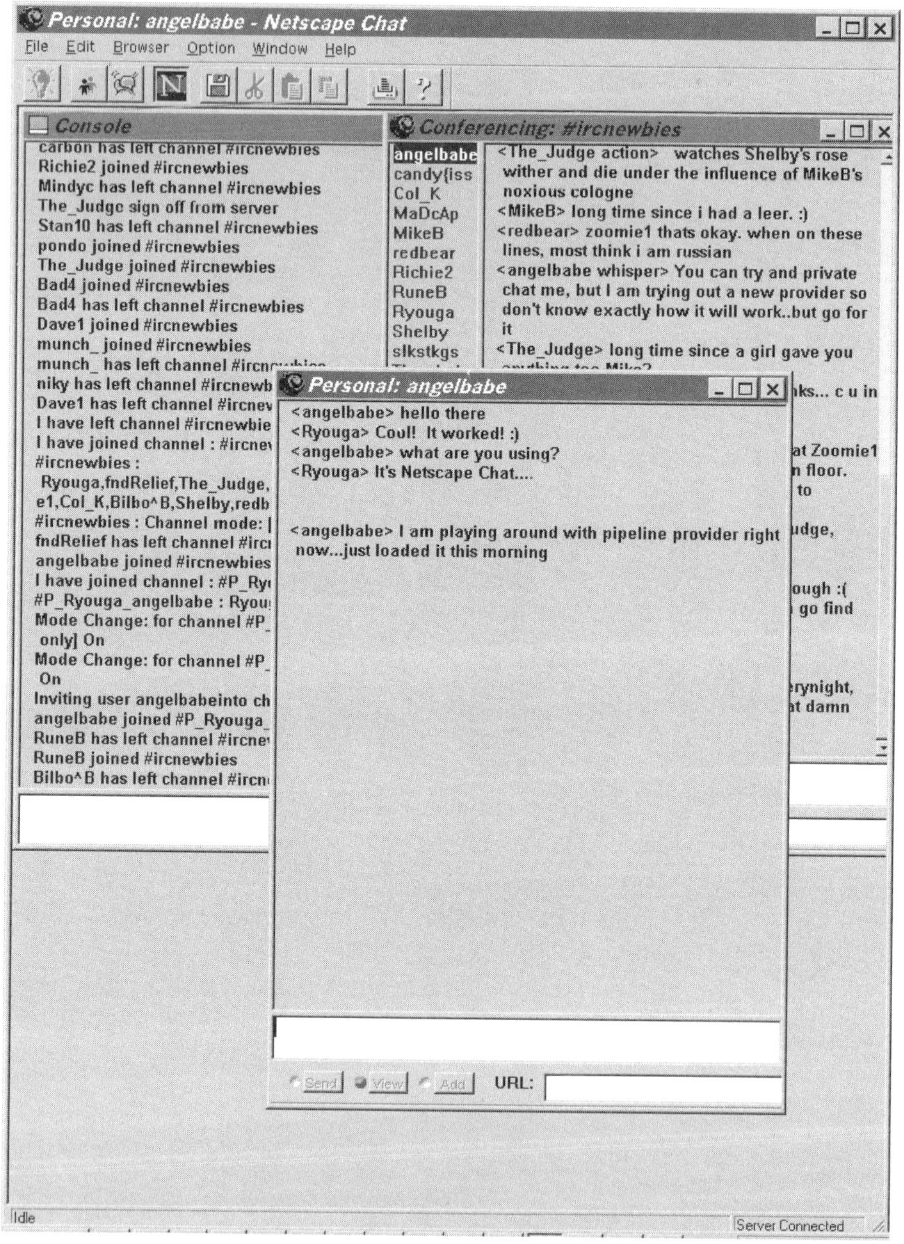

Figure 19.6 Personal conversation

You can send any of the IRC commands that Netscape supports by typing a slash mark followed by the command, as in the /me example given below. For example, to change your nickname, type /nick followed by the new nickname you want to use. To change your nickname from Ryouga to Akane, for instance, type /nick Akane. To get information about somebody you're talking to, type /whois followed by that person's name (for example, /whois Laura displays information about the person using the nickname Laura).

To perform an action, type a slash mark in the Chat notepad, followed by *me*, and the description of the action you want to perform:

```
/me El Viejo sits down beside Lacy and orders an Anchor Steam
Beer
```

You'll see the results of your action in the conversation window:

```
<El Viejo action> El Viejo sits down beside Lacy and orders
an Anchor Steam Beer
```

Ignoring Someone

You may find that you're not really interested in the comments being made by an individual in the conversation—at the best, perhaps they're interfering, or not contributing; at the worst, you may find that you're being harassed by some infantile jerk. Happily, there's a cure: You can ignore him.

To ignore a person:

1. From the File menu, choose Personal Conversation. You'll see the Show People window.
2. Highlight the harasser's name.
3. Click Ignore On.
4. If you like, you can ignore additional people by repeating steps 2 and 3.
5. Click the Close button to close the Show People window.

Note that your ignore list isn't saved when you quit Chat.

If you would like to give the miscreant a reprieve, you can do so by following the instructions below.

To de-ignore a person:

1. From the File menu, choose Personal Conversation. You'll see the Show People window.
2. Highlight the name of the person you're ignoring.
3. Click Ignore Off.
4. If you like, you can de-ignore additional people by repeating steps 2 and 3.
5. Click the Close button to close the Show People window.

Compiling a List of Web Pages to Share

One of Chat's neatest characteristics is its close integration with Netscape. You can send Web pages to others, and if they're using Chat, they'll see the page in their copy of Netscape.

To send Web pages to others, you begin by compiling a list of one or more URLs to send.

To compile a list of URLs:

1. In Netscape, locate and display the first Web page that you want to send, or just type the URL in the URL box.
2. Repeat step 1 until you've finished your list. You'll find the URLs in the list box. You can display the list—and then choose any of the URLs you've collected—by clicking the down arrow.

Sending a Web Page to Someone

Once you've compiled a list of one or more URLs, you can send a Web page to other people in the channel you're using.

To send a Web page:

1. In the URL pane, select the Web page that you want to send.
2. If you would like to send the Web page to just one person, highlight that person's name in the Nicknames List. To send the page to everyone, just skip this step.
3. Click Send in the URL toolbar.

If any of the people you're chatting with are using Netscape Chat, they'll see the page you've sent displayed automatically in their copy of Netscape. (The automatic display of pages sent in this manner is controlled by the Auto Start option in Chat's Preference menu, which is activated by default. If this option is turned off, Netscape won't display pages conveyed via IRC.)

Printing a Transcript

If something memorable has happened while you're on IRC, you can print the transcript. To do so, click the Print button.

Exiting a Channel

When you're finished chatting, it's polite to say goodbye. To exit the conversation, just click the Close box, or choose Exit Conversation from the File menu.

Starting Your Own Channel

If you don't see a channel that pertains to a subject you'd like to discuss, try starting one. There's no guarantee that anyone will join your conversation—in fact, there's no guarantee of *anything* on IRC! Try it and see what happens.

To start a channel:

1. From the File menu, choose Group Conversation. You'll see the Conversation Channels dialog box.
2. Choose Conferencing (the default) or Auditorium. In the Conferencing mode, anyone can speak to anyone. In the Auditorium mode, participants must get permission from the moderator to start speaking to the group. If you choose Auditorium, you become the moderator of the auditorium by default. If you would like to appoint others to be co-moderators, you can do so by selecting their names and choosing Grant Moderator from the Auditorium menu. You might wish to do this if you choose to leave a moderated channel you've created, because IRC will cancel an auditorium that doesn't have a moderator.

3. To start the channel, just click Join. IRC creates the new channel, and its name appears on the list of channels that other IRC participants are viewing.

Using an Auditorium

If you're participating in an auditorium, you must ask permission to speak—and if you're a moderator, you must decide whether to grant it. You'll know when you're participating in an Auditorium—if you are, you'll see the Auditorium menu on Chat's menu bar.

To ask for permission to speak:

1. Select a moderator's name from the Nickname pane.
2. From the Auditorium menu, choose Request Microphone.
3. In the Chat Notepad, compose your request and press Enter. This sends the message to the moderator you've selected.
4. Check the transcript pane for a message from your moderator.
5. If you're granted permission to speak, use the Notepad to communicate with the audience.

To grant permission to speak:

1. Highlight the name of the person who has asked to speak.
2. From the Auditorium menu, choose Grant Speaker.

If you wish to remove permission to speak, highlight the person's name, open the Auditorium menu, and choose Revoke Speaker.

From Here

- Access Gopher archives with Chapter 20's help.
- Get free software from FTP archives; find out how in Chapter 21.
- Get into the fray in Usenet newsgroups in Chapter 22.

Chapter 20

Digging Around in Gopher

Gopher got its start as a campus-wide information system at the University of Minnesota, the mascot of which is—you guessed it. It enables people to access all kinds of different information with the same easy menu-based browsing system. Those nice University of Minnesota folks made the program freely available, and what do you know? Colleges and universities everywhere used Gopher to make information available. A few private organizations did, too.

Before the Web came along, Gopher was the Latest Best Thing for accessing Internet resources, and it grew wildly. But the Web's success has choked off Gopher's growth. Still, there are lots of useful resources available in Gopher menus, mainly because people haven't had the time to put them on the Web yet. But no matter; clever Netscape can navigate Gopher menus

directly. You can also use services called Veronica and Archie to find Gopher-based information.

This chapter covers the use of Gopher menus with Netscape. Although Gopher is easy to use, this chapter includes some yummy tips for locating great Gopher sites and searching Gopherspace effectively. Even if you've navigated Gopher already, you'll still want to skim this chapter.

Accessing Gopher Sites

To access a Gopher site, you have two options:

- **Click a Gopher hyperlink** A hyperlink to a Gopher site looks like any other hyperlink. After you click the link, you'll see a Gopher menu instead of a Web page.
- **Type a Gopher URL directly** A Gopher URL looks like a Web URL, except that it starts with gopher:// instead of http://, as in the following:

  gopher://gopher.well.sf.ca.us/

Understanding Gopher Menus

After you've accessed a Gopher site, you'll see a Gopher menu, such as the one shown in Figure 20.1.

As displayed by Netscape, a Gopher menu is a list of hyperlinks—but they're of different kinds. You may see one or more of the following items, each with its own icon:

Another Gopher menu Click this item to display the items in this folder.

A document If you click this link, you will see a plain-text document, which you can read on-screen.

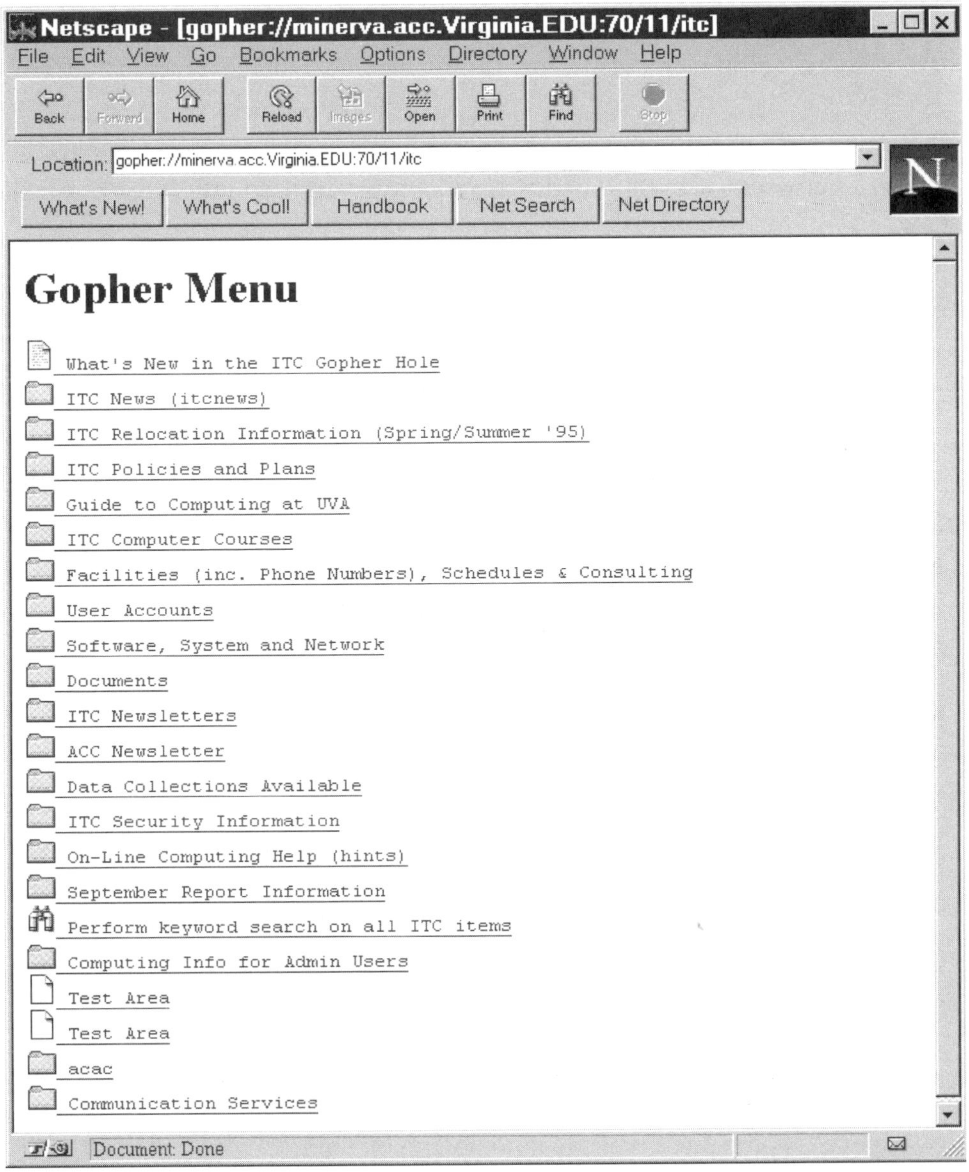

Netscape - [gopher://minerva.acc.Virginia.EDU:70/11/itc]

File Edit View Go Bookmarks Options Directory Window Help

Back Forward Home Reload Images Open Print Find Stop

Location: gopher://minerva.acc.Virginia.EDU:70/11/itc

What's New! What's Cool! Handbook Net Search Net Directory

Gopher Menu

What's New in the ITC Gopher Hole

ITC News (itcnews)

ITC Relocation Information (Spring/Summer '95)

ITC Policies and Plans

Guide to Computing at UVA

ITC Computer Courses

Facilities (inc. Phone Numbers), Schedules & Consulting

User Accounts

Software, System and Network

Documents

ITC Newsletters

ACC Newsletter

Data Collections Available

ITC Security Information

On-Line Computing Help (hints)

September Report Information

Perform keyword search on all ITC items

Computing Info for Admin Users

Test Area

Test Area

acac

Communication Services

Document: Done

Figure 20.1 Gopher menu

	**A binary file**	If you click this link, Netscape will begin downloading the file.
	**A graphic**	If you click this link, Netscape will display the graphic.
	**Perform a search**	If you click this link, you'll see a search document. Type one or more keywords, and click the Search button to initiate the search.
	**Access a Telnet session**	If you click this link, Netscape will start your Telnet helper application. For more information on Telnet, see Chapter 23.

When you've gone "down" into a Gopher submenu (otherwise known as a "Gopher hole"—get it?), you can go back "up" again to the menu you just viewed. To do so, click the Back button.

For the Time-Challenged

- Gopher is a menu-driven information system that Netscape can access directly. Gopher menus may contain links to Gopher submenus, documents, binary files, graphics, or search utilities.
- If you've gone "down" into a Gopher submenu, click the Back button to get out of the "hole."
- Check out TradeWave Galaxy's Gopher Jewels list for some terrific Gopher sites.
- You can search Gopher directory titles and document names with Veronica, but you'd be wise to access this overloaded service in the wee hours of the morning.
- It isn't obvious from Veronica's search screen, but the software has some very sophisticated search capabilities.

Gopher Jewels

Looking for good stuff on Gopher? Check out Gopher Jewels, accessible via TradeWave Galaxy (http://galaxy.einet.net/GJ/). You'll see a list of hyperlinks to great Gopher sites, which are classified by subject; there are over 2,300 Gopher sites accessible in this way. Table 20.1 lists the subject categories currently found in the Gopher Jewels list. Have fun!

Table 20.1 Subject Categories in Gopher Jewels (TradeWave Galaxy)

Agriculture and Forestry	Internet Cyberspace Related
AIDS and HIV Information	Internet Resources by Type (Gopher, Phone, USENET, WAIS, Other)
Anthropology and Archaeology	Internet Service Providers
Architecture	Journalism
Arts and Humanities	Language
Astronomy and Astrophysics	Legal or Law Related
Biological Sciences	Library Information and Catalogs
Books, Journals, Magazines, Newsletters, and Publications	List of Lists Resources
Chemistry	Manufacturing
Computer Related	Math Sciences
Country Specific Information	Medical Related
Disability Information	Meteorology
Economics and Business	Military
Education (includes K–12)	Miscellaneous Items
Employment Opportunities and Resume Postings	Museums, Exhibits, and Special Collections
Engineering Related	News Related Services
Environment	Patents and Copyrights
Federal Agency and Related Gopher Sites	Physics
Free-Nets and Other Community or State Gophers	Political and Government
Fun Stuff and Multimedia	Products and Services—Store Fronts
Genealogy	Psychology
General Reference Resources	Radio and TV Broadcasting
Geography	Religion and Philosophy
Geology and Oceanography	Safety
Global or World-Wide Topics	Social Sciences
Grants	State Government
History	Technical Reports
	Technology Transfer
	Travel Information

Searching Gopher: Veronica

Veronica is a search engine that's designed to find resources in Gopherspace (the world of accessible Gopher items). To do so, Veronica scans an automatically compiled index of titles of Gopher directory titles and document names. Note that this index does *not* include words found within the text of these files. Jughead is essentially a version of Veronica that searches for directory titles only.

To access Veronica, click the Veronica hyperlink in HOME.HTM, or use the following URL:

gopher://gopher.ed.gov:70/11/other_gopher/veronica

Note that you can search two ways:

- **Directory Titles Only (Jughead)** This is a good place to start your search. If you're lucky, you'll find a Gopher menu that groups a lot of resources pertaining to the subject in which you're interested.
- **Searching All Gopherspace (Veronica)** This search examines Gopher document names as well as directory titles. You'll get a lot more items from this search, but much of it will be irrelevant junk.

To initiate the search, decide whether you're going to search directory titles or Gopherspace, and click a server name. You'll see a search page.

It says, "Too many connections—Try again soon"! What, you're trying to search Veronica during the *day*? With so many gazillions of people using the Internet, Veronica has become an early-morning-hours service, unless you're very lucky.

Simplified Searching

On some Veronica servers, you'll see an item called "Simplified Veronica Search." This option uses automated techniques to find an available server. It gives you the best chance of actually getting something out of your Veronica search.

Interpreting the Results of the Search

If the search is successful, you'll see a Gopher menu containing the items the server has retrieved. You can navigate this Gopher menu just like any other Gopher menu.

If the search is unsuccessful, you'll see a message informing you that the server returned no data. Try again, using more general keywords.

Advanced Veronica Searches

Like many of the Internet's search services (see Chapter 17), Veronica searches are more capable than you'd think, looking at that simple search page. By default, Veronica performs a case-insensitive search; if you type two or more words, Veronica ANDs them (no document is retrieved unless all of the keywords are present in the document title). In addition, Veronica performs a whole-word search; if you type "cat," you'll get documents with the word "cat" in the title, but not "concatenate."

You can override Veronica's default search settings in the following ways:

- **OR Operator** To search with an OR operator so that Veronica retrieves documents that have any of the keywords in their titles, separate the words with OR ("cats or dogs").
- **NOT Operator** To exclude documents containing a certain word in their titles, type NOT followed by the word you want to exclude ("cats not dogs").
- **Parenthetical Statements** For a finely honed search, you can embed Boolean operators in parentheses. For example, a search for "recipes and (indian or thai)" retrieves Indian as well as Thai recipes, but nothing else pertaining to India or Thailand.
- **Searching for Resources of a Certain Type** The -t operator enables you to restrict the retrieval list to certain types of documents. For example, the following retrieves graphics (GIFs) and sounds pertaining to Star Trek: Star Trek -tgs. To restrict the search in this way, type -t followed by a code and the text you're searching for. For a list of the -t codes, see Table 20.2.
- **Specify the Maximum Number of Hits** By default, Veronica retrieves 200 hits. To increase this number, use the -m operator. The following retrieves 1,000 Star Trek documents: Star Trek -m1000. (You can combine this code with the -t code, if you wish: Star Trek -m1000 -tg retrieves 1,000 Star Trek GIFs, which is assuredly more than you'll ever need.)

Table 20.2 Codes for Restricting Veronica Searches with the -t Operator

0	Text file	s	Sound
1	Directory	e	Event (not in 2.06)
2	CSO name server	I	Image (other than GIF)
4	Mac HQX file	M	MIME multipart/mixed message
5	PC binary	T	TN3270 session
7	Full Text Index (Gopher menu)	c	Calendar (not in 2.06)
8	Telnet session	g	GIF image
9	Binary file	h	HTML, Hypertext Markup Language

From Here

- Hunt down some files with FTP; you'll find the lowdown in Chapter 21.
- Join the tumult on Usenet newgroups with Netscape's excellent newsreading and mail capabilities; check out Chapter 22 for the details.
- See Chapter 23 for information on using Telnet with Netscape.

Chapter 21

Ransacking FTP File Archives

FTP is short for File Transfer Protocol, and its full name pretty much describes what it does. Using FTP, you can exchange program or text files with anyone connected to the Internet. Netscape gives you partial FTP capabilities—specifically, to get files. (You can send files with Netscape's mail capabilities, as discussed in Chapter 18, but that is mail, not FTP—there is a difference.)

You can't just browse around in anyone's computer in search of files. Normally, you need an account and a password to access someone else's computer on the Internet. But some kind people have created publicly accessible file archives. This is also called "anonymous FTP," since you had to log into these computers as "anonymous" when you were using one of those old, clunky FTP programs (which are still needed to upload files to FTP sites). Netscape logs you in to anonymous sites automatically.

For the Time-Challenged

- Netscape accesses anonymous FTP file archives smoothly, showing you a graphical version of server file directories. Just click the items you want. To go back up to a parent directory, be sure to use the hyperlink, not the Back button.
- Archie searches a database of thousands of FTP archives. With Netscape, you can access Archie through a gateway such as ArchiePlex.
- The Virtual Software Library (VSL) provides an easy way to obtain software from the largest and best shareware archives. Don't miss it!

Most of the files in these publicly accessible file archives are programs, including tons of Microsoft Windows programs. You can obtain these and soup up your computer to just an incredible degree. (Mine shows a picture of the Starship Enterprise on start-up, plays the theme from Star Trek, and then you hear a "beam-me-up" transporter sound. OK, it's dumb, but it's more fun than looking at the Windows logo.) These programs are either freeware (copyrighted but freely copiable as long as you don't sell them) or shareware (you really ought to pay that registration fee, you know). The moral: Use FTP to get your hands on extremely cool programs, and they're free (or really cheap). Netscape gives you wonderful tools for browsing FTP file archives (see Figure 21.1), and the WinZip software included with this book automatically decompresses the files after you download them.

If you're interested in obtaining software from the Internet, this chapter's for you!

Accessing Anonymous FTP File Archives

FTP is smoothly integrated with Netscape. You can access anonymous FTP file archives in two ways:

- **Clicking an FTP Hyperlink** You see an FTP file directory.
- **Typing the URL Directly** To access an anonymous FTP archive, you can type ftp:// followed by the archive's name, such as ftp://ftp.virginia.edu/.

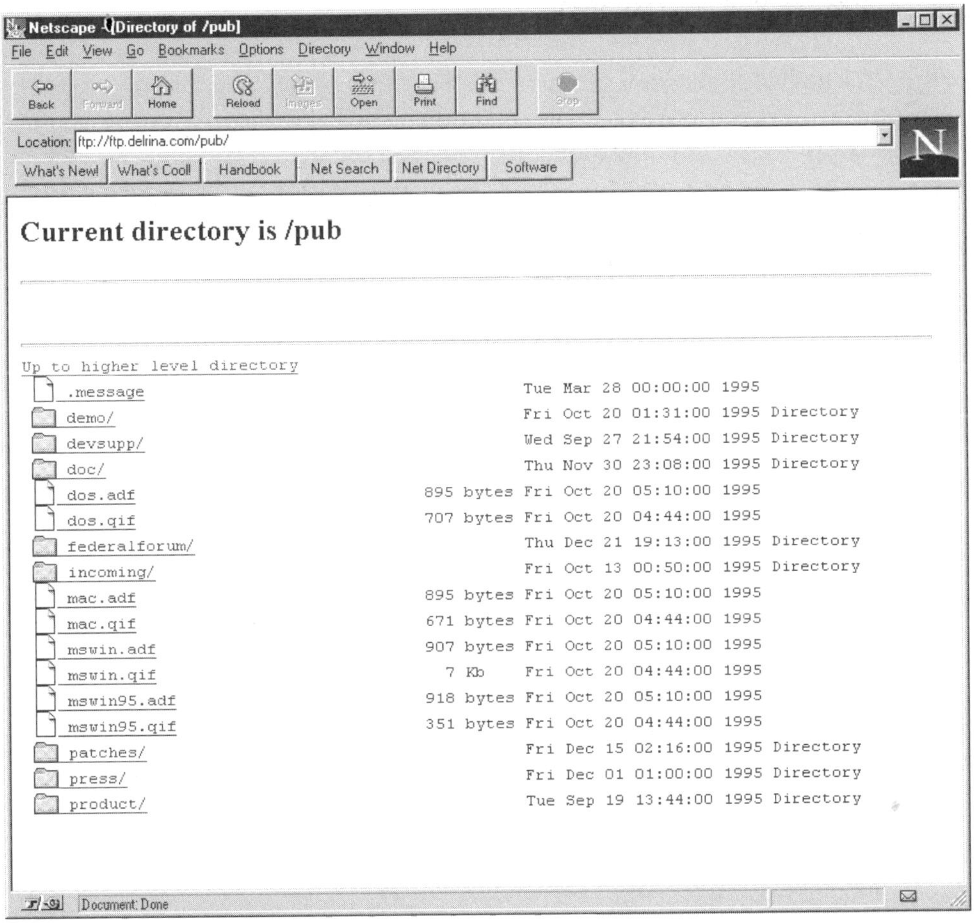

```
Netscape - [Directory of /pub]
File  Edit  View  Go  Bookmarks  Options  Directory  Window  Help
Back  Forward  Home  Reload  Images  Open  Print  Find  Stop
Location: ftp://ftp.delrina.com/pub/
What's New!  What's Cool!  Handbook  Net Search  Net Directory  Software

Current directory is /pub

Up to higher level directory
.message                    Tue Mar 28 00:00:00 1995
demo/                       Fri Oct 20 01:31:00 1995 Directory
devsupp/                    Wed Sep 27 21:54:00 1995 Directory
doc/                        Thu Nov 30 23:08:00 1995 Directory
dos.adf         895 bytes   Fri Oct 20 05:10:00 1995
dos.qif         707 bytes   Fri Oct 20 04:44:00 1995
federalforum/               Thu Dec 21 19:13:00 1995 Directory
incoming/                   Fri Oct 13 00:50:00 1995 Directory
mac.adf         895 bytes   Fri Oct 20 05:10:00 1995
mac.qif         671 bytes   Fri Oct 20 04:44:00 1995
mswin.adf       907 bytes   Fri Oct 20 05:10:00 1995
mswin.qif         7 Kb      Fri Oct 20 04:44:00 1995
mswin95.adf     918 bytes   Fri Oct 20 05:10:00 1995
mswin95.qif     351 bytes   Fri Oct 20 04:44:00 1995
patches/                    Fri Dec 15 02:16:00 1995 Directory
press/                      Fri Dec 01 01:00:00 1995 Directory
product/                    Tue Sep 19 13:44:00 1995 Directory

Document: Done
```

Figure 21.1 An FTP archive viewed with Netscape

NAVIGATING FTP DIRECTORIES

As a Windows user, you've surely plowed around in lots of MS-DOS directories. If you have, you're already familiar with UNIX directories, since DOS was modeled on UNIX. Netscape makes it even easier by providing a highly graphical interface, as shown in Figure 21.1.

To navigate within FTP directories, do the following:

- To open a subdirectory, click one of the folders.
- To go back to the parent directory (the next directory up in the directory tree), click "Up to higher level directory," a hyperlink you'll find at the top of the file list. Do not click the Back button. If you do, you'll get disoriented and lose track of the directories' hierarchical arrangement.

What's in the Files?

Netscape uses little icons to tell you which kind of file you're viewing. Here's a handy guide:

	**A text document**	Click here to read the document. If it's called README, chances are it contains important and useful information about the files in this directory.
	**A graphic**	Click here to download the graphic.
	**A document or file that Netscape couldn't identify**	Click it and see what happens.
	**A movie or animation**	Click here to download an MPEG or QuickTime movie.
	A program	Click here to download the software.

	A compressed file	Click here to download and decompress the file.
	A sound	Click here to hear the sound.
	A subdirectory	Click here to see another directory of files, and possibly additional subdirectories.

Looking for Shareware with the Virtual Software Library

Originally the spare-time activity of Dr. Ziga Turk, a professor at the University of Ljubljana in Slovenia, the Virtual Software Library (VSL) has become the preeminent tool for hunting down publicly available programs on the Internet. VSL permits you to search the text of file descriptions and provides very nice search tools. Though Archie (a search tool covered later in this chapter) indexes the contents of more anonymous FTP sites, VSL covers the biggest and best ones—including the fabled CICA archive at the University of Indiana—and it's a sure bet that you'll find all the most popular shareware at VSL.

To access VSL, click the hyperlink in HOME.HTM, or use the following URL:

http://vsl.cnet.com/

You'll see VSL's welcome screen, shown in Figure 21.2.

To search for files in VSL, choose one of the buttons below the search options heading on the welcome page. Your options are:

Quick Search Gives you a simple but useful search form—usually all you'll need.

Most Popular Shows a list of the most frequently downloaded files for an operating system that you specify.

New Arrivals Lists the software most recently added to the archive for a given operating system.

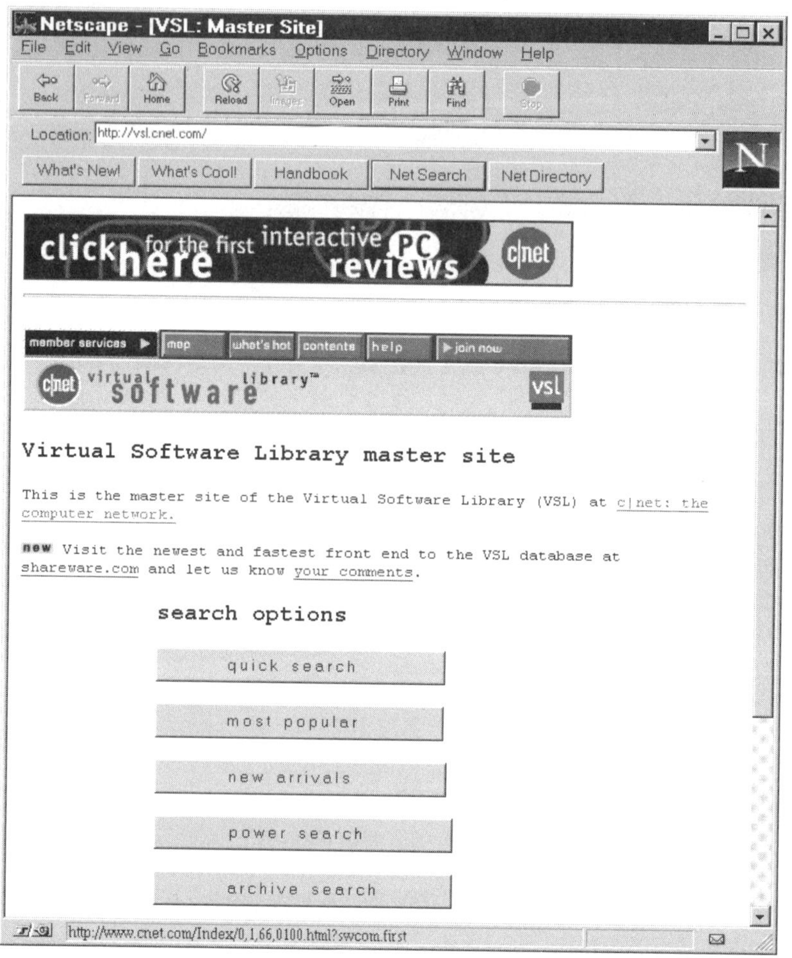

Figure 21.2 The Virtual Software Library welcome screen

Power Search	Lets you tailor your search extensively with an elaborate form. The power search form appears in Figure 21.3.
Archive Search	Lets you specify a particular software archive that you want to search.

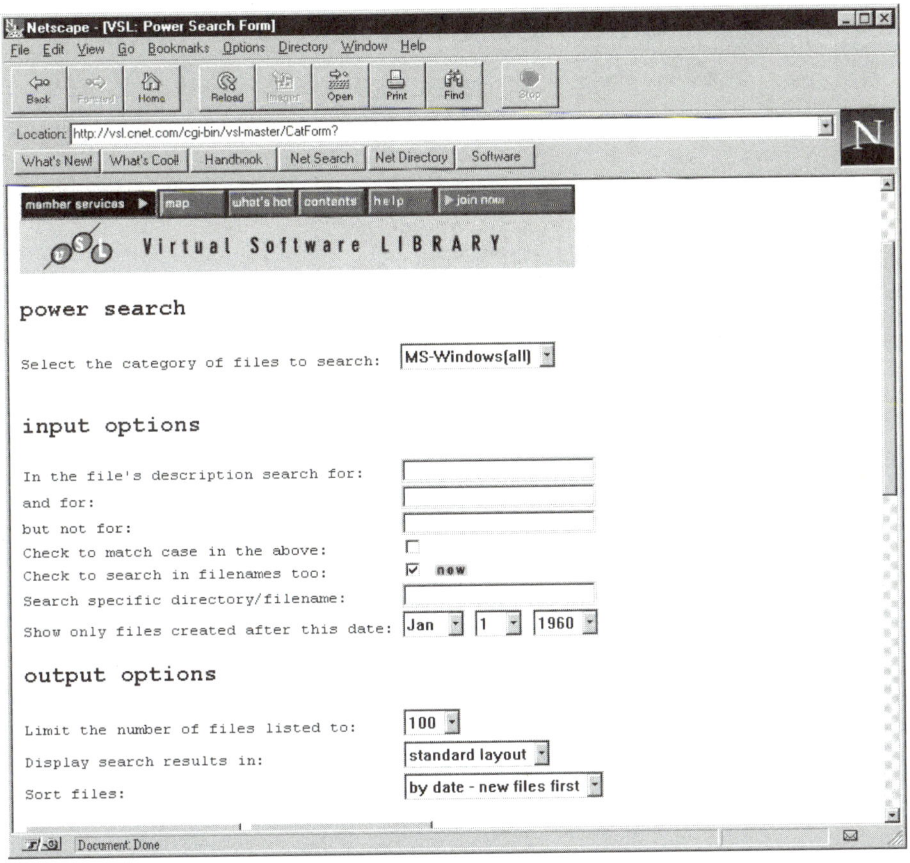

Figure 21.3 The VSL power search form

These instructions describe how to use the power search form.

1. In the "Select the category..." list box, choose the operating system for which you want software. You'll want to choose either MS-Windows(all), MS-Windows 3.x, MS-Windows95, or MS-WindowsNT, but, as an indicator of VSL's comprehensiveness, note that Atari and Amiga are options, too.

2. In the text box labeled "In the file's description search for," type the first word you want to match.
3. If you would like to perform an AND search, type a second keyword in the "and for" box. VSL will retrieve a file only if it matches both the keywords you have typed.
4. If you would like to exclude files with certain words in their descriptions, type the unwanted word in the "and not for" box.
5. If you want to perform a case-sensitive search, click the "match case" check box.
6. If you want to search file names, as well as descriptions, for your search terms, click the "Check to search in filenames too" check box.
7. Unless you know exactly which directories you want to search, leave the "Search specific directory/filename" box blank.
8. To search for files of a certain age, enter a month, day, and year in each of the three date list boxes.
9. To increase the number of files retrieved, choose a larger number in the "Limit the number of files listed to" list box.
10. You can opt to display your search results in Standard or Compact layouts—the two options are nearly the same—by choosing options from the "Display search results in" list box.
11. You can tell the VSL search engine to sort the results of your search by date or by directory path by choosing an option from the "Sort files" list box.
12. Click the Start Search button.

You'll see a new page reporting the results of your search (Figure 21.4). If VSL couldn't find any files, you won't see any file names. If you do see file names, click the one that looks like it meets your needs. You'll see another page of hyperlinks for downloading the file; click the one nearest you to begin downloading.

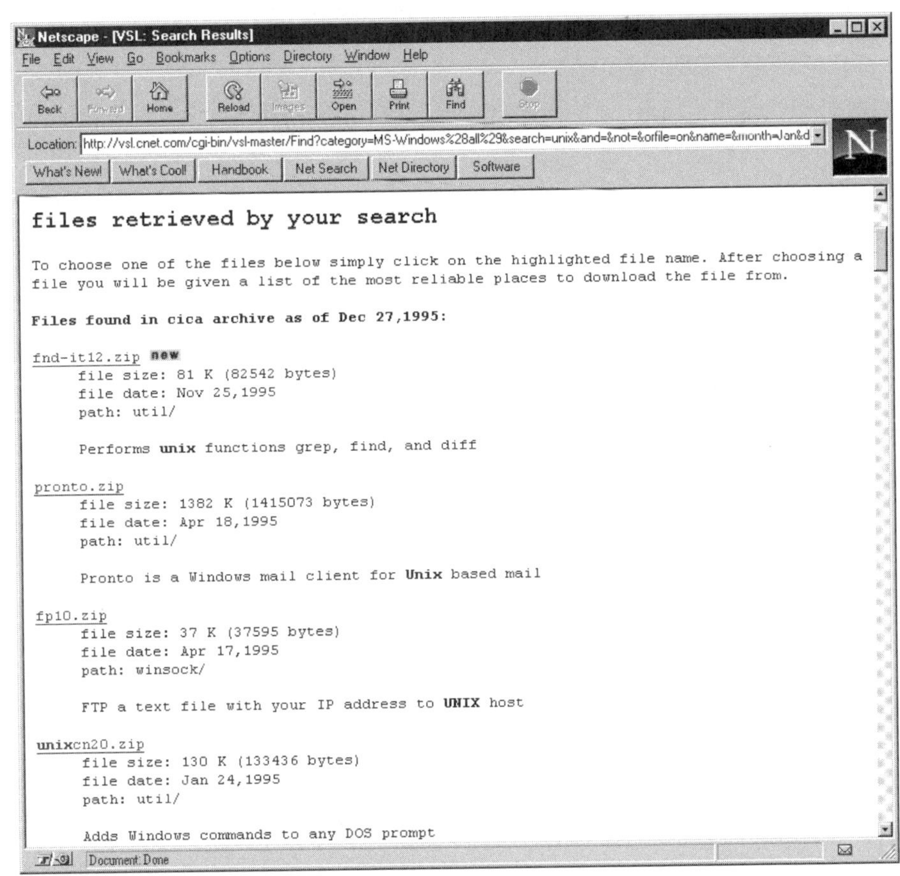

Figure 21.4 The results of a VSL search

Finding FTP Resources: Archie

There are thousands of anonymous FTP file archives out there—but how do you find them? A service called Archie enables you to search for a file, but there's a rub—you pretty much need to know the name of the file you're

looking for. Suppose someone tells you about a file called uudecode.exe that you just have to have. Since you know the name, Archie can help you find an anonymous FTP file archive that contains it, if there is one.

Archie is a UNIX program, but there are lots of Web gateways that enable Netscape and you to communicate with Archie. One of the best is the ArchiePlex gateway, at the following URL:

http://pubweb.nexor.co.uk/public/archie/archieplex/archieplex.html

After accessing ArchiePlex, you'll see the page shown in Figure 21.5.

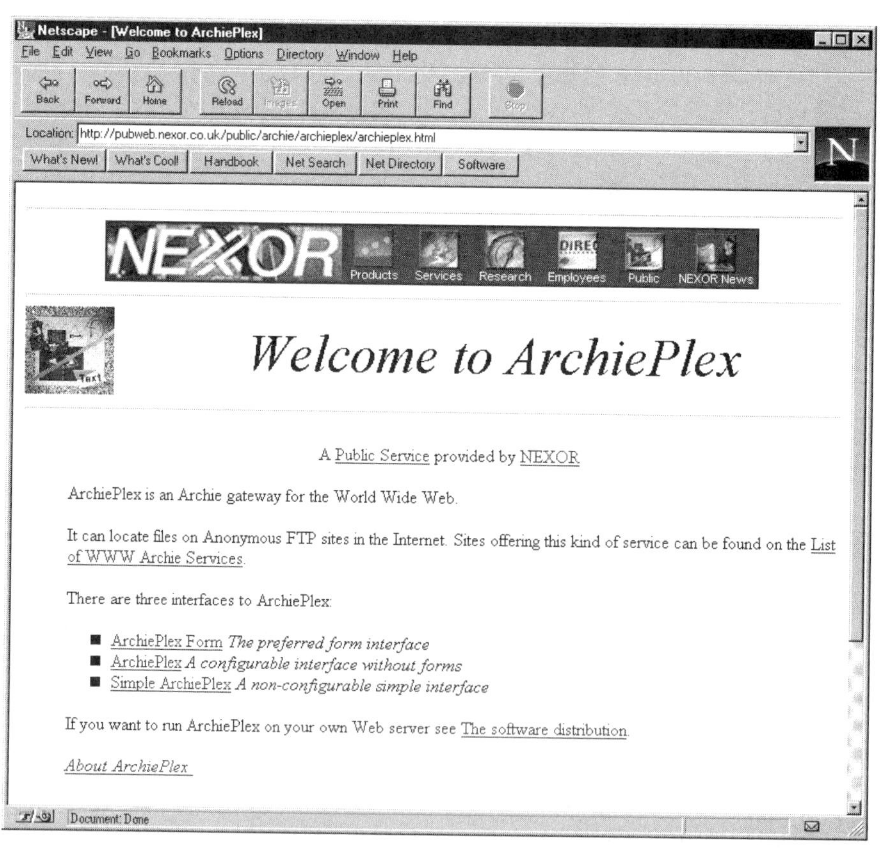

Figure 21.5 The ArchiePlex welcome page

If you haven't already read Chapter 17, take a look at the section called "Understanding Search Techniques." It will help you use ArchiePlex more effectively.

To use ArchiePlex, follow these steps:

1. The easiest way to use ArchiePlex is with the interface that takes advantage of Netscape's forms capability. Click the "ArchiePlex Form" hyperlink on the welcome page. One of the other two search facilities is for browsers without forms capability; the other isn't very flexible. The ArchiePlex form appears in Figure 21.6.
2. In the Search For box, type the name of the file you want to retrieve. If you don't know the whole name, that's OK—type as much as you know for sure. The default search setting, Case Insensitive Substring Match, is a good one for Archie. It allows you to get hits on, say, "EasyWriter," if you typed "Easywriter" in the Search For box.
3. If you wish, change the default output sort order (click By Date to see the most recent version of the file first).
4. Next to "Several Archie Servers can be used," pick the Archie server nearest you, geographically.
5. Choose other options, if you wish, although the defaults are fine. In particular, be nice to other users.
6. Click Submit. If you made a mistake, click Reset and start over with step 2.

If Archie finds any files matching your request, you'll see a new page listing the anonymous FTP sites that have the file for which you're looking.

It says "Server timed out"! Welcome to the club. Here, unfortunately, is yet another of those overloaded Internet services that is becoming increasingly difficult to access. If the server is busy, you're likely to see this message. As the saying goes, "try again later". . . like at 3:30 AM.

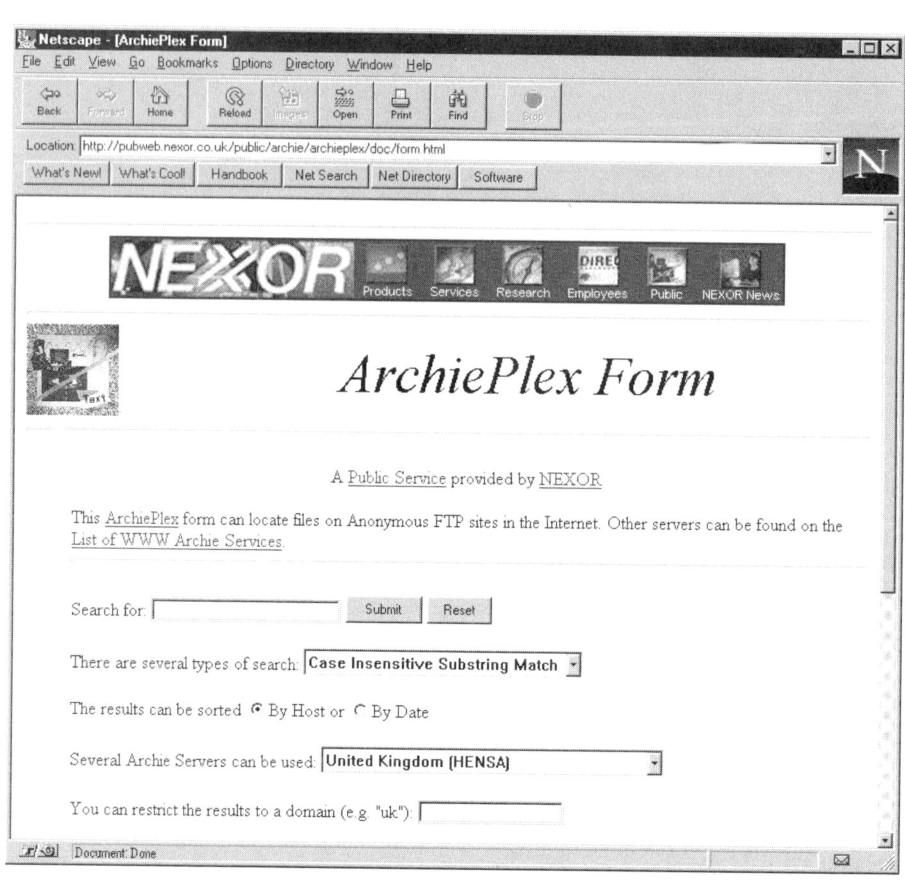

Figure 21.6 The ArchiePlex form

From Here

- Feeling brave? Venture into the wilds of Usenet, with Netscape as your helper. See Chapter 22.
- Don't forget you can access Telnet sessions with Netscape, as you'll learn in Chapter 23.

Chapter 22

Ranting and Raving in Usenet Newsgroups

Usenet is a computer-based discussion system that's widely distributed on the Internet. The idea underlying Usenet is devilishly clever: The Usenet software works behind the scenes, copying and relaying the messages users contribute, so that in time every participating computer (called a *Usenet site*) has an exact copy of every message contributed to the network. The software knows how to organize these messages into topical categories, called *newsgroups*, which you can read. In addition, you can contribute your own messages to these newsgroups. With more than 160,000 Usenet sites connected to the network worldwide, more than 15,000 newsgroups, and an estimated 7 million regular users, contributing to Usenet may be the ultimate act of self-publishing—or self-immolation, if you break any of Usenet's none-too-explicit rules or guidelines. Whatever else you do with Usenet, read newsgroups for a good while before attempting to post your own messages.

Usenet got its start in 1979 as a method of sharing information about UNIX computer systems, and the network still plays a major role in providing computer support. From its earliest days, though, participants showed even more interest in discussing social and political issues, including controversial ones such as abortion and the death penalty. Since then, Usenet has grown wildly, but the growth has not been without controversy. Usenet's strong points lie in the discussions of computer hardware and software, hobbies, entertainment, and recreation. But many people have concluded that Usenet is not very well suited for the discussion of controversial social issues. It's just too easy for obnoxious twerps to ruin the discussion, leading to a "low signal-to-noise ratio," as experienced Usenet hands term it. I'll promise you one thing: After reading Usenet for a while, your estimate of the number of obnoxious twerps in the world will go up by a very substantial percentage.

One of Usenet's worst problems is its own success. Every day, Usenet contributors post the equivalent of 80,000 pages of text—the days are long gone, obviously, when anyone could hope to read all or most of the newsgroups. Most people follow just one or two of them and ignore the rest—but even so, many newsgroups receive dozens or hundreds of messages per day.

Still, Usenet is a wonderful resource. Many newsgroups offer intelligent discussion, particularly the moderated ones, in which all submissions must pass the scrutiny of a human moderator, who checks to see whether they are relevant to the newsgroup's goals. Generally speaking, the technically oriented newsgroups are of the greatest value; there's a real spirit of information exchange and resource sharing. One of the best things about Usenet are the FAQs (Frequently Asked Questions), which attempt to provide answers to the questions people are most likely to ask. There are hundreds of these, and some of them are among the best sources of information on a topic that you can obtain anywhere.

To read and contribute to Usenet newsgroups, you need software called a *newsreader*. But don't go out on the Net hunting down FTP sites—you already have one of the best newsreaders available: Netscape. Whether you want to join in the hue and cry or just access FAQs, Netscape provides wonderful tools for accessing Usenet. You can read messages, post your own messages on a new subject, or reply—either by a follow-up post or an e-mail message—to messages others have left. Compared to the most powerful newsreading programs, Netscape lacks only a few advanced functions. It's the perfect tool for reading Usenet on a daily basis. This chapter thoroughly explores Netscape's Usenet capabilities.

For the Time-Challenged

- To get started with Usenet, you must name your NNTP server in the Mail and News Preferences dialog box.
- To download the newsgroup names, click Show All Newsgroups in the Options menu.
- To read a newsgroup, click its name in the Subscribed Newsgroups window. You'll see a list of current article titles. To read an article, click its title.
- Netscape organizes articles so that you can see the "thread" of discussion; original articles are listed with their replies.
- Use the Next and Previous buttons to navigate through the articles, or just click the article you want to read.
- Don't even think about posting until you fully understand the rules of netiquette.
- Create your signature file before posting.
- To post an article, click the To: News button at the newsgroup's article title level.
- Consider posting an e-mail reply instead of posting a follow-up message to the group. To post a reply to the group, click Re: News. To post an e-mail reply, click Re: Mail.

New for 2 The new version of Netscape offers vastly improved newsreading capabilities, as you'll find in this chapter. Netscape's now as good as most of the stand-alone newsreader programs available today.

They flamed me! To be "flamed" means to receive a lot of unfriendly e-mail letters. If you break the rules of Usenet "netiquette," flaming may be the result. Please do not post messages to a Usenet newsgroup until you fully understand the newsgroup's purpose and the range of acceptable discussion subjects. Most of all, please do not post questions that have already been answered in the newsgroup's FAQ (Frequently Asked Questions), if there is one (not all newsgroups

have FAQs). This chapter shows you how to access Usenet FAQs; please read this section carefully and obtain the FAQ for any newsgroup to which you're thinking of posting a message. Carefully observe the rules of netiquette, which boil down to good manners, basically: be polite, don't "shout" (using all capital letters), give credit where credit is due, and don't post anything in anger.

Introducing Usenet Newsgroups

With at least 15,000 Usenet newsgroups available from most servers, some kind of organization is needed to make sense of the lengthy list of newsgroup names. This organization is hierarchical, and works in the following way:

- Every newsgroup is part of a top-level hierarchy, such as comp (computer-related subjects), rec (recreation), or soc (social newsgroups).
- Every newsgroup has at least one other part to its name, with the parts separated by dots (such as misc.test or alt.censorship).
- Many newsgroups are further subdivided by adding additional names, as in the following examples:

  alt.fan.tolkien
  alt.fan.woody-allen
  comp.sys.ibm.pc.games.action
  comp.sys.ibm.pc.games.adventure

Newsgroups are organized into two broad categories:

- **Standard Newsgroups** These newsgroups have been established by a formal voting procedure. Every Usenet site is expected to carry the standard newsgroups; not all do, however, owing to problems with disk storage space.
- **Alternative Newsgroups** Anyone who knows the correct UNIX command can create a newsgroup in the alternative (alt.*) hierarchy—but no Usenet site is obligated to carry it. However, many sites offer all or many of the alt newsgroups, which range from important and useful (alt.censorship) to completely silly (alt.barney.dinosaur.die.die.die).

The standard newsgroups fall into the following hierarchies:

bionet	Biology and the environment
biz	Business discussions and advertising
ClariNet	A do-it-yourself on-line newspaper consisting of feeds from major wire services, such as UPI and AP
comp	Computers and computer applications
K12	Primary and secondary education
misc	Anything that doesn't fit into the other categories
news	Newsgroups about Usenet itself
rec	Hobbies and sports
sci	The sciences generally
soc	Social issues and socializing
talk	No-holds-barred controversy, flaming, verbiage—and occasionally, interesting discussion and debate

Usenet may be among the world's most ephemeral communications media: Every article is set to expire after a certain period (usually, two weeks), in which case the message simply disappears from the Net. With hundreds of megabytes of new articles streaming in daily, many Usenet sites have no choice but to decrease the expiration period down to as little as 24 hours. If you don't read the newsgroup regularly, then, you'll miss the action—and you won't have a clue about why a certain topic has become the day's cause célèbre.

What's in a Newsgroup?

A newsgroup consists of articles that have been contributed by Usenet's participants. They fall into two categories:

- **Posts** An original message, with a new topic, that somebody contributed.
- **Follow-up Posts** A reply to the original message, which usually contains some quoted text from the original message. The title of a

follow-up post usually echoes the original post's title, with the addition of "re:" at the beginning of the title.

To enhance your ability to follow the thread of discussion, Usenet software can organize posts and follow-up posts into groups (called *threads*). Not all newsreaders are threaded, though, in which case they throw the messages at you in chronological order. Happily, Netscape can thread the messages—and that makes it an above-average newsreader. Other features take it into the "very good" category, as you'll see in the pages to follow.

Why won't Usenet work? To access Usenet, you need access to an NNTP server, a program that makes Usenet newsgroups accessible to newsreading software. Generally, access to an NNTP server is included with Internet service subscriptions. If you're not sure, call your service provider, and be sure to get the NNTP server's domain name. The next section shows you how to tell Netscape which server to use.

Configuring Netscape to Access Usenet

To configure Netscape to access Usenet, you supply the program with the domain name of your NNTP (Usenet) server. To tell Netscape which NNTP server to use, follow these steps:

1. From the Options menu, choose Mail and News Preferences.
2. Click the Servers tab. You'll see the Servers page, shown in Figure 22.1.
3. In the NNTP server box (News area), type the domain name of your NNTP server.
4. Click OK.

Understanding the News Window

The News window is very similar to the Mail window discussed in Chapter 18—in fact, if you've already learned how to send and receive e-mail

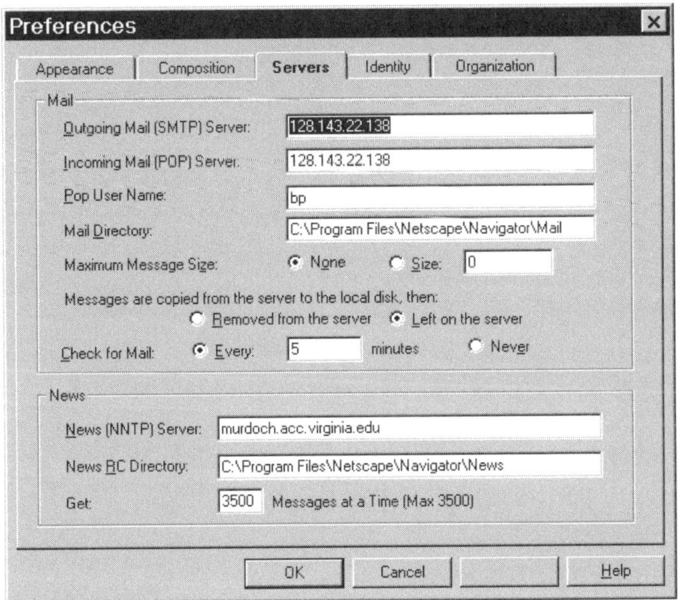

Figure 22.1 Servers page of Mail and News Preferences dialog box

with Netscape, you know a lot of how to get into the swing of things on Usenet.

The window is divided into three panes (see Figure 22.2):

- **Newsgroup Pane** In this window, you see the newsgroups to which you are currently subscribed. By default, you'll be subscribed to newsgroups helpful to new Usenet users. Learn Usenet by reading these first. If you enlarge this window slightly by dragging the right frame border, you'll see the number of current unread and total messages for each newsgroup.
- **Message Header Pane** In this window, you see the author and title of the messages currently available in the newsgroup that's selected in the newsgroup pane. Each item has several items of information, organized in columns. First is the sender's name, followed by a "Hot

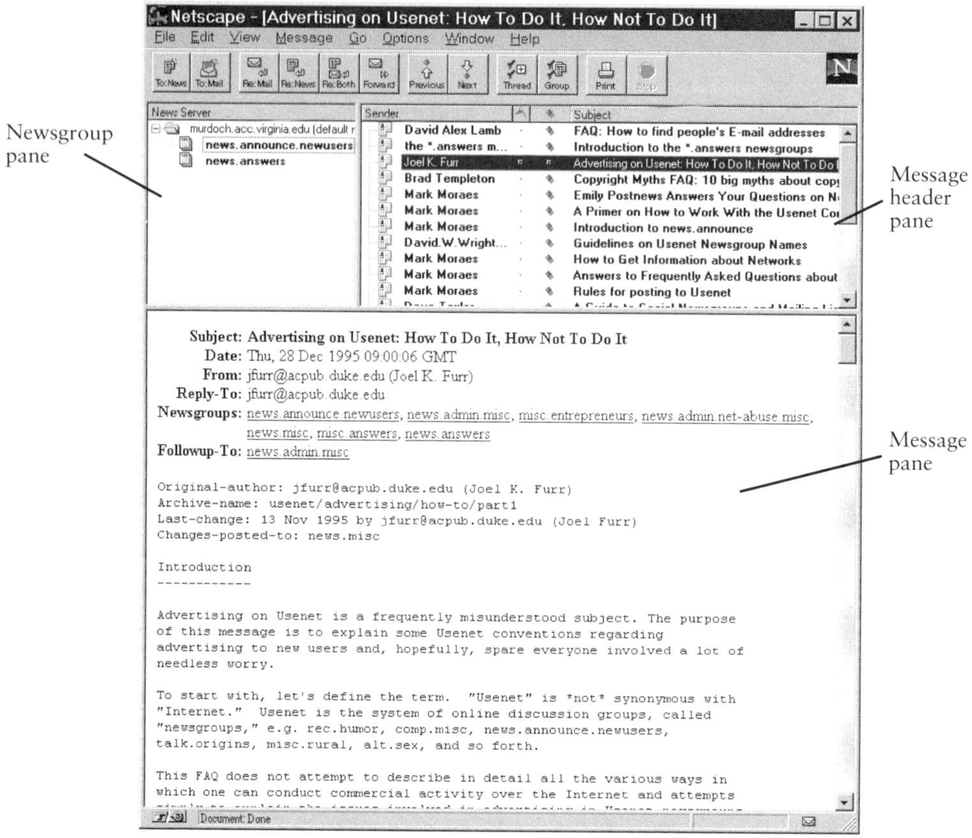

Newsgroup pane

Message header pane

Message pane

Figure 22.2 The three panes in the News window

Item" flag that you activate (if you wish), a read/unread icon, the message's subject, and the date the message was written.

- **Message Pane** This window shows the text of the message currently displayed in the message header pane.

The News window also has its own button bar. Here's a guide to the buttons you'll find:

To: News Click this button to post a new message to the newsgroup that's currently selected in the newsgroup pane.

To: Mail Click this button to mail a message to someone.

Re: Mail Click this button to send a reply via e-mail to the person who wrote the message that's currently displayed.

Re: News Click this button to post a follow-up article to the message that's currently being displayed.

Re: Both Click this button to send a reply via e-mail and post a follow-up article at the same time.

Forward Click this button to forward the current article to someone's e-mail address.

Previous View the previous message.

Next View the next message.

Thread Mark entire thread as read. You won't see this thread the next time you open the newsgroup.

All Mark entire newsgroup as read. You won't see any of the current messages the next time you open the newsgroup.

Print Print the current message.

Stop Stop downloading the current message.

Understanding Threading

By default, Netscape sorts the messages by *threads*. The term thread comes from the phrase "follow the thread of a discussion." In thread sorting, original message are grouped with their replies.

Here's an example. Suppose I post a message asking people in rec.boats which marinas they recommend in the Deltaville area of the Chesapeake Bay. Soon, several people reply. The message header pane looks like this:

```
Suggestions for marinas near Deltaville?
   Re: Suggestions for marinas near Deltaville?
   Re: Suggestions for marinas near Deltaville?
```

Now suppose somebody responds to one of the Re: messages. Netscape will add the message as follows:

```
Suggestions for marinas near Deltaville?
     Re: Suggestions for marinas near Deltaville?
     Re: Suggestions for marinas near Deltaville?
       Re: Suggestions for marinas near Deltaville?
```

Threading is a great feature. You're going to love it. Without threading, you'd have to search through the message list to find replies—and that really takes the fun out of Usenet.

About Crossposting

One of the things you'll notice in Usenet is that some messages are posted to more than one newsgroup. This is called *crossposting*. You'll see a lot of flames about crossposting, a fact that's attributable to new users' misconceptions about it. So let's get this straightened out right now.

Crossposting isn't a bad thing in itself. Often, it makes sense to crosspost. For example, suppose I'm describing marinas in Virginia. I might want to post my message to rec.boats.cruising and crosspost it to a local Virginia newsgroup. Nobody would object to that.

What gets people in trouble with crossposting is overdoing it. People who abuse Usenet—for example, by posting irrelevant advertisements in newsgroups on completely unrelated subjects—tend to crosspost wildly, sometimes crossposting to dozens or even hundreds of newsgroups. There have been several infamous incidents of crass individuals trying to post ads to every newsgroup in existence.

If you try crossposting to too many newsgroups, you're sure to get flamed. Worse, you could become the Cancelmoose's next target. The Cancelmoose is a shadowy figure, whose identity is thought to be known to Usenet gurus but is carefully hidden from the public and the media. Cancelmoose busies himself by running a secret, hacked program that seeks out and cancels messages posted by people who have been known to abuse Usenet. It isn't very ethical to cancel somebody else's message—in fact, it's not even supposed to be possible—but nobody's complaining. Think of the Cancelmoose as something like the Lone Ranger, and you'll have the idea.

What's in the Header?

For each message, you'll see a *header*, which contains a lot of information about the message you're viewing, including the message's subject, date, the e-mail address (and sometimes the name) of the person who contributed the message, and the newsgroups to which the message was posted. Sometimes you'll see additional information, including the following:

- **Reply To** This field indicates the e-mail address to which you should reply, if you wish to do so.
- **Followup-To** If the message was posted to more than one newsgroup, this field indicates the group to which you should send the reply.
- **References** If you're viewing a reply, the references identify the original messages. These are links; if you click the first reference (number 1), you'll see the original message, if it's still available (it might have been deleted by the server).

Downloading the Newsgroups List

Your next step is to download the full newsgroups list from your news server. Depending on how many newsgroups your server carries, this may take a minute or several minutes.

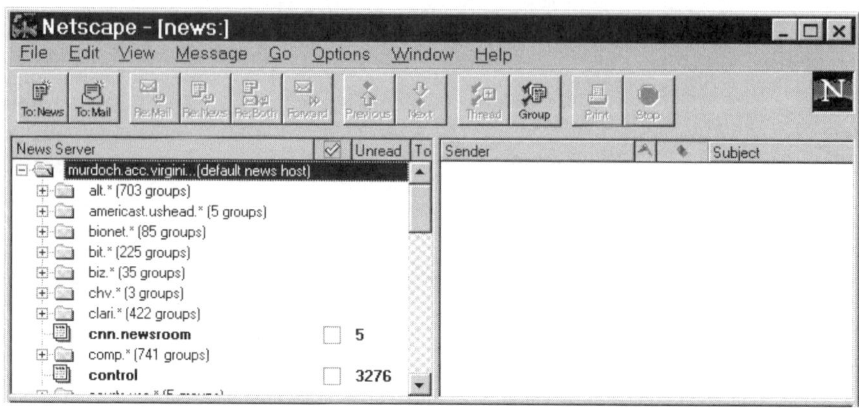

Figure 22.3 Newsgroups pane after downloading all the newsgroup names

To download the newsgroups list: From the Options menu, choose Show All newsgroups. Netscape downloads all the newsgroup names, and you see them listed in the newgroups pane (Figure 22.3).

The newsgroup list is arranged into folders and subfolders, making it easy for you to navigate. That's a good thing, because there may be as many as 13,000 names in this list! To see the newsgroups within a folder, click the plus sign next to the folder. You'll see folders within folders, which helps even more to keep the list organized.

Browse around in the newsgroup list for a while until you get the hang of how it's organized. Next, you'll subscribe to the newsgroups that you want to read on a regular basis.

Subscribing to Newsgroups

Once you've downloaded the newsgroups list, as described in the previous section, it's time to select the newsgroups that you think you'll want to read on a regular basis.

The term "subscribe" is something of a misnomer, since it doesn't affect anything at the server level. On the contrary, it's a setting that's local to your system. After you've subscribed to some of the newsgroups in the total list,

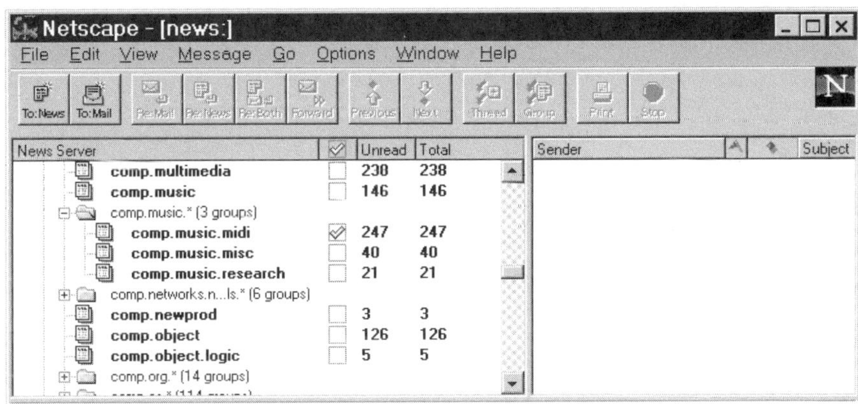

Figure 22.4 Subscribing to newsgroups

you can change the list display so that the newsgroup panel displays only those newsgroups to which you've subscribed. That's convenient.

To subscribe to a newsgroup, select the newsgroup's name in the newsgroup pane and click the check box. You may need to move the right border frame to bring the check box into view (Figure 22.4).

To display only the newsgroups to which you've subscribed, choose Show Subscribed Newsgroups from the Options menu. I recommend this option; in the newsgroups pane, you'll see only the newsgroups to which you've subscribed, saving you the trouble of having to hunt them down in the long, huge list.

Reading the News

To read the articles in a newsgroup, click its name in the newsgroups pane. To read an article, just click the article's subject header in the header pane.

I read this cool article the last time I logged on to this newsgroup, but now it's gone! There are two possible reasons for this. First, the article may have expired (most Usenet

servers keep articles for only a couple of weeks). Second, Netscape always hides the articles you've already read. To redisplay the read messages, choose Show All messages from the Options menu.

As you read the news, you'll commonly perform the following actions:

- **Go to the next article.** Click the Next button.
- **Go to a previous article.** Click the Previous Article button.
- **Read the article that started all this ruckus.** If you're reading a follow-up article, look in the header for a References field, and click the first number you see. The original article may have expired, though.
- **Mark an article as read.** When you read an article, Netscape removes the little green icon next to the article's name in the message header pane. This indicates that the article has been read. You'll still see the article for the rest of this session, but it won't appear the next time you access this newsgroup (unless you choose Show All Articles from the Options menu). To mark an article as read without reading it, just click the little green icon so that it disappears. Netscape will also remove the bold from the article's subject header. You won't see this article the next time you access this newsgroup.
- **Bag all the articles in this thread and go on to the next thread.** Click the Thread button. Netscape marks the entire article as read and displays the first article in the next thread. You won't see the marked articles the next time you log on to this group.
- **Mark every current article as read.** If there's nothing of interest, mark all the articles as read so that you won't have to page through them the next time you access the newsgroup. To mark every article as read, click the Group button.
- **Leave this newsgroup entirely and choose another newsgroup.** Click another newsgroup name in the newsgroup pane.
- **Subscribe to another newsgroup.** If you're displaying only the newsgroups to which you've subscribed, as the previous section recommended, choose Show All Newsgroups from the Options menu. Subscribe to the newsgroups you wish to read.
- **See if there are any interesting new newsgroups.** From the Options menu, choose Show New Newsgroups. You can subscribe to any of these.

Many graphic images are posted to the alt.binaries.pictures.* newsgroups—and not just the naughty ones you've heard about. There are plenty of fun and perfectly legal pictures, too (while browsing alt.binaries.pictures.animals, I found a really cute picture of some kittens—and it's now my Windows wallpaper). Netscape can display these images, as long as they're posted in one part (look for 1/1 in the subject line). If the image is posted in two or more parts, Netscape can display only the first part.

Printing a Message

You can print the text of any Usenet post you see. Just open the File menu and choose Print. Alternatively, you can press Ctrl + P or click the Print button.

Posting Your Own Messages

After you 've read a newsgroup for a while, you may wish to try posting your own messages. But please be sure you know what you're doing before posting.

Netiquette

Before you post to Usenet, you should make sure you know what you're doing. If you don't, you may find yourself on the wrong end of lots of angry posts and e-mail messages. Usenet people aren't difficult to get along with—as long as you follow the rules. Here's a quick overview:

- Don't crosspost (post to more than one newsgroup) unless there's a compelling reason to do so. Since you're a beginner, you wouldn't know any such reasons, so don't do it.
- Make sure you are posting to the right newsgroup.
- Read the newsgroup for at least two weeks before posting.

- Read the FAQ (Frequently Asked Questions) for the newsgroup. Don't ask questions that have already been answered in the FAQ. To locate the FAQ for a newsgroup, use Infoseek or one of the other search engines discussed in Chapter 17, and search for the newsgroup's name and FAQ.
- Do not criticize anyone's spelling or grammar. Lots of people who post to Usenet speak English as a second or third language.
- Keep your cool. Never post in anger.
- Ignore messages that contain obvious inaccuracies ("Francis Ford Coppola directed *Star Wars*"). These messages may be a trap (called a *troll*) to tempt you to make a fool out of yourself.
- Do not post a follow-up message if an e-mail reply will do.
- Don't post anything you wouldn't want to see on your boss's desk tomorrow morning—or your mother's.
- Do not post "test" messages to an ordinary newsgroup. There are newsgroups for this purpose, such as alt.test.

Creating Your Signature

It's not strictly necessary, but you may wish to create a *signature*, a text file containing your name, address, phone, and fax numbers, so that people can find out how to contact you (other than through e-mail).

To create a signature file, follow these steps:

1. From Program Manager (Windows 3.x) or the Start menu (Windows 95), open the Accessories program group.
2. Double-click the Notepad accessory.
3. Type a signature of no more than four lines. Include your name, title, organization, city, state, zip, phone, and fax. Don't get cute.
4. From the File menu, choose Save, and save the file using the name sig.txt. Make a note of where you've saved the file.
5. In Netscape, open the Options menu and choose Mail and News Preferences.
6. Click the Identity tab.

7. In the Signature File area, type the location and file name of your signature file.
8. Click OK.

Posting an Original Message

Assuming you've carefully read the "Netiquette" section above and you're confident you know what you're doing, you can use Netscape to post a message to Usenet. For your first post, use alt.test.

To post your message:

1. Open the newsgroup to which you want to post.
2. Click the To: News button. You'll see a window that's identical to the one you use to create e-mail (see Chapter 18), shown in Figure 22.5. If you created a signature file, Netscape automatically adds it. In addition, the program has automatically placed the current newsgroup's name in the Newsgroups box.
3. In the Subject area, type a brief but descriptive title for your document. This is what people will see in the newsgroup's article title list. Don't type "Help" or "A Question." Titles such as this will be ignored. Be specific.
4. Type the message.
5. Carefully proofread your post for spelling and typographical errors. You can't get it back once it has been sent!
6. Click Send. Netscape posts your message.

I don't see my message on the article list! Don't worry, everything's OK with your post. Usenet software has a low priority for processing; the posts you contribute are kept in a storage area until there's enough computer capacity to take care of them. This might be minutes, or even hours, from the time you actually post the message.

Replying by E-mail

If you want to reply to somebody's post, consider sending an e-mail reply rather than posting to the group. Suppose, for example, that somebody has

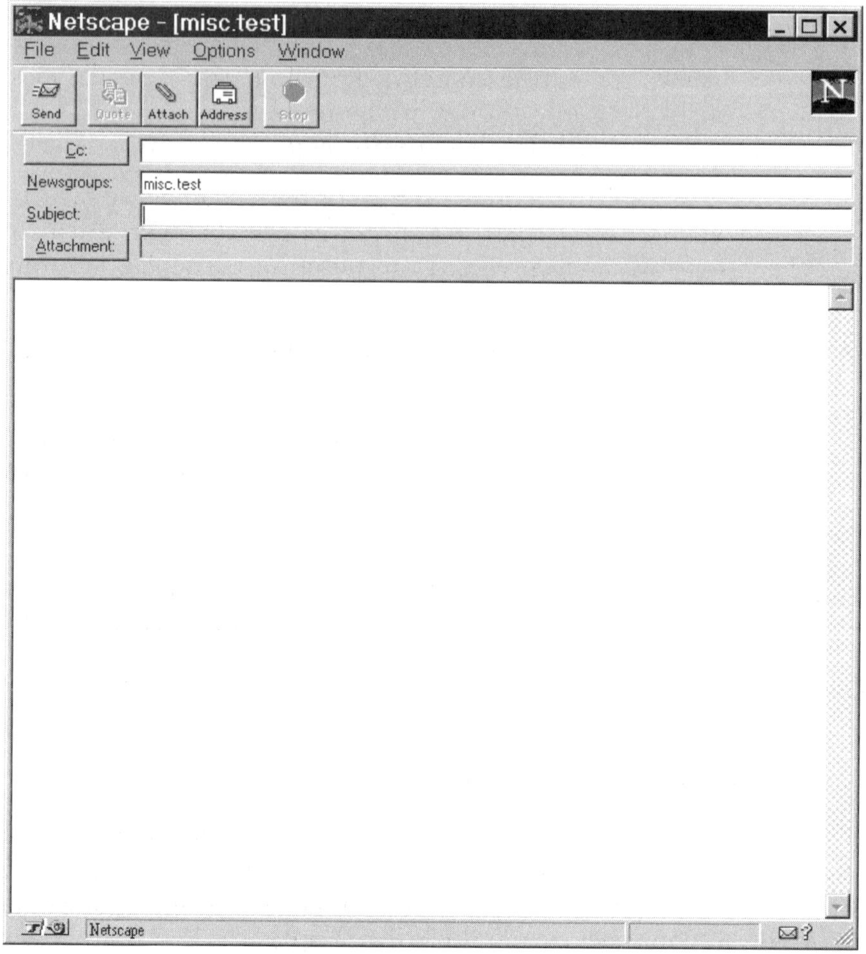

Figure 22.5 Posting an article

posted a question and you know the answer. Do you think the whole group would be interested? If so, then post a follow-up reply, as explained in the next section. If you think only the person asking the question would be interested, then send an e-mail reply.

To send an e-mail reply, follow these steps:

1. Display the article to which you want to reply.
2. On the Netscape button bar, click Re: Mail. You'll see the message window, like the one shown in Figure 22.5. Netscape has echoed the person's e-mail address in the To box.
3. If you would like to quote the text of the document to which you are replying, click Quote. By all means edit this text down to just the part to which you want to respond. In particular, edit out the person's signature.
4. Type your reply. You can insert this within the quoted text, if you like.
5. Carefully check your typing and spelling, and make sure that you've deleted the newsgroup name from the Newsgroups field.
6. Click Send.

I changed my mind! I don't want to send this! No problem. Just click the close box. You'll see a message asking if you really want to abandon the message. Click Yes.

Posting a Follow-up Message

Post a follow-up message only if you're sure you want the whole newsgroup to see your reply. It's OK to post such a message, as long as you really think that it's worth reading and that it falls within the newsgroup's guidelines.

To post a follow-up message, follow these steps:

1. Display the article to which you want to reply.
2. Click the Re: News button. You'll see the message window, like the one shown in Figure 22.5. Netscape has echoed the subject and placed "Re:" before it.
3. If you would like to quote the text of the document to which you are replying, click Quote. By all means edit this text down to just the part to which you want to respond. In particular, edit out the person's signature.

4. Type your reply. You can insert this within the quoted text, if you like.
5. Carefully check your typing and spelling.
6. Click Send.

Searching Today's Usenet Postings

If you're looking for specific information on Usenet, you can easily go nuts trying to search manually through the thousands of postings that appear each day. Why not let the computer do it for you?

There are several services on the Web that enable you to search Usenet posts. You can access them by clicking the Net Search button. All of these services enable you to view the articles retrieved by the search. Here's a quick overview:

- **Infoseek Guide** To search newsgroups, click the Newsgroups option button. Type the words for which you want to search, and click Search.
- **Alta Vista** Click the Alta Vista link. In the Alta Vista page, choose Usenet from the drop-down list box after Search. Type the words for which you want to search, and click Submit.
- **Deja News Research Service** Click the Deja News link. In the Deja News page, click Search. Type the words for which you want to search, and click Submit.

Searching Usenet FAQs

To make sure you don't post a question that others have asked before, you should read the FAQ for a newsgroup to which you want to post. Not all newsgroups have FAQs, but you should make an effort to find one in case there is.

Happily, it's easy to search for Usenet FAQs. Just click Netscape's Net Search directory button. In the Infoseek area, click Usenet FAQs. Type the name of the newsgroup, and click Search.

From Here

- There's only one portion of the Internet you've yet to traverse: Telnet. Flip to the next chapter to complete your training!

Chapter 23

Surviving Telnet and 3270 Sessions

Some computers cannot connect to the Internet. Among the worst offenders are IBM mainframe computers, which don't speak the same language that most other computers do. Fortunately for you if you need information stored on one of these dinosaurs, Telnet (and the similar 3270) lets you access information stored on mainframes via your Web browser. In addition to mainframe computers, the roster of Telnet sites includes thousands of bulletin board systems (BBSs) all over the world, and a good sprinkling of freenets (community information services). All in all, there's a lot of interesting stuff out there, as long as you're willing to forgo multimedia—Telnet is strictly text-only.

In order to access the information stored on Telnet resources, you'll need a Telnet and a 3270 helper application, as discussed in Appendix B. Basically, a Telnet helper application turns your computer into a primitive, dumb VT100 terminal, which allows you text-only access to mainframe

computer data. A 3270 session is virtually the same species of beast, save that your computer is taught to emulate an IBM 3270 terminal. Like Telnet, 3270 sessions are text-based, but 3270 sessions can include text of varying color (wow!) and even primitive ASCII-style graphics.

This chapter isn't of much value unless you really need to access a Telnet resource, such as a university library card catalog. If so, read on, and good luck.

Using NCSA Telnet for Windows

When you see a hyperlink that leads to a Telnet session, you can access the data contained in this resource. To do so, follow these instructions:

1. Click the Telnet hyperlink. You may see a dialog box telling you what to type after your Telnet client starts. If you do, click OK to proceed.
2. After NCSA Telnet for Windows appears on-screen (Figure 23.1), you may need to press Enter once or twice before things start happening.
3. If you were instructed to type something special to log on (see step 1), do so now.
4. If the Telnet server asks you what type of terminal you are using, type VT100 and press Enter.
5. To end your Telnet session, just double-click the Control menu icon (the large hyphen in the left corner of the application's title bar). If you're using Windows 95, click the Close button (the one with an X in it) on the title bar. When the program asks if you want to close the Telnet session, click the OK button.

In most Telnet sessions, you can type a question mark (?) and press Enter to see an on-screen list of your options.

From now on, you're at the mercy of the mainframe programmer who created the application you're using. Like MS-DOS applications, each Telnet session you encounter will have its own unique user interface, which might be very good or very bad. Figure 23.2, for example, shows the Telnet screen of PALS, the catalog at the State University of New York at Fredonia's Reed Library. PALS' user interface is reasonably easy to use; the commands you need to know appear on a menu, and help screens are provided.

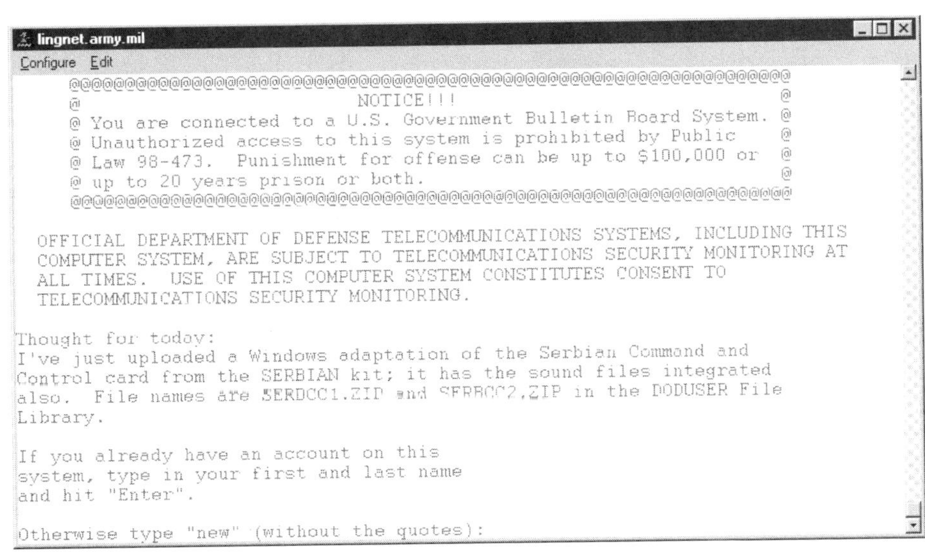

Figure 23.1 NCSA Telnet for Windows in action

For the Time-Challenged

- By means of Telnet and 3270 links, you can access the resources of thousands of mainframe computers, bulletin board systems (BBSs), and freenets worldwide. But it's strictly text-only.
- When you click a Telnet hyperlink, Netscape starts NCSA (National Center for Supercomputing Applications) Telnet for Windows. Watch for a dialog box telling you how to log on. If nothing happens, press Enter. To quit the Telnet session and return to Netscape, double-click the Control menu icon or click the close button.
- When you click a 3270 hyperlink, Netscape starts QWS3270. You may be able to use your computer's function keys (F1 through F10) to perform certain functions. The application may paint the screen with vivid colors and text-based graphics. To exit, choose Close and then Quit from the File menu.

```
LIBRARY.FREDONIA.EDU
Configure  Edit

BEGIN SESSION ON      PALS 01-05-96 21:49:31 ID/WA: P00004/041  VSN: 8R1.00

 The Basic Search Command forms are:

     AU Last-name First-name Middle-name         (Search by Author)
     TI First 4 Title words                      (Search by Title)
     TE Word <BO> Word <BO> Word ...             (Search by Term/Topic)
        *Where <BO> is a boolean operator (AND, OR, or NOT)
     SU First 4 Subject Heading words            (Search by Subject)
     CO Author-last-name First-title-word        (Search by Combination)
     CA Call Number                              (Search by Call Number)
     BR <IN> Name-or-Word                        (Browse Catalog Indexes)
        *Where <IN> is an Index Symbol (AU, TI, TE, SU, CO, or CA)

     Send messages by pressing the RETURN, ENTER or NEWLINE key
     Use the BACKSPACE or BS key to backup and type over mistakes
CATALOG-FRE=>_
```

Figure 23.2 The PALS library catalog at SUNY-Fredonia—a typical Telnet session

Here are some things to remember about Telnet sessions:

- If the screen is blank, press Enter.
- If you need to correct a typing mistake, you can usually do so by pressing the Backspace key to rub out what you've typed. If this doesn't work, open the Configure menu and activate the Backspace option.
- If you get lost or confused, just quit the session by double-clicking the Control menu icon or the close box. You'll see the Web page containing the Telnet hyperlink; you can start over, if you wish.

Using QWS3270 (3270 Telnet Sessions)

3270 sessions closely resemble their Telnet brethren, save that your computer emulates an IBM 3270 mainframe terminal. Generally, that's good news—you'll see colored text and even some primitive graphics, which may make the application easier to use. As in all things Telnet, though, that depends on the programmer's skill.

If you click a hyperlink to a 3270 session, Netscape starts QWS3270, (you can learn to install this application in Appendix B). You'll see the QWS3270 screen, as shown in Figure 23.3. You can't see the colors very well in this book's screen shot, admittedly, but it's much better than garden-variety Telnet: red and bright blue against a black background, which all adds up to an easier-to-use interface. In addition, you'll see a row of buttons along the bottom of the application's window. You can click these buttons to perform special tasks (just what they do depends on how the programmer set up the application you're accessing). Otherwise, QWS3270 looks and works pretty much the same way NCSA Telnet does.

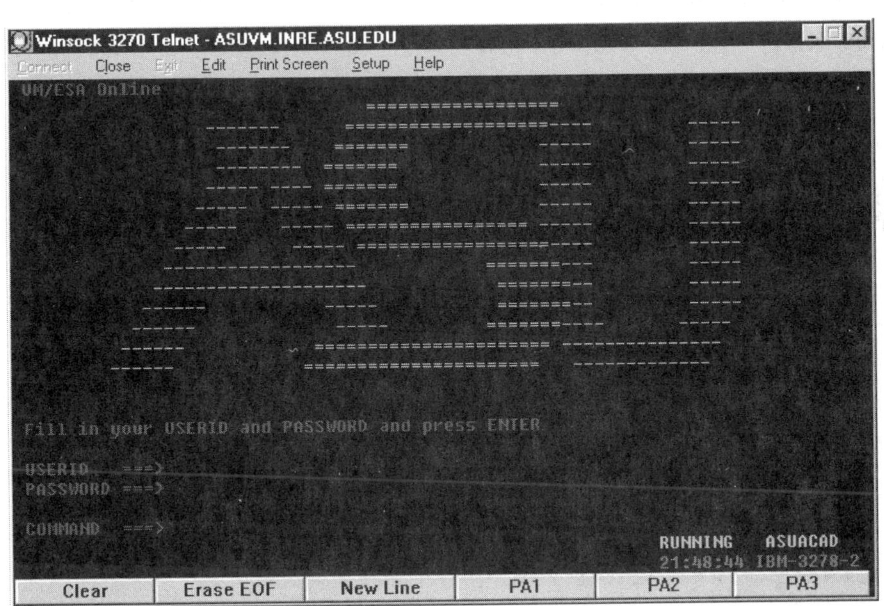

Figure 23.3 A typical 3270 session—this one's at Arizona State University. The text appears in various colors.

Here are some things to remember about 3270 sessions:

- If the interface tells you to press a PF key to do something, press the corresponding function key on your keyboard. For example, PF1 corresponds to F1.
- If the interface tells you to press a PA key to do something, click the corresponding PA button at the bottom of QWS3270's window.
- If you need to correct a typing mistake, you can usually do so by pressing the Backspace key to rub out what you've typed.
- To delete the word to the right of the cursor, hold down the Ctrl key and press Del.
- To erase everything you've just typed, click the Erase Input button.
- You can move the cursor by pressing the arrow keys on your keyboard.
- If the screen display doesn't look right, click the Clear button.

Searching for Telnet Resources with HyTelnet

What's out there in Telnet-land? To find out, you can search a database of Telnet and 3270 gateways called HyTelnet. To access HyTelnet's search page, use the following URL:

http://galaxy.einet.net/hytelnet/HYTELNET.html

You'll see the search page shown in Figure 23.4.

The result of a HyTelnet search is a Web page that lists Telnet sites that include your search words in their descriptions. To access one of these sites, click the hyperlink; you'll see another Web page with the Telnet site's description. Included in the description page is a Telnet or 3270 session link.

Figure 23.4 The HyTelnet search page. Enter your search terms in the box at the bottom of the page.

From Here

- You've surfed the Web and explored the Internet. So what's left? How about the future? Check out Part VI for information about the exploding world of on-line commerce, which you can access by means of Netscape's secure protocols.

Part VI

The Netscape Marketplace

Chapter 24

Understanding Secure Transactions

A revolution's under way: The Web is going commercial. In the coming years, more and more businesses will open shop on the Web, allowing you to access on-line catalogs and providing the means for you to order on-line. And for payment? Use your credit card. Thanks to Netscape's security technology, you can rest assured that nobody can intercept your credit card number or expiration date while it's in transmission via the Internet.

This chapter is for anyone who would like to understand Netscape's security capabilities, but it's not really necessary to read. This technology functions in the background. If you access a secure site, you see a message and the broken key becomes a whole key. You can have confidence at this point that your transmissions cannot be intercepted or read by a third party.

For the Time-Challenged

- Security actually involves three different aspects: authentication (knowing who's sending you something), confidentiality (knowing that no third party can intercept and read the information you exchange with someone), and integrity (knowing that your message has not been tampered with or altered while en route).
- Public key cryptography, the technology that underlies Netscape's security features, enables any two people to exchange undecipherable messages without needing to exchange decoding keys via a secure channel.
- Netscape's security standard, called Secure Socket Layer (SSL), uses public key cryptography to enable you to establish a secure connection with a Web server.
- There is no single Web security standard yet; in fact, there are several competing standards. In the years to come it is likely that a single standard will emerge.
- Your credit card information cannot be intercepted en route, but you still need to use common sense when ordering via the Web. Order from trusted, well-established firms, and make sure you understand their policies.

What Is Security?

In the computer world, security has three distinct shades of meaning: authentication, confidentiality, and integrity, as the following sections discuss. Of greatest interest to you, as a potential customer of commercial Web services, are confidentiality and integrity.

Authentication

In brief, *authentication* ensures that you are really who you say you are when you log on to a server. Most Web servers demand no authentication at all—they just let you in. However, virtually all Web servers support simple protection by password: You must type a login name (user name) and password to access the service. An example of a Web service that requires password authentication is HotWired, the online version of *Wired* magazine.

When you access HotWired for the first time, you're asked to create a login name and password and to supply your e-mail address. You then receive an automatically generated e-mail message that includes an authorization number. You must then supply this authorization number to access the system. What's gained from this? A modicum of assurance that you aren't accessing the site using someone else's name and e-mail address.

Confidentiality

Confidentiality refers to the protection of information while it is en route to its destination. It's not nice to think about, but none of the information you are transmitting via the Web is free from prying eyes. Hackers, criminals, or investigators can easily intercept, record, and print all the information you transmit.

Integrity

Integrity refers to the exact preservation of the transmitted data so that it reaches its destination without any alteration, accidental or deliberate. As with confidentiality, the Web provides absolutely no means of ensuring the integrity of transmitted data. It could be altered while en route, either by chance or deliberate interference, and the receiving computer would have no way of knowing.

The Need for Encryption

The solution to the Web's confidentiality and security problems lies in the use of encryption. In essence, *encryption* is the process of converting a plaintext message (a message that could be read by anyone) into an unreadable ciphertext by means of a key (a method of transforming the message so that it appears to be gibberish). The message can be read only by the intended recipient, who possesses the key and uses it (in a process called *decryption*) to make the text readable again.

A simple encryption technique is ROT-13, which "rotates" all letters in the alphabet thirteen characters to the right. The ciphertext looks like gibberish, but it is easily decrypted by rotating the letters thirteen characters to

the left. Encryption ensures integrity as well as confidentiality; if anyone or anything has altered the message en route, it won't decode 100% correctly, so you'll know that something has gone wrong.

ROT-13 is a poor encryption technique because its key is so simple. In fact, it's used on Usenet only to keep adult-oriented material away from the eyes of children or those who would rather not have such material thrown in their faces. More complicated keys are needed to ensure confidentiality and integrity. With more complicated keys, though, another problem arises: how to transmit the key to the recipient. Traditionally, this has been done by courier, but this is costly and time-consuming.

A new cryptographic method called *public key cryptography* eliminates the need to deliver the key and raises the possibility that people who have never previously exchanged messages could send encrypted messages to each other that could not be intercepted by a third party. In public key cryptography, there are two different keys, an encryption key and a decryption key:

- **Public Encryption Key** You make your encryption key public; people use it to send an encrypted message to you.
- **Decryption Key** This key is kept private. You use it to decode the messages sent to you. Nobody else can read the message without this key.

With public key cryptography, there is no need to establish a secure channel to exchange the decryption key; the person who wishes to send an encrypted message to you merely obtains the public encryption key, encrypts the message, and sends it to you. Nobody along the way can decode the message, even if they have intercepted the encryption key; they would need the decryption key, and you keep that secret. Rightfully, public key encryption has been described as a revolution in cryptography. It will make cryptography available to ordinary people.

Introducing the Secure Socket Layer Security Protocol

To provide secure transactions via the World Wide Web, Netscape Communications Corporation has proposed a standard called the Secure Socket Layer

(SSL) protocol. This proposed Internet standard seeks to provide secure public key encryption capabilities so that people can exchange information securely via any established Internet protocol, including not only the Web but also Gopher, FTP, Telnet, and others. What's more, SSL seeks to do this without placing undue demands on users; much or all of the SSL processing goes on in the background, without requiring any intervention from the user.

An SSL session begins when an SSL-capable client (such as Netscape Navigator) contacts an SSL-capable server (such as Netscape's secure Web servers). A brief exchange of public keys occurs; from that point on, the client and server can exchange secure, encrypted messages, and no third party can intercept them. In addition, SSL includes integrity-checking features that assure both parties that the message has not been tampered with or altered during its transmission.

I read that somebody cracked the security scheme! Due to limitations stemming from Cold War–era export restrictions, Netscape's security can indeed be cracked—but only by running several expensive workstations for days on end. That's worth doing to make a point, perhaps, but not to decode your $29.95 order to Victoria's Secret.

What about Standards?

As of this book's writing, there is no official standard for the secure transmission of sensitive data on the World Wide Web. In an effort to gain acceptance for its SSL protocol as the standard security protocol for the Web, Netscape has published SSL's specifications and made the technology widely available. However, competing firms are attempting to do the same. The worst-case scenario is that two or more competing but incompatible security standards will exist. If this happens, the Web's budding commercial ventures could die on the vine; a user of Netscape would be able to access only Netscape-friendly secure sites, while users of competing browsers (such as Spyglass's Enhanced NCSA Mosaic) would be able to access only those sites conforming to Spyglass's protocol.

The most likely outcome of this struggle, in the short run, is that two or three competing security standards will exist and Web servers will have to recognize them all. This situation is very much to the disadvantage of the online business community, as well as to online consumers; it means that you may

have to run Netscape to access one secure service, and Internet Explorer (or some other browser with a proprietary security scheme) to access another.

An April, 1995 accord may have paved the way for a *de facto* security standard. Netscape Communications announced that the company would back S-HTTP, a competing Web security protocol developed by Terisa Systems, in addition to its own SSL, in both Netscape Navigator and its server products. However, Visa International and Microsoft Corporation recently announced yet another competing security protocol, called Secure Transaction Technology (STT), so the problem of competing security protocols is far from resolved.

Accessing a Secure Server

You'll know when you access a secure server because you'll see the dialog box shown in Figure 24.1. This dialog box informs you that you are accessing a secure document. In addition, the broken key on the status bar is suddenly made whole.

If you don't want to see this warning again, deselect the check box next to Show This Alert Next Time.

Another way you can tell that you've accessed a secure server is to look at the Location box: A secure server's URL begins with https//:.

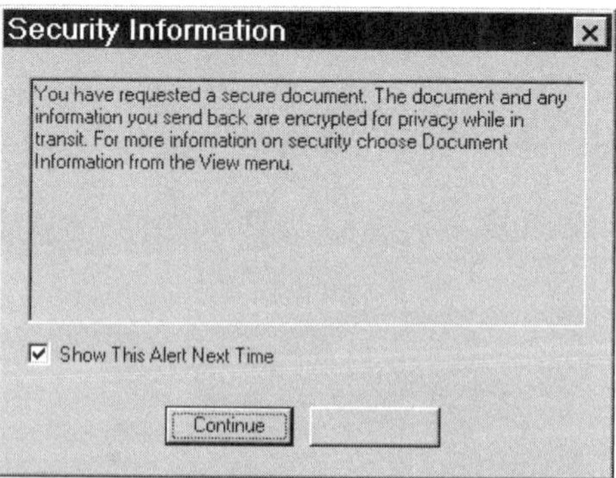

Figure 24.1 Secure server (CDNOW)

To get more information about the document you have accessed, open the View menu and choose Document Info. This command displays the dialog box shown in Figure 24.2. When you access a secure document, you see the server's authentication certificate, which tells you that you really are accessing the service you think you're accessing (and not some clever hacker's "mock" service). This dialog box also indicates the level of security that has been established.

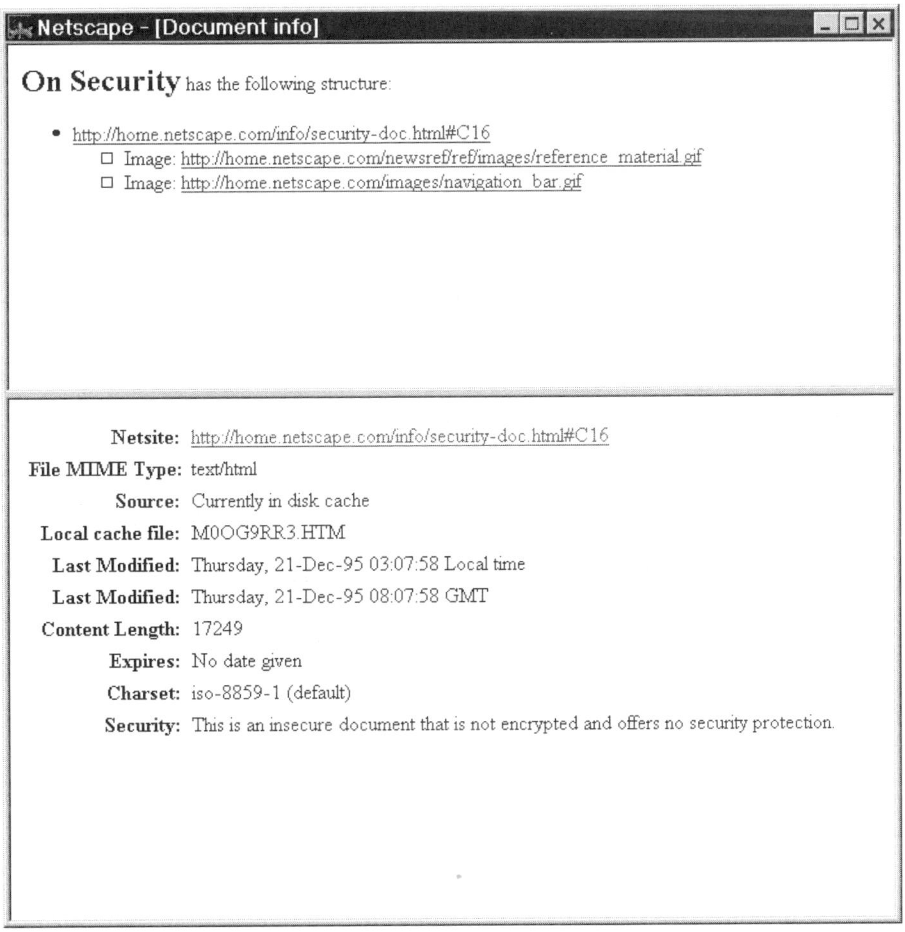

Netscape - [Document info]

On Security has the following structure:

- http://home.netscape.com/info/security-doc.html#C16
  - Image: http://home.netscape.com/newsref/ref/images/reference_material.gif
  - Image: http://home.netscape.com/images/navigation_bar.gif

Netsite:	http://home.netscape.com/info/security-doc.html#C16
File MIME Type:	text/html
Source:	Currently in disk cache
Local cache file:	M0OG9RR3.HTM
Last Modified:	Thursday, 21-Dec-95 03:07:58 Local time
Last Modified:	Thursday, 21-Dec-95 08:07:58 GMT
Content Length:	17249
Expires:	No date given
Charset:	iso-8859-1 (default)
Security:	This is an insecure document that is not encrypted and offers no security protection.

Figure 24.2 Document Info dialog box (insecure document)

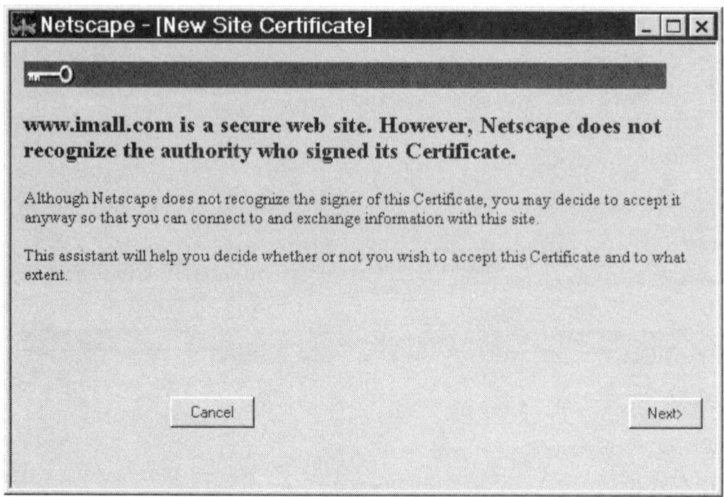

Figure 24.3 Certificate authentication warning

It says the certificate can't be authenticated! A security certificate ensures that the service you're accessing is actually what it says it is, and not some fly-by-night imposter. In order to obtain the certificate, on-line vendors must pay a fee—and not all of them are willing to do so, seemingly. Even some of the sites featured in Netscape's Galleria (see Chapter 25) aren't certificated. So you'll see the scary-looking dialog box shown in Figure 24.3. I wouldn't worry about this too much; just click your way to Finish and see what's on-line.

Is My Credit Card Information Really Safe?

Once you've accessed a secure server, you can transmit your credit card number without fear of its being intercepted along the way. Does that mean your credit card information is safe? With Netscape's security features, you can be assured that nobody can obtain your credit card number by tapping

VeriFone/Netscape Deal Makes It Easier to Offer On-Line Ordering

When you charge something at a store, the clerk takes your card and swipes it through a little verifying machine. It's actually an on-line device; the card reads your information, contacts the verification service, and determines whether your card's valid and how much credit is available. Right now, there's no software available that does this automatically when you order on-line, unless vendors develop the software themselve—an expensive proposition. So somebody has to manually check all the orders before they can be processed. But that's about to change.

The maker of about 75% of those "swiping" devices, VeriFone, announced an agreement with Netscape to develop automatic verification for Netscape's Commerce Server. One of the Web-based vendors that welcomes this development is the Internet Shopping Network, of Palo Alto, CA, which currently processes some $1.4 million in credit card orders each month.

your Internet connection. But sending your credit card number via a secure link is very much like giving it to somebody over the telephone: You're still dependent on the honesty and integrity of the person on the other end. In the end, ordering on the Web won't be any safer than any other form of mail or telephone order.

If you're thinking about ordering something by credit card on the Web, use all the common-sense rules that you would when ordering by telephone or mail. Order from well-established firms with good reputations. Make sure you fully understand the firm's policies regarding the delivery of ordered goods, returns and exchanges, and refunds.

FROM HERE

- Want to take a look at some Web commerce pioneers? Check out Chapter 25.

Chapter 25

Let's Go Shopping!

Secure Web Commercial Sites

To promote Web vendors who have adopted Netscape's secure server technology, Netscape Communications has developed a Galleria page (Figure 25.1) featuring growing numbers of commercial Web servers. To access the Galleria, open the Directory menu and choose Netscape Galleria. What you'll find, as this chapter attests, is that Web commerce is still in the experimental phase. What's going to sell on the Web? Are there some types of merchandise that aren't well suited to the Web commercial idiom? Do you offer just a few high-profile items or your whole catalog? Are Web commercial sites best deployed for one-of-a-kind, special-interest items or for huge shopping enterprises on a department store scale? As of yet, nobody knows, but there are plenty of experiments in all directions.

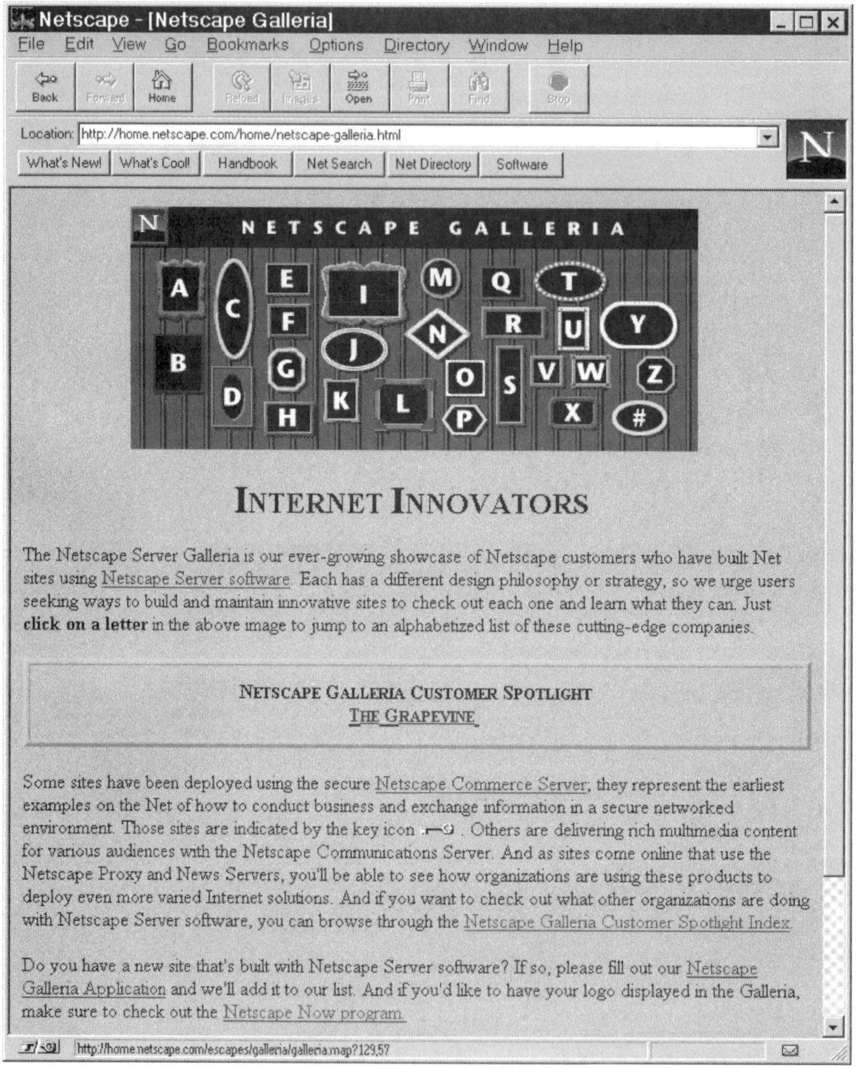

Netscape - [Netscape Galleria]

File Edit View Go Bookmarks Options Directory Window Help

Back Forward Home Reload Images Open Print Find Stop

Location: http://home.netscape.com/home/netscape-galleria.html

What's New! What's Cool! Handbook Net Search Net Directory Software

NETSCAPE GALLERIA

A B C D E F G H I J K L M N O P Q R S T U V W X Y Z #

INTERNET INNOVATORS

The Netscape Server Galleria is our ever-growing showcase of Netscape customers who have built Net sites using Netscape Server software. Each has a different design philosophy or strategy, so we urge users seeking ways to build and maintain innovative sites to check out each one and learn what they can. Just **click on a letter** in the above image to jump to an alphabetized list of these cutting-edge companies.

NETSCAPE GALLERIA CUSTOMER SPOTLIGHT

THE GRAPEVINE

Some sites have been deployed using the secure Netscape Commerce Server; they represent the earliest examples on the Net of how to conduct business and exchange information in a secure networked environment. Those sites are indicated by the key icon. Others are delivering rich multimedia content for various audiences with the Netscape Communications Server. And as sites come online that use the Netscape Proxy and News Servers, you'll be able to see how organizations are using these products to deploy even more varied Internet solutions. And if you want to check out what other organizations are doing with Netscape Server software, you can browse through the Netscape Galleria Customer Spotlight Index.

Do you have a new site that's built with Netscape Server software? If so, please fill out our Netscape Galleria Application and we'll add it to our list. And if you'd like to have your logo displayed in the Galleria, make sure to check out the Netscape Now program.

http://home.netscape.com/escapes/galleria/galleria.map?129,57

Figure 25.1 Netscape Galleria page

This chapter provides an in-depth look at a few of the most interesting commercial Web sites that were on-line at the time of this book's writing; the Galleria page will certainly list additional vendors, so take a look.

For the Time-Challenged

- If you run into a secure Web commercial site, scope it out one step at a time. Be sure to display and read the fine print—when will your order be delivered, and how? What happens if you want to return it? Don't shut off your shopping smarts just because you're ordering on-line.
- You won't find full on-line catalogs—at least, not yet. The dominant philosophy seems to be "Let's offer a few good deals, and see who bites."
- Don't assume that the price is right—at least, not without checking around. Is it really worth the thrill to order something on-line if you could get the same article for less money at a local retail store?

Don't be shy about browsing these sites—there's no obligation. You can even fill out order forms, and then change your mind and cancel at the last moment.

Need a Visa card? Well, how about getting one on-line? Access the Bank of America Credit Card & Loans page at http://www.bankamerica.com/p-finance/creditov.html. You'll find an on-line application form for BankAmericard Gold, which features a low introductory APR and no annual fee (at this writing). The rest of the site's well worth browsing; you'll find on-line money tips, special offers, and information about the bank's many services.

THE GRAPEVINE

Here's a challenge. You own a winery. But most of your visitors and customers aren't young. How do you reach the younger generation and introduce them to the pleasures of fine wine?

The Grapevine (http://www.winery.com/) is one answer. It's a complete guide to wine, featuring the creations of more than 30 vineyards (Figure 25.2). To keep things fresh, the site features current news and events, such as the catalog from a recent Sonoma County wine auction. By means of an

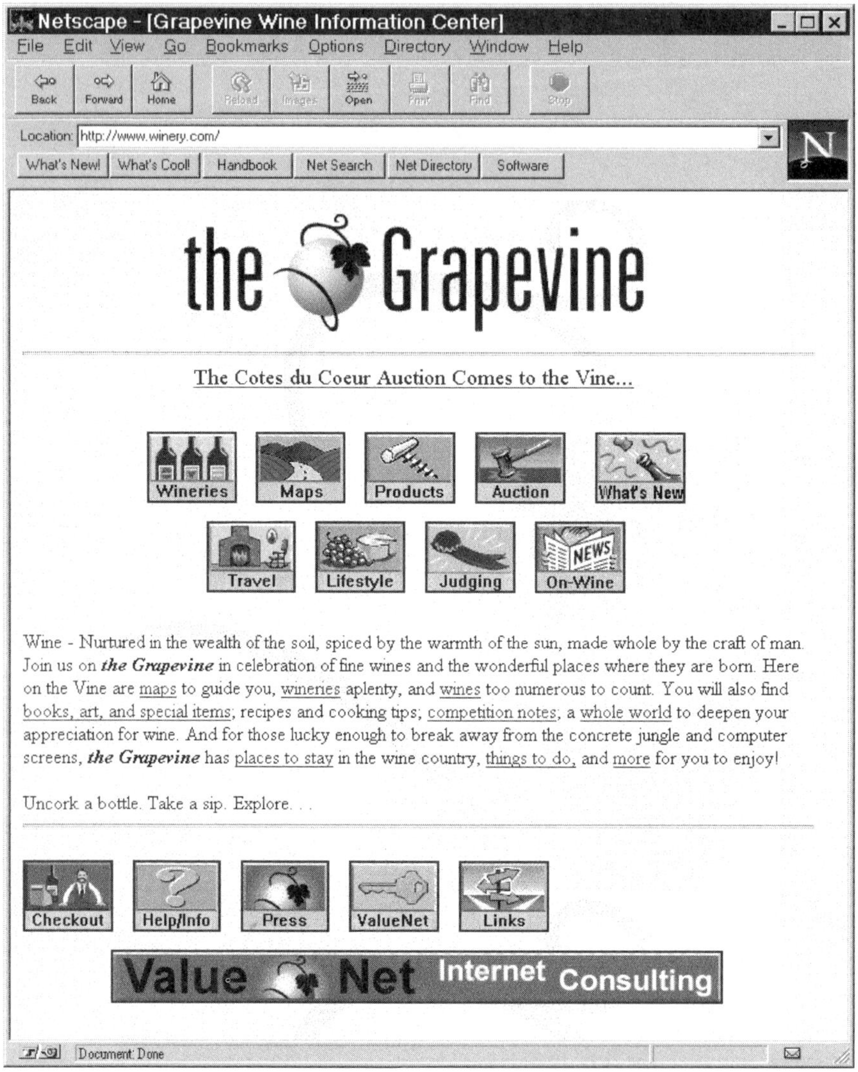

Netscape - [Grapevine Wine Information Center]

File Edit View Go Bookmarks Options Directory Window Help

Back Forward Home Reload Images Open Print Find Stop

Location: http://www.winery.com/

What's New! What's Cool! Handbook Net Search Net Directory Software

the Grapevine

The Cotes du Coeur Auction Comes to the Vine...

Wineries Maps Products Auction What's New

Travel Lifestyle Judging On-Wine

Wine - Nurtured in the wealth of the soil, spiced by the warmth of the sun, made whole by the craft of man. Join us on ***the Grapevine*** in celebration of fine wines and the wonderful places where they are born. Here on the Vine are maps to guide you, wineries aplenty, and wines too numerous to count. You will also find books, art, and special items; recipes and cooking tips; competition notes; a whole world to deepen your appreciation for wine. And for those lucky enough to break away from the concrete jungle and computer screens, ***the Grapevine*** has places to stay in the wine country, things to do, and more for you to enjoy!

Uncork a bottle. Take a sip. Explore. . .

Checkout Help/Info Press ValueNet Links

Value Net Internet Consulting

Document: Done

Figure 25.2 The Grapevine

on-line toteboard, people browsing the site could relay their bids to the auctioneers!

The Grapevine relies on heavy-duty equipment: Several Sun workstations and Netscape's Commerce Server, which enables secure on-line ordering.

Once within the site, you can navigate by means of well-designed icons (Wineries, Maps, Products, Auction, What's New, Travel, Lifestyle, Judging, and On-Wine, an on-line wine newspaper).

What about the wineries? One of the things that's worrisome about Web commerce is that the vendors might not represent the best of the lot. But you'll find some of California's best wineries on Grapevine, including the superb Matanzas Creek Winery, makers of what many wine aficionados believe is one of the finest Merlots in the entire world. And it's not just California that's represented. You'll find Oregon, Australian, and even Texas wineries in Grapevine—and doubtless more by the time you read this book.

SOFTWARE.NET

As an indication of what software retailing might be like in the future, software.net (Figure 25.3) goes the whole nine yards—not only can you take advantage of on-line ordering via secure Netscape transactions but you can also obtain some programs via electronic links. No packaging to fill up landfills, no old buggy versions to worry about, no truck making its way across the United States, no week-long delay—just instantaneous, environmentally responsible delivery. Don't think that the software distributed electronically is strictly no-name, low-quality stuff: For those taxing moments before April 15, for example, you can obtain H&R Block's TaxCut or Novell's TaxSaver.

software.net (http://www.software.net/index.htm) illustrates the First Rule of Web Marketing: Provide some freebies that make the site attractive to people. Not a site to mince words, software.net offers a Free Stuff page full of genuinely interesting stuff. At this writing, you could obtain the latest version of the Norton virus scanning software and a half-dozen sampler programs (full-featured but with built-in expiration dates). There's even a Usenet-like discussion system for software.net's products and services. To help you make the best selection, you can search a database of over 50,000 magazine articles from 16 major computer publications.

INTERNET SHOPPING NETWORK

It had to happen: Cable TV's Home Shopping Network was one of the first commercial ventures on the Internet, and it figures (Figure 25.4). After all, who else has more experience in high-tech marketing? Don't expect to find

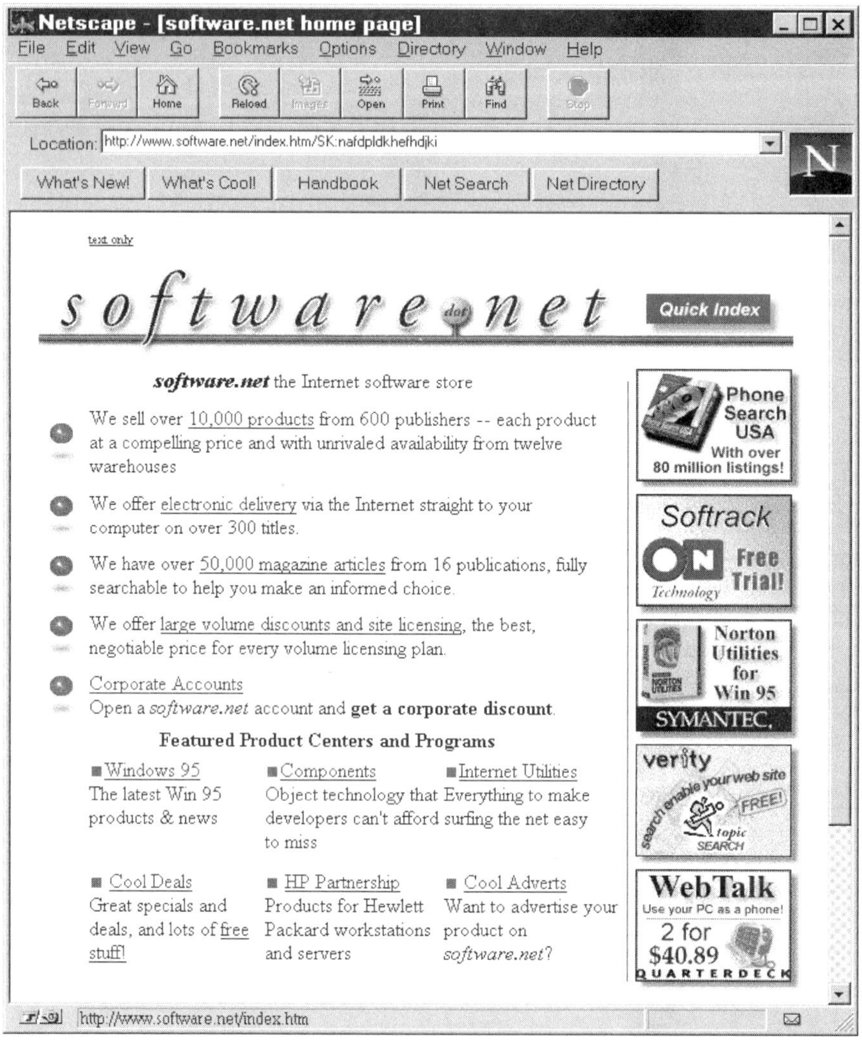

Figure 25.3 software.net

everything under the sun at ISN, though—the site specializes in the stuff its youthful browsers like to buy. Specifically, you'll find software, computer and electronics gear, photo and video stuff, equipment for home offices, and—naturally—flowers for those with romantic yearnings.

So how do you order? It's easy. When you find something you like—and I like the 28.8 Kbps modem for $99—you click the Buy button, and the server shifts into the secure mode. You'll see a page inviting you to become a member of ISN, if you're not already. If you don't feel comfortable about giving your credit card information on-line, despite the security protection, or if you're accessing ISN from behind a firewall that disables security, you

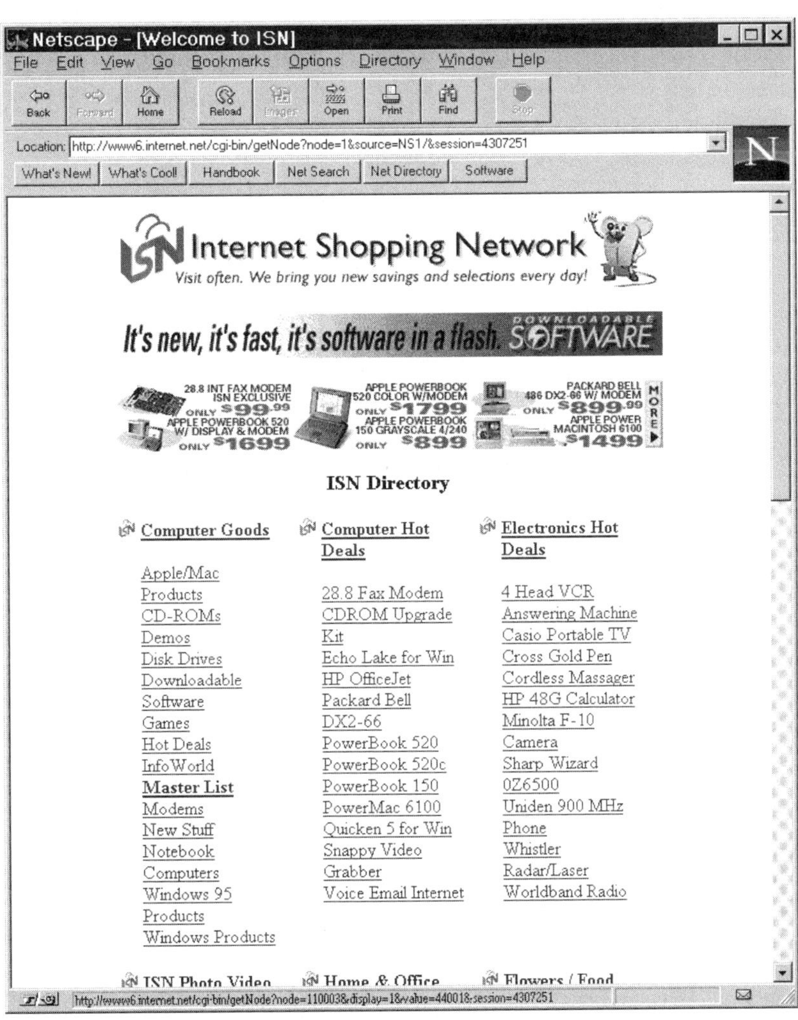

Figure 25.4 Internet Shopping Network

can call an 800 number, or fax the membership form. There's no charge for the membership.

Save The Earth Foundation

It's not all about profit. Save The Earth Foundation is a 20-year-old nonprofit organization that supports environmental research and education. To raise money for its programs, the Foundation decided to create a Web-based auction of rock-music posters and memorabilia. At this writing, the first auction was closed—and presumably a success—but another one was in the wings. Access Save The Earth Foundation's ArtRock Auction page (Figure 25.5) at http://www.commerce.com/save_earth/auction/auction.html.

marketplaceMCI

The Web shopping arm of internetMCI (Figure 25.6), the long-distance company's foray into the Internet service provider sweepstakes, marketplaceMCI offers a number of storefronts. Each of them is accessible by means of Netscape's secure communications technologies. Here's what's available at this writing:

- **Aetna Insurance** Get quotes on-line!
- **Art Access** Fine art celebrating nature
- **Andy's Garage Sale** Featuring all sorts of junk dirt cheap! Andy's is an offshoot of Fingerhut Corporation, a direct mail marketing company.
- **Border's Books** For your favorite books and CDs.
- **Covey Leadership Center, Inc.** Leadership training featuring the "Seven Habits of Highly Effective People"
- **DAMARK** Electronics, sporting goods, housewares, and more
- **Doneckers** Fine women's apparel, restaurants, guest houses, and more
- **Dun & Bradstreet Information Services** Global business intelligence

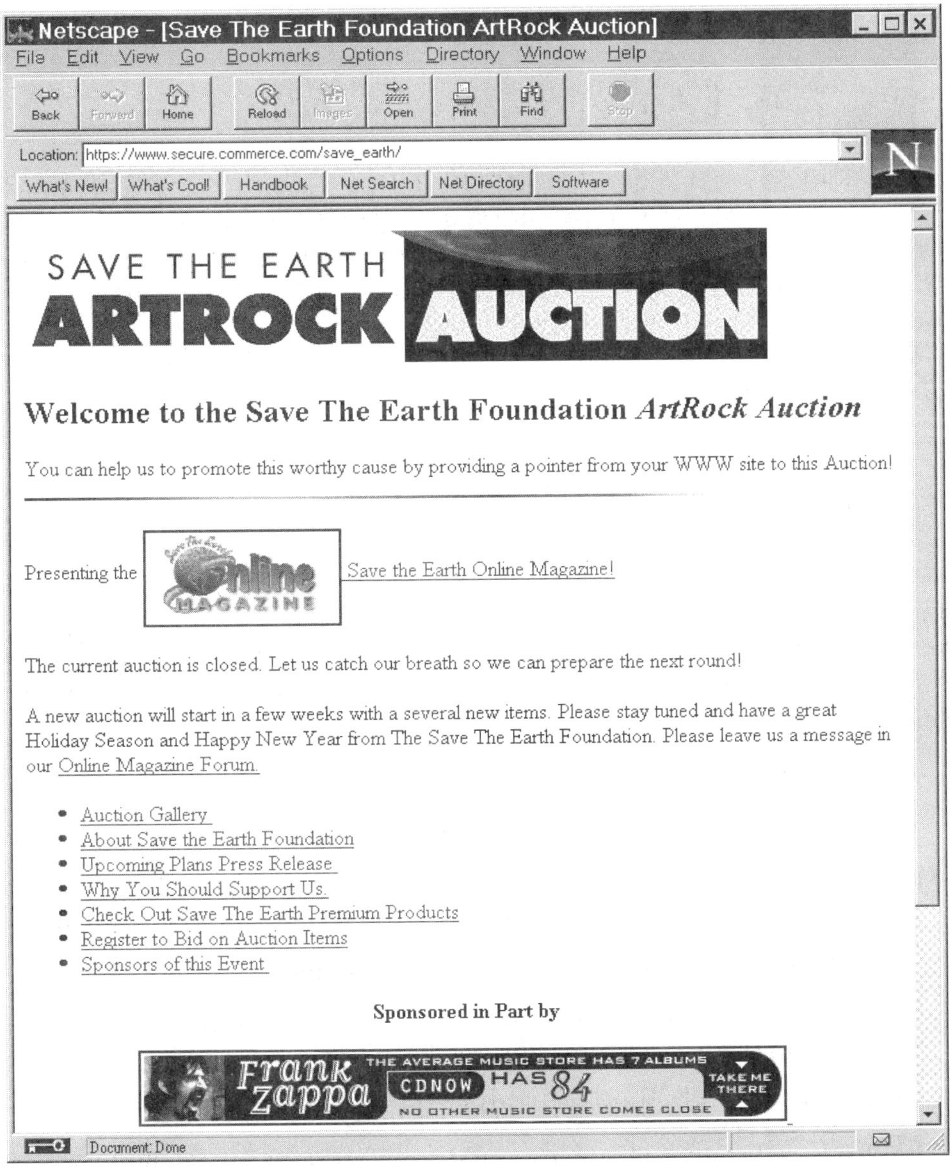

Netscape - [Save The Earth Foundation ArtRock Auction]

File Edit View Go Bookmarks Options Directory Window Help

Back Forward Home Reload Images Open Print Find Stop

Location: https://www.secure.commerce.com/save_earth/

What's New! What's Cool! Handbook Net Search Net Directory Software

SAVE THE EARTH
ARTROCK AUCTION

Welcome to the Save The Earth Foundation *ArtRock Auction*

You can help us to promote this worthy cause by providing a pointer from your WWW site to this Auction!

Presenting the Online Magazine Save the Earth Online Magazine!

The current auction is closed. Let us catch our breath so we can prepare the next round!

A new auction will start in a few weeks with a several new items. Please stay tuned and have a great Holiday Season and Happy New Year from The Save The Earth Foundation. Please leave us a message in our Online Magazine Forum.

- Auction Gallery
- About Save the Earth Foundation
- Upcoming Plans Press Release
- Why You Should Support Us.
- Check Out Save The Earth Premium Products
- Register to Bid on Auction Items
- Sponsors of this Event

Sponsored in Part by

Frank Zappa THE AVERAGE MUSIC STORE HAS 7 ALBUMS CDNOW HAS 84 NO OTHER MUSIC STORE COMES CLOSE TAKE ME THERE

Document: Done

Figure 25.5 Save The Earth Foundation's ArtRock Auction

- **FTP Software, Inc.** Go anywhere networking
- **Hammacher Schlemmer & Co.** Since 1848, a wide range of products as unique as their name
- **Intercontinental Florist** Flowers available for worldwide delivery
- **The Mac Zone** and **The PC Zone** Low prices and overnight delivery of the hottest computer products
- **MCI Store** Communications products and services
- **OfficeMax OnLine** Grand opening specials on office supplies, computers, accessories, and business machines
- **Omaha Steaks** For that fantastic T-bone
- **Proxima, Inc.** Internet applications, technologies, design, and commerce
- **QUALCOMM Incorporated** Eudora (Internet-native) e-mail software
- **Reiter's Scientific & Professional Books** 60,000 books in stock, established 1936, worldwide shipping
- **Reveal Computer Products** Computer hardware, software, and accessories

DAMARK

I'm sure you've received a DAMARK catalog—you know, the mail-order catalog with all those great electronic close-out items. The Web incarnation of DAMARK appears in marketplaceMCI, and it's worth a visit—if only to see how a well-endowed direct marketing firm conceptualizes the possibilities of the Web market. Plus, you might find a bargain or two!

Access DAMARK's catalog at the following URL:

http://www2.pcy.mci.net/markeplace/damark/html/d10000.html

You'll see buttons that enable you to visit audio/video, home improvement, home office, home furnishing, computer, and "hot deal" sections. A few of the hot deals available at this writing are shown in Figure 25.7

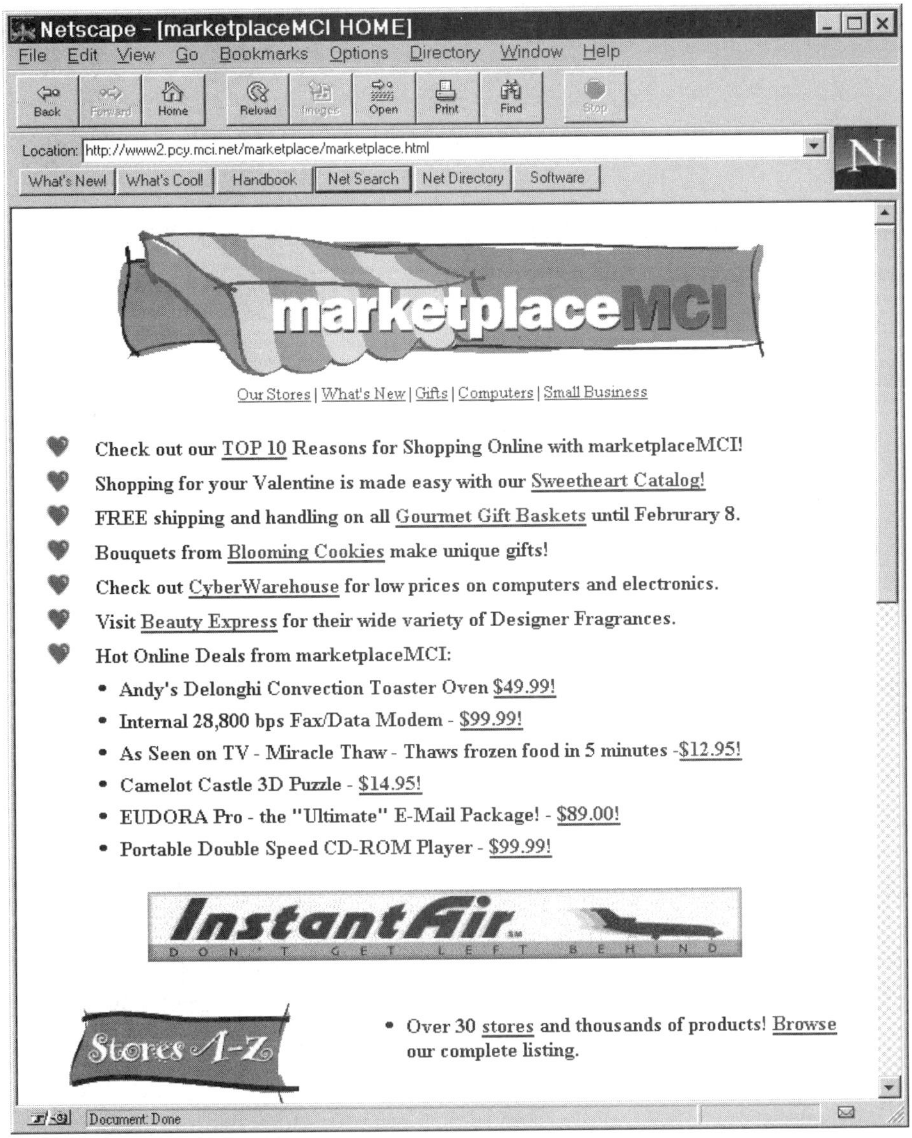

Netscape - [marketplaceMCI HOME]

File Edit View Go Bookmarks Options Directory Window Help

Back Forward Home Reload Images Open Print Find Stop

Location: http://www2.pcy.mci.net/marketplace/marketplace.html

What's New! What's Cool! Handbook Net Search Net Directory Software

marketplaceMCI

Our Stores | What's New | Gifts | Computers | Small Business

- Check out our TOP 10 Reasons for Shopping Online with marketplaceMCI!
- Shopping for your Valentine is made easy with our Sweetheart Catalog!
- FREE shipping and handling on all Gourmet Gift Baskets until Februrary 8.
- Bouquets from Blooming Cookies make unique gifts!
- Check out CyberWarehouse for low prices on computers and electronics.
- Visit Beauty Express for their wide variety of Designer Fragrances.
- Hot Online Deals from marketplaceMCI:
  - Andy's Delonghi Convection Toaster Oven $49.99!
  - Internal 28,800 bps Fax/Data Modem - $99.99!
  - As Seen on TV - Miracle Thaw - Thaws frozen food in 5 minutes -$12.95!
  - Camelot Castle 3D Puzzle - $14.95!
  - EUDORA Pro - the "Ultimate" E-Mail Package! - $89.00!
  - Portable Double Speed CD-ROM Player - $99.99!

InstantAir DON'T GET LEFT BEHIND

Stores A-Z

- Over 30 stores and thousands of products! Browse our complete listing.

Document: Done

Figure 25.6 marketplaceMCI (with special Valentine's Day decor!)

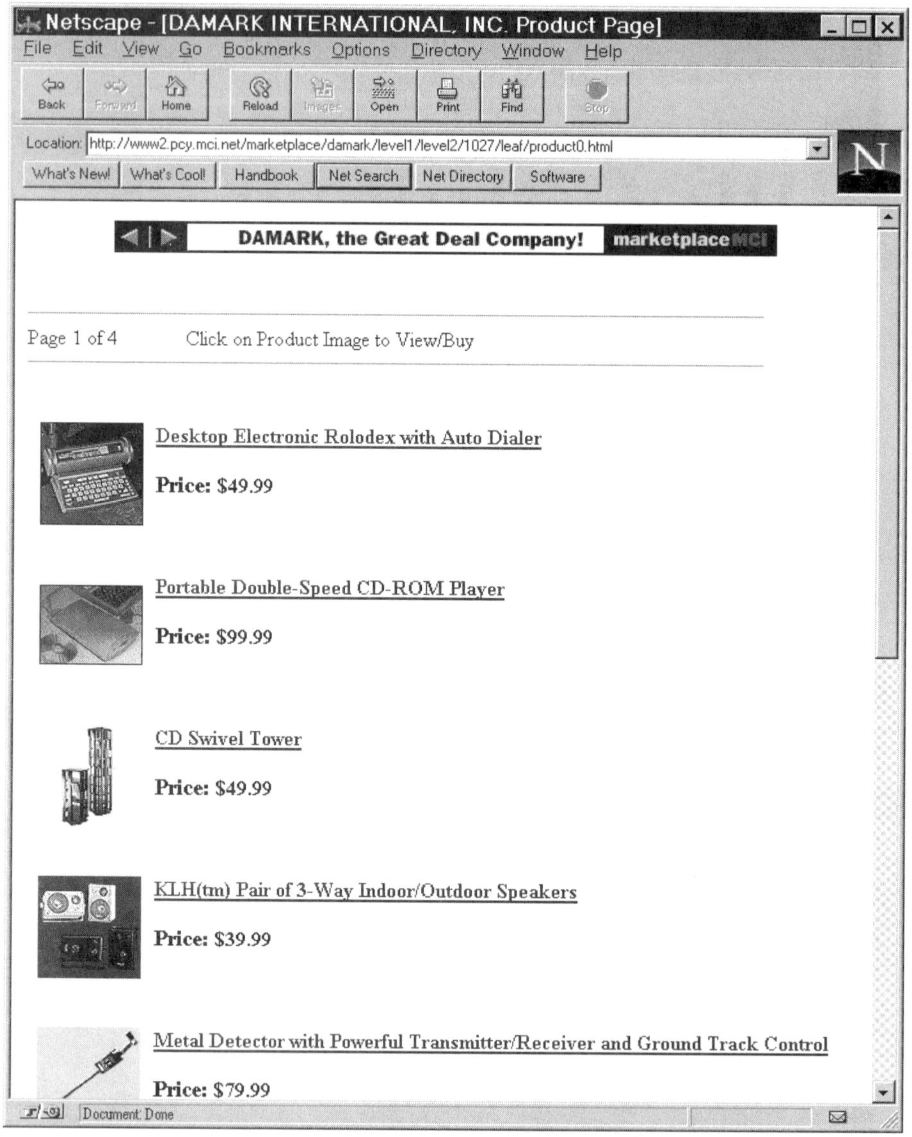

Netscape - [DAMARK INTERNATIONAL, INC. Product Page]

File Edit View Go Bookmarks Options Directory Window Help

Back Forward Home Reload Images Open Print Find Stop

Location: http://www2.pcy.mci.net/marketplace/damark/level1/level2/1027/leaf/product0.html

What's New! What's Cool! Handbook Net Search Net Directory Software

DAMARK, the Great Deal Company! marketplaceMCI

Page 1 of 4 Click on Product Image to View/Buy

Desktop Electronic Rolodex with Auto Dialer

Price: $49.99

Portable Double-Speed CD-ROM Player

Price: $99.99

CD Swivel Tower

Price: $49.99

KLH(tm) Pair of 3-Way Indoor/Outdoor Speakers

Price: $39.99

Metal Detector with Powerful Transmitter/Receiver and Ground Track Control

Price: $79.99

Document: Done

Figure 25.7 DAMARK's Web store

From Here

- With this chapter, we've come to the end of this book. I hope you'll enjoy Netscape and the Web as much as I do!

Part VII

APPENDICES

Appendix A

Getting Connected

To determine which parts of this appendix you should read, please note the following:

- If you already have a copy of Netscape Navigator 2.0 and you're already connected to the Internet, you don't need to read this appendix. It's for people who don't have the program.
- If you don't have Netscape, and you aren't yet connected to the Internet, read on. If you are in the United States, this book's CD-ROM disc contains Netscape Navigator 2.0 and all the software you'll need to connect to EarthLink Network, a U.S.-based nationwide Internet service provider. Go the section entitled "Connecting with EarthLink Network TotalAccess."

- Do you already have a connection with an Internet service provider or live outside the United States? You can obtain a copy of Netscape Navigator by using the Internet, as explained later in this appendix. Go the section beginning on page 408.

Connecting with EarthLink Network TotalAccess

This book's CD-ROM disc contains all the software you'll need to connect to the Internet, including Netscape Navigator 2.0. The software comes in two versions:

- **Microsoft Windows 3.1** This version is for users of Microsoft Windows 3.1 and Microsoft Windows for Workgroups 3.1.
- **Microsoft Windows 95** This version is for users of Microsoft Windows 95 systems.

Please note that the version of Netscape Navigator that's included with the EarthLink Network TotalAccess package is designed to operate only with an EarthLink Network connection. If you already have an Internet connection through another service provider or live outside the United States, you can download the latest version of Netscape Navigator by following the instructions given later in this chapter.

For information on installing the EarthLink TotalAccess software, including Netscape Navigator 2.0, please see Appendix E.

What You'll Need

To access the Internet with TotalAccess, you'll need the following:

- A Microsoft Windows 3.1 or Windows 95 computer with 8 MB of free disk space
- A high-speed modem (at least 9600 Kbps; 14.4 Kbps is better, and 28.8 Kbps is best)
- A credit card

Understanding Your EarthLink Access Options

You can access EarthLink in the following ways:

- **TotalAccess USA** If you live in one of the more than 100 U.S. cities in which this service is offered, this is a great deal. At this writing, EarthLink was charging $19.95 per month (plus a $25 one-time startup fee) for unlimited access to the Internet. A very good deal!
- **TotalAccess USA 800** If you don't live in one of the cities covered by TotalAccess USA, you can cannect using EarthLink's 800 number. You'll pay $24.95 per month (plus a $25 one-time startup fee); included are five free hours per month. You'll pay $4.95 per hour for additional connect hours per month.
- **TotalAccess Southern California** If you live in Southern California, you can take advantage of local dialup numbers throughout this area. You'll pay $19.95 per month (plus a $25 one-time startup fee) for *unlimited* access to the Internet.

What's Included in the TotalAccess Package

The TotalAccess software (included on this book's CD-ROM disc) includes the following:

EarthLink Network Registration	This software enables you to establish your EarthLink account in five minutes or less.
TotalAccess Internet Dialer	With this program, establishing your Internet connection is completely automatic.
Netscape Navigator 2.0	For Windows 3.1 and Windows 95.
Eudora	The most highly respected e-mail package in the business. Of course, you can also use Netscape for e-mail.
Online Help	Just press F1 for help at any time.
Free Technical Support	EarthLink's ready to help you, should you run into a technical snag.

Where Is Earthlink TotalAccess USA Available?

EarthLink USA access is currently available in the areas listed in Table A.1. To find out whether your city is served by EarthLink TotalAccess USA, look up your telephone area code in this table.

Please note that EarthLink may have added additional local dialup numbers since this book was published. For more information, call EarthLink at 1-800-395-8425.

Table A.1 EarthLink TotalAccess USA Dialup Connections

Area Code	Prefix	State	City
201	622	NJ	Newark
202	222	DC	Washington
203	357	CT	Stamford
203	724	CT	Hartford
206	441	WA	Seattle
208	381	ID	Boise
209	463	CA	Stockton
210	352	TX	San Antonio
212	238	NY	New York
213	620	CA	Los Angeles
214	741	TX	Dallas
214	438	TX	Irving
215	448	PA	Philadelphia
216	253	OH	Akron
216	579	OH	Cleveland
217	527	IL	Springfield
219	239	IN	South Bend
302	576	DE	Wilmington
303	575	CO	Denver
305	486	FL	Fort Lauderdale
305	358	FL	Miami
309	434	IL	Bloomington
310	338	CA	Compton
312	986	IL	Chicago
313	225	MI	Detroit
314	886	MO	Columbia
314	213	MO	Saint Louis
315	442	NY	Syracuse
316	383	KS	Wichita
317	977	IN	Indianapolis

Table A.1 *Continued*

Area Code	Prefix	State	City
318	676	LA	Shreveport
319	341	IA	Iowa City
319	333	IA	Davenport
334	431	AL	Mobile
334	223	AL	Montgomery
404	817	GA	Atlanta
404	432	GA	Smyrna
405	270	OK	Oklahoma City
407	648	FL	Orlando
407	681	FL	West Palm Beach
408	751	CA	Salinas
408	268	CA	San Jose
408	492	CA	Santa Clara
409	833	TX	Beaumont
410	727	MD	Baltimore
412	394	PA	Pittsburgh
413	846	MA	Springfield
414	227	WI	Milwaukee
415	322	CA	Palo Alto
415	357	CA	San Francisco
419	246	OH	Toledo
501	375	AR	Little Rock
502	583	KY	Louisville
504	525	LA	New Orleans
508	628	MA	Framingham
510	704	CA	Oakland
513	621	OH	Cincinnati
515	323	IA	Des Moines
518	426	NY	Albany
603	594	NH	Nashua
609	586	NJ	Mercerville
609	569	NJ	Pleasantville
612	321	MN	Minneapolis
614	222	OH	Columbus
615	756	TN	Chattanooga
615	524	TN	Knoxville
615	748	TN	Nashville
617	927	MA	Boston
617	672	MA	Waltham
619	320	CA	Palm Springs
619	338	CA	San Diego
702	382	NV	Las Vegas
704	342	NC	Charlotte
706	821	GA	Augusta
708	241	IL	Hinsdale
708	480	IL	Northbrook

Table A.1 *Continued*

Area Code	Prefix	State	City
713	567	TX	Houston
713	625	TX	Westheimer
714	871	CA	Anaheim
714	726	CA	Santa Ana
716	843	NY	Buffalo
716	327	NY	Rochester
803	799	SC	Columbia
803	673	SC	Florence
804	947	VA	Lynchburg
804	533	VA	Norfolk
804	674	VA	Richmond
805	892	CA	Santa Barbara
812	433	IN	Evansville
813	573	FL	Feathersound
813	247	FL	Tampa
817	850	TX	Fort Worth
818	340	CA	Sherman Oaks
901	761	TN	Memphis
903	234	TX	Longview
909	460	Canada	Ontario
909	875	Canada	Rialto
912	651	GA	Savannah
913	368	KS	Topeka
914	451	NY	Poughkeepsie
914	681	NY	White Plains
915	544	TX	El Paso
916	447	CA	Sacramento
918	582	OK	Tulsa
919	872	NC	Raleigh
919	361	NC	Durham
919	972	NC	Rocky Mount

Obtaining the Latest Version of Netscape

This section is for readers who already have an Internet service connection, but don't have Netscape. By following the instructions in this section, you

can obtain a free evaluation copy of the latest version of Netscape Navigator from the Internet. You can do this the *really* easy way, the easy way, or the slightly more difficult way, as explained in the following sections.

The Really Easy Way

Did your service provider give you a Web browser other than Netscape? You can use this browser to download Netscape Navigator 2.0. To do so, simply type the following URL into your browser's Location box:

http://www.netscape.com

and follow the links to download the latest version of Netscape.

According to Netscape's current licensing restrictions, individuals, businesses, and government organizations may evaluate Netscape Navigator free of charge for up to 90 days. After that time, you should purchase your copy of Netscape. Students, faculty, and staff members of educational institutions and employees of charitable nonprofit organizations may use Netscape free of charge.

The Easy Way

Purchase a copy of Netscape Navigator. You can buy Netscape from just about any place that sells software, including office supply stores, software stores at shopping malls, and mail-order software suppliers.

The Slightly More Difficult Way

You can also obtain Netscape by using the Internet. To obtain Netscape Navigator this way, you'll need an FTP program. FTP is short for File Transfer Protocol. With FTP, you can obtain files on computers that have set up *anonymous FTP* services. In anonymous FTP, the computer accepts requests from anyone who accesses the site, and lets you browse around the computer's file directories. When you find a file you want—here, Netscape 2.0, of course—you can download it to your computer.

Where can you get an FTP program? If you're using Windows 3.1, ask your service provider. If you're using Windows 95, you're in luck—there's an FTP program included with Windows 95's Internet software. It's called FTP.EXE. To run the program, click the Start menu, click Run, type FTP.EXE in the dialog box, and click OK.

Once you've gotten your FTP program running, you'll need to configure the program to access a site from which you can download the Netscape software. For details on how to do this, consult the documentation of the FTP program you're using. In brief, you'll need to supply the FTP address of the computer that contains a copy of the Netscape software. Once you've contacted this computer, you'll need to navigate the computer's file directories so that you can locate and download Netscape.

This isn't quite as hard as it sounds. With most FTP programs, accessing an FTP server is as easy as typing the FTP address. To obtain Netscape, the address you'll need is one of Netscape's FTP servers. At this writing, the following servers at Netscape Communications contained copies of the Version 2.0 software:

ftp2.netscape.com
ftp3.netscape.com
ftp4.netscape.com
ftp5.netscape.com
ftp6.netscape.com
ftp7.netscape.com
ftp8.netscape.com

It says "User anonymous access denied!" No, don't worry, Mozilla still loves you. The problem is that so many people are trying to access Netscape's server that the server can't even send you a message informing you that it's too busy. Check out the list of *mirror sites*, which are anonymous FTP sites that also have copies of Netscape's software. You'll find this list in Table A.2. Note that not all of these sites have Netscape 2.0 (or at least, not yet)—but once you've obtained *any* copy of Netscape, you can then obtain the latest version The Really Easy Way, as explained earlier in this section.

Once you've accessed one of these FTP sites, you may need to do some directory navigation to find the folder containing Netscape. If you see a list of directories after you log on, look for the /pub directory—this is the one that usually contains files to download. You may need to hunt around a bit to find Netscape. To learn how to navigate directories using your FTP client, see your program's documentation.

Table A.2 Netscape FTP Mirror Sites

ftp://wuarchive.wustl.edu/packages/www/Netscape/netscape1.1/
ftp://ftp.cps.cmich.edu/pub/netscape/
ftp://ftp.utdallas.edu/pub/netscape/netscape1.1/
ftp://unicron.unomaha.edu/pub/netscape/netscape1.1/
ftp://server.berkeley.edu/pub/netscape/
ftp://SunSITE.unc.edu/pub/packages/infosystems/WWW/clients/Netscape/
ftp://ftp.orst.edu/pub/packages/netscape/
ftp://magic.umeche.maine.edu/pub/Mirrors/nscape/
ftp://consult.ocis.temple.edu/Big_Kahuna/Pub/MAC/Comm/
ftp://ftp.adelaide.edu.au/pub/WWW/Netscape/
ftp://ecto.curtin.edu.au/pub/internet/clients/netscape/
ftp://sunsite.dcc.uchile.cl/pub/WWW/netscape/netscape/
ftp://sunsite.doc.ic.ac.uk/computing/information-systems/www/Netscapes/
ftp://ftp.sunet.se/pub/www/Netscape/netscape1.1/
ftp://ftp.luth.se/pub/infosystems/www/netscape/netscape/
ftp://sunsite.ust.hk/pub/WWW/netscape/
ftp://ftp.sun.ac.za/pub/archiving/www/mcom/netscape/
ftp://bash.cc.keio.ac.jp/pub/inet/netscape/
ftp://SunSITE.sut.ac.jp/pub/archives/WWW/netscape/
gopher://SunSITE.sut.ac.jp:70/11/archives/WWW/netscape/
http://SunSITE.sut.ac.jp/arch/archives/WWW/netscape/
ftp://bash.cc.keio.ac.jp/pub/inet/netscape/
ftp://ftp.glocom.ac.jp/pub/net/netscape/
ftp://ftp.pu-toyama.ac.jp/pub/net/WWW/netscape/
ftp://ftp.cs.titech.ac.jp/pub/net/WWW/netscape/netscape1.1/
ftp://ftp.nc.nihon-u.ac.jp/pub/network/WWW/client/netscape/
ftp://ftp.elcom.nitech.ac.jp/pub/netscape/
ftp://ftp.leo.chubu.ac.jp/pub/WWW/netscape/netscape1.1

Appendix B

Configuring Support and Helper Applications

If you just want to browse the Web and view the text and graphics you'll find, you can use Netscape just as soon as you've established your network connection. However, you'll need to do some configuration and program installation if you would like to take full advantage of Netscape, including:

- Listening to sounds
- Viewing movies
- Accessing Telnet sessions

This appendix walks you through the entire configuration process, step by step. For information on configuring Netscape for e-mail access, see

Chapter 18. For information on configuring Netscape for Usenet access, see Chapter 22.

Before proceeding, you will want to install the support and helper applications that are included on this book's CD-ROM disc. For more information, see Appendix E.

Why Netscape Needs Support and Helper Applications

By itself, Netscape can deal with GIF and JPEG graphics, as well as Sun/NeXt (*.au) and Apple/Silicon Graphics (*.aiff) sounds. But there are many more types of multimedia files out there. Netscape needs the help of several helper applications to deal with sounds, animations, movies, and compressed files. In addition, if you want to be able to access Telnet resources (see Chapter 23), you need to configure Netscape to use support applications.

Configuring Support Applications

If you've installed Telnet and TN3270 helper applications, which enable you to access mainframe computer resources (see Chapter 23), you need to tell Netscape where these programs are located.

To configure your Telnet support applications:

1. From the Options menu, choose General Preferences. You'll see the Preferences dialog box.
2. Click the Apps tab. You'll see the Apps page.
3. In the Telnet Application box, click the Browse button, and locate your Telnet helper application.
4. In the TN3270 box, click the Browse button, and locate your TN3270 helper application.
5. Click OK.

Configuring Helper Applications

When Netscape encounters a file that it can't directly read, the program examines the file's *extension*. An *extension* is a three- or four-letter addition to a file's name. For example, "mov" is the extension of the file "sailboat.mov." Any file with the extension "mov" is a QuickTime graphics file. The program then examines a table that associates QuickTime graphics files with a helper program. If a program is listed, Netscape starts the helper. If no program is listed, you see an on-screen error message informing you that Netscape can't display the data you've downloaded. You can save the data to disk, or you can browse for an application capable of displaying the data.

To prevent this error message, you should take a few minutes to link the various file types to applications. It's easy, and once you've done this, you can forget about it.

To link multimedia file types with helper applications:

1. From the Options menu, choose General Preferences.
2. Click the Helpers tab. You'll see the Helpers page. Take a moment to look at this dialog box. In the list box, you see the various file types. If an application is already associated with a file type, you see the application's name in the Action column; otherwise, you see Ask User.
3. Find and select a file type. Start with application/x-zip-compressed.
4. Click the Browse button, and use the Open dialog box to select and open the WinZip application you installed from this book's CD-ROM disc (see Appendix E).
5. In the Action area, make sure the Launch the Application button is selected.
6. Repeat steps 3 through 5 for the rest of the file types you're going to configure. See Table B.1 for a list of the file types and applications to install.

The file type's not listed! Depending on which version of Netscape you're using, one or more of the file types in Table

B.1 may not appear in the file type list. But don't worry—you can add new file types easily:

1. Click the Create new Type button.
2. In the Configure New MIME Type dialog box, type the part of the file type that comes before the slash mark (for "audio/x-mpeg," you type "audio").
3. In the MIME Sub Type box, type the part of the file type that comes *after* the slash mark (for "audio/x-mpeg," you type "x-mpeg." Do *not* type the slash mark—Netscape adds that automatically).
4. Click OK.
5. With the new type still selected, type the extension or extensions in the File Extensions box (separated by commas—no spaces, please).
6. Click Launch the Application.
7. Now, associate your new file type with an application, as you've done for the other file types.

Table B.1 File Types and Applications

File Type	Application	Extensions
application/pdf	Adobe Acrobat Reader	pdf
application/x-compress	WinZip	x
application/x-gzip	WinZip	Z
application/x-pan-realaudio	RealAudio Player	ra
audio/midi	MidiGate	mid
audio/x-mpeg	XingSound Audio Player	mp2
video/fli	Autodesk Animation Player	fli
video/mpeg	NET TOOB	mpg, mpeg
video/quicktime	QuickTime for Windows	mov, qt
video/x-msvideo	Windows Media Player	

Appendix C

Netscape Quick Reference

File Menu

The File menu (Figure C.1) enables you to manage Web documents; specifically, you can open additional windows or open documents by typing the URL directly or loading them from disk. You can save files, both in HTML and plain text; you can even mail documents to other Internet users. You can view hidden information about a document, including its security status. You can preview the printed appearance of a document on-screen and then print the document. A final option enables you to save all your preferences and exit Netscape.

New Web Browser

Opens a new Netscape window and displays the default home page. *Note*: By default, you can open a maximum of four Netscape windows. To

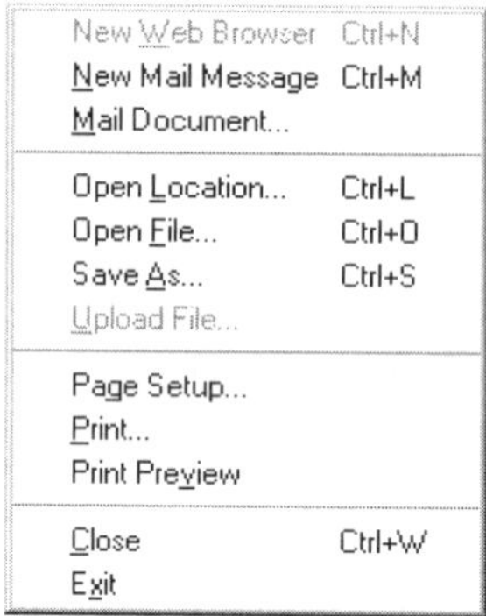

Figure C.1 File menu

increase this number, open the Options menu, choose Network Preferences, and click the Connections tab. Type the number of windows you want to open in the Number of Connections box.

Note that increasing the number of connections may slow down each of the connections. For optimum performance, set the number of connections at four.

New Mail Message

Displays the Message Composition window, which enables you to send an electronic mail message via the Internet.

Mail Document

Displays the Message Composition box, which enables you to send an electronic mail message via the Internet. Netscape automatically attaches the document you're currently viewing, and the program echoes the document's URL in the body of the message.

Open Location

Displays the Open Location dialog box, which enables you to type a URL directly.

It's easier to just type the URL in the Location box. To do so, click the current URL, and press Delete to erase it. Type your URL, and click OK.

Open File

Displays an Open dialog box that enables you to open a local file. Netscape can display HTML documents, JPEG and GIF graphics, and text files.

Save As

Saves the current document to a local disk drive. You can save the document with the HTML formatting (source) or as plain text (HTML codes are stripped from the document).

Upload File

Enables you to select a file to upload to an FTP server, as long as you have write permission on this server. You can also upload a file by dragging a file from the desktop into Netscape's window.

Page Setup

Choose margins, headers, footers, and other printing options with this menu command before you choose Print.

Print

Displays the Print dialog box, which prints the document you are currently viewing. You can select from a variety of print options, including number of copies, page range, and others (depending on your printer's capabilities).

Print Preview

Shows what your document will look like when printed. The Print Preview window draws on Microsoft Windows resources to display a one- or two-page graphic rendition of Netscape's print output. You can zoom in for a closer look, if you wish, and page through the print output. If it looks good, you can initiate printing from within this window without having to use the Print command.

Undo	Ctrl+Z
Cut	Ctrl+X
Copy	Ctrl+C
Paste	Ctrl+V
Select All	Ctrl+A
Find...	Ctrl+F
Find Again	F3

Figure C.2 Edit menu

Close

Closes the current window. If only one window is open, this command quits Netscape.

Exit

Saves the current configuration and quits Netscape.

Edit Menu

The Edit menu (Figure C.2) includes the standard Windows commands for editing text. There are great keyboard shortcuts for all of these commands (see Appendix D).

Undo

Reverses the last editing action, if possible. For example, suppose you type a new URL in the Location box. If you choose Undo, you see the previous URL. *Note:* This command is available only when it is able to reverse the last action.

Cut

Deletes the current selection and places a copy of the selection in the Clipboard. *Note:* This command is available only when it is possible to delete the selection (for example, you may use it within the Location box but not within a Web document).

Copy

Copies the current selection to the Clipboard.

Paste

Pastes the Clipboard's contents at the insertion point's location. *Note*: This command is available only when it is possible to paste text (for example, into the Location box).

Select All

Selects all the available text or items.

Find

Displays the Find dialog box, which enables you to search for a word or phrase within the currently displayed document.

Find Again

Repeats the search, using the settings you previously supplied in the Find dialog box.

View Menu

The View menu (Figure C.3) enables you to choose options for the display of Web documents; you won't use it much, though, because the most commonly accessed commands have more convenient equivalents on the Toolbar.

Reload

Retrieves a fresh copy of the current document from the cache or, if the original document has changed, from the Web server.

Reload Frame

Retrieves a fresh copy of the frame that's currently active (selected).

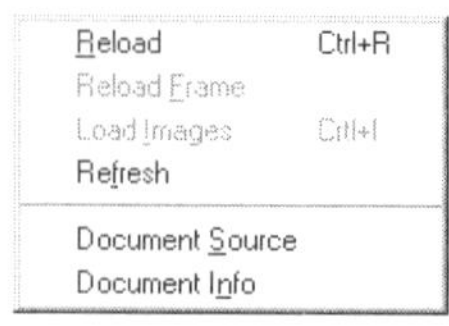

Figure C.3 View menu

Load Images

If you have turned off the automatic display of in-line images (see Options), this command reloads all the in-line images in the current document. To load in-line images selectively, click the image you want to see with the right mouse button, and choose View This Image.

Refresh

Refreshes the screen from the cache, clearing distortion or errors in the display of fonts, colors, or backgrounds.

Document Source

Displays the HTML source code of the document you are currently viewing. In the Source window, you can scroll through the document. You can also copy text to the Clipboard (select the text and press Ctrl + C).

Document Info

Displays a View Source window that provides information about the Web page you're currently viewing, including security settings.

Go Menu

The Go menu (Figure C.4) provides navigation commands. You won't use the commands much, though, because the Toolbar offers a more convenient way

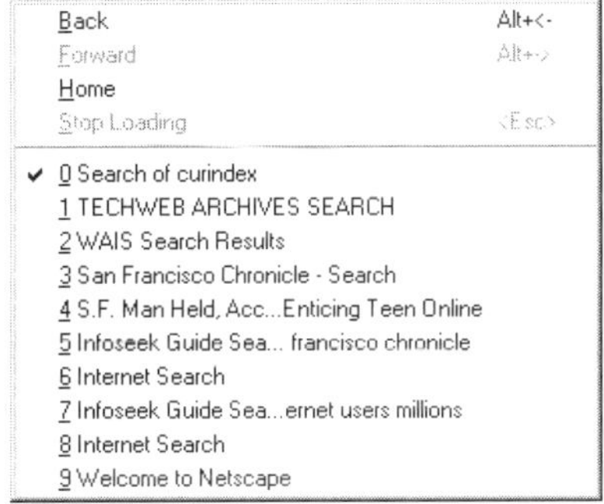

Figure C.4 Go menu

of choosing these commands. The best thing about the Go menu is that it lists the last few Web pages you've visited, allowing you to go back to a page you viewed several pages ago without clicking the Back button over and over.

Back

Displays the previous document (same as clicking the Back button). This option is dimmed if the current document is the first you've displayed in a new Netscape window.

Forward

Displays the document that was displayed prior to clicking the Back button or choosing Back from the Go menu (same as clicking the Forward button). This option is dimmed if you have not chosen Back or clicked Back.

Home

Displays the default start page (the document listed in the Home Page Location field of the Appearance page, Preferences dialog box).

Stop Loading

Stops the retrieval of the current document (same as clicking Stop).

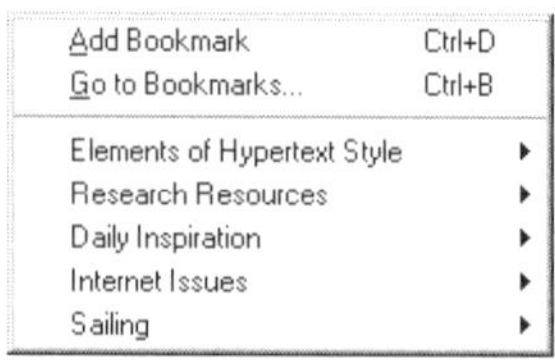

Figure C.5 Bookmarks menu

History Items (0, 1, 2, 3, etc.)

Choose one of these options to redisplay previously viewed documents.

Bookmarks Menu

The Bookmarks menu (Figure C.5) enables you to add, view, edit, and organize bookmarks. Bookmarks that you've added appear on the lower portion of the menu.

Add Bookmark

Adds the current document to the bookmark folder that is currently selected in the Set to New Bookmarks Folder text box (Bookmarks window)

Go to Bookmarks

Displays the Bookmarks window. You can use this dialog box to store and organize your favorite bookmark items.

Options Menu

The Options menu (Figure C.6) enables you to choose options for Netscape's operation, as well as to specify program configuration settings, the location of helper programs, and much more.

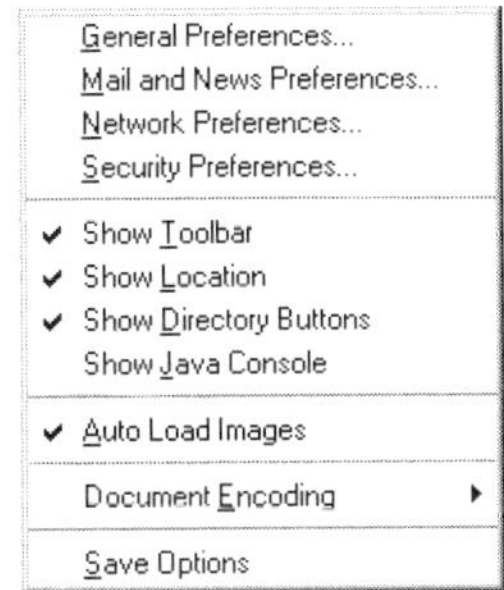

Figure C.6 Options menu

General Preferences

Displays the Preferences dialog box, which has the following seven pages. Note that essential configuration options are discussed in Appendix B.

Appearance	Choose Toolbar, startup, and link style options.
Fonts	Choose a different language encoding for foreign languages, if you're using Netscape in a non-English-speaking country. In addition, you can choose a font for the body text (proportional spacing) and the fixed font.
Colors	Choose colors for links, followed links, text, and background. You can also determine whether Netscape should override a document's colors.
Images	Choose options for displaying images, and determine when images are displayed (while loading or after loading).
Apps	Specify the location for supporting Telnet, TN3270, and text editor applications, and specify the default directory for storing files temporarily.
Helpers	Specify helper applications, as discussed in Appendix B.

Language	Specify which languages Netscape will accept when you download pages.

Mail And News Preferences

In this Preferences page, you choose options for electronic mail and Usenet newsgroups. You'll find the following tabbed pages:

Appearance	Choose the font to display e-mail messages and Usenet articles. You can also choose a character style for quoted text. In the Windows 95 version of Netscape Navigator, you can choose between Netscape and the Microsoft Exchange client to send and receive e-mail (I recommend Netscape).
Composition	Choose the encoding method for sending and receiving e-mail and articles (8-bit or MIME-compliant). You can also specify an e-mail address or a file to which to send copies of your e-mail and articles.
Servers	Here you specify the addresses of your mail and Usenet servers.
Identity	In this dialog box you type your name and e-mail address, as well as the location of your signature file.
Organization	Choose options for displaying e-mail addresses

Network Preferences

This option displays a dialog box that enables you to choose cache, connection, and proxy information. You don't need to worrry about the proxy information unless you're using Netscape behind a firewall. There are three tabbed pages, as follows:

Cache	Choose the size of the memory and disk cache, specify the cache location, and choose how Netscape verifies documents.
Connections	Specify the number of network connections that Netscape can establish at any one time. Also, spec-

	ify the size of the network buffer (the memory space set aside for network data transmission).
Proxies	If you are using Netscape behind a firewall, ask your network administrator how to fill out this dialog box.

Security Preferences

In this dialog box, you can choose how you want Netscape to handle communication with secure servers. You'll see two tabbed pages:

General	In this page, you can disable Java. You can also specify when Netscape displays those rather annoying security alert boxes.
Site Certificates	Here, you see a list of the site certificates that you have accepted. These certificates establish that the site you're contacting really is the site you think you're contacting.

Show Toolbar

Hides or displays the Toolbar.

Show Location

Hides or displays the Location box.

Show Directory Buttons

Hides or displays the Directory buttons.

Show Java Console

Hides or displays a window that monitors the execution of Java applets.

Auto Load Images

Disables or enables the automatic decoding of in-line graphics. If this option is switched off, you can view a single graphic by clicking it with the

Netscape's Home
What's New!
What's Cool!
Netscape Galleria
Internet Directory
Internet Search
Internet White Pages
About the Internet

Figure C.7 Directory menu

right mouse button and choosing View This Image from the pop-up menu; alternatively, you can choose Load Images from the View menu to view all the images in the current document.

Save Options

Saves the current preferences and options, including window sizes. Netscape saves options automatically when you quit using the Exit command (File menu).

Directory Menu

The Directory menu (Figure C.7) provides menu equivalents (and then some) for the Directory buttons.

Netscape's Home

Displays Netscape Communications Corporation's home page, which is the default home page for Netscape (unless you've changed the setting in the Appearance page of the Preferences dialog box).

What's New!

Displays Netscape Communications Corporation's What's New page, which lists new Web sites of unusual interest. Same as clicking the What's New! button.

What's Cool!

Displays a selection of unusual, interesting, or pioneering Web pages; well worth a look. Same as clicking the What's Cool! button.

Netscape Galleria

Displays a list of Web servers that offer secure transactions using Netscape's Secure Socket Layer (SSL) technology.

Internet Directory

Displays a document that enables you to access Yahoo and other subject trees. Same as clicking Net Directory.

Internet Search

Displays a document that enables you to access search engines such as Lycos and WebCrawler. Same as clicking Net Search.

Internet White Pages

Displays a page that enables you to search for people on the Internet, using services such as Netfind.

About the Internet

Displays a page that enables you to access information about the Internet.

Window Menu

This menu (Figure C.8) enables you to access Netscape Mail, Netscape News, the Address Book, the Bookmarks window, and the History window.

Netscape Mail

Opens a new Mail window.

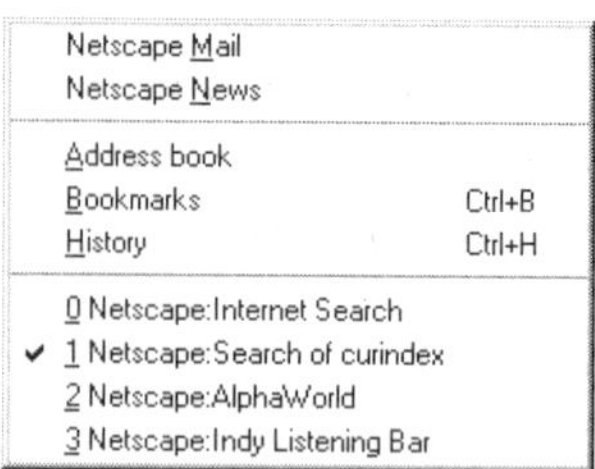

Figure C.8 Window menu

Netscape News

Opens a new Usenet window.

Address Book

Opens the Address Book window, which enables you to add new e-mail addresses to your Address Book.

Bookmarks

Opens the Bookmarks window, which enables you to organize your bookmark items.

History

Displays the History dialog box.

Open Windows (0, 1, 2, 3, Etc.)

At the bottom of the Windows menu, you'll see a list of the Netscape browser windows that are currently open.

HELP MENU

The Help menu (Figure C.9) accesses documents stored on Netscape Communications Corporation's server. It's loaded with interesting and helpful information, including an on-line Netscape handbook.

About Netscape

Displays a dialog box indicating which version of Netscape you're using.

About Plug-ins

Displays a page of information concerning the Version 2.0 plug-ins.

Registration Information

Displays information enabling you to register your copy of Netscape.

Software

Displays a page of information about Netscape Communication Corporation's software offerings.

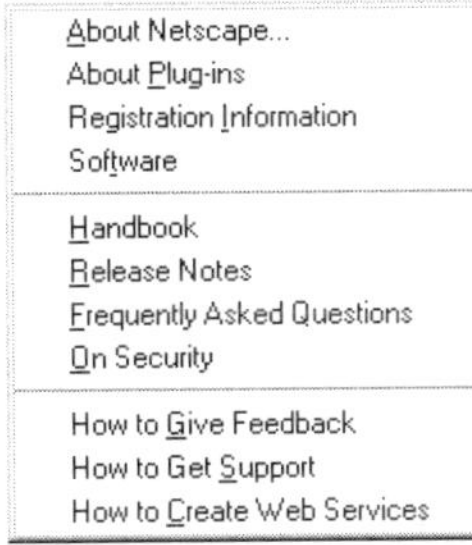

Figure C.9 Help menu

Handbook

Accesses Netscape Communications Corporation's on-line help manual for Netscape.

Release Notes

Displays a page of notes about the version of Netscape you are using.

Frequently Asked Questions

Displays a page of frequently asked questions (and answers) about Netscape Navigator.

On Security

Displays information about Internet security and Netscape's Secure Sockets Layer (SSL) security technology.

How to Give Feedback

Displays a page providing instructions about submitting bug reports and providing feedback on Netscape Navigator.

How to Get Support

Displays a page providing instructions for obtaining technical support for registered users.

How to Create Web Services

Displays a page about creating World Wide Web sites. Tons of links to Internet-based information.

Appendix D

Netscape's Keyboard Shortcuts

To Do This	Press These Keys
Add bookmark	Ctrl + D
Close a window	Ctrl + W
Copy selection to the Clipboard	Ctrl + C
Create a new mail message	Ctrl + M
Cut selection to the Clipboard	Ctrl + X
Display Bookmarks dialog box	Ctrl + B
Find again	F3
Find text in current document	Ctrl + F
Go back	Alt + <
Open a local file	Ctrl + O (the letter)
Open a new browser window	Ctrl + N
Paste from the Clipboard	Ctrl + V
Print current document	Ctrl + P
Reload current document	Ctrl + R
Save a file to disk	Ctrl + S
Select all	Ctrl + A
Stop loading	Esc
Type a URL directly (Open Location)	Ctrl + L
Undo your last editing action	Ctrl + Z
View all in-line images	Ctrl + I
View the history list	Ctrl + H

Appendix E

Using This Book's CD-ROM Disc

If you already have a copy of Netscape Navigator

To access the programs and additional goodies on this book's CD-ROM disc, do the following:

1. Place the CD-ROM disc in your CD-ROM drive.
2. If necessary, start Netscape Navigator.
3. From the File menu, choose File Open.
4. In the Open dialog box, select the CD-ROM disc.
5. Select the file WELCOME.HTM.
6. Follow the instructions and links in WELCOME.HTM.

To access the EarthLink TotalAccess software:

Use the Windows File Manager (Windows 3.1) or My Computer icon (Windows 95) to open the CD-ROM disc. Do one of the following:

1. If you are using Windows 3.1, double-click the win31 folder.
2. If you are using Windows 95, double-click the win95 folder.
3. Double-click the file called SETUP.EXE.
4. Follow the on-screen instructions.

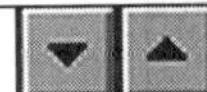

Index

LIMITED WARRANTY AND DISCLAIMER OF LIABILITY

ACADEMIC PRESS, INC. ("AP") AND ANYONE ELSE WHO HAS BEEN INVOLVED IN THE CREATION OR PRODUCTION OF THE ACCOMPANYING CODE ("THE PRODUCT") CANNOT AND DO NOT WARRANT THE PERFORMANCE OR RESULTS THAT MAY BE OBTAINED BY USING THE PRODUCT. THE PRODUCT IS SOLD "AS IS" WITHOUT WARRANTY OF ANY KIND (EXCEPT AS HEREAFTER DESCRIBED), EITHER EXPRESSED OR IMPLIED, INCLUDING, BUT NOT LIMITED TO, ANY WARRANTY OF PERFORMANCE OR ANY IMPLIED WARRANTY OF MERCHANTABILITY OR FITNESS FOR ANY PARTICULAR PURPOSE. AP WARRANTS ONLY THAT THE MAGNETIC DISC(S) ON WHICH THE CODE IS RECORDED IS FREE FROM DEFECTS IN MATERIAL AND FAULTY WORKMANSHIP UNDER THE NORMAL USE AND SERVICE FOR A PERIOD OF NINETY (90) DAYS FROM THE DATE THE PRODUCT IS DELIVERED. THE PURCHASER'S SOLE AND EXCLUSIVE REMEDY IN THE EVENT OF A DEFECT IS EXPRESSLY LIMITED TO EITHER REPLACEMENT OF THE DISC(S) OR REFUND OF THE PURCHASE PRICE, AT AP'S SOLE DISCRETION.

IN NO EVENT, WHETHER AS A RESULT OF BREACH OF CONTRACT, WARRANTY OR TORT (INCLUDING NEGLIGENCE), WILL AP OR ANYONE WHO HAS BEEN INVOLVED IN THE CREATION OR PRODUCTION OF THE PRODUCT BE LIABLE TO PURCHASER FOR ANY DAMAGES, INCLUDING ANY LOST PROFITS, LOST SAVINGS OR OTHER INCIDENTAL OR CONSEQUENTIAL DAMAGES ARISING OUT OF THE USE OR INABILITY TO USE THE PRODUCT OR ANY MODIFICATIONS THEREOF, OR DUE TO THE CONTENTS OF THE CODE, EVEN IF AP HAS BEEN ADVISED OF THE POSSIBILITY OF SUCH DAMAGES, OR FOR ANY CLAIM BY ANY OTHER PARTY.

Any request for replacement of a defective CD-ROM disc must be postage prepaid and must be accompanied by the original defective disc, your mailing address and telephone number, and proof of date of purchase and purchase price. Send such requests, stating the nature of the problem, to Academic Press Customer Service, 6277 Sea Harbor Drive, Orlando, FL 32887, 1-800-321-5068. APP shall have no obligation to refund the purchase price or to replace a disc based on claims of defects in the nature or operation of the Product.

Some states do not allow limitation on how long an implied warranty lasts, nor exclusions or limitations of incidental or consequential damage, so the above limitations and exclusions may not apply to you. This Warranty gives you specific legal rights, and you may also have other rights which vary from jurisdiction to jurisdiction.

THE RE-EXPORT OF UNITED STATES ORIGIN SOFTWARE IS SUBJECT TO THE UNITED STATES LAWS UNDER THE EXPORT ADMINISTRATION ACT OF 1969 AS AMENDED. ANY FURTHER SALE OF THE PRODUCT SHALL BE IN COMPLIANCE WITH THE UNITED STATES DEPARTMENT OF COMMERCE ADMINISTRATION REGULATIONS. COMPLIANCE WITH SUCH REGULATIONS IS YOUR RESPONSIBILITY AND NOT THE RESPONSIBILITY OF AP.